Greek Religion
A Sourcebook

Valerie M. Warrior

focus *an imprint of*
Hackett Publishing Company, Inc.
Indianapolis/Cambridge

Cover: Macron Vasepainter. Young man pouring a libation on an altar. Center medallion of a red-figured cup (around 480 BCE) Inv. G 149. Location : Louvre, Paris, France. Photo Credit : Erich Lessing / Art Resource, NY. Background image © istockphoto / Peter Zelei.

ISBN 13: 978-1-58510-031-6

Previously published by Focus Publishing, R. Pullins Co.

Focus an imprint of
Hackett Publishing Company, Inc
P.O. Box 44937
Indianapolis, Indiana 46244-0937

www.hackettpublishing.com

CONTENTS

Figures and Maps

Figures

Maps

PREFACE

HERODOTUS, HISTORIES 8.144. Being Greek means having the same blood and language, common shrines of the gods and sacrifices, and the same kinds of customs.

Writing in the mid-fifth century BCE, the historian Herodotus discerned the commonality of Greek religious practice. The Greeks performed their worship through prayer and sacrifice at altars marked off as sacred space, often located in sanctuaries. In modern Greece one can visit the spectacular sites of Delphi and Olympia — ruined panhellenic sanctuaries with magnificent temples.[1] However, prominent Greek remains also can be found to the east in modern Turkey and around the Black Sea, and to the west in Sicily, southern Italy, and the shores of eastern and southern Spain.

The Greeks had no single word for religion. *Theous sebasthai* —to be in awe of the gods, to feel and express respect for them — is probably the best approximation for what we loosely call religion. The noun *sebas* implies a combination of awe, respect, and reverence. *Eusebeia* — proper or right observance of *sebas* — is often translated as piety but more precisely means "doing the right or proper thing."[2] Impiety, *asebeia*, is lack or denial of respect for the gods.

Just as the Greeks did not have an all-embracing word for religion, so too with the concept of ritual. Many ritual activities are described as *ta nomizomena* —the customary things—or *ta ethea* —customs. Isocrates (436—380 BCE), an advocate of panhellenism, emphasizes the essential conservatism of Greek religion: "[Our ancestors'] sole concern was not to destroy any of the ancestral practices and not to add anything that was not traditional. For they thought that piety (*eusebeia*) consists, not in paying out large sums of money, but rather in not disturbing any of the rites that their ancestors had handed down to them" (*Areopagiticus* 30).

---

1   *panhellenic*: shared or open to all Greeks.

2   *eusebeia*: *eu* - means well or good.

How this book works

This book presents, in translation, selected ancient sources on the religion of the people of the Greek-speaking world, as practiced from the eighth century down to approximately the end of the fourth century, BCE. The ancient sources include literary texts, inscriptions, and other sources of Greek writings, as well as a much smaller selection of visual representations. Some sources are from later antiquity but all speak about earlier practices, at least apparently.

The key feature of this book is a *narrative* of what the Greeks themselves said about their gods and their worship. The ancient sources, text and visual, have been selected and arranged to form *one ongoing story* which gradually introduces traditional Greek religion.

My view is that the ancient sources should be regarded as the primary means by which an accurate understanding of the past can be gained. Modern interpretations are secondary, though sometimes helpful as aids to learning.

With this in mind, commentary generally is brief. Explanation and elaboration does follow after most ancient testimony, and commentary sometimes also comes before to provide context or a transition from earlier material. However, my aim is a gloss on the ancient evidence, not an alternative account.

After an introductory chapter, this book proceeds by theme. First come the gods and the cult practices of family and communities. Next come prayer and sacrifice and various key practices and venues of worship. Then evolving views of justice are set out. Finally, the story proceeds over disparate branches—mystery religions, the philosophers and other challenges, fringe practices such as magic, and the introduction of new cults and gods.

The ancient sources

Study of the ancient sources on Greek religion can be like trying to piece together a jigsaw puzzle that has far too many missing pieces. The surviving pieces are highly disparate, a mix of evidence that extends over several centuries and derives from many different places. There is a constant danger of distorting historical reality by making misleading analogies or introducing modern preconceptions. "Consider the source" is a rule that must be constantly borne in mind.

The literary testimony ranges from the works of Homer and Hesiod (late eighth century BCE) to later authors such as the geographer Strabo, the traveler Pausanias, the biographer Plutarch, to the early Christian writers of the second and third centuries CE, and to scholia, notes made in the margin of a manuscript of a particular literary work. Ancient historians such as Herodotus and Thucydides include in their narrative mention of religious ceremonies, omens, prophecies, and the consultation of oracles—all of which were an integral part of Greek life. Philosophers such as Plato offer reflections, both positive and negative, on Greek religious practices.

The poems of Homer and Hesiod, together with the tragic dramas of Aeschylus, Sophocles and Euripides, and the comedies of Aristophanes, are among our most important sources concerning Greek religion. These works reached a very wide audience through oral tradition, conventional education, and public performance at religious festivals. In these literary works are embedded many precepts and rituals presented as traditional Greek religion. However, none of these literary texts were canonical. Mainstream traditional Greek religion had *no sacred literature*.

Important non-literary evidence is varied and increasingly accessible. Long widely known are vase paintings and sculpted images portraying religious ceremonies and myths. Archaeological discoveries include graves with various kinds of commodities, coins depicting a deity or myth, and inscriptions recording dedications or thank-offerings and laws that govern religious sanctuaries. Epitaphs from tombs yield valuable information about the lives of ordinary people who would not otherwise have found their way into the history books. Other epigraphic evidence includes religious calendars noting festivals, financial accounts of sanctuaries, prayers, curses, and mystical texts. The discovery of inscribed tablets relating to Orphic teachings yields a tantalizing glimpse of beliefs that are very different from the religion of the world of Homer and Hesiod or that of the classical Greek city state. Many of these materials are chance survivals from different places and periods, underscoring the fact that the totality of these disparate sources still is but a part of the jigsaw puzzle that constitutes our information about Greek religion.

Translations and acknowledgments

My transliteration of Greek is flexible rather than consistent. For the most part I use the more familiar Romanized form of names, for example, Achilles rather than the Greek form Akhilleus, and Clytemnestra rather than Klytaimestra. In the case of Oedipus, I have retained the Greek Oidipous only in the case of the heading of the translations from Ruby Blondell's *The Theban Plays*. Both Greek and Roman names are listed in the glossaries.

Excerpts are taken from translations in the following works in the Focus Classical Library: Aristophanes, *Clouds*, translated by Jeffrey Henderson (1992); Euripides, *Medea, Hippolytus, Heracles, Bacchae*, ed. Esposito (2002); Hesiod, *Theogony*, translated by Richard S. Caldwell (1987);[3] *The Homeric Hymns*, translated by Susan C. Shelmerdine (1995); Sophocles, *The Theban Plays: Antigone, King Oidipous, Oidipous at Colonus*, translated by Ruby Blondell (2002).

The excerpts from Euripides' *Trojan Women* in chapter 10 are from Shirley Barlow's translation of Euripides, *Trojan Women* (Aris and Philips 1986). The

---

3   Excerpt 9.9 *Works and Days* also is from Caldwell's Focus volume.

translations of the Bacchic gold tablets in chapter 11 are those of Fritz Graf and Sarah Iles Johnston, *Ritual Texts for the Afterlife* (2007).

I am deeply indebted to Ruby Blondell, who translated the many passages from Homer's *Iliad* and *Odyssey*. Shirley Barlow kindly offered her unpublished translation of Aeschylus' *Suppliant Women* 86–100.

The remaining translations are my own. In translating verse I make no claim to versification, attempting merely to preserve individual lines insofar as possible. By contrast with my transliteration, my translations attempt to be quite literal rather than free. Similarities to like-minded published translations are inevitable, especially in the case of inscriptions, and of fragments from works otherwise lost.

Acknowledgments

My sincere thanks go to Ruby Blondell and Fred Naiden for their helpful comments on early drafts, to my anonymous readers for their constructive criticism, and to Robert Garland, Christine Kondoleon, and Rebecca Sinos for comments along the way.

Ron Pullins provided encouragement and patient support throughout the project. It has been a pleasure to work with Linda Diering, Amanda Pepper, Cindy Zawalich, and the rest of the team at Focus.

1. Introduction

1.1 THALES, *KRS* no. 91.[1] All things are full of gods.

1.2 THEOGNIS 1179–1180.

Respect and fear the gods because this prevents an individual

from doing or saying anything that is impious (*asebes*).

1.3 PLATO, *EUTHYPHRO* 14 b. If someone knows how to say and do what is pleasing to the gods when praying and sacrificing, these things are holy and protect individual households and the common interests of the city. But the opposite of what pleases the gods is impiety, which overthrows and destroys everything.

1.4 PLATO, *TIMAEUS* 27 c. All people who have even a little good sense (*sophrosyne*) always invoke a god at the beginning and end of any undertaking, be it great or small.

> The work of the early Greek thinker Thales (first half of the sixth century BCE) only survives in fragments quoted by later authors. The dates of the poet Theognis are uncertain, but he probably lived before 480 BCE. The philosopher Plato (c. 429–347 BCE) notes that worship of the gods is integral to the well-being of societal groups ranging from the family (*oikos*) to the city state (*polis*).

1.5 HOMER, *ILIAD* 1.37–41.

"Hear me, god of the silver bow, protector of Chryse

and sacred Cilla, ruling in might over Tenedus, Smintheus:[2]

if ever I built and roofed a temple to give you joy,

---

1 The fragments of authors whose works have mostly been lost are collected in *KRS* = Kirk, G. S., Raven, J., and Schofield, M., *The Presocratic Philosophers*, 2nd edition, Cambridge 1983. The fragments are individually numbered, and KRS provide a Greek text, an English translation, commentary and notes. I have used the KRS Greek text in making my translation.

2 *Chryse, Cilla, Tenedus*: places near Troy where Apollo was worshipped. *Smintheus*: this problematic cult title, which probably means "mouse-god," only occurs here.

1

if ever I burned rich fat from the thighs of bulls or goats   40
for you in sacrifice, I beg you, fulfill my desire."

This prayer of the Trojan priest of Apollo is one of the first actions related in Homer's *Iliad* (probably second half of eighth century BCE but reaching final form in the sixth century BCE). Before making his actual request, the priest reminds the god of the previous animal sacrifices he has made. Prayer, usually accompanied by the offering or sacrifice of an object that was of value to the donor, was the essential ritual preface to any initiative, whether in domestic affairs or in the broader arenas of politics and warfare.

The aim of regular prayer and sacrifice was to win and maintain the gods' favor and to avoid their anger. "I am giving so that you may sometime return the favor."[3]

Figure 1.1 A sacrificial procession depicted on an oil flask (*lekythos*) c. 520–510 BCE. On the right, a girl leads the procession; in front of her is an Ionic column with a fillet or ribbon tied around it. On her head she holds a basket containing the sacrificial knife and barley corns for the consecration of the sacrificial victims. Two cows adorned with fillets follow her; they are attended by two youths wearing wreathes or crowns on their heads. Photograph © 2008 Museum of Fine Arts, Boston.

Durable objects, often of considerable value, were deposited as offerings in the sanctuary of a particular god to indicate the donor's respect or piety, either in anticipation of, or in gratitude for, a favor. Such votive offerings include gold, silver, and bronze vessels; weaponry; bronze or terracotta figurines; statues; paintings; and elaborately woven garments. Votive offerings were made by private individuals as well as by officials acting on behalf a community such as a city.

Less permanent offerings ranged from the expensive sacrifice of animals to the giving of a simple object such as a special cake made from the fruits of the earth or a liquid offering (libation) of wine, milk, or honey. A seventh

---

3   As Price 1999: 38–39 has noted, "like other systems of gifts and counter-gifts, the Greek ritual system assumed choice on both sides. Gifts to the gods were not a way of buying the gods, but of creating goodwill from which humans might hope to benefit in the future." See also Pulleyn 1997: 16–38.

Figure 1.2. Mantiklos "Apollo." A votive bronze statuette of Apollo, c. 700–675 BCE. Inscribed on the front of the thighs of the nude male figure is the dedication: "Mantiklos donated me as a tithe to the far shooter, the bearer of the silver bow. You Phoebus [Apollo] give something pleasing in return." Photograph © 2008 Museum of Fine Arts, Boston.

century BCE Athenian law is quoted by Porphry, the late third century CE scholar, philosopher, and student of religions.

1.6 PORPHYRY, *ON ABSTINENCE FROM KILLING ANIMALS* 4.22. A law of Dracon is also remembered, a ruling to last for ever among the inhabitants of Attica. Honor the gods and local heroes, in public following the ancestral practices, and in private as best as one can, with pious language, the first-fruits of crops, and annual offerings of cakes. The law required that the divine be honored with the first-fruits of those crops that people use and with cakes.

> The Greek concept of piety (*eusebeia*) implied the assiduous outward observance and proper performance of ritual, but it did not necessarily involve the worshiper's mental attitude. The correct performance of ritual was the essence of traditional Greek religion, not faith, nor belief defined by creed or doctrine.

> Homer describes the offering of a libation of wine to Zeus, the son of Cronus, before a feast.

1.7 HOMER, *ILIAD* 7.480–481.

They poured wine on the ground from their cups, nor did anyone dare to drink until he had poured a libation to the all-powerful son of Cronus.

When the Trojan warrior Hector returns from the battlefield, he refuses to make a libation until he has cleansed himself by washing the blood from his hands.

1.8   HOMER, *ILIAD* 6.266–268.

Reverence keeps me from pouring gleaming wine to Zeus
in libation with hands unwashed;[4] no one splattered with blood
and gore can pray to the son of Cronus, lord of the dark clouds.

In *Works and Days*, a poem about farming written c. 700 BCE, the poet Hesiod warns that the gods will not respond to the prayer of anyone who is ritually unclean.

1.9   HESIOD, *WORKS AND DAYS* 724–726.

After dawn, never pour a libation of sparkling wine to Zeus
with unwashed hands, nor to the other immortal gods.
For they will not hear you, and will spit your prayers back.

In the *Iliad* and *Odyssey* of Homer and the *Works and Days* and *Theogony* of Hesiod we see anthropomorphized gods—stronger, more powerful, and more beautiful than humans. These gods are said to be immortal, never to die. However, they are not eternal and are not the creators of the universe or of humans, but are themselves created.

Zeus, Hera, Athena, Poseidon, Aphrodite, Hermes, Hephaestus, Ares, and Demeter are generally depicted as living on Olympus, a mountain in northeastern Greece. Their family relationships are complex. Zeus, the head of the family, is the son of Cronus and Rhea. Hera is both Zeus' sister and wife. Poseidon and Demeter are Zeus' brother and sister. Hestia, a more shadowy Olympian deity who is goddess of the hearth, is another daughter of Cronus and Rhea. Apollo and Artemis are Zeus' children by Leto. Zeus also is the father of Athena by Metis, of Ares by Hera, of Hermes by Maia, and of Dionysus by Semele. Hera is said to be the sole parent of Hephaestus. Hades, the brother of Zeus and Poseidon, is king of the underworld. His wife is Persephone, the daughter of Hades' sister Demeter and of Zeus.

In addition to the complexity of these family relationships involving marriage with close kin, inconsistencies about a particular god's parentage are apparent. For example, in Homer Aphrodite is the daughter of Zeus and Dione, whereas in Hesiod she is born from the foam of the sea created by the severed genitals of Ouranos (Sky).

Many gods were addressed with a variety of cultic epithets, or titles, that describe their function in a particular sphere.[5] For example, Zeus is invoked as Hupatos (most high) Soter (savior, protector), Polieus (of the city), Meilichios (gentle). In the home (*oikos*) he is variously invoked as Zeus Philios

---

4   *Reverence keeps me:* the Greek verb *hazomai* literally means "I stand in awe and dread, and so do not dare to do" a certain thing.

5   For the various functions of the Olympian gods, see the brief summaries pp. 265–266, and Dowden in Ogden 2007: 41–55.

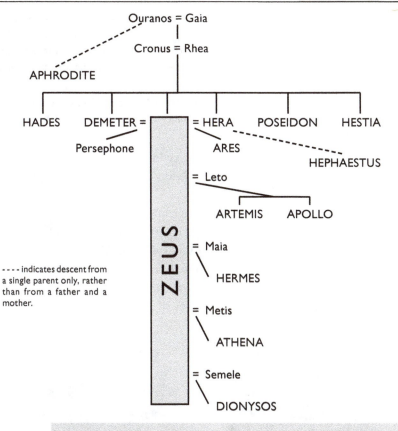

Figure 1.3. The Family of Zeus (adapted from Garland 1994 Table 1)

(friendly one), Herkeios (protector of the enclosure), Ktesios (guardian of property), Kataibates (averter of lightning), and Xenios (protector of strangers and god of hospitality). In Athens, Athena was worshiped as Parthenos (maiden), Polias (of the city), and Promachos (leader in battle).[6]

There were minor deities such as pastoral Pan, half man and half goat,[7] and non-anthropomorphized divine powers (*daimones*) both kindly and malicious. Misfortune often is attributed to an unspecified *daimon*. The *agathos daimon* (Good Spirit) protects the *oikos* (house and home) and, thus, the family.

More sinister and malign deities were thought to dwell in or beneath the earth. These powers are generally referred to a "chthonic " from the Greek *chthon*, earth. The Furies or Erinyes were chthonic spirits who avenged the murder of blood relatives.

---

6   On cults, see Larson 2007.

7   On nature gods in Greek religion, see Larson in Ogden 2007: 56–70.

Also worshiped were heroes and heroines, figures intermediary between gods and humans, real or imaginary persons said to have accomplished superhuman deeds.[8] Generally a hero cult was restricted to the particular area in which the hero was said to have performed the deeds that resulted in heroization.

Hesiod notes the birth of the hero Heracles, son of Zeus and the mortal Alcmena, who was granted immortality after completing his labors.

1.10   HESIOD, *THEOGONY* 943–955.

And Alcmena bore mighty Heracles, having
joined in love with cloud-gathering Zeus.

....

The strong son of fair-ankled Alcmena, mighty   950
Heracles, having finished his painful labors,[9] took
Hebe, child of great Zeus and gold-sandled Hera,
as his modest wife in snowy Olympus; he is
happy, who finished his great work and lives with
the immortals, carefree and ageless for all days.   955

Figure 1.4. Silver tetradrachm of Alexander the Great of Macedon, (ruled 336–323 BCE), depicting on the reverse a seated statue of Zeus holding a long staff in his left hand. An eagle, a symbol of Zeus, perches on his extended right arm. The legend on the right of the coin reads "of Alexander." On the obverse is the head of the hero Heracles, a son of Zeus, wearing a lion skin.[10] Alexander traced his ancestry to Heracles. © istockphoto/Georgios Kollidas.

---

8 On hero cult, see Ekroth, "Heroes and Hero Cults," in Ogden 2007: 100–114; Kearns, "Between god and man: status and function of heroes and their sanctuaries," in Schacter and Bingen 1992: 63–99, and "The Nature of Heroines" in Blundell and Williamson 1998: 98–110.

9 *painful labors*: as a slave of King Eurytheus, Heracles was forced to perform twelve labors to gain his freedom.

10 *lion skin*: an allusion to the killing of the lion of Nemea, one of Heracles' twelve labors.

Often the focal point of hero worship was the hero's tomb or reputed place of burial within a sacred area. Marathon, a local territorial district (*deme*) of Attica where the Athenians defeated the invading Persians in 490 BCE, mantained the cult of a legendary hero named Marathon. The geographer Pausanias (mid-second century CE) notes this cult of Marathon, as well as a cult of the men who fell in the battle, and also the cult of the deified Heracles.

1.11 PAUSANIAS 1.32.4. The people of Marathon worship both those who died in the fighting, calling them heroes, and secondly Marathon, from whom the people take their name, and then Heracles because they say that they were the first among the Greeks to acknowledge him as a god.

In Euripides' *Iphigenia in Tauris* (413 BCE), the goddess Athena tells Iphigenia, the daughter of Agamemnon, that she will return to Greece and become a priestess of Artemis at Brauron in Attica.[11] After death, she will be worshiped, receiving the garments of women who have died in childbirth.

1.12 EURIPIDES, *IPHIGENIA IN TAURIS* 1462–1467.

And you, Iphigenia, by the holy meadows

of Brauron must be a priestess of this goddess

When you die, you will be buried there,

and people will dedicate to you beautifully woven garments

that women who die in childbirth

leave in their homes.

The gods were thought to communicate their will to humans by sending signs, for example, in the flight of birds or in dreams. These various signs were interpreted by seers or prophets (*manteis*) who were specialists in divination (*mantike techne*), the discernment of the gods' will as a guide to action.[12]

Xenophon (c.430–c.354 BCE) notes that both Greeks and non-Greeks use divination, believing that the gods are omniscient.

1.13 XENOPHON, *SYMPOSIUM* 4.47–49. It is apparent that both Greeks and non-Greeks believe that the gods know everything, the present and the future. At any rate, all cities and peoples use divination to ask the gods what they should or should not do.

1.14 XENOPHON, *MEMORABILIA* 1.1.3. Believers in divination rely on birds, oracles, signs, and sacrifices. They do not think that the birds or humans they encounter know what is advantageous for the inquirer, but rather that they are the means by which the gods send signs.

---

11 In this play, Iphigenia was not sacrificed by her father Agamemnon before he sailed to Troy, as in Euripides' later play, *Iphigenia at Aulis*. She was rescued and sent to the land of the Taurians in the Black Sea area.

12 On seers and divination, see Johnston and Struck, ed., 2005 and Flower 2008.

In Sophocles' *King Oidipous* the Leader of the Chorus, who generally expresses traditional religion, advises Oedipus to consult the seer Tiresias regarding the meaning of a response received from the oracle of Apollo at Delphi.

1.15 SOPHOCLES, *KING OIDIPOUS* 284–286.

I know the lord whose vision is the closest to
Lord Phoebus is Tiresias; look into this
with his help, lord, and you'll most clearly learn the truth.

The gods intervene in human lives, for both good and ill, but their intervention often seems based on whim rather than reason.

1.16 HOMER, *ILIAD* 24.527–533.

Two storage-jars stand full of gifts in the storeroom of Zeus,
one of them holding the evils he gives and the other one blessings.
If Zeus who hurls the thunder-bolt gives someone a mixture
of both he sometimes meets with evil and sometimes with good.   530
But if he gives someone only woeful gifts he degrades him;
evil starvation drives him over the splendid earth,
and he wanders deprived of honor from gods and mortals alike.

Solon, the late seventh-early sixth centuries BCE Athenian lawgiver whom later generations regarded as a sage, remarks on the gods' inscrutability.

1.17 SOLON, Frag. 17 Diehl.[13]

The purpose of the immortals is obscure to mortals.

Several passages in early Greek literature connect Moira, Fate or Destiny, with the gods. A number of Greek words often are translated by "fate" or "destiny" but these English words can be problematic in a Greek context. *Moira* is the general word used to denote a portion or share, and hence one's portion, lot, fate, destiny, or span of years. Although the gods intervene in human lives, these interventions apparently do not overrule *moira*. In Hesiod's *Theogony* three *Moirae* are personified: Klotho, the Spinner who spins the thread of life; Lachesis, the Allotter, who measures the thread; and Atropos, the Unbending One who determines and terminates that thread, usually by cutting it.

1.18 SOLON, Frag.1.63–64, Diehl.

Indeed Fate (*Moira*) brings to mortals both evil and good,
and the gifts of the immortal gods are inescapable.

1.19 HESIOD, *THEOGONY* 904–906.

the Moirae, to whom wise Zeus gave most honor,
Klotho and Lachesis and Atropos, who give   905
mortal men to have both good and evil.

---

13 Diehl = *Anthologica Lyrica Graeca*, ed. E. Diehl, 1949 Leipzig.

Moira notwithstanding, in the literary sources there is a growing emphasis on the gods' concern for justice (theodicy). In *Works and Days* Hesiod advises rulers not to be unjust to their subjects because Zeus is watching out for justice.

1.20 HESIOD, *WORKS AND DAYS* 238–239.

But for those who practice wicked violence and cruel deeds,
Zeus the loud-voiced decrees justice (*dike*).

1.21 HESIOD, *WORKS AND DAYS* 266–269.

The eye of Zeus, seeing and understanding all things,
observes these things too, if he so wills. Nor does it escape his notice
what sort of justice it is that the city keeps within itself.

In Homer's *Odyssey*, Zeus Xenios is said to protect strangers and suppliants, as Odysseus asks the Cyclops Polyphemus for "guest-friend gifts."[14] The ritual act of supplication is described, whereby the suppliant falls at the feet of the Cyclops, thus acknowledging the latter's superior power. The Cyclops, however, refuses Odysseus' request, thereby putting himself outside the norms of civilized behavior.[15]

1.22 HOMER, *ODYSSEY* 9.266–276.

"But as for us, having reached here we fall at your knees
as suppliants, hoping that you will provide us with guest-friend gifts
or other kinds of gifts, as it's right to do for a stranger.
Respect the gods, most mighty one! We are suppliants;
strangers and suppliants both have their honor protected by Zeus,   270
Zeus Xenios who attends on strangers, who should be respected."
So I spoke; he replied at once, relentless of heart:
"How naive you are, stranger, or else you have come here from far away,
you who urge me to dread the gods or avoid their wrath;
we Cyclopes pay no attention to Zeus who carries the aegis,[16]   275
or the rest of the blessed gods, since we are stronger by far."

By contrast, later in the *Odyssey*, Odysseus' swineherd Eumaeus spontaneously offers hospitality to a beggar, the disguised Odysseus.

---

14 *Xenios*: this adjective refers to the concept of guest friendship, deriving from the noun *xenos* which can mean a guest, host, foreigner, or stranger, depending on the context. *suppliant*: one who makes a humble entreaty usually in the name of a particular god, begging for some kind of assistance from an individual who is in a more powerful position. *guest-friend gifts*: an exchange of gifts to establish a lasting bond or relationship, *xenia*, between two individuals who are strangers to each other and unrelated by blood. *Xenia* is a contract whereby each individual will assist or protect the other when needed.

15 For a detailed analysis of this episode see Naiden 2006: 139–140.

16 *aegis*: a goatskin cloak or shield with tassels that was said to be immortal. When shaken, it struck fear into an enemy.

1.23 HOMER, *ODYSSEY* 14.56–58.

"Stranger, it is not right for me to dishonor a stranger,
even one worse off than yourself; all strangers and beggars are sent
by Zeus, and a gift that is small to the giver means friendship to them."

> Gods were invoked when an oath was sworn and a sacrifice was made. In
> the *Iliad*, three deities are to be invoked as witnesses to an oath establishing
> a truce between the Greeks and Trojans: the goddess Earth, the Sun (Helios)
> who sees everything, and Zeus to whom oaths are sacred.

1.24 HOMER, *ILIAD* 3.103–107.

Bring here two lambs, a male that is white and a female, black,
for Earth and Helios;[17] we shall bring another for Zeus;
and have strong Priam brought here as well, to cut the oaths   105
himself—for his sons are irresponsible, not to be trusted—
lest someone transgress and destroy the oaths that are sacred to Zeus.[18]

> Homer describes King Agamemnon's invocation of Zeus as the king swears
> the oath on behalf of the Greeks.

1.25 HOMER, *ILIAD* 3. 276–280.

"Zeus father, master of Ida, greatest in glory and might,
and Helios, you who can see all things and hear all things,
you rivers, and earth, and you, the agents of vengeance against
dead humans under the earth if anyone swears an oath
that is false: bear witness and guard the oaths that we place our trust
  in.[19]   280

> Xenophon (c. 430–354 BCE) reports how the Greek commander Clearchus
> articulated the sanctity of the oaths and pledges that he had just exchanged
> with the Persian governor.

1.26 XENOPHON, *ANABASIS* 2.5.7–8. A man who has consciously disregarded these oaths is not a man whom I would call fortunate. I do not know how a man who is at war with the gods could swiftly make his escape, nor where he might flee, nor into what darkness he could run, nor how he could withdraw into a secure place of refuge. For everything in everyplace is subject to the gods, and the gods control all things equally. Such are my feelings about the gods and the oaths that we swore, the oaths that we placed in the gods' keeping when we made our pact.

---

17 The white male lamb is for Helios, the Sun, whereas the black female victim is for the goddess Earth.

18 *Priam*: the Trojan king, who is to take the oath on behalf of the Trojans. *oaths that are sacred to Zeus*: an allusion to Zeus Horkios, the protector of oaths (*horkoi*).

19 The invocation encompasses the entire universe, with the Sun, Zeus, Earth, and the powers of the underworld. In *Iliad* 15. 36–38, Hera swears by the Earth, Heaven (Ouranos), and the down-flowing water of the river Styx, which is the "greatest and most awesome oath for the blessed gods."

The breaking of an oath incurred the gods' anger, affecting and thus polluting not only the wrong-doer, but also all who came in contact with him. Pollution (*miasma*) could be caused by breaking an oath, voluntary or involuntary homicide, contact with the dead or with childbirth, giving birth, or sexual intercourse.[20]

In Euripides' tragedy *Medea* (first produced in 431 BCE), the foreign princess Medea has murdered her children because her husband Jason has repudiated her. Jason calls for vengeance, but Medea points out that oath-breakers and deceivers of foreigners cannot expect the gods to favor them.

1.27 EURIPIDES, *MEDEA* 1389–1393.

Jason

May the childrens' Fury and Justice,[21]

avenger of murder, destroy you!

Medea

What god, what spirit, listens to you,

breaker of oaths and a deceiver of friends?

Jason

You polluted slayer of your children!

At the end of Euripides' *Electra* (first produced c. 416 BCE), the god Castor, who with his brother Pollux protected seafarers, declares that they do not protect those who are polluted. He warns mortals not to go on a sea voyage with an oath breaker because the gods' anger could be manifested at any time, especially by means of shipwreck.

1.28 EURIPIDES, *ELECTRA* 1350–1356.

Castor

We do not help those who are polluted,   1350

but those to whom righteousness and justice are dear

throughout their lives, these we protect

and deliver from all distress.

Let no one wish to be unjust

and let no one sail with men who have broken their oaths.   1355

I, a god, proclaim this to mortals.

Impiety (*asebeia*) is literally a lack or denial of *sebas* (respect or reverence for the gods) and includes such actions as breaking oaths, malicious damage to property or rituals or representations of the gods, killing suppliants, entering certain temples when not permitted, introduction of new gods or cults not officially recognized by the state, and holding unorthodox views concerning the gods. The penalty for *asebeia* could be death, the most conspicuous example being the condemnation of Socrates on the last two

---

20 On pollution see Parker 1983, second edition 1996.

21 *childrens' Fury*: the Furies (*Erinyes*) pursued those who had murdered their own kin.

counts. *Asebeia*, however, does not include blasphemy or presenting the gods in what we might consider an irreverent or derogatory manner.

The Athenian orator Antiphon (c. 436–338 BCE) notes that impiety deprives the wrong-doer of hope. In the *Oeconomicus*, a treatise by Xenophon on estate management, the protagonist expresses his concept of piety and its benefits. Isocrates (436–338 BCE), the Athenian orator and advocate of panhellenism, gives advice on piety and morality.

1.29 ANTIPHON, *ON THE CHOREUTES* 5. An individual who acts impiously and commits transgressions against the gods would deprive himself of the very hope that is the greatest of human blessings.

1.30 XENOPHON, *OECONOMICUS* 11.8. I think I have learned that the gods made it impermissible for human beings to succeed without knowing what must be done and without taking care that these things are done. To some who are wise and diligent they give prosperity, but not to others. Therefore I begin by serving the gods, but I try, as is right for me when I pray to the gods, to act in a way to find health and strength of body, honor in the city, goodwill among friends, honorable safety in war, and wealth that is honorably increased.

1.31 ISOCRATES, *ANTIDOSIS* 282. You should realize that those who receive more from the gods both now and in the future are those who are most pious and most diligent in their devotions to them; and that those who fare better with their fellow humans are those who are the most conscientious in dealing with their associates, whether in their homes or in public, and are consequently most highly esteemed.

2. The Gods in Hesiod's *Theogony* and Homer's *Iliad*

2.1 HERODOTUS, *HISTORIES* 2.53. But from where each of these gods came into existence, and whether all of them had always existed, and what they looked like, all this was not known until the day before yesterday, so to speak.

For I believe that Hesiod and Homer, who were four hundred years before my time,[1] and no more than that, made for the Greeks the genealogies of the gods, giving them their appropriate titles, assigning their honors and skills, and describing their appearance.

> Writing in the mid-fifth century BCE, Herodotus discusses the origin and nature of the gods, noting that Homer and Hesiod gave systematic accounts of the gods' origins, genealogies, appearance or form, and gave them their various titles.[2] Herodotus' statement, however, does not mean that these poets invented Greek religion. Rather, they put together a version of the various myths concerning the gods that became the generally accepted tradition. The poems of Homer and Hesiod are a culmination of the long Greek tradition of oral poetry.

> The dating and authorship of the *Iliad* and *Odyssey* have long been the subject of scholarly discussion. Both epics are focused on the period during and immediately after the siege of Troy by the Greeks, an event that is generally dated c. 1200 BCE, but most scholars agree that the two epics were composed by Homer in the second half of the eighth century, and probably did not reach their final form until the sixth century BCE.

---

1 *four hundred years*: Herodotus overestimates the dates of Homer and Hesiod; modern scholars date them to the eighth rather than the ninth century BCE.

2 *titles*: either patronymics, such as "Zeus, son of Cronus," or cult titles such as Zeus Xenios, the protector of strangers.

Hesiod is thought to have been writing c. 700 BCE. In his poem *Theogony* Hesiod relates the origin and genealogies of the gods.[3] He distances himself from the stories he is about to relate by attributing his inspiration to the Muses who, he says, know both truth and fiction and mingle them as they wish.

2.2   HESIOD, *THEOGONY* 22–34.

Once they [the Muses] taught Hesiod beautiful song
as he watched his sheep under holy Helicon;
this is the first thing the goddesses told me,
the Olympian Muses, daughters of Zeus Aigiochos:[4]   25
   "Rustic shepherds, evil oafs, nothing but bellies,
we know how to say many lies as if they were true,
and when we want, we know how to speak the truth."
   This is what the prompt-voiced daughters of great Zeus said;
they picked up and gave me a staff, a branch of strong laurel,   30
a fine one, and breathed into me a voice
divine, to celebrate what will be and what was.[5]
They told me to sing the race of the blessed who always are,
but always to sing of themselves first and also last.

   Hesiod asks the Muses how the world and its gods were created.

2.3   HESIOD, *THEOGONY* 104–115.

Greetings, children of Zeus; grant me lovely song,
and praise the holy race of immortals who always are,   105
who were born from Gaea and starry Ouranos,
and from dark Nyx, and those salty Pontus raised.[6]
Tell how at first gods and earth came to be,
and rivers and vast sea, violent in surge,
and shining stars and the wide sky above,   110

---

3   For commentary on Hesiod's *Theogony*, see Caldwell 1987.

4   *Helicon*: a mountain in Boeotia, about halfway between Thebes and Delphi. *Olympian Muses*: the Muses were the divine patronesses of song and singers; they were called "Olympian" because of their father Zeus' connection with Mount Olympus. *Aigiochos*: literally the one who carries the aegis, a large goatskin cloak or shield with tassels that was said to be immortal. When shaken, it struck fear into the enemy. The attaching of a distinctive epithet to the name of a god or mortal is a convention of epic poetry, e.g, Poseidon is described as the "Earth-Shaker" in *Theogony* 456 (2.6), Athena as "owl-eyed" in *Theogony* 895 (2.7).

5   *staff*; in the Homeric assembly of chieftains, the staff was the symbol of the authority to speak, and was held by kings or princes, priests, prophets, heralds, and speakers. *laurel*: the laurel was sacred to Apollo as god of prophecy; hence Hesiod's claim "to celebrate what will be and what was."

6   *Gaea*: Earth. *Ouranos*: Sky. *Nyx*: Night. *Pontus*: Sea.

[and the gods born from them, givers of good]
how they divided their wealth and allotted honors
and how first they held valed Olympus.[7]
Tell me these things, Muses with Olympian homes,
from the first, say which of them first came to be.   115

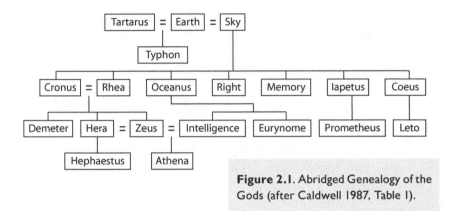

Figure 2.1. Abridged Genealogy of the Gods (after Caldwell 1987, Table 1).

The Muses reply that the first stage of the cosmogony occurred without sexual intercourse. First there was Chaos, then Gaea (Earth), Tartaros, and Eros (Desire). Erebus and Night were born from Chaos, and Night and Erebus produced Aether and Day. Finally Gaea produced Ouranos (Sky), the mountains and the sea. Then, in the second stage, Ouranos and Gaea had intercourse and produced twelve children, the last of whom was Cronus. These twelve came to be called the Titans.

2.4   HESIOD, *THEOGONY*, 116–138.

First of all Chaos came into being; but next
wide-breasted Gaea, always safe foundation of all
immortals who possess the peaks of snowy Olympus,
and dim Tartarus in a recess of the wide-pathed earth,
and Eros, most beautiful among the immortal gods,   120
limb-weakener, who conquers the mind and sensible thought
in the breasts of all gods and all men.[8]
From Chaos were born Erebus and black Nyx,

---

7   *valed Olympus*: the Greek literally means "with many folds," a reference to the many valleys in the mountain range.

8   *Chaos*: Abyss, an opening or gap, not disorder or chaos in a modern sense. *Gaea*: the earth, and also the primal mother. *Tartarus*: generally the lowest part of the underworld, but here, apparently, the lowest part of the earth. *Eros*: Love, Desire, the power of generation.

from Nyx were born Aether and Hemera,

whom she conceived and bore, joined in love with Erebus.[9]   125

Gaea first bore a child equal to herself,

starry Ouranos to cover her all over, and

to be an always safe home for the blessed gods.

She bore the high Ourea, pleasing homes of divine

nymphs, who dwell in the valed mountains.[10]   130

She also bore the barren sea, violent in surge,

Pontus, without love's union; but next

she lay with Ouranos and bore deep-whirling Oceanus,

and Koios and Kreios and Hyperion and Iapetus,

and Theia and Rhea and Themis and Mnemosyne   135

and gold-crowned Phoebe and attractive Tethys.

After them was born the youngest, crafty Cronus,

most terrible of children; he hated his lusting father.[11]

> At the instigation of Gaea, Cronus castrated Ouranos, and from the severed
> genitals sprang the goddess Aphrodite.

2.5   HESIOD, *THEOGONY* 188–208.

As soon as he [Cronus] cut off the genitals with adamant,

they were carried over the sea a long time, and white   190

foam arose from the immortal flesh;[12] within a girl

grew; first she came to holy Cythera, and

next she came to wave-washed Cyprus.[13]

An awesome and beautiful goddess emerged and

grass grew under her supple feet. Aphrodite   195

[foam-born goddess and well-crowned Cythereia]

gods and men name her, since in foam she grew;

and Cythereia, since she landed at Cythera;

---

9 *Erebus*: Darkness. *Aether*: Brightness, the upper air. *Hemera*: Day

10 *Ourea*: Mountains

11 *Oceanos*: a river that encircled the earth as opposed to Pontus, Sea, which lay in the middle of the landmass. *Themis*: Right or Established Custom. *Mnemosyne*: Memory or Remembrance. These twelve children of Ouranos and Gaea are later named Titans by their father; see *Theogony* 207 in 2.5.

12 The name Aphrodite contains the word *aphros*, Greek for "foam", and thus is generally thought to mean "born from the foam." Caldwell (1987: 40) suggests that foam symbolizes semen. The goddess of sexual desire was born from a god's genitals, just as Athena, the goddess of wisdom, was born from the head of the god Zeus; see 2.8.

13 *Cythera*: an island off the southern coast of the Peloponnese in Greece. *Cyprus*: a large island in the eastern Mediterranean. Both places were centers of Aphrodite's worship, especially Paphos in Cyprus.

and Cyprogenes, since she was born in wave-beat Cyprus;

and "Philommeides," since she appeared from the genitals.   200

Eros accompanied her, and fair Himeros followed,

when first she was born and went to join the gods.[14]

She has such honor from the first, and this is her

province among men and immortal gods:

girls' whispers and smiles and deceptions,   205

sweet pleasure and sexual love and tenderness.

    Great Ouranos, their father, called his sons Titans,

reproaching the sons whom he himself begot.

> Rhea and Cronus produce Hestia (Hearth), Demeter, Hera, Hades, Poseidon
> and Zeus. To avoid being superceded by his children, Cronus eats them at
> birth.[15]

2.6   HESIOD, *THEOGONY* 453–506.

    Rhea lay with Cronus and bore illustrious children:

Hestia, Demeter, and gold-sandaled Hera and

strong Hades, who lives in a palace under the ground   455

and has a pitiless heart, and loud-sounding Earth-Shaker[16]

and wise Zeus, the father of gods and men,

by whose thunder the wide earth is shaken.

Great Cronus would swallow these, as each

would come forth from the holy womb to his mother's knees,   460

intending that none of Ouranos' proud line but

himself would hold the right of king over the immortals.

For he learned from Gaea and starry Ouranos

that it was fate that his own son would overthrow him,

---

14 *Philommeides*: literally means genital-loving. Hesiod is punning on the similar-
   ity of pronunciation between *medea*, genitals, and *meid-* , laughter. *Philommeides*,
   laughter-loving, is an epithet used of Aphrodite in Homer, *Iliad* 3. 424, *Odyssey* 8.362
   and Hesiod, *Theogony* 989. *Himeros*: Longing, Desire.

15 See Figure 1.3 for genealogy.

16 *Hestia*: goddess of the hearth, the focal point of the home (*oikos*) who has little
   mythical function but was very important in people's lives. *Demeter*: goddess of
   grain, vegetation, and fertility. *Hera*: goddess of weddings and marriage. In myth
   she is portrayed as the powerful but jealous wife of Zeus, a resentful stepmother who
   bears Hephaestus without having sexual intercourse because of her anger at Zeus'
   many affairs and his illegitimate offspring; see below 2.8, *Theogony* 927–929. *Hades*:
   god of death and the underworld. *Earth-Shaker*: Poseidon, god of the sea, who is also
   connected with earthquakes and horses.

although he was powerful, by the plans of great Zeus.[17]   465
So he kept no blind man's watch, but alertly
swallowed his own children; incurable grief held Rhea.

> With the help of her parents Gaea and Ouranos, Rhea deceives Cronus
> by substituting a stone for the infant Zeus, who is reared on the island of
> Crete.

But when she was about to bear Zeus, father of gods
and men, she begged her own dear parents,
Gaea and starry Ouranos, to help her think   470
of a plan by which she might secretly have
her son, and make great crafty Cronus pay the
Erinyes of her father and the children he swallowed.[18]
They heard and obeyed their dear daughter
and told her what was destined to happen   475
concerning king Cronus and his strong-hearted son.
They sent her to Lyctus, to the rich land of Crete,
when she was about to bear her youngest son,
great Zeus; vast Gaea received him from her
in wide Crete to tend and raise.   480
Carrying him through the swift black night, she came
first to Lycos; taking him in her arms, she hid him
in a deep cave, down in dark holes of holy earth,
on Mount Aegaeum, dense with woods.
Rhea wrapped a huge stone in a baby's robe, and fed it   485
to Ouranos' wide-ruling son, king of the earlier gods;
he took it in his hands and put it down his belly,
the fool; he did not think in his mind that instead
of a stone his own son, undefeated and secure, was left
behind, soon to overthrow him by force and violence and   490
drive him from his honor, and rule the immortals himself.

> Cronus is forced to disgorge his older children, first vomiting the stone which
> Zeus places at Delphi. Zeus receives his thunderbolts from the Cyclopes.

Swiftly then the strength and noble limbs
of the future lord grew; at the end of a year,
tricked by the clever advice of Gaea,
great crafty Cronus threw up his children,   495

---

17 *For he learned...*: see Caldwell 1987: 54: "Gaia and Ouranos foretell, but do not deter-
    mine, the future. Their prophecy to Cronus may put him on the alert, but his efforts
    will necessarily fail."

18 *Erinyes*: underworld goddesses of revenge, who avenge the killing of blood relatives.

defeated by the craft and force of his own son.
First he vomited out the stone he had swallowed last;
Zeus fixed it firmly in the wide-pathed earth
at sacred Pytho in the vales of Parnassus,
to be a sign thereafter, a wonder to mortal men.[19]   500
        He released from their deadly chains his uncles,[20]
Ouranos' sons, whom their father mindlessly bound.
They did not forget gratitude for this help,
and gave him thunder and the fiery lightning bolt
and lightning, which vast Gaea earlier had hidden;   505
relying on these, he is king of mortals and immortals.[21]

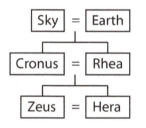

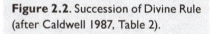

Figure 2.2. Succession of Divine Rule
(after Caldwell 1987, Table 2).

The gods make Zeus their supreme ruler and he gives them their various
honors. When Metis, his first wife, was about to give birth to Athena, Zeus
swallowed her.

2.7   HESIOD, *THEOGONY* 881–900
        But when the blessed gods had finished their work
        and decided the matter of rights with the Titans
        by force, they urged wide-seeing Olympian Zeus
        to be king and rule the immortals, by Gaea's
        advice; and he divided their honors among them.[22]   885

---

19 *Pytho*: Delphi. *Parnassus*: the mountain range in the hinterland of Delphi. *stone*:
    Hesiod identifies this stone with the famous *omphalos*, the navel stone at Delphi,
    which was said to mark the center of the universe.

20 *uncles*: the Cyclopes, also children of Ouranos and Gaea; see Caldwell 1987: 56.

21 Caldwell 1987: 55, "Zeus is a sky-god like his grandfather Ouranos, associated
    especially with rain, storms, and lightning. He is king of the gods because he is most
    powerful, but he is also most wise. He seems to be connected with no particular
    city or region, but is the most panhellenic of the gods. He is also the most sexually
    active."

22 For Homer's account of the honors assigned to Poseidon, Hades, and Zeus himself,
    see Homer *Iliad* 15. 187–193, below 2.19.

Zeus, king of gods, made Metis his first wife,[23]
she who knows most of gods and mortal men.
But when she was about to bear the owl-eyed
goddess Athena, then he deceived her mind with a
trick of wily words, and put her down in his belly,[24]   890
by the advice of Gaea and starry Ouranos. Thus
they advised him, so that no other of the eternal
gods would hold the office of king but Zeus.
For from her wise children were fated to be born:
first a daughter, owl-eyed Tritogeneia,[25]   895
like her father in strength and wise counsel,
but then she was going to bear a son
proud of heart, king of gods and men;
but first Zeus put her into his own belly,
so the goddess might advise him on good and evil.   900

Hesiod lists Zeus' other children by different mothers, including the gods
Apollo, Ares, Hermes, Dionysus, and the goddesses Athena and Artemis.
Hera produces Hephaestus "without love's union."

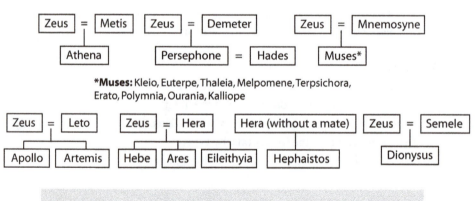

Figure 2.3. The "wives" of Zeus (adapted from Caldwell 1987, Table 14).

---

23 *Metis*: the name means "crafty intelligence", she is a daughter of Oceanus (*Theogony* 358).

24 *put her down in his belly*: i.e, swallowed her; see Caldwell 1987: 77: "Since Metis, like all water-deities, can change her shape, Zeus seems to have tricked her ("with wily words") into assuming a shape in which she could easily be swallowed." On Athena's birth from Zeus' head, see *Theogony* 924 in 2.8.

25 *Tritogeneia*: another name of Athena. *owl-eyed*: Athena is often associated with the owl, especially in Athens.

2.8   HESIOD, *THEOGONY* 912–942.

Next he came to the bed of nurturant Demeter;
she bore white-armed Persephone, whom Aedoneus
seized from her mother; but Zeus allowed it.[26]

Then he loved fair-haired Mnemosyne,[27] who bore   915
the nine Muses with golden headbands,
whose delight is banquets and the pleasure of song.

And Leto, joined in love to Zeus Aigiochos,
bore Apollo and archeress Artemis, beautiful
children beyond all of Ouranos' descendants.   920

Lastly he made Hera his blooming wife;
she bore Hebe and Ares and Eileithyia,[28]
having joined in love with the king of gods and men.

He himself bore from his head owl-eyed Athena,
the awesome, fight-rousing, army-leading, unweary   925
mistress whose delight is din and wars and battles;
but Hera, who was angry and at odds with her husband,
without love's union bore famous Hephaestus,
excellent in arts beyond all of Ouranos' descendants.

....

And the Atlanteid Maia bore to Zeus glorious Hermes,
herald of the gods, after going up to his holy bed.
And the Cadmeid Semele bore an illustrious son,[29] much-   940
cheering Dionysus, after joining Zeus in love,
mortal with immortal; now they both are gods.

---

26 Persephone, the daughter of Zeus and Demeter, was carried off by Hades to be
   his bride in the underworld. She was restored to her mother for part of the year,
   during which time the crops grew. During Persephone's absence in the underworld,
   Demeter mourned, thus neglecting the crops. *Aedoneus:* a longer form of the name
   Hades, god of the underworld.

27 *Mnemosyne:* see 2.4 with n. 11.

28 Hebe was the goddess of youth, Ares, the god of war, and Eileithyia goddess of childbirth.

29 *Cadmeid Semele:* Semele was a daughter of Cadmus, king of Thebes.

The gods in Homer's *Iliad*

The genealogies of the gods as related in Hesiod's *Theogony* are essential for understanding the dysfunctional Olympian family depicted in Homer's *Iliad* and *Odyssey*. The plot of the *Iliad* is driven by the divisions among the Olympian gods, who take sides during the siege of Troy. Of the more important male gods, Apollo sides with the Trojans and Poseidon with the Greeks. The goddesses Hera and Athena are on the side of the Greeks, whereas Aphrodite is on the side of the Trojans. This alignment assumes familiarity with the story of the judgment of Paris, the Trojan prince who preferred the gift of Aphrodite to those of Hera and Athena. Aphrodite's gift to Paris was the most beautiful woman in the world. And so Paris abducted Helen, the wife of the Greek Menelaus, causing Menelaus' brother Agamemnon to lead an army against the Trojans.

Divine intervention should be regarded in light of Thales' statement, which begins this book, that all things are full of gods. In the struggle between the Greeks and Trojans, often a god initially intervenes in human disguise and is seen by only one individual. Stories from more historical times continue this tradition of divine intervention. For example, Herodotus reports that Pan appeared to the Athenian runner sent to Sparta to ask for help before the battle of Marathon in 490 BCE.[30] As Lloyd-Jones observes, "we must acknowledge that Homer's gods are effective and his religion real, but that his human characters are free to decide and are responsible for their decisions."[31]

Early in Book 1 of the *Iliad* Athena warns Achilles not to kill Agamemnon, who has refused to accept the ransom offered by the Trojan priest Chryses to retrieve his daughter.[32] Achilles tries to reason with Agamemnon but a quarrel ensues. Achilles is considering what action to take when Hera sends Athena to restrain him. Achilles recognizes the goddess, who is seen only by him, and realizes that he must obey; otherwise, he will lose the gods' favor.

2.9   HOMER, *ILIAD* 1.188–222.

So he spoke, and distress came over the son of Peleus;[33]
the heart in his shaggy chest pondered, this way and that,
whether to draw the sharpened sword from beside his thigh,   190
scatter the crowd and slaughter the son of Atreus,[34] or
to put a stop to his rage and hold his heart in check.

---

30 See 1.1 and 14.7.

31 Lloyd-Jones 1983: 10.

32 The priest's daughter had been captured by the Greeks and was Agamemnon's concubine.

33 *son of Peleus*: Achilles.

34 *son of Atreus*: Agamemnon.

While he debated this in his mind and heart, and was starting
to pull his mighty sword from the scabbard, Athena came
down from the sky; the white-armed goddess Hera had sent her,   195
her heart full of love and concern for both of the men alike.
She stood behind Peleus' son and grasped his tawny hair
appearing to him alone; none of the rest of them saw her.
Achilles turned round, stunned, and recognized her at once,
Pallas Athena; her two eyes shone with a terrible light.   200
He addressed her, speaking words that flew from his lips on wings:
"Why on earth have you come here, offspring of Zeus who carries the
    aegis?[35]
To observe the outrageous behavior of Atreus' son, Agamemnon?
Now I shall tell you something that will, I think, be accomplished:
the arrogance he is displaying is soon going to cost him his life."   205
The grey-eyed goddess Athena addressed him then in his turn:
"I've come to put a stop to your fury, if you'll be persuaded,
down from the sky; the white-armed goddess Hera has sent me,
her heart full of love and concern for both of you men alike;
come, cease from this strife; do not pull out your sword with your
    hand;   210
instead abuse him with verbal insults regarding the future;
for I shall tell you something that will indeed be accomplished:
one day you'll have three times the amount of splendid gifts
because of this outrage; hold back therefore, persuaded by me."
    Answering her, swift-footed Achilles addressed her in turn: 215
"Goddess, I must pay careful attention to what you say,
despite the rage in my heart; for this is the better way;
if someone obeys the gods they listen to him in return."
    He spoke, and checked his weighty hand on the silver hilt
and drove the mighty sword back inside its scabbard, obeying   220
the word of Athena; and she went back to Olympus to join
the rest of the gods in the palace ruled by Zeus who carries the aegis.

> Achilles withdraws from the fighting and asks his mother Thetis to go as a
> suppliant to Zeus, begging him to help the Trojans so that the Greeks will
> regret Achilles' absence from the battlefield.[36]

---

35 *Zeus who carries the aegis*: see above 2.2 with n. 4.

36 *Thetis*: a sea nymph, daughter of the sea god Nereus, and thus immortal. Achilles'
    father Peleus was mortal.

2.10   HOMER, *ILIAD* 1.498–516.

She [Thetis] found the resounding son of Cronus sitting apart

from the rest, on the topmost peak of many-folded Olympus;

she sat before him, taking hold of his knees with her left   500

hand, her right hand touching his chin from underneath,[37]

and addressed lord Zeus, the son of Cronus, in supplication:

"Zeus father, if ever I brought you benefit, either by word

or by deed among the immortals, I beg you, fulfill my desire:[38]

honor my son, who is doomed to the shortest life among mortals.   505

Agamemnon, lord of men, has done him dishonor by taking

and keeping his due reward, which he stripped from him in person;

you honor him therefore, Olympian Zeus, deviser of counsels;

bestow victorious power on the Trojans until the Achaeans

pay my son his due and enrich his standing with honor."   510

So she spoke; cloud-gathering Zeus addressed her not,

but sat for a long time silent. Thetis clung to his knees

tightly, without letting go, and spoke for a second time:

"Promise me truly and bow your head in assent, or else

refuse—since you're untouched by fear—so that I may know   515

for sure how far I'm the most dishonored of all the gods."

> Zeus gives his promise, despite fear of his wife Hera's anger. The details of his
> plan to help Achilles, however, are not revealed until later in the poem.

2.11   HOMER, *ILIAD* 1.517–530.

Then greatly upset, cloud-gathering Zeus addressed her in turn:

"What a dreadful business this is! You will stir up hatred between

myself and Hera, who always provokes me with words of abuse.

As it is she is constantly casting reproaches against me among   520

the immortal gods; she says I am helping the Trojans in battle.

But go away now, so that Hera may not notice you here;

I'll make these things my own concern and see them accomplished.

Come, I shall bow my head in assent, that you may be persuaded;

for this is the mightiest guarantee that I can provide   525

among the immortals: nothing can be reneged on, revoked

or left unaccomplished, once I have bowed my head in assent."

The son of Cronus spoke and nodded his blue-black brows;

---

37 *touching his chin...*: the ritual act of a suppliant, one who humbles himself in order to
   ask a favor. Another way of supplicating was to grasp the knees of the person being
   supplicated; see below line 512.

38 *if ever I brought you benefit...*: an allusion to an earlier story that Thetis had saved
   Zeus when the other gods wished to bind him (*Iliad* 1.396–406).

the ambrosial locks of hair on the lord's immortal head
fell tumbling forward, making mighty Olympus shake.   530

> When Hera learns of Thetis' visit, a domestic argument ensues, in which
> Zeus asserts not only his supremacy over his wife, but also his right to
> withhold his thoughts from the other gods.

2.12 HOMER, *ILIAD* 1. 544–550.

The father of men and gods said, answering her in reply:
"Hera, do not expect to have knowledge of all that I say,   545
for it will be hard on you, even though you are my wife;
if something is fitting for you to hear, then no one at all,
whether god or human, will know about it before yourself;
but if I wish to reflect on something away from the gods,
don't keep on questioning me about that and asking for details."   550

> Peace is restored within the Olympian family as Hera's son Hephaestus
> advises his mother to stop quarreling with Zeus about mortals, since he has
> the power to overthrow them all. Book I of the *Iliad* ends with a description
> of the gods feasting on Olympus.

2.13 HOMER, *ILIAD* 1. 571–604.

And then the famous craftsman Hephaestus began to address them,
in an act of kindness to white-armed Hera, his own dear mother:
"What a dreadful business this will be, no longer supportable,
if the two of you are to quarrel like this on account of mortals,
and persist in raising a ruckus among the gods; there will be   575
no pleasure at all in this good feast if the worse wins victory.
I advise my mother—although she already knows this herself—
to act with kindness towards our own dear father Zeus,
that our father may not reproach her again and disrupt our feast.
For if he wishes, he the Olympian lightning-lord   580
can hurl us out of our seats; for he is the strongest by far.
Approach him and try to appease him with soft and gentle words,
and then the Olympian lord will at once be gracious to us."
    So he spoke, and darting up he placed in the hand
of his own dear mother a two-handled drinking-cup and addressed
    her: 585
"Endure, my mother; despite your sorrow submit to his will,
for fear these eyes of mine may see you, dear as you are,
being beaten; and then I won't have the power to protect you, despite
my distress; it is harsh to pit oneself against the Olympian...."

....

So he spoke, and Hera, the white-armed goddess, smiled,   595
and smiling accepted the drinking-cup from the hand of her child;
and then he poured sweet nectar for all the rest of the gods,[39]
which he drew from a mixing-bowl and served from left to right;
and when they saw Hephaestus the cripple hobbling about
in the palace, unquenchable laughter arose from the blessed gods.   600
    And so they feasted all day long till the sun went down,
and none of their hearts was deprived of an equal share of the feast,
or of the sound of the beautiful lyre in Apollo's hands,
or of the Muses, who sang and responded with beautiful voice.

> As Athena intervened on behalf of Achilles,[40] so the goddess Aphrodite
> intervenes on behalf of the Trojan prince Paris. Menelaus, the former husband
> of Helen, is about to capture Paris and drag him by his helmet to the Greek
> army. The goddess breaks the helmet strap and takes him back to Troy.

2.14 HOMER, *ILIAD* 3.369–384.

He [Menelaus] spoke, and darting forward took hold of the horsehair-
    shaded
helmet, twisted him [Paris] round and started to drag him towards   370
the finely-greaved Achaeans;[41] the richly-embroidered strap
was choking his tender neck—the tight strap holding the helmet
under his chin. And he would have got him there and reaped
unquenchable glory, but Aphrodite, daughter of Zeus,
quickly noticed and broke the strap made out of the hide   375
of an ox once killed by force. The helmet came away empty
in the hero's sturdy hand; he whirled it around and threw it
towards the finely-greaved Achaeans; his stalwart comrades
retrieved it; but he went rushing back, heart set on killing
the man with a spear of bronze; but Aphrodite had seized him,   380
easily—being a goddess—and cloaked him densely in mist,
and set him down in his perfumed bedroom fragrant with incense.
Then she went herself to summon Helen; she found her
high on a tower, with a crowd of Trojan women around her.

> Unlike Achilles, who acknowledged the power of the gods, Helen challenges
> Aphrodite and refuses to go to Paris, whom Homer calls Alexandros.
> Enraged, Aphrodite threatens to withdraw her favor.

---

39 *nectar*: the gods' equivalent of wine.

40 See 2.9.

41 *finely-greaved*: the greaves are armor protecting the lower part of the leg. *Achaeans*:
    Greeks.

2.15   HOMER, *ILIAD* 3.399–420.

"Troubling divinity, why do you long to deceive me like this?
Will you take me even further away, to a well-inhabited   400
city in Phrygia somewhere or charming Maeonia,
if there's some mortal man there too who is dear to your heart?
Is it because Menelaus has now won victory over
glorious Alexandros [Paris], and wants to bring me back home—
loathsome as I am—is this the reason you're standing here   405
at my side now, heart full of trickery? *You* go and sit with him!
Retreat from the paths of the gods and direct your feet no more
to Olympus; devote yourself to grieving for him and protecting
him till he makes you his wife or his concubine—his slave!
But *I* won't go to him—that would rightly bring me reproach—   410
to attend to that man's bed; all of the Trojan women
will blame me later. Infinite is the distress in my heart."
      Glorious Aphrodite addressed her then in a rage:
"Do not provoke me, you stubborn fool, lest in my rage
I abandon you and hate you exceedingly—just as much   415
as I love now—and devise woeful hatred for you from both
Danaans and Trojans alike, and an evil doom destroy you."[42]
      So she spoke, and dread filled Helen, daughter of Zeus;
wrapped in her brightly gleaming robe she went in silence,
unseen by the Trojan women, the goddess leading the way.   420

> In attempting to rescue her son Aeneas from battle, Aphrodite is wounded
> by the Greek warrior Diomedes, son of Tydeus. Apollo intervenes and saves
> Aeneas. Diomedes taunts the goddess.

2.16   HOMER, *ILIAD* 5.334–354.

But when he found her [Aphrodite], pressing hard on her heels through
   the throng,
the son of Tydeus [Diomedes] mighty of heart leaped forward at her, 335
reaching and wounding her dainty wrist with his sharpened spear;
the spear stabbed into her skin, straight through the ambrosial gown
that the Graces themselves had worked for her, and cut her hand
close to the heel; immortal blood came flowing out
from the goddess—the ichor that flows in the veins of the blessed
   gods.   340
For the gods do not eat grain, or drink any gleaming wine;[43]

---

42 *Danaans*: Greeks.

43 *gleaming wine*: the gods drink nectar, not wine; see above *Iliad* 1.597 in 2.13.

that is why they have no blood and are called the immortal ones.
Crying out loud she dropped her son; but Phoebus Apollo
saved him from the battle with his own hands, by wrapping around him
a blue-black cloud, so that no one among the Danaans swift   345
of horse might strike his chest with bronze and strip him of life;
Diomedes, great at the war-cry, shouted loudly at her:
"Daughter of Zeus, retreat from war and the battle's heat;
is it not enough to use your deceptions on women, who have
no strength? Yet if you do make war your business, I think   350
you will shudder to hear about warfare even from far away."
    So he spoke; she left in a frenzy, sorely distressed;
wind-footed Iris took her and led her away from the throng,
burdened with pain, her beautiful skin stained dark by the wound.[44]

> Zeus' plan of helping the Trojans goes into abeyance when Hera seduces
> him and Poseidon rallies the Greeks. When Zeus awakes, he reestablishes
> control and reveals details of his plan.

2.17 HOMER, *ILIAD* 15.59–77.

"Let Phoebus Apollo urge on Hector into the battle,
breathe vigor [*menos*] into him once again and make him forget   60
the pain distressing him in his mind;[45] then let him again
turn back the Achaeans, driving them into a strengthless rout,
and in their flight let them fall back on the many-benched ships
of Peleus' son, Achilles; and he will rouse into action
his comrade Patroclus,[46] whom glorious Hector will kill with his spear 65
in front of Troy, when he has destroyed many more young men
in their prime, including glorious Sarpedon, my own son.
Enraged at Hector, glorious Achilles will kill him in turn,
then I shall engineer a continuous counterattack
pushing ceaselessly back from the ships until the Achaeans   70
capture steep-walled Troy in accord with the plan of Athena.[47]
Before that I won't put a stop to my rage, or allow
any other immortal to go down there and protect the Danaans,
not until the desire of Peleus' son is fully accomplished,

---

44 *Iris*: the messenger of the gods.

45 *Hector*: a son of Priam; he is the best of the Trojan warriors. *breathe vigor into him*:
   the Greek *menos* is defined by Dodds 2004: 8 as a "mysterious access of energy;" or "a
   new confidence or eagerness."

46 *Patroclus*: the friend and companion of Achilles.

47 "*Then I shall engineer…*": these events go beyond the scope of the *Iliad* which ends
   with the funeral of Hector.

as I promised him at the outset, bowing my head, on the day   75
when the goddess Thetis came as a suppliant, grasping hold
of my knees, and begged me to honor Achilles, sacker of cities."

> Hera acknowledges Zeus' supremacy.

2.18 HOMER, *ILIAD* 15.104–109.

"How naive and senseless we are to set our hearts against Zeus!
Our desire is to get close up and stop him by means of words   105
or else by force; but he just sits apart and ignores us,
paying us no attention, because he says that among
the immortal gods he is clearly supreme in power and strength.
That is why each one of you suffers whatever evil he sends you."[48]

> Zeus continues to have problems with his family. Ordered by Zeus to leave
> the battlefield, Poseidon points out that he, Zeus, and Hades drew lots for
> the allocation of the world.

2.19 HOMER, *ILIAD* 15.185–195.

"Oh no! As great as he is, these arrogant words are too much,   185
if he's going to force me, his equal in honor, against my will.[49]
There are three of us brothers, the sons of Cronus, whom Rhea bore,
Zeus and myself and Hades, the third, who rules down below.
All things were divided in three, with honor allotted to each;
when the lots were drawn I won the grey salt sea as my share   190
to dwell in forever, the misty darkness was Hades' share,
and Zeus's share was the brightness and clouds of the broad sky above;
earth remains common to all and so does lofty Olympus.
Therefore I shall not live as Zeus is minded, but let him
remain content in his own third share, powerful though he is."   195

> When confronted by the imminent death of his son, the Trojan Sarpedon,
> Zeus wonders whether to rescue him. But his wife Hera reminds him of
> Sarpedon's mortality.

2.20 HOMER, *ILIAD* 16.431–443.

And when he saw them, the son of Cronus, deviser of crooked
schemes, addressed these words to Hera, his sister and wife:
"Oh no! It is destiny that Sarpedon, dearest of men,
be overcome at the hands of Patroclus, son of Menoetius.
My heart is divided in its desire and my mind is debating: 435
should I seize him out of the tearful battle and take him away
from here, and set him down in Lycia's flourishing land,

---

48 See Hephaestus' advice to Hera in 2.13.
49 This message is intended for Zeus.

or should I overcome him now at Patroclus' hands?"

Then Hera the ox-eyed lady answered him in reply:

"Most dreaded son of Cronus, what word is this you have said!   440
Do you wish to release from woeful death a man who is mortal,
one who was destined from long ago to meet this fate?
Do it, then. But we won't all praise you, the rest of us gods."

> After convincing Zeus that he should yield to destiny, Hera suggests that
> Sarpedon's body be sent to his homeland for full burial honors. Zeus weeps
> for his son.

2.21   HOMER, *ILIAD* 16.450–461.

"But if he is dear to you indeed and your heart is lamenting,   450
let him remain in the powerful clash of the battlefield
to be overcome by the hand of Patroclus, son of Menoetius,
but when the spirit and breath of life have left him, then
send Death and refreshing Sleep to bear him away from the fighting
and carry him off until they reach broad Lycia's people;   455
there his brothers and friends will pay him proper respect
with a mound and a marker-stone—the due reward of the dead."

So she spoke and the father of men and gods was persuaded.
He poured a rain of bloody tear-drops onto the ground
to honor his own dear child, who was going to be destroyed   460
by Patroclus in fertile Troy, far from his land of his fathers.[50]

> After Patroclus is killed by Hector, Achilles is willing to accept Agamemnon's
> apology and return and fight to avenge Patroclus' death. Agamemnon
> disclaims responsibility for his behavior by blaming the intervention of *Ate*
> or Delusion.

2.22   HOMER, *ILIAD* 19.86–96.

"... But I am not responsible,
Zeus is, and Fate, and the Fury who wanders shrouded in mist;
they filled my mind with savage Delusion (*Ate*) at the assembly,
on the day when I stripped from Achilles his due reward in person.
But what could I have done? Gods always accomplish their will.   90
Delusion, the eldest daughter of Zeus, deludes us all
to our ruin; her feet are tender—she never touches the ground,
but walks on the heads of men doing damage to human minds,
entangling first one person and then the next in her snares.
Even Zeus was blinded once by Delusion—Zeus who says   95

---

50   After Sarpedon is killed, Zeus sends Apollo to rescue the body (*Iliad* 16.666–683).

that he is supreme among men and gods."[51]

Since Achilles is returning to the battlefield, Zeus holds a council of gods and orders them to take sides and join in the fighting. But when challenged by Poseidon to join the fray, Apollo remarks that humans should fight their own battles.

2.23 HOMER, *ILIAD* 21.462–467.

Earth-Shaker, you would say I've taken leave of my senses,
if I'm to go to war with you for the sake of mortals,
wretches who are like leaves, one moment warm and alive
as they eat the fruits of the plowed-up earth, but a moment later   465
perishing lifeless. Come, let us put a stop to our fighting
as quickly as possible; let them strive on their own behalf.

Zeus asks the gods whether Hector should be rescued.

2.24 HOMER, *ILIAD* 22.167–187.

The father of men and gods was the first to speak among them:
"Oh no! I see with my own eyes a man who is dear to me
being chased around the wall of the city. My heart is lamenting
for Hector, who burned for me the thigh-bones of many oxen   170
on the peaks of many-folded Ida, at other times too
in the highest part of the citadel; yet now glorious Achilles
is chasing him round the city of Priam on his swift feet.
Come, tell me what you think, you gods, and help me devise
the proper counsel: should we save him from death, or should we   175
overcome him, good man though he is, at the hands of Achilles?"
The grey-eyed goddess Athena addressed him then in her turn:
"Father, lord of bright thunder and dark clouds, what have you said!
Do you wish to release from woeful death a man who is mortal,
one who was destined from long ago to meet this fate?   180
Do it, then. But we won't all praise you, the rest of us gods."[52]
Answering her, cloud-gathering Zeus addressed her in turn:
"Tritogeneia, my own dear child, take heart, for I spoke
without eagerness in my heart and I wish to be gentle towards you;
act in the way that your mind directs you and stop holding back."   185

---

51 *Even Zeus was blinded…*: see the comments of Lloyd-Jones 1983: 23, " That helps
Agamemnon to save face, but it does not cancel his responsibility," and of Garland
1994: 21, "Though we do not need to assume that Homer is endorsing Agamemnon's
face-saving explanation of his poor behaviour, there is no reason to doubt that belief
in *ate* was widespread."

52 Note the identical words of Hera in 2.20.

So speaking he urged on the already eager Athena,

and she went darting down from the craggy peaks of Olympus.

> Zeus weighs the fates of Hector and Achilles on the golden scales, and Apollo abandons Hector.

2. 25 HOMER, *ILIAD* 22.208–213.

But when in their running they came to the springs for the fourth time, then

the father held out a golden balance, and placed in its pans

two heavy fates of death with its endless burden of grief,   210

one for Achilles, the other for Hector, tamer of horses;

he grasped the center and raised it, and Hector's destined day

sank down to the realm of Hades, and Phoebus Apollo left him.

> Realizing that he was deceived by Athena, who had disguised herself as his brother Deiphobos, Hector accepts his fate.

2.26 HOMER, *ILIAD* 22.294–305.

Shouting loudly he summoned Deiphobus of the white shield,

asking for a long spear, but his brother was nowhere near him;   295

then Hector knew in his mind what had happened, and said out loud:

"Oh no! The gods have clearly called me to meet my death.

I thought that the hero Deiphobus stood here close by my side;

but he is safely within the wall, and Athena deceived me.

Now evil death is near me and stands no more at a distance;   300

there's no escape; it turns out that this was dear all along

to Zeus and Zeus's son, the far-shooter,[53] who in the past

were eager to keep me safe; but now my destiny's found me.

In that case let me not be destroyed without struggle and glory,

performing some mighty deed that those in the future will hear of."[54] 305

> The dying Hector warns Achilles that he will be killed by Paris, aided by Apollo. Achilles declares his acceptance of fate.

2.27 HOMER, *ILIAD* 22.355–366.

Gleaming-helmeted Hector addressed him in turn as he died: 355

"I could foresee this, knowing you well; I would never have

persuaded you, for the heart in your breast is made out of iron.

Take heed lest I become a cause of wrath from the gods

upon your head, on the day when Paris and Phoebus Apollo

destroy you, good man though you are, at the Scaean gates."   360

---

53 *the far-shooter*: Apollo.

54 *some mighty deed*: …: concern for future fame was the prime motivation of the epic hero.

So he spoke, and the end of death was folded around him;
the spirit flew from his limbs and down to the realm of Hades,
lamenting its lot and leaving behind his manhood and youth.
Glorious Achilles addressed him in turn even though he was dead:
"Die! As for me, I'll accept my fate at whatever time   365
Zeus and the other immortal gods may wish to fulfill it.

3. FAMILY AND COMMUNITY

3.1 DIODORUS SICULUS 5.68. It is said that Hestia invented the establishment of *oikoi* (households),[1] and because of this blessing her shrine has been set up in every home by almost all peoples, where she receives her share of honor and sacrifices.

3.2 PLATO, *LAWS* 5.729 c. By paying honor and respect to one's kinsfolk and all who share in the worship of the gods of the tribe and who also share descent and blood, a person will also enjoy the favor of the gods of the household (*oikos*) who will be well disposed toward his own begetting of children.

> The *oikos*, generally translated as household or family, consisted of both persons and property, including the slaves and cattle. The head of the *oikos* was the oldest male family member, who was responsible for the worship of the gods within his own household and so acted as its priest.
>
> Diodorus, writing in the second half of the first century BCE, attributes the institution of the *oikos* to Hestia, goddess of the hearth. Because the household is a great gift, Hestia is honored almost everywhere. The philosopher Plato (c.429–347 BCE) describes an individual's obligation to the gods and the ensuing benefits.
>
> Religion permeated all societal groups: the *oikos* (household or family), the *genos* (kinship or descent group), the *deme* (local territorial district), social groups such as phratries (brotherhoods), and the larger community of the *polis* (city state).[2] Birth, entry into adulthood, marriage, and death, the major life transitions, were marked by important rituals that were celebrated by

---

1 *Hestia*: goddess of the hearth, daughter of Cronos and Rhea, and so the sister of Zeus, Poseidon, Hera, Hades, and Demeter.

2 A phratry or brotherhood was a religious and political association of alleged kinsmen from different *oikoi* who acknowledged common ancestors and shared a common cult.

both the immediate family (*oikos*) and the societal groups within the polis. The evidence for these rituals, however, is scanty and extremely diverse, deriving from a disparity of both literary and epigraphic sources that range over several centuries and indicate variations in the different Greek communities throughout the Mediterranean world. Many of the generalizations that follow are based on the evidence for practices in Athens or Sparta, two city states that had very different social structures.

The treatise *Constitution of Athens* (the authorship is disputed) indicates that, when an Athenian was standing for political office, his credentials were carefully examined by members of the Council.

3.3   ARISTOTLE? *CONSTITUTION OF ATHENS* 55.3. "Who is your father and what deme does he belong to? Who is your father's father? Who is your mother and what deme does she belong to?" After that they ask him, "Do you have an Apollo Patroos and Zeus Herkeios and, if so, where are their shrines?[3] Do you have any family tombs and, if so, where are they? Do you treat your parents well? Do you pay your taxes? Have you taken part in military campaigns?"

From birth to early adulthood

The goddesses who presided over childbirth were Artemis, Eileithyia (the one who brings to light), Demeter Kourotrophos (nurturer of the young), and Hera (goddess of marriage and thus of childbirth). Generally a midwife, a woman beyond the age of bearing children, would officiate at the birth, together with married women of the household. Various potions or drugs (*pharmaka*) would be administered, spells intoned, and the appropriate deities invoked.[4]

Two excerpts from a late fourth-century BCE sacred law of the Greek colony of Cyrene in North Africa define the extent of the pollution caused by childbirth and the pollution caused by miscarriage.

3.4   RO no. 97,[5] side A, lines 16–20. The woman in childbed pollutes the house; she pollutes anyone inside the house, but she does not pollute anyone outside the house, unless he comes inside. Any person who is inside shall

---

3   *Apollo Patroos*: through Ion, a son of Apollo, the god was regarded as the ancestor of all Athenians. *Zeus Herkeios*: Zeus as protector of the enclosure (*herke*), and thus also of the *oikos*.

4   See Garland 1990: 61–64, 66–68.

5   RO no. 97 is number 97 in Rhodes and Osborne 2003, a collection of Greek historical inscriptions more widely available than earlier publications. For each inscription RO provide a full Greek text, often revised on the basis of new evidence, together with citations of earlier publications, an English translation, and commentary. Where an RO Greek text is available, I have used that text for my translation, but have consulted earlier publications. On this law which is attributed to the oracle of Apollo, see also the remarks of Parker 1983: 332–351.

be polluted for three days, but he will not pollute anyone else, no matter wherever this person goes.

3.5   RO no. 97, side B, lines 106–109. If a woman has a miscarriage, if it is distinguishable,[6] they are polluted as if a person has died; but if it is not distinguishable, the house itself is polluted as if from childbirth.

> On the fifth or seventh day, the newborn child was brought from the women's quarters and ritually carried around the hearth of the *oikos*, in a ceremony called the *amphidromia*, literally "running around."[7] This act symbolized the acceptance of the infant into the *oikos*. At this ceremony the child was given a name. The probable reason for waiting a few days was to be reasonably sure that the child was going to survive, as Aristotle notes.

3.6   ARISTOTLE, *HISTORY OF ANIMALS*. 588 a 8–10. The majority of deaths in infancy occur before the child is a week old; therefore it is customary to name the child at that age because it is thought that the child then has a better chance of survival.

> Death in childbirth was a constant threat. In Euripides' *Medea*, Medea compares the risks of childbirth with those of death in battle.

3.7   EURIPIDES, *MEDEA* 248–251.

They [men] say that we [women] spend all our time at home,
and live safe lives, while they go out to battle.
What fools they are! I'd rather stand three times
behind a shield than bear a child once!

> A late inscription (second century CE) from the island of Paros bears the following epitaph for a woman who died in childbirth.

3.8   *IG* XII. 5.310.

Nicander was my father, Paros my country.
My name is Socrateia. When I died, my husband
Parmenion buried me, granting me this favor
so that my good conduct in life be remembered
by future generations. The cruel Fury of childbirth,
implacable, with a hemorrhage took me from my happy life.
By my pains I could not bring the child into the light
but he lives in my womb among the dead.
In my third decade of life, I reached the sixth year.
I left my husband male offspring: two for my father
and husband; for myself, because of the third,
I am in this grave.

---

6   *distinguishable*: the issue is whether the foetus is recognizable as a person.

7   See Dillon 2002: 254 and Garland 1990: 93–95.

We should be aware of not only the high mortality rate of both mothers and children but also the exposure of unwanted infants. Girls were more likely to be exposed than boys. A letter from a Greek soldier who was serving in Alexandria away from home and sending money to his pregnant wife indicates the practice of exposing babies. This letter is preserved on a first-century BCE papyrus.

3.9 *OXYRHYNCHUS PAPYRUS* 744. I send you my warmest greetings, I want you to know that we are still in Alexandria. Don't worry if I remain in Alexandria when the others return. I beg and beseech you to take care of the child and, if I receive my pay soon, I will send it to you. If you have the baby before I return, if it is a boy, let it live; if a girl, expose it. You sent a message with Aphrodisias, "Don't forget me." How could I forget you? Please don't worry.

> In most Greek states the decision not to rear a child was made within the *oikos*, usually by the infant's father, but in Sparta the choice was made by tribal elders who represented the community as whole. An infant rejected in Sparta was thrown to its death down a chasm known as the Place of Throw-aways or Disposal (*Apothetae*).

3.10 PLUTARCH, *LYCURGUS* 16.1–2. A father did not have authority over raising his offspring. Instead, he took his child and brought to a place called Lesche,[8] where the elders of the tribe were seated. They examined the child, and if it was well-formed and strong, ordered it to be raised, assigning it one of the nine-thousand lots of land. But if the child was ill-born and deformed, they got rid of it in the so-called *Apothetae*, a kind of chasm near Mount Taygetus, on the grounds that it was not advantageous for it to live, either for itself or for the state, if it were not well-formed and strong right from the start.

> Before the age of one, the son of an Athenian citizen was presented by the father to his phratry, a religious and political grouping of several different *oikoi*, at the festival of the *Apatouria*, a three-day festival held in October/November. As the child was presented, the father took an oath on the phratry altar that he was indeed the father of the child and that its mother was an Athenian by birth, thus ensuring the child's citizenship. When the boy was about sixteen years old, he was re-introduced for admission to membership of his father's phratry, thus confirming his right to Athenian citizenship. The following excerpt from an early fourth-century BCE inscription, from the deme of Decalea in Attica, indicates the strict control exercised by the phratry to ensure the legitimate admission of young boys into membership.

3.11 RO no. 5, side B, lines 108–126.[9] The oath of the witness at the introduction of the boys:

---

8   *Lesche*: a public building or meeting place.

9   For the full Greek text of this inscription with a translation and commentary, see Rhodes and Osborne 2003: 26–39.

I bear witness that this candidate whom he is introducing is his own legitimate son by a wedded wife. This is the truth, by Zeus Phratrios: if I keep my oath, may much good befall me, but if I swear falsely, the opposite.

Menexenus proposed:

It should be resolved by the members of the phratry concerning the introduction of the boys in other respects in accordance with the previous decrees. But, in order that the members of the phratry may know those who are going to be introduced, they shall be recorded with the leader of the phratry in the first year after the *koureion* sacrifice,[10] by name, the name of the father, his deme, and by the mother and her father's name and deme; and, when they have been recorded, the leader of the phratry shall display the record wherever the Decaleans congregate, and the priest shall inscribe the record on a white tablet and display it in the sanctuary of Leto.[11] The priest is to inscribe the phratry decree on a stone marker...

> The phratry functioned as the intermediary between family and the state. At the age of about eighteen, a young man was enrolled on the register of his father's *deme*, the local territorial district. There were 139 demes in Attica, each having its own particular cults of both gods and heroes and its own political organization with its own assembly and officials.
>
> Two late sources, Hesychius and the Suda,[12] refer to the ritual of the *koureion* sacrifice that was held on the third day of the festival of the Apatouria when young men cut their hair, offered an animal sacrifice, and were inducted into their phratries. At this point, an Athenian youth was no longer a *pais* (child) but an *ephebe*, literally "one who is on the threshold of adulthood."[13]
>
> The first action of the newly enrolled *ephebe* was to make a tour of all the deme sanctuaries of Athens. The ephebe then swore the oath recorded on the following fourth century BCE inscription. This oath put the young man's civic duties, including his service in the military, under divine sanction. If he broke the oath, he would incur the anger of the gods.

3.12 *GHI* 2.204. I will not bring shame upon these sacred weapons nor will I abandon my comrade-in-arms wherever I am in battle order. I will defend things both holy and profane. I will not leave the fatherland smaller than

---

10 *koureion sacrifice*: this sacrifice was offered when a son reached military age and became a full member of the phratry. At this ceremony the young man's hair was cut: see Garland 1990: 179.

11 *Leto*: the mother of Apollo and Artemis.

12 *Hesychius*: the author, probably fifth century CE, of a lexicon of rare Greek words found in poetry or in Greek dialects. *Suda*: the name of a lexicon that was compiled about the end of the tenth century CE.

13 Polinskaya in Dodd and Faraone 2003: 104 n. 14 discerns two senses of the term "ephebe": "(1) ephebes as an age-group, from the onset of puberty to twenty years of age when young men gained full access to citizenship rights; (2) ephebes as young men of eighteen-twenty undergoing military training and service in Attica in the fourth century BCE and later."

I found it, but larger and better, so far as I am able with the assistance of all the citizens. I will obey the officials who always govern wisely and the laws, both those which are already established and those that are wisely established in the future. If anyone overthrows them, I will not allow it, so far as I am able with the assistance of all the citizens. I will honor the ancestral sanctuaries. The following gods are witnesses: Aglaurus, Hestia, Enyo, Enyalius, Ares and Athena Areia, Zeus, Thallo, Auxo, Hegemone, Heracles, the territory of the fatherland, the wheat, barley, vines, olive-trees, and fig-trees.[14]

> During their childhood, both boys and girls performed religious functions, serving in minor roles in festivals and other religious ceremonies. Such service was a mark of high honor both for them and for their family. Pre-pubescent Athenian girls participated in religious rituals in honor of the two virgin goddesses, Artemis and Athena. In Aristophanes' comedy *Lysistrata*, the women of the chorus emphasize the nobility of their birth and list the sacral duties that they had performed as children.

3.13 ARISTOPHANES, *LYSISTRATA* 637–647.

All you citizens, we are beginning

by offering useful advice to the city.

And rightly so, since she raised me in magnificent luxury.

As soon as I was seven, I served as an *Arrephoros*.

Then, at ten, I was an *aletris* for the foundress.

Then, shedding my saffron robe, I was a bear at the Brauronia.[15]

And once, as a lovely girl, I carried the basket, wearing a necklace of dried figs.[16]

> Every four years the Athenians sent select girls between the ages of five and ten to serve the goddess Artemis in her sanctuary at Brauron in Attica. The mythical explanation of this custom is that Artemis was angry because a bear had been killed in the area for harming a girl. When Artemis sent a plague upon the Athenians, the Delphic oracle ordered that Athenian girls

14 *Aglaurus*: a daughter of Cecrops, a mythical king of Athens; she sacrificed herself to save her country in time of war. *Enyo, Enyalius, Ares and Athena Areia*; all are military deities, thus underscoring the military orientation of ephebes. Zeus: probably in his capacity as protector of oaths. *Thallo, Auxo*: both names are personifications of growth and increase. *Hegemone*: the feminine of *hegemon*, leader.

15 *Arrephoros*: the significance of the title is obscure: *-phoros* means "carrier," but the first part of the title, *arre-*, is variously interpreted as "things that must not be mentioned," i.e., sacred objects (Parke 1977; 141) or as "dew." Burkert 1985: 229 notes, "*Arrhephoros* seems to mean dew carrier, with dew symbolizing both impregnation and new offspring;" see also Rosenzweig 2004: 119. n. 1. *aletris*: usually denotes a female slave who ground grain. In this context, however, it apparently refers to the *arrephoroi* making the sacrificial cakes. *foundress*: Artemis, the patron goddess of the Brauronia, a festival celebrated in her honor at Brauron on the east coast of Attica.

16 The basket contained the sacrificial knives; figs were a symbol of fertility.

should "play the bear." The culmination of this festival was the *Arcteia*, the Ritual of the Bear, in which the girls shed their saffron-colored robes and danced, probably naked, impersonating bears.[17]

Each year two Athenian girls between the ages of seven and eleven were chosen from the most noble Athenian families to be *Arrephoroi* and live on the Acropolis in the service of Athena Polias (Guardian of the City). The girls' main function was to help weave a robe for Athena that was carried in the Panathenaic procession. Writing in the second century CE, Pausanias gives an account of the sacred duties that the *Arrephoroi* performed by night at the festival of the *Arrephoria* to mark the end of their service to Athena. The descent to the precinct of Aphrodite in the Gardens symbolizes their passage to puberty and entry into that goddess' sphere.

3.14 PAUSANIAS 1.27.3. What surprised me is something that is not generally known, and so I will describe what happens. Two young maidens live not far from the temple of Athena Polias; the Athenians call them the *Arrephoroi*.[18] For some time they live near the goddess, but when the time of the festival comes they perform the following rituals at night.[19] They place on their heads the sacred objects that the priestess of Athena gives them to carry, but neither she who gives nor those who carry them know what they are. There is a precinct (*peribolos*) in the city which is not far away from the so-called Aphrodite in the Gardens, with a natural entrance leading underground.[20] This is the way that the maidens go down. Below they leave what they were carrying and receive something else that is covered; this they bring back. Then these maidens are discharged, but others are brought to the acropolis in their place.

Betrothal, wedding, and marriage

3.15 DIODORUS SICULUS 9.10.4. Most Greeks call the marriage contract *engue*.

Diodorus notes the first formal stage in the enacting of a marriage, *engue*, the pledging or betrothal. Marital unions were generally negotiated between two families by the heads (*kurioi*) of these families, sometimes several years before the actual wedding. In Athens the bridegroom was not infrequently considerably older than the bride, in which case he probably had some say

---

17 See Price 1999: 90–95 and Faraone in Dodd and Faraone 2003: 43–68.

18 *Athena Polias*: Athena of the city, who was worshiped in the "Old Temple" that later became part of the Erechtheum.

19 Simon 1983: 39–46, followed by Rosenzweig 2004: 48, suggests that the festival of the *Arrephoria* was celebrated in the month of Skiophorion, at the height of summer, with the *Arrephoroi* going to the Gardens of Aphrodite to obtain vegetal fertility material to refresh Athena's sacred olive tree on the acropolis, and thus all the olive trees of Attica.

20 *not far away*: this phrase is open to question as the exact location is much disputed.

in the negotiations. The girl had little if any choice and may not even have been present at the *engue*.[21]

An Athenian law cited by Demosthenes indicates that the *engue* defined the distinction between a legitimate wife and a concubine by granting only the wife the capacity to produce children who would become citizens. The emphasis is on legitimacy, citizenship, and the continuity of the civic community.

3.16 DEMOSTHENES, *AGAINST STEPHANUS* 2.18. If a woman is pledged for lawful marriage by her father, or by a brother who is a son of the same father, or by her grandfather on her father's side, her children shall be legitimate.

The primary purpose of marriage was the procreation of children. At the betrothal or pledging (*enguesis*), the bride's *kurios* would make a pledge and specify the dowry.

3.17 MENANDER, *THE GROUCH* 842–844.

I now betroth my daughter
for the plowing of legitimate children.
And I add three talents dowry.

For females the all-important rite of passage was that of marriage. The deities connected with marriage were Artemis, Aphrodite, and Hera.[22] Before her wedding a bride dedicates the things of her childhood to Artemis, the goddess of virginity.

3.18 PALATINE ANTHOLOGY 6.280.

Before her wedding, Timareta dedicated her tambourine, her pretty ball,
to you, Artemis of the Lake, a maid to a maid, as is fitting;
also the net that shielded her hair, her dolls too, and her dolls' dresses.
You, daughter of Leto, hold your hand over the child Timareta
daughter of Timaretus, and purely keep her in purity.

Three clauses from the sacred law from Cyrene (see 3.4) show that, at least in this Greek community, girls immediately before marriage, brides, and pregnant women were obliged to observe certain rituals in honor of Artemis. Penalties for pollution were imposed if they failed to do so.

3.19 RO no. 97 side B, lines 83–100.[23] A bride before she goes to the bedchamber must go down to Artemis, but she herself must not be under the same roof as

---

21 For a general discussion of the evidence for the age at marriage and selection of a partner, see Garland 1990: 210–217. On the *engue,* see Ferrari, in Dodd and Faraone 2003: 31.

22 Other divinities connected with marriage include Zeus Teleios (the fulfiller), Demeter, Hermes, the Graces, the Nymphs, the Fates (Moirai), and Athena, the goddess of handicrafts.

23 For the complete Greek text with a translation and commentary, see Rhodes and Osborne 2003: 494–505.

her husband, nor shall she be polluted [by sexual intercourse] until she comes to Artemis. Any woman who has not done these things and deliberately incurs pollution must purify the sanctuary of Artemis and, as a penalty, she must sacrifice a full-grown animal and then go to the bedchamber. But if she incurs pollution involuntarily, she must purify the sanctuary.

A bride must go down to the bridal chamber to Artemis, whenever she wishes at the Artemisia, but the sooner the better. Any bride who fails to go down must make an additional sacrifice to Artemis as ordained at the Artemisia. And because she has not gone down, she must purify the Artemision and sacrifice as a penalty a full-grown animal.

A pregnant woman is to go down to the bridal chamber to Artemis and she herself must also give to the bear the feet, head, and skin.[24] If she does not go down before giving birth, she must go down with a full-grown animal.

> The poet of the *Homeric Hymn to Aphrodite* (perhaps c. 675 BCE) reflects on Aphrodite's power.

3.20 *HOMERIC HYMN TO APHRODITE,* 1–44.

Muse, sing to me the deeds of golden Aphrodite
of Cyprus,[25] who roused sweet longing in the gods
and overwhelmed the tribes of mortal men
and the birds of the air and all the beasts,
as many as the land nourishes and the sea;   5
for the deeds of fair-wreathed Cytherea are a care to all.[26]

...

But for the rest of us there is no escaping Aphrodite,
neither for blessed gods nor mortal men.   35
She even led astray the mind of Zeus who delights in the thunderbolt,
he who is the greatest and has the greatest share of honor.
And, whenever she wished, deceiving his wise mind,
she easily mated him with mortal women,
making him completely forget Hera, his sister and wife,   40
who is by far the best in form among the immortal goddesses
and the most glorious child born to crafty-minded Cronus

---

24 *bear*: Rhodes and Osborne 2003: 504–505 suggest that this is possibly an allusion to a ritual similar to that of young girls "playing the bear" in honor of Artemis at Brauron in Attica. Parker 1983: 345 suggests that "the bear" is a priestess. *feet, head, and skin*: of a sacrificial animal.

25 *deeds*: the Greek *erga* refers not only to myths about the goddess' actions, but also to her domain—sexual attraction, the power of erotic love. *Cyprus*: Aphrodite is said to have been born from the foam of the sea and to have come to shore on the island of Cyprus.

26 *Cytherea*: a common epithet of Aphrodite. She is said to have floated by the island of Cythera, south of the Peloponnese, before coming to Cyprus.

and mother Rhea. And Zeus, who knows imperishable plans,
made her his devoted wife.

Diodorus Siculus remarks on the predominance of Aphrodite in the life of a
bride immediately before her marriage and in her wedding ceremonials.

3.21 DIODORUS SICULUS 5.73.2. To Aphrodite was entrusted the time in girls'
lives in which they are expected to marry, the rest of the observances which
are even now a part of wedding ceremonies, together with the sacrifices
and libations that humans make to this goddess.

Hera was the deity who protected the legitimacy of the union and often was
invoked as Teleia, the one who accomplishes. In anticipation of marriage, a
bride makes a dedication to Hera.

3.22 PALATINE ANTHOLOGY 6.133.

Alcibia dedicated the sacred veil for her hair
to Hera, when she reached the time of her lawful wedding.

Much of our information about the weddings derives from vase paintings.[27]
Wedding rituals were enacted in both the *oikos* of the bride and that of the
groom. After a prenuptial bath in her old home, the bride was ceremonially
adorned with her bridal dress, a crown, and special sandals. A sacrifice was
made and the wedding feast held.

3.23 MENANDER, *THE WOMAN FROM SAMOS* 673–674.

They are holding your wedding; the wine is mixed, the incense is burning,
the ritual has begun, and offerings have been kindled in Hephaestus' fire.

During the feast, the bride sat with the women, apart from the men and
probably veiled. Before leaving her parental home, she uncovered her face,
retaining the veil over her head.[28] In the early evening she was escorted
on foot or by wagon to her husband's *oikos*. Hymns were sung in honor
of Hymeneus, the god of marriage. On entering her new *oikos*, she was
received by the bridegroom's parents. As she was led around the hearth of
her new home, she was showered with various fertility symbols, nuts and
dried fruits, and given a basket of bread. Then she removed her veil and
entered the nuptial-chamber with her groom. Outside the door a wedding
song (*epithalamion*) was sung.

Artemis continued to be worshiped by women after marriage. A larger than
life-size marble statue (c. 650 BCE) dedicated by an otherwise unknown
Nikandre to the goddess Artemis was discovered in that goddess' sanctuary
on the island of Delos, the birthplace of Artemis and Apollo, with the
following inscription:

---

27 For illustrations of wedding scenes with commentary and further literary sources,
see Oakley and Sinos 1993.

28 For discussion of the problem of the formal unveiling of the bride (the *anakalupt-
eria*), see Ferrari 2003: 32 and Oakley and Sinos 1993: 25–26.

Figure 3.1. Marriage scenes depicted on an Attic red-figure *loutrophoros*, c. 425 BCE.[29] At the left, a young man dressed as a traveler clasps the hand of an older bearded man, evidently the prospective bride's *kurios*, at the *engue*. In the center is the bridal procession as the young groom takes his bride by the hand and leads her to the bedchamber. Behind the bride are three attendants. From left to right, one carries a vessel containing perfumes or unguents; another carries a small chest probably containing the bride's jewelry and cosmetics in her right hand and a basket in her left. Between them are a fan and a goose, a bird often depicted with Aphrodite. A third attendant adjusts the bride's veil to reveal her bridal crown. Two Erotes (Cupids) fly on either side of the bride. At the right, the groom's mother stands in the doorway of her home holding two bridal torches. At the lower right, an Eros flies out of the door where the groom's mother stands. Inside the house, in front of the bedchamber, is another woman, her arms raised, apparently expressing surprise at the Eros that has emerged from the bedchamber. Behind her the scene of the *engue* begins with the bride's father. Photograph © 2008 Museum of Fine Arts, Boston.

3.24 *IG* XII 5.2 p. xxiv 1425 b. Nikandre dedicated me to the goddess [Artemis] the far-shooting rainer of arrows,[30]

Nikandre, the pre-eminent daughter of Deinodeikes of Naxos,

sister of Deinomenes, and now wife of Phraxus.

> Two further dedications to Artemis, one by a mother Telostodike, and the other by Telostodike and her husband Demokydes. The second inscription is from the island of Paros, the provenance of the first is less certain. The woman named on the two inscriptions is possibly one and the same person.

3.25 *IG* XII 5.1 216.

Telestodike dedicated this statue to you, Artemis.

She is the mother of Asphalius, and daughter of Therseleos.

---

29 *loutrophoros*: literally "bathcarrier," in which water for the bride's bath was carried into her home.

30 *far-shooting rainer of arrows*: the arrows from Artemis' bow were a metaphor for the deaths of women, especially in childbirth.

3.26 *IG* XII 5.1 215.

Demokydes and Telestodike together vowed

and dedicated this statue to the virgin Artemis,

the daughter of aegis-bearing Zeus, on her sacred land.

Grant increase to their family and livelihood, free from suffering.

> A couple makes more mundane dedications to Artemis in gratitude for the
> delivery of a son, and the father prays for the child's well-being.

3.27 *PALATINE ANTHOLOGY* 6.271.

Artemis, the son of Cichesias has dedicated these sandals to you,

and Themistodike her simple folded robe.

because you gently held your two hands

over her in labor, coming without your bow.[31]

Lady Artemis, grant that Leon may yet see his son   5

grow to be great and strong.

> A brief excerpt from a fourth-century BCE inscription from the sanctuary of
> Artemis at Brauron provides an inventory of elaborate and costly garments
> dedicated to the goddess by various women, probably in gratitude for a
> safe delivery.

3.28 *IG* II 2 1514. In the year of Callimachus' archonship [349/8 BCE]: Callippe
[dedicated] a short tunic, scalloped, and embroidered with interwoven
letters. Chaerippe and Eucoline, a dotted tunic in a box. Philumene, a tunic
made of linen from Amorgos. In the year of Theophilus' archonship [348/7
BCE]: Pythias, a long spotted robe. In the year of Themistocles' archonship
[342/1 BCE]: an embroidered purple tunic in a display box... and Eucoline
dedicated it. Phyle [dedicated] a woman's belt; Pheidylla a woman's white
cloak in a display box. Mneso a frog-green garment. Nausis a woman's
cloak, with a broad purple border in a wave design.

Marriage contested

> Zaidman and Pantel note that "No ancient Greek city devised a precise
> legal definition of marriage. Certain types of union were privileged, but the
> boundary between marriage and a non-marital union was often a fine one"[32]
> Their remarks are corroborated by cases that came before the Athenian
> law courts contesting the legitimacy of particular marital unions.

> The following excerpt is from a speech delivered in a private Athenian lawsuit
> during the fourth century BCE that is concerned with proving the legality of
> a marriage. The plaintiff, speaking on behalf of a woman, is claiming a share of
> the estate of a man, Ciron, who is alleged to be the woman's grandfather.

---

31 *Artemis...coming without your bow*: i.e., promoting successful birth, cf. 3.24 with n.
      30.

32 Zaidman and Pantel 1992: 68.

One argument hinges on the acceptance of the woman's assertion that her grandfather included her in all the family rituals and that she attended religious ceremonies that were only open to the legitimate wives of Athenian citizens.

3.29 ISAEUS, *ON THE ESTATE OF CIRON* 15–16. We also have other proofs that we are the children of Ciron's daughter. For, as was natural because we are the children of his own daughter, he never performed a sacrifice of any kind without us; whether the sacrifice was small or great, we were always there, taking part in the sacrifice. Moreover, we were not only invited on such occasions, but he also took us to the country for the Dionysia. We always went with him to the public spectacles and we sat by his side. And we went to his house to celebrate all festivals.

When he sacrificed to Zeus Ktesios,[33] a ritual to which he was especially devoted, he never admitted slaves or free persons outside his own family. He performed all the rites himself, and we shared in them, laying our hands with his on the victims and placing our offerings along with his; and we participated in all the other rites. He prayed for our health and prosperity, as was proper for a grandfather.

> The spokesman also points out that the plaintiff's mother was received with honor by her father's demesmen and that her father gave a marriage banquet at his phratry, later presenting their children to the phratry. A further mark of the honor accorded to the plaintiff's mother is that she was chosen to preside at the Thesmophoria, an honor only accorded to legally married Athenian citizen women. [34]

3.30 ISAEUS, *ON THE ESTATE OF CIRON* 18–20. Therefore it is clear from these proofs that not only is our mother the legitimate daughter of Ciron, but there is also the evidence of what our father has done for us and the attitude of the wives of his demesmen towards our mother. When our father took her in marriage, he held a wedding feast and summoned three of this friends in addition to his relatives. He also gave a marriage banquet for the phratry according to their established customs. After this, the wives of his demesmen chose our mother to preside at the Thesmophoria along with the wife of Diocles of the deme Pithus and conduct the customary ritual together with her.

In addition to this, when we were born, our father introduced us to the phratry, and took an oath according to the established customs that he was introducing children born from an Athenian citizen and a lawfully wedded wife. None of the members of the phratry made any objections or disputed that this was the truth, although there were many of them and they always make a thorough investigation.

If our mother was the kind of woman that our opponents allege, do you think that our father would have given a wedding-feast or a marriage

---

33 *Zeus Ktesios*: Zeus the guardian of the possessions of the *oikos*.

34 *Thesmophoria*: a women's festival held in honor of Demeter; see 7.22–7.26.

banquet? Rather he would have concealed the whole affair; nor would the wives of the other demesmen have chosen her to conduct the Thesmophoria with Diocles' wife and put her in charge of the sacred objects.

No indeed, they would have turned instead to one of the other wives for these matters. Nor would the phratry have admitted us; rather they would have objected and proved their objections, if there had not been complete agreement that our mother was the legitimate daughter of Ciron.

Death and death rituals

In the *Odyssey*, Odysseus goes to the entrance to Hades and encounters the ghosts of various people he has known.[35] The ghost of his mother explains the nature of death.

3.31 HOMER, *ODYSSEY* 11.218–222.

This is the way things are for mortals, after they die;
the sinews no longer hold together the flesh and bones;
the powerful fury of blazing fire overcomes all that   220
on the pyre, as soon as the vigor of life has left the white bones,
and the spirit flutters about and flies away like a dream.

The ghost of Achilles tells Odysseus that he would rather work as a laborer for a tenant farmer than be king of the underworld.

3.32 HOMER, *ODYSSEY* 11.488–491.

Don't try to comfort me for my death, resplendent Odysseus.
I'd rather work on top of the earth as a laborer,
for a landless tenant farmer with little to live on himself,[36]   490
than rule down here as lord over all of the perished dead.

In contrast to the Homeric concept of the soul as an insubstantial ghost fluttering aimlessly in the underworld, Pythagoras (late sixth century BCE) is said to have promoted a doctrine of reincarnation and the transmigration of souls (*metempsychosis*). He migrated to the Greek colony of Croton in southern Italy c. 530 BCE, where he organized a society that involved initiation, secret doctrines, and a code of special dietary laws and burial rites. Plato contrasts the legacy of Homer with that of Pythagoras.

3.33 PLATO, *REPUBLIC* 600 a–b. Well, if Homer has no reputation for public services, do we hear that in his lifetime he was the personal guide and educator of any private individuals? Are there any who loved him for his company and handed down to later generations a Homeric way of

---

35 See 13.37 for Homer's description of the ritual enacted by Odysseus to communicate with the dead in the underworld.

36 *landless tenant farmer*: such an individual was in a less secure situation than a slave, who at least was the property of a master who would feed and clothe him.

life? Pythagoras was himself especially loved for this, and even today his followers are conspicuous for what they call the Pythagorean way of life.

> Xenophanes (c. 570–475 BCE) is reported to have made the following jest, probably at the expense of an individual who believed in the doctrine of reincarnation.

3.34 XENOPHANES, *KRS* no. 260 as quoted by DIOGENES LAERTIUS 8.36. On the subject of reincarnation, Xenophanes bears witness in an elegy which begins:

"Now I will turn to another tale and show the way."

What he says about him [Pythagoras] goes like this:[37]

Pythagoras was once passing by when a puppy was being whipped.

Taking pity on the animal, he said,

"Stop. Don't beat it. It's the soul (*psyche*) of a friend;

I recognized him from his voice."

> The philosopher Empedocles (c. 492–432 BCE) from Acragas in Sicily also posited a theory of reincarnation. He believed that he had been reduced to mortality, like other divine spirits (*daimones*), but that eventually he would regain divinity after a cycle of reincarnations. In the following excerpts, he describes the cycle of reincarnation that befell wrong-doers like killers and oath-breakers.

3.35 EMPEDOCLES, *KRS* no. 401.

There is an oracle of Necessity, ancient decree of the gods,

eternal, sealed with broad oaths:

when anyone does wrong and pollutes his own limbs with bloodshed,

he who by his error falsifies the oath he swore,

—spirits whose have as their lot a long life—   5

for thrice ten thousand years he wanders apart from the blessed,

being born throughout that time in all manner of forms of mortal
   things,

exchanging one hard path of life for another.

The force of the air (*aither*) pursues him into the sea,

the sea spews him out onto the floor of the earth, the earth casts   10

him into the rays of the blazing sun, and the sun into the eddies of the
   air;

one takes him from the other, but all abhor him.

Of these I too am now one, an exile from the gods and a wanderer,

trusting in raving Strife.

---

37 *Pythagoras*: although he is not mentioned specifically in this quotation, it is generally agreed that the reference is to him.

3.36   EMPEDOCLES, *KRS* no. 417.

I have already been once a boy and a girl,

a bush and a bird, and a leaping traveling fish.

> In a victory ode written in 476 BCE Pindar offers some of the earliest
> testimony about the belief in punishments and rewards in an afterlife, and
> in reincarnation.

3.37   PINDAR, *OLYMPIAN* 2.57–78.

The helpless spirits of the dead

immediately pay the penalty—and the wrongs committed here in this
   realm of Zeus

are judged beneath the earth by one

who makes pronouncements with hateful necessity.   60

But for evermore, in equal nights,

and equal days, enjoying the sun,

the good receive a life of less toil,

not vexing the soil with the strength of their hands

nor the water of the deep,

for a bare living. But in the presence of the honored   65

gods, all who rejoiced in keeping their oaths

lead a life that knows no tears,

while others endure a toil that none can bear to see.

And those that have been courageous to have lived three times

in either world, keeping their souls completely free from wrongdoing,

they travel the highway of Zeus   70

to the tower of Cronus. There on the Island of the Blessed,[38]

the ocean breezes blow, and flowers of gold blaze,

some on shore from shining trees, while others are nourished by water.

With garlands they entwine their hands, making crowns,

according to the just counsels of Rhadymanthys[39]—   75

for he sits ready with advice beside the Great Father,[40]

the husband of Rhea,

who has the highest seat of all.

---

38 The highway of Zeus and Tower of Cronus are otherwise unknown. *Island of the
   Blessed*: see Homer, *Odyssey* 563-569, Hesiod, *Works and Days* 169-173, and Plato,
   Gorgias 523 a–e.

39 *Rhadymanthys*: ruler and judge of the dead in Elysium, the realm of the blessed.

40 *Great Father*: Cronus.

In Sophocles' *Oidipous at Colonus* (produced posthumously in 401 BCE), Oedipus realizes that the appointed time has come for him to die. He prepares for death, asking his daughters to perform the rituals that precede a funeral.

3.38 SOPHOCLES, *OIDIPOUS AT COLONUS* 1597–1603.

Messenger

he [Oedipus] sat down; then he loosed his filthy garments. Next
he called his children and commanded them to bring
fresh water, both for washing and for offerings.[41]
The two of them went over to the hill of green   1600
Demeter, which was in our view, and in a short
time fetched their father what he ordered and attended
him with washing and the customary clothes.[42]

> The laying out of the corpse (*prothesis*) was generally done by women who performed the ritual washing of the corpse, dressed it in white garments and a winding sheet, and laid it out on a bier in the entrance to the house, with the head resting on a cushion and the face exposed. The women then enacted the ritual mourning, tearing their hair and scarring their cheeks with their nails, beating their breasts, weeping, and uttering cries of lamentation or keening. Outside the home of the deceased a vessel was placed containing lustral water for the mourners to use for purification before they entered the house. The duration of the pollution varied according to the degree of kinship with the deceased.

> Homer describes the *prothesis* of Hector's body that Priam had ransomed from Achilles.

3.39 HOMER, *ILIAD* 24.719–724.

And after they had brought him inside the glorious palace
they laid him out on a well-constructed bed, and beside him   720
set singers in place to lead the dirge; they mourned for him,
with the singers leading the dirge while the women wailed in response.
Among them white-armed Andromache began the lament,[43]
as she held in her arms the head of Hector, slayer of men.

> The need for burial is the crux of Sophocles' *Antigone*. When King Creon forbade the burial of his nephew Polyneices because he had made war on his native city, Polyneices' sister, Antigone, performed burial rites for him. Brought before Creon, she declares the laws of the gods transcend those of mortals.

---

41 *washing*: a ritual bath. *offerings*: funerary libations to the gods of the underworld (*choai*, as opposed to *spondai* which were libations to the Olympian gods).

42 *washing and customary clothes*: corpses were ritually washed and dressed in white funeral garments.

43 *Andromache*: Hector's wife.

3.40 SOPHOCLES, *ANTIGONE* 450–457.

Antigone

It was not Zeus who made this proclamation;   450
nor was it Justice dwelling with the gods below
who set in place such laws as these for humankind;
nor did I think your proclamations had such strength
that, mortal as you are, you could outrun those laws
that are the gods', unwritten and unshakable.   455
Their laws are not for now or yesterday, but live
forever; no one knows when first they came to light.

> Homer's *Iliad* ends with the funeral of Hector. The ashes are placed in a
> golden chest in the ground and covered with a mound of earth. The burial
> is followed by a feast.

3.41 HOMER, *ILIAD* 24.776–804.

So she spoke, in tears, and the Trojan people wailed
in response. Then the old man Priam addressed the mass of the people:
"Trojans, gather up firewood to bring to the city; you need not
dread in your hearts any secret Argive ambush; Achilles,
when he sent me away from their black ships, assured me of this: 780
they will give us no more suffering till the twelfth dawn comes.
    So he spoke, and they yoked to the wagons oxen and mules,
and quickly gathered together in front of the city walls.
For nine whole days they went and collected a boundless supply
of wood; when dawn appeared for the tenth time, shedding its light   785
on mortals, they carried valiant Hector forth from the house,
in tears, then placed his corpse on the pyre, and set it alight.
    When rosy-fingered early-rising dawn had appeared,
the mass of the people gathered round glorious Hector's pyre;
and when they had gathered together there and assembled in full,   790
first they poured on gleaming wine to quench the pyre's embers,
all of it, everywhere that the furious fire had extended;
then his brothers and comrades, weeping, collected together
his white bones, and abundant tears poured down from their cheeks.
They took the bones and placed them inside a golden chest,   795
after enfolding them gently in fine soft purple robes.
This they quickly placed in a hollow grave, and above it
they spread a close-set covering layer of mighty stones.
They hastily built up a mound to mark the place, with guards
watching all sides in case the well-greaved Achaeans attacked.   800
After building the mound to mark the place they returned to Troy.

Then, properly gathered together, they ate a magnificent feast
within the palace of Priam, a king who is nurtured by Zeus.

> The historian Thucydides describes the state funeral celebrated for the
> men who had been killed in the first year of the Peloponnesian War (432/1
> BCE).

3.42 THUCYDIDES 2.34. During the same winter, the Athenians, following the
custom of their ancestors, celebrated at public expense the funeral rites of
the first who had died in this war. The ceremony is as follows. The bones
of the deceased lie in a tent erected for that purpose for a period of three
days, and each person brings to his own dead whatever offering he wishes.
On the day of the funeral (*ekphora*), coffins of cypress wood are carried on
wagons, one for each tribe, and the bones of each are in his tribe's coffin.
One empty bier, covered with a pall, is carried for the missing, whose bodies
could not be found for burial.

Anyone who wishes, both citizen and foreigner, may join in the funeral
procession. The female relatives attend the burial, making lamentation. The
coffins are laid in the public tomb, which is situated in the most beautiful
suburb of the city.[44] This is the place where they always bury the men from
their wars, except those who fell at Marathon. They were buried on the
battlefield because the Athenians judged their valor to be exceptional.

But when the bones have been covered with earth, a man is chosen by the
state whose intellectual gifts are highly regarded and who is foremost in
public esteem. This man delivers an appropriate eulogy, after which the
people depart. This is the burial procedure. Throughout the entire war,
whenever the occasion arose, they followed this custom.

> After a burial, members of the deceased's family visited the tomb to make
> offerings. The Athenian speech-writer Isaeus (c. 420–340 BCE) tells how
> he and his wife cared for his stepfather both in life and death, performing
> the necessary rituals after the burial and ensuring that Menecles' name
> lived on.

3.43 ISAEUS, *ON THE ESTATE OF MENECLES* 2.36. I, the adopted son,
with the help of my wife, the daughter of this man Philonides, cared for
Menecles while he was alive, and I gave his name to my little son so that
the name would continue in the family. When he died, I buried him in a
manner worthy both of him and myself. I set up a fine monument to him
and performed the customary rituals on the ninth day and all the other
rituals required at the tomb in the best possible way; for this I won the
praise of all my demesmen.

---

44 The outer part of the Ceramicus (the Potter's Quarter), immediately outside the
Dipylon Gate.

Epitaphs

The poet Simonides composed an epitaph for the Athenians who died fighting the Persians at the battle of Plataea in 479 BCE, and also for Spartans, and for a Cretan.

3.44 *PALATINE ANTHOLOGY 7.253.*

If a noble death is the greatest part of virtue,

Fortune (Tyche) has granted this to us above all others.

For we, who hastened to bestow freedom upon Hellas,

lie here enjoying praise that will never grow old.

3.45 *PALATINE ANTHOLOGY 7.251.*

These men bestowed unquenchable glory upon their dear country,

taking upon themselves the dark mist of death.

They have died, but are not dead, since their valor

glorifies them and brings them up from the house of Hades.

3.46 *PALATINE ANTHOLOGY 7.254 a.*

A Cretan by birth, I, Brotachus of Gortyn, lie here;

I came for trade, not for this!

Figure 3.2. Grave marker in the form of an oil flask (*lekythos*), late fifth century BCE. A seated woman is waited upon by her slave girl. The woman is admiring herself in a mirror that she holds in her left hand. The servant holds a box, containing either jewels or cosmetics. Photograph © 2008 Museum of Fine Arts, Boston.

4. PRAYER AND SACRIFICE

4.1   DEMOSTHENES, *EPISTULA* 1. It is proper for a person who is beginning any serious discourse or task to begin first with the gods.

4.2   HESIOD, *WORKS AND DAYS* 465–468.
Pray to Zeus of the earth and to pure Demeter
that the sacred corn of Demeter be full and heavy,
when first you begin plowing.

4.3   PLATO, *EUTHYPHRO* 14 c. Is it then the case that sacrificing is making a gift to the gods, whereas praying is asking them for something?

4.4   PLATO, *POLITICUS* 290 c–d. Priests, as tradition says, are experts in giving gifts from us to the gods through sacrifices and making requests of gods on our behalf in prayers for the acquisition of good things.

4.5   PLATO, *LAWS* 4.716 d. To make sacrifice and commune with the gods continually by prayers, offerings, and devotions of every kind is most noble and good and conducive to the happy life, and also most fitting for the good person.

> Most of the extant traditional Greek prayers are petitionary, invoking the gods and making a request to win the gods' favor or mitigate their anger. There are also prayers of supplication, dedication, and thanksgiving, as well as hymns, vows or promises, and oaths invoking a god as witness.
>
> In the domestic sphere, prayer and sacrifice were made by individual males and females on behalf of themselves or their family, usually without the assistance of a priest or priestess. By contrast, most public and state rituals were administered by a male or female priest, who served a particular deity. A priest acted as an intermediary between a deity and a worshiper, not as advisor or pastor. The overall duty of a priest was to attend to sacred matters (*hiera*), which included sacrifices and other offerings and the maintenance of the sanctuary of a particular god or goddess and the property within that sanctuary.

Underlying the rituals of prayer and sacrifice is the pragmatic concept of a contractual relationship that works on three implicit principles: the giving of a gift in the hope that the favor will be returned when needed, the promise of a gift in return for the granting of a prayer, and the request of a favor in return for previous gifts. The scale of the sacrifice would have varied according to the occasion and number of participants, be it public or private Gifts ranged from the deposit in a god's sanctuary of valuable durable offerings like the Mantiklos' Apollo statuette (Fig. 1.2), large statues, or gold and silver vessels to perishable commodities like a cake, produce of the earth, or the meat of a sacrificial animal.[1] The impression given by the literary and epigraphic sources is that the bigger and better the gift and the louder the prayer, the greater was the chance that the gods would pay attention and respond to the request.

The Trojan priest Chryses prays to Apollo because his daughter has been captured by the Greeks and King Agamemnon has refused the priest's offer of ransom. Chryses first reminds Apollo of previous animal sacrifices he has made. He then asks Apollo to punish the Greeks because Agamemnon has dishonored him. The invocation specifies particular locations and a cult title in order to identify Apollo precisely, since otherwise the god may not respond. The prayer is immediately answered, as Apollo sends a plague upon the Greeks.

4.6   HOMER, *ILIAD* 1.37–52.

"Hear me, god of the silver bow, protector of Chryse
and sacred Cilla, ruling in might over Tenedus, Smintheus:[2]
if ever I built and roofed a temple to give you joy,
if ever I burned rich fat from the thighs of bulls or goats   40
for you in sacrifice, I beg you, fulfill my desire:
use your arrows to make the Danaans pay for my tears."[3]

So he spoke in prayer, and Phoebus Apollo heard him;
he went down the craggy peaks of Olympus, rage in his heart,
bearing his bow and close-covered quiver slung on his shoulders;   45
the arrows he bore on his shoulders rattled and clanged with his stride
as he moved along, full of rage; he advanced on them like the night.
He took a position away from the ships and let fly a shaft;
a terrible clanging noise rang out from the silver bow.
First he aimed at the mules and swift-running dogs; but then   50
he released a piercing arrow towards the men themselves
and struck them; countless pyres of corpses ceaselessly burned.

---

1   For the valuable gifts at Olympia and Delphi, see 6.5, 6.6, 6.12 and 6.13.

2   *Chryse, Cilla, Tenedus*: places near Troy where Apollo was worshipped. *Smintheus*: this problematic cult title, which probably means "mouse-god", only occurs here.

3   *Danaans*: Greeks.

Blood and other sacrifice

The sacrifice of animals is especially prominent in Homer, and is a recurrent theme in Greek iconography. This ritual was performed at public festivals throughout the Greek world and at family events such as weddings.[4]

In sacrifice to the Olympian gods, part of the animal was burned as an offering to the deity and the rest was consumed by the worshipers at a communal feast. However, the victim was generally not consumed in sacrifices to heroes, to the dead, to chthonic deities, nor in sacrifices performed before battle or before crossing a river or other boundary, taking an oath, or making a purification.

The most prestigious and expensive sacrificial victims were cattle. Sheep and goats were the more usual victims. Pigs also were sacrificed, especially to Demeter. Also attested is sacrifice of cocks, dogs, birds and fish.

The sacrificial victims were carefully scrutinized for purity to ensure that they were without blemish and tested for their behavior under stress. Plutarch (c. 50-120 CE), himself a Delphic priest, relates that the reason for pouring liquid on a sacrificial animal was to test the vitality and so prove its suitability for sacrifice to the god.[5]

4.7 PLUTARCH, *MORALIA* 437 a–b. For when priests and holy men say that they are offering sacrifice and pouring a libation over a victim and observing its movements and its trembling, how do they interpret this except as an sign that the god will prophesy or not? For what is being offered as a sacrifice must be pure, unblemished, and unmarred, both in body and in spirit.[6]

It is not difficult to observe indications of the body, but the spirit is tested by placing meal before bulls and peas before boars. If the animal does not taste the food, they deem it unsound. The test for a goat is cold water. For apathy and a lack of reaction when doused is not a normal characteristic.

Homer describes the sacrifice of the animals sent by Agamemnon to propitiate Apollo when the daughter of the priest Chryses was returned to her father. Chryses prays to Apollo to stop the plague.

4.8 HOMER, *ILIAD* 1.440–474.

Then much-devising Odysseus led the girl to the altar,   440

placed her back in her own dear father's arms and addressed him:

"Chryses, the lord of men Agamemnon has sent me to bring you

back your child and slaughter a sacred hecatomb

---

4 Scholars are divided in their interpretation of the origins and purpose of animal sacrifice; see Bremmer in Ogden 2007: 132–144 with bibliography. For discussion of the iconography and literary testimony, see Van Straten 1995.

5 On the scrutiny of animal behavior as a criterion for determining suitability for sacrifice, see Naiden 2007: 61–73; see also 4.15 with n. 27 and 5.8.

6 *spirit*: in this context the Greek *psyche* means spirit or vitality.

to Phoebus on the Danaans' behalf, to propitiate
the lord who has sent the Argives sorrows full of lament."[7]   445
   So speaking he placed her back in his arms; he accepted
his own dear daughter joyfully. Swiftly and in due order
they stood a sacred hecatomb round the well-built altar;
then washed their hands and took up handfuls of barley corns.[8]

Chryses lifted his arms and prayed in a mighty voice: 450
"Hear me, god of the silver bow, protector of Chryse
and sacred Cilla, ruling in might over Tenedus:[9] once
before you heard me indeed as I lifted my voice in prayer,
honored me greatly, and harshly smote the Achaean army;[10]
now once again, as before, I beg you, fulfill my desire,   455
drive back this foul plague and turn it from the Danaans."
   So he spoke in prayer, and Phoebus Apollo heard him.
When they had prayed and cast the barley corns on the victims,
they pulled back the animals' heads, cut their throats and skinned them;
then they cut out the thigh-bones and folded a layer of fat   460
around them on both sides, and placed on them pieces of flesh;
these the old man burned on a wooden stick, then poured
on gleaming wine; beside him young men held in their hands
five-pronged forks. Then, after consuming the thighs with fire
and tasting the entrails,[11] they cut up the rest of the meat and
   pierced it   465
with spits, and roasted it skillfully; then they drew off the pieces.
After the work was done and the feast was ready, they feasted,
and no one's heart was deprived of an equal share of the feast.
And when their desire for food and drink had been satisfied,
young men filled mixing bowls to the brim with drink and served it 470

---

7 *hecatomb*: properly the offering of a hundred oxen, but generally used of a large
   number of sacrificial victims. *Phoebus*: Apollo. *Danaans... Argives*: Greeks.

8 *washed their hands*: a ritual purification before beginning the sacrifice. *barley corns*:
   grains of barley that were scattered on its head, indicating its consecration.

9 *"Hear me..."*: note the precision of the invocation which is a repetition of the prayer
   formula used earlier at lines 37–38 in 4.6. The ritual must be correctly performed if
   the prayer is to be fulfilled.

10 *Achaean*: Greek.

11 *tasting the entrails*: the heart, liver, lungs, kidney and stomach. This was a ritual
   tasting, taking a share of the gods' portion. Sometimes these portions were eaten as a
   first course, as the entrails were considered a tasty treat by the ancients.

Figure 4.1. Mixing bowl (*krater*, c. 425 BCE) depicting a sacrifice. On the left two youths wearing garlands are leading a ram to an altar, where a priest is standing. One youth plays the double flute, the other tends the victim. The priest is washing his hands in a basin held by a youth named Hippocles. In his left hand Hippocles holds a flat tray that serves as a basket for the sacrificial knife and the barley corns for consecrating the sacrificial victim. Between these two figures hangs a horned skull decorated with a ribbon or fillet. On the right, a bearded man named Aresias holds a staff and stands watching. Photograph © 2008 Museum of Fine Arts, Boston.

to everyone, starting first with libations from every cup.[12]
All day the young Achaean men propitiated
the god by singing a beautiful paean to honor him
who works from afar; and hearing it, his heart was delighted.[13]

> A passage from the *Odyssey* supplies further details of sacrificial ritual. King Nestor of Pylos is giving a feast in honor of Telemachus, the son of Odysseus, and he orders a sacrifice in fulfillment of a vow to Athena. The victim's horns are gilded and the women prepare the feast, uttering a ritual cry as Nestor's sons kill the heifer.

---

12 *mixing bowls*: wine was usually diluted with water in a mixing bowl. *starting first with libations from every cup*: each participant made a libation before drinking, an indication that men and gods were sharing in the sacrificial feast.

13 *paean*: a song or hymn, usually sung in honor of Apollo. *the one who works from afar*: Apollo the archer.

4.9   HOMER, *ODYSSEY* 3.415–472.

The hero Pisistratus came among them and made a sixth,   415
and they brought and seated beside them godlike Telemachus.[14]
Then Nestor, Gerenian horseman, began to speak among them:
"Swiftly, my own dear children, I beg you, fulfill my desire,
that I may propitiate first among gods Athena, who came
to me in visible form at the sumptuous feast of the god.[15]   420
Come, one of you go to the plain for a heifer, that it may arrive
as quickly as possible, driven here by an herdsman.[16] Another
go to the place where Telemachus, great of heart, has left
his black ship; bring all his comrades, leaving two of them only.
Let a third man go and summon Laerces, who works in gold,   425
to come here that he may plate with gold the horns of the heifer.
The rest of you all remain here together; direct the women
servants inside the house to prepare for a glorious feast,
to arrange the seats and firewood and bring us splendid water."
So he spoke, and all of them busied themselves. The heifer   430
arrived from the plain; great-hearted Telemachus' comrades arrived
from their speedy well-balanced ship; the metal-smith arrived
with his metal-working tools in his hands, the tools that defined
his skill, the well-constructed tongs, the anvil and hammer
with which he worked the gold; Athena arrived to attend   435
her rites.[17] The old man Nestor, the charioteer, gave gold
to the smith, who plated the heifer's horns with particular care,
to give the goddess joy when she looked on the splendid gift.
Then glorious Echephron and Stratius led in the heifer
by the horns; Aretus arrived from within with a flowered bowl   440

---

14 *Pisistratus*: one of Nestor's sons.

15 Nestor had earlier recognized that Telemachus' companion was the goddess Athena
in disguise; see *Odyssey* 3.371–373.

16 *heifer*: the gender of this sacrificial animal is specified earlier, at *Odyssey* 3.382–383,
when Nestor, after recognizing the disguised Athena, vowed to sacrifice to her "a
year-old, unbroken heifer, with a wide forehead, that no man has yet led beneath
the yoke." Thus, as a victim, this unbroken yearling was unblemished. The Roman
poet Virgil, (*Georgics* 3.60—61) notes that cows do not calve before their fourth year.
The offering of such a heifer represented a considerable "sacrifice" because, having
successfully reared the animal, Nestor was depriving himself of the heifer's future
offspring, and also her milk. The sacrifice of a young ox would not have been such an
economic loss.

17 *Athena*: is not only the intended recipient of this sacrifice, she is also the goddess of
handicrafts.

of water;[18] his other hand held barley corns in a basket.
Thrasymedes, stalwart in war, stood by them holding a sharp
axe in his hand, to strike the heifer, while Perseus held
the bowl for the blood. The old man Nestor, the charioteer,
began with the water and barley corns, and with lengthy prayers   445
to Athena, casting hairs from the heifer's head in the fire.[19]

When they had prayed and cast the barley corns on the victim,
at once Thrasymedes, Nestor's son, the mighty of heart,
stood close and struck; the axe cut the tendons of the neck
depriving the heifer of vigor. They let out a piercing cry—   450
the daughters of Nestor, his daughters-in-law and respected wife,
Eurydice, eldest-born of the daughters of Clymenus.[20]
The others raised up the victim's head from the broad-pathed earth
and held it back as Pisistratus slaughtered it, leader of men.
After the black blood flowed and the vigor of life had left   455
the bones they quickly dismembered the heifer and cut out the thigh-
    bones,
all in the proper way, and folded a layer of fat
around them on both sides, and placed on them pieces of flesh;
these the old man burned on a wooden stick, then poured
on gleaming wine; beside him young men held in their hands   460
five-pronged forks. Then after consuming the thighs with fire
and tasting the entrails, they cut up the rest of the meat and pierced it
with spits, and roasted it, holding the pointed spits in their hands.
....

    When they had roasted the outer flesh and drawn off the pieces   470
they sat and feasted; good men attended to them as they ate,
pouring streams of wine into drinking-cups made out of gold.

> In another description of sacrifice from the *Odyssey*, Eumaeus, the swineherd
> on Odysseus' farm grants hospitality to a stranger who is Odysseus in
> disguise.[21] Eumaeus sacrifices his prize boar, as he prays for Odysseus' safe
> return.

---

18 *flowered bowl of water*: a bowl, garlanded with flowers, containing water for purification.

19 *head hairs*: these symbolize the consecration for sacrifice.

20 *let out a piercing cry*: a ritual cry or scream, *ololuge* in Greek, typically uttered by
   women when a death occurs.

21 On hospitality, see 1.22 and 1.23 with notes 14 and 15.

4.10 HOMER, *ODYSSEY* 14.419–438.

And the men brought in a very fat boar that was five years old
and stood it beside the hearth; the swineherd did not forget   420
the immortal gods, for he was a man who possessed good sense;
he began by casting into the fire some hairs from the head
of the white-tusked boar, and then he prayed to all of the gods
for clever Odysseus to come back home again to his house.
He drew himself up and struck the boar with a piece of oak   425
left over from splitting; the spirit left it.[22] They slaughtered it,
singed it, then quickly dismembered it; the swineherd placed
some pieces of flesh, from each of the limbs, above the rich fat;
he sprinkled ground-up barley on top of these then cast them
into the fire; they cut up the rest of the meat and pierced it   430
with spits, and roasted it skillfully, then drew off the pieces,
and placed it all on platters; the swineherd himself stood up
to divide the feast; for he was a most fair-minded man.
He cut up the meat and shared it all into seven portions;
the first he assigned to the nymphs and Hermes, Maia's son,   435
with a prayer;[23] the rest he distributed to each man there;
he awarded Odysseus the lengthy strips of meat from the back
of the white-tusked boar and glorified the heart of his lord.

> Hesiod tells the story of Prometheus, son of the Titan Iapetus, who
> attempted to deceive Zeus. This myth explains the practice of offering the
> bones to the gods and retaining the flesh for mortals.

4.11 HESIOD, *THEOGONY* 535–557.

For when gods and mortal men made a settlement   535
at Mekone, then he (Prometheus) cleverly cut up a big ox and
set it before them, trying to deceive the mind of Zeus.
For Zeus he set out meat and innards rich with fat
on the skin, covering it with the stomach of the ox;
but for men he set the white ox-bones, with crafty skill   540
arranging them well and covering them with shining fat.
Then the father of gods and men said to him:
    "Son of Iapetus, distinguished of all gods,
sir, how unjustly you divided the portions."   544
    Thus Zeus, knowing deathless plans, spoke and mocked him.

---

22 *struck the boar…*: probably to stun it before slitting its throat.

23 *the nymphs*: lesser female deities of the woodlands. *Hermes*: the son of Zeus and
   Maia; he was the god who guides people, especially travelers.

But clever Prometheus answered him, gently
smiling, and did not forget his crafty trick:
"Zeus, most honored and greatest of eternal gods,
take of these whichever the spirit within tells you."
He spoke with the trick in mind; but Zeus knowing deathless   550
plans, knew and did not miss the trick; in his heart
he foresaw evils which were going to happen to mortal men.[24]
With both hands he lifted up the white fat,
but he was angry in mind and rage came to his spirit,
when he saw the white ox-bones in the crafty trick.   555
Therefore the tribes of men of earth burn to the
immortals white bones on reeking altars.

> A character in a comedy by Menander (c. 344/3–292/1 BCE) comments on
> the giving of the inedible parts of the victim to the gods, suggesting that
> sacrifices are in part an excuse for a feast.

4.12 MENANDER, *THE GROUCH* 447–453.

How these rogues sacrifice!
They bring their picnic boxes and wine jars, not for the gods
but for themselves. The incense is a pious offering,
also the sacrificial cake.[25] The god gets all of these   450
when they are put on the fire. And the tail
and the gall bladder they give to the gods because they are inedible;
the rest they guzzle themselves.

> In Aristophanes' comedy *Peace*, first produced in 421 BCE during the
> Peloponnesian war, Trygaeus and the god Hermes are attempting to haul
> the goddess Peace out of a deep pit. They start with a prayer and libation.

4.13 ARISTOPHANES, *PEACE* 431–437.

Trygaeus
Well, then. Hold out the bowl,
so that we can start the work, as we pray to the gods.

Hermes
Pour libations, pour libations!
Auspicious language, please!

Trygaeus
As we pour, we'll pray that this day   435
may be the beginning of every good for the Greeks.

---

24 *evils*: an allusion Prometheus' theft of fire from the gods and Zeus' order for the
creation of Pandora, the first woman, who is said to have opened a box or jar that
released evil into the human world.

25 *sacrificial cake*: a simple offering made from cereals.

And may anyone who toils with us this day at the ropes
never be forced to bear a shield again.

> After rescuing the goddess, Trygaeus prepares to make a sacrifice to her. He
> sends his slave to find a sheep, while he finds an altar and other necessities
> for sacrifice. This humorous account is the most detailed literary evidence
> for the technical details of an ordinary animal sacrifice as opposed to the
> more elaborate sacrifices described in Homer.

4.14 ARISTOPHANES, *PEACE* 936–965.

Trygaeus

Go then, and bring the sheep as quickly as possible.   938
I'll provide an altar on which we'll sacrifice.

....

Trygaeus

O, look! Here's an altar right in front of the door.

....

Slave

Here's the basket with barley corns, and a garland and a knife.
And here's the kindling. The only thing we're missing is the sheep.

Chorus

The two of you should have a contest with each other.   950
For if Chaeris sees you,[26]
he'll come, uninvited, to play his pipes.
And then, I know full well,
for his puffing and toiling
you'll end up having to pay him.   955

> After the sheep is produced, Trygaeus gives further instructions to the
> slave, while he dips some kindling in water and sprinkles it over the sheep,
> telling it to shake.

Trygaeus

Here take the basket and the vessel with lustral water.
Walk quickly round the altar from left to right.

Slave

OK. What's the next order? I've done the circuit.

Trygaeus

Right, I'll take this firewood and dip it in the water.

---

26 *Chaeris*: a notoriously bad musician.

(to the sheep) You there, be quick and shake.[27] *(To the slave)* You, hand
   me some of the barley corns.   960

Hand me the container and wash your hands.

Now throw some of the barley to the audience.

Slave

OK.

Trygaeus

You've already thrown it?

Slave

Yes, by Hermes.

There's not a single one of the spectators

who hasn't got a barley corn.   965

    An oracle-monger, Hierocles, arrives, offering more hindrance than help.[28]

4.15 ARISTOPHANES, *PEACE* 1051–1062.

Hierocles

What's this sacrifice and to which of the gods are you sacrificing?

Trygaeus

Keep roasting; and don't speak. And keep off the tail-piece.

Hierocles

Won't you say to whom you are sacrificing? This tail looks good.

Trygaeus

The tail is good.   1055

Slave

It sure is good. Dear Lady Peace!

Hierocles

Come then, begin, and then give me the first offerings.[29]

Trygaeus

Better to roast it first.

Hierocles

But these are already roasted.

---

27 *shake*: this movement of the victim has generally been thought to indicate its assent
to being sacrificed. Naiden 2007: 61–73, however, shows that the evidence for sacrificial animals signifying consent to their death is flimsy at best. Iconographic and literary evidence is cited to show that victims were far from docile and sometimes had
to be tied and dragged to the altar. Demonstration of the victim's vitality (*psyche*),
not its acquiescence, was the objective of dousing the victim with water; see also 4.7
and 5.8.

28 *oracle-monger*: a seer or prophet who specialized in reading the future from the
entrails of sacrificial victims. Payment was usually required for their services.

29 *first offerings*: the entrails were merely tasted by the sacrificer, and then the rest was
given to the gods.

Trygaeus

You are a busy-body, whoever you are.

(*To the slave*) Start carving.

Slave

Where's the table?

Trygaeus

Bring the wine.[30]

Hierocles

The tongue is cut separately.[31]   1060

Trygaeus

We know. But do you know what you should do?

Hierocles

Tell me.

Trygaeus

Don't speak a word to us. For this is a sacrifice to Peace.

Trygaeus refuses to let Hierocles taste the entrails and pour the libation.

4.16 ARISTOPHANES, *PEACE* 1102–1109.

Trygaeus

Pour on the libation, and hand me a piece of the entrails.

Hierocles

If that's your idea, I'll serve myself too.

Trygaeus

Pour libation! Pour libation!

Hierocles

Pour it for me too, and give me a share of the entrails.   1105

Trygaeus

That's not what the blessed gods want.

Before that happens, we'll make the libation.

As for you, get out! O Lady Peace, remain with us throughout our life.

Two inscriptions from religious calendars from different areas indicate some of the mundane preliminaries for a public sacrifice. A mid-fourth century BCE religious calendar from the Aegean island of Cos describes the selection and preparations for the sacrifice of an ox to Zeus Polieus (Zeus of the City). This festival, the biggest civic festival of the year, was celebrated in the month Batramios (the approximate equivalent of January) in the agora or market place, within the sanctuary of the Twelve Gods. The inscription also gives specifications for the different sacrifices, the duties of individual

---

30 *table*: the meat was placed on a table where it was cut for distribution. *wine*: to be poured as a libation over the victim as it roasted.

31 The tongue was customarily given to the priest.

priests, perquisites for various people, and the disposition of the meat which must either be kept within the city or consumed in the sanctuary.

The first part of the inscription deals with the selection of the sacrificial ox. On the day before the sacrifice takes place, nine oxen, three from three different groups were driven into the market place (*agora*), where they were observed by a priest who was sitting at a table wearing his sacred garb, with the *hieropoioi* (the managers of the sacred rites) on each side of the table. The ox selected for sacrifice was the one that made a bow to the goddess Hestia, goddess of the hearth and one of the Twelve Gods.

4.17 RO no. 62,[32] side A, lines 19–59. It is sacrificed if it makes a deep bow (*mega hypokrupsei*) to Hestia.[33] The kings' share-receiver makes the sacrifice and provides offerings and offers in addition a half *hekteus* of offerings. He takes his share, the skin and a leg, the *hieropoioi* take a leg, and the remaining meat belongs to the city.[34]

The heralds lead the ox selected for Zeus to the agora. After reaching the agora, the owner of the ox or the person deputizing for him calls out: "For the people of Cos I am providing the ox; let the Coans give the price to Hestia." And let the chief magistrates immediately take an oath and make a valuation; when a valuation has been made, let the herald announce how much the valuation was. Then they drive the ox to Hestia Hetaeraea and make the sacrifice.[35] The priest puts a ribbon upon the ox and pours a cup of wine mixed with water as a libation in front of the ox. Then they lead the ox away, together with the burnt offering, seven cakes, honey, and the ribbon. As they leave, they call for respectful silence. At this point they untie the ox and begin the sacrificial ritual with olive and laurel. The heralds burn a pig and its entrails upon the altar, pouring on libations of honey and milk. After washing the intestines, they burn them beside the

---

32 RO no. 62 is number 62 in Rhodes and Osborne 2003, a collection of Greek historical inscriptions more widely available than earlier publications. For each inscription RO provide a full Greek text, often revised on the basis of new evidence, together with citations of earlier publications, an English translation, and commentary.

33 Naiden 2007: 64 notes that the bowing is required, not elicited as in the case of the sheep in Aristophanes' *Peace*. He also notes that the verb *hupokuptein* does not mean "nod" or "assent."

34 The kings' share-receiver is otherwise unknown and is probably an ancient title that has survived, despite its obsolescence. The duty of making the sacrifice and the perquisites here assigned to this official seem inconsistent with the later stipulations concerning the slaughterer (lines 37–38) and the assigning of the perquisites to "a priest" (lines 49–50).

35 *Hetaeraea and make the sacrifice*: the text at this point is problematic. The ensuing lines are also difficult to interpret, since the ox is not killed until the following day (line 46); see Rhodes and Osborne 2003: 309.

altar. And once they are burnt without wine,[36] let him [the herald?] pour upon them a libation of honey and milk.

(35) Let the herald announce that they are celebrating the annual festival as a feast for Zeus Polieus. Let the priest make an additional offering together with the intestines, incense, and cakes, libations mixed and unmixed, and a ribbon. Then let the priest and herald go the *hieropoioi* at the public building, and let the *hieropoioi* entertain the priest and the herald during this night.[37] When they make libations, let the priest choose one of the *hieropoioi* as slaughterer of the ox that is being sacrificed to Zeus Polieus, and let him proclaim that the slaughterer shall be pure from woman and man during the night.[38] And let the heralds choose whoever they want from their own number as slaughterer of the ox and let whoever of them wishes proclaim the choice to the person chosen.

(44) On the same day: to Dionysius Scyllites, a pig and a kid. The pig meat is not to be taken away [from the sanctuary].[39] The priest makes the sacrifice and provides the offerings. As perquisites, he takes the skin and leg.

On the twentieth: the selected ox is sacrificed to Zeus Polieus. What has to be wrapped is wrapped in the skin.[40] On the hearth a sacrifice is made of half a *hekteus* of barley, two half-*hekteus* loaves, one shaped like a cheese, and the things wrapped in skin. On these the priest pours a libation of three mixing bowls of wine. Perquisites from the ox: for the priest the skin and a leg (the priest provides the offerings) and half of the breast and half the stomach; for the incense-bearer the hip-end of the leg given to the *hieropoioi*; for the heralds, a double portion of meat from the back, shoulder meat, a three-spit share of blood meat; for the Nestoridae, a double portion of meat from the back; for the doctors,[41] meat, for the flute-player, meat; to the smiths and potters, the brain. The rest of the meat is for the city. All of these are not taken out of the city.

(55) On the same day: to Athena Polias, a pregnant sheep. The priest makes the sacrifice and provides the offerings. As perquisites, he takes the skin and a leg.

---

36 *burnt without wine*: Rhodes and Osborne 2003: 309 suggest that this kind of sacrifice indicates that chthonic elements in the cult of Zeus Polieus; likewise the libation of honey and milk.

37 *hieropoioi*: managers of the sacred rites, whose job was to ensure that every detail of the ritual was correctly performed.

38 *pure from woman and man*: see Rhodes and Osborne 2003: 310–311: "The insistence on the sexual purity of the slaughterers is unusual, a mark of the high dignity of the occasion, and this is the only early text that specifies that the purity should be from homosexual as well as from heterosexual intercourse."

39 *not to be taken away*: i.e., it must be eaten in the sanctuary.

40 *what has to be wrapped*: the parts of the victim that are sacrificed to the gods.

41 *doctors*: the temple of Asclepius on Cos was one of the most important centers of healing in the Greek world and the location of the Hippocratic school.

On the twenty-first: to Dionysius Scyllites a pig and a kid: the meat of the pig is not to be taken away. The priest makes the sacrifice and provides the offerings. As perquisites he takes the skin and a leg.

> An excerpt from the beginning of a an early fourth-century BCE sacrificial calendar from the deme of Marathon in Attica gives the cost of providing animals and other offerings for the official sacrifices held by the deme each month.[42]

4.18 IG II^2 1358, col. 2.[43] [The deme-leader of the Ma]rathonians makes the following sacrifices [in the first quarter of the year: ...within] ten days. To the Hero, [a pig, 3 drachmas; to the Heroine,] a pig, 3 drachmas. A table for the Hero [and the Heroine, 1 drachmas.] In the month Boedromion, before the Mysteries [- - -] an ox, 90 drachmas, a sheep, 12 drachmas; to Kourotrophos [...].[44]

In the second quarter: in the month Posideon [- - -] an ox, 150 drachmas; a sheep, 12 drachmas; to the Heroine, [a sheep, 11 drachmas, priestly portion,] 7 drachmas.[45] To Ge [Earth] "in the Fields," a pregnant cow, 70 [drachmas, priestly portion - - -]. To Telete, *spylia*, 40 drachmas.[46]

Ritual purity and pollution

> In several of the passages we have examined, the need for cleanliness before making a sacrifice is expressed. When Hector returns from the battlefield, he reminds his mother of the need for cleansing himself before making a libation, as he asks her to make an offering and prayer to Athena.

4.19 HOMER, *ILIAD* 6.264–278.

"Lady mother, do not lift honey-sweet wine to my lips,
or my limbs may lose their fury and I may forget my strength.   265
Reverence keeps me from pouring gleaming wine to Zeus
in libation with hands unwashed; no one splattered with blood
and gore can pray to the son of Cronus, lord of the dark clouds.
But collect the older women together and go to the temple
of Athena driver of spoils, with offerings to be burned;   270
and take a gown, the most delightful and largest that

---

42 Parke 1977: 48 estimates the average day-wage of an Athenian in the mid-fourth century BCE to be between one and a half to two drachmas.

43 For a translation of the entire inscription, see Rice and Stambaugh 1979: 113–115.

44 *table*: a table would have been spread with meats and offerings. *Boedromion*: the Athenian month of Boedromion roughly coincided with late September–late October. *Mysteries*: the Eleusinian Mysteries, on which see Chapter 11. *Kourotrophos*: Nurturer of Youth.

45 *Posideon*: this Attic month occurred approximately in late November–late December.

46 *Telete*: perhaps a goddess of initiation. *spylia*: the meaning is unknown.

you have in the palace, the one that is dearest to you yourself,
and place it upon the lovely-haired goddess Athena's knees;
promise that we will sacrifice in her temple twelve
unbroken yearling heifers,[47] if only she will take pity   275
on our city, and on the Trojans' wives and innocent children,
and keep the son of Tydeus away from sacred Troy,
Diomedes the savage spearman and powerful master of fear.

> Hector's mother goes with her attendants to Athena's temple and gives a
> gown to the priestess, who prays on their behalf to the goddess. At the end
> of this excerpt, Homer remarks that Athena did not grant their prayer.

4.20 HOMER, *ILIAD* 6.297–311.

And when they reached Athena's temple, up on the citadel,
Theano of the lovely cheeks threw open the doors for them,
daughter of Cisseus and wife of Antenor tamer of horses,
for the Trojans had appointed her as Athena's priestess.   300
With a piercing cry, all lifted up their arms to Athena;
Theano of the lovely cheeks took hold of the gown
and placed it upon the lovely-haired goddess Athena's knees,
and prayed, invoking the aid of the daughter of mighty Zeus:
"Lady Athena, defender of cities, glorious goddess,   305
break Diomedes' spear, and grant that he himself
fall headlong onto his face in front of the Scaean gates,
and we will immediately sacrifice in your temple twelve
unbroken yearling heifers, if only you will take pity
on our city, and on the Trojans' wives and innocent children."   310
So she spoke in prayer; but Pallas Athena refused her.[48]

> Hesiod's advice on ritual purity:

4.21 HESIOD, *WORKS AND DAYS* 724–726.

After dawn, never pour a libation of sparkling wine to Zeus
with unwashed hands, nor to the other immortal gods.
For they will not hear you, and will spit back your prayers.

4.22 HESIOD, *WORKS AND DAYS* 336–341.

In so far as you can, make sacrifice to the immortal gods
in purity and cleanliness, and burn the shining thigh bones.
At other times, propitiate them with libations and incense,
both when you go to bed and when the sacred light returns,

---

47 *unbroken yearling heifers*: see 4.9 with n. 16.

48 Diomedes continues to have success against the Trojans and ultimately, in accordance with Zeus' plan, Hector is killed by Achilles.

so that their hearts and minds may be propitious to you,   340

and that you may buy the property of others and not have someone else
buy yours.

> Although fear of pollution becomes more pervasive in the literature and
> history of the period after Homer and Hesiod, this does not mean that
> it was not perceived earlier. A late fourth-century BCE law on pollution
> from Cyrene gives stipulations about a man making sacrifice after sexual
> intercourse.

4.23 RO no. 97, side A, lines 11–13.[49] A man coming from a woman after sleeping
with her by night, may sacrifice whatever he wishes. If he has slept with her
during the day, once he has washed, he may go — — wherever he wishes,
except to — — —

> The most abhorrent pollution was caused by homicide, whether voluntary or
> involuntary. The orator Demosthenes (384–322 BCE) cites a law of Dracon,
> the late seventh century BCE lawgiver, listing the various bans imposed upon
> a murderer, thus making the offender a complete social outcast.

4.24 DEMOSTHENES, *AGAINST LEPTINES* 158. Among the laws of his kind,
Dracon marked the terrible crime of homicide by banning the offender
from lustral water, libations, the mixing bowls, sacrifices, and the market
place.[50] Thus he enumerated everything that he thought would be a likely
deterrent to homicide.

> The situation of Oedipus, as portrayed in Sophocles' *King Oidipous*,
> epitomizes the worst kind of pollution, that of a man who has unknowingly
> killed his own father. At the beginning of the play, the priest of Zeus describes
> the pollution that is afflicting the entire community of Thebes because of
> an unsolved murder.

4.25 SOPHOCLES, *KING OIDIPOUS* 22–30.

Priest

As you yourself can see, the city's now so badly
storm-tossed that it can no longer keep its head
from sinking down beneath the tossing waves of blood;
it is decaying in the fruitful husks of earth,   25
decaying in the herds of pastured cattle and
in women's barren labor-pains; and the fire-bearing
god,[51] most hateful plague, has swooped to scourge

---

49 For the complete Greek text with a translation and commentary see Rhodes and
Osborne 2003: 494–505.

50 *mixing bowls*: the large bowls in which wine was mixed with water before being
dispensed at a feast.

51 *fire-bearing god*: Apollo.

the city, emptying the house of Cadmus while

black Hades is enriched with groaning and laments.[52]   30

> When Oedipus is told by the oracle of Apollo that the cause of the plague is the murderer of Laius, he invokes a terrible curse that makes the murderer a complete social outcast. Ironically, Oedipus has no idea that he himself is the murderer of the long-dead Laius and that Laius was his father.

4.26 SOPHOCLES, *KING OIDIPOUS* 236–243.

Oedipus

I solemnly prohibit anyone within

this land whose power and throne are mine to take him in—

the man who did this[53]—or address him, or allow

him to participate in prayers or sacrifices

to the gods, or let him share the lustral water;   240

no, all must thrust him from their homes, since he's the source

of the polluting taint upon us, as the god's

Pythian oracle has just revealed to me.[54]

> In Aeschylus' *Eumenides*, Orestes, who has killed his mother Clytemnestra to avenge his father's murder, goes to Apollo's shrine at Delphi to be purified from the pollution incurred by matricide. He describes how he was purified by the blood of a slaughtered pig.

4.27 AESCHYLUS, *EUMENIDES* 276–283.

Orestes

Schooled amid evil, I know

many ways of purification, and I know where speech is right

and likewise silence; and in this case

I am ordered to speak by a wise teacher.

For the blood upon my hand becomes sleepy and dies away,   280

and the pollution (*miasma*) of my matricide is washed away.

At Apollo's hearth, while still fresh,

it was expelled by Phoebus' cleansing with the slaughter of a pig.

> The philosopher Heraclitus (active c. 500 BCE) comments on the futility of ritual of purification by means of blood.

---

52 *house of Cadmus*: Cadmus was an earlier king of Thebes, but here the reference is to the suffering of all the people of Thebes.

53 *the man who did this*: note the attempted precision of the definition, even though the identity of Laius' murderer is unknown.

54 *Pythian oracle*: the Pythia was the priestess of Apollo at Delphi. Inspired by the god, she delivered his message

4.28 HERACLITUS, *KRS* no. 241. In vain [humans] purify themselves of blood-guilt by defiling themselves with blood, as though one who had stepped into mud were to wash with mud. Anyone noticing him doing this would think him mad.

Some ancestral practices

In Xenophon's *Memorabilia*, Socrates speaks of the advice of Apollo who said that the god's favor was best obtained by following the custom (*nomos*) of the city.

4.29 XENOPHON, *MEMORABILIA* 4.3.16. You see that the Delphic god, when someone asked him how he might win favor with the gods, answered, "by following the custom of the city."[55] For, I suppose, everywhere it is the custom to propitiate the gods to the best of one's ability with offerings. How better, then, can a man honor the gods with due reverence than by doing their bidding?

The following excerpts indicate three different contexts in which ancestral customs prevailed. In Aeschylus' *Seven against Thebes* (produced 467 BCE), Eteocles, the army commander, prays for the gods' support, vowing magnificent gifts in the event of victory.

4.30 AESCHYLUS, *SEVEN AGAINST THEBES* 266–278.
Make the better prayer; "May the gods fight on our side!"
Listen in your turn to my prayer; then
raise the sacred cry of jubilation, the paean,
the customary Greek invocation at sacrifices,
which emboldens our friends and delivers us from battle fear.   270

To the guardian gods of my country,
whether they dwell in the plain or keep watch over the market-place,
to the springs of Dirce, to the waters of the Ismenus,[56]
I now promise that, if all goes well and the city is saved,
I will offer on the altars of the gods the blood of sheep,   275
and the sacrifice of bulls. Thus I vow
to set up trophies,[57] and I shall drape our sacred places
with our enemies' garments, pierced by our spears.

Thucydides describes the prayers and libations that were offered when the Athenian fleet set out for Sicily to begin a new campaign (415 BCE).

---

55 *Delphic god*: Apollo, as god of prophecy.

56 The springs of Dirce and the river Ismenus were in the city of Thebes.

57 *trophies*: a trophy was a monument consisting of the arms taken from the enemy that was erected at the site of the victory.

4.31 THUCYDIDES 6.32. When the ships had been manned and loaded with everything that they were going to take with them, silence was proclaimed by a blast on the trumpet. They offered the prayers that were customary before making a voyage, not each ship individually, but altogether, led by a herald. Throughout the whole army, marines and officers mixed the wine and poured libations in gold and silver cups. The rest of the throng of citizens on the shore and any others who wished them well prayed with them. When they had sung the paean and finished the libations, they set sail.

> A poem by the philosopher Xenophanes (c.570–478 BCE) describes the religious preparations for a symposium (drinking party).[58]

4.32 XENOPHANES, *DK* Frag. 1.[59]

Now the floor is clean, and the hands
of every guest, and the drinking cups. Someone puts garlands on our
heads; another hands around sweet-scented myrrh in a dish.
The mixing bowl stands full of good cheer;
and more wine is ready to hand, wine which promises never to run
    short,   5
sweet wine in the wine-jars, smelling of flowers.
In the midst incense sends up its sacred odor,
and there is cold water, sweet and pure.
Golden loaves are set out, and there is a magnificent table
loaded with cheese and rich honey.   10
The altar in the middle is a mass of flowers,
and song and festivity fill the house.
Men of good cheer must first hymn the god
with reverent words and pure speech,
pouring libations and praying to act righteously—   15
for this is more within our reach.
It is not excessive for a man to drink as much
as can carry him home without the help of an attendant (unless he is
    very old).
I praise the man who as he drinks reveals noble thoughts,
displaying his memory and his striving for virtue.   20
He never recounts the battles of Titans or Giants
or Centaurs, the fancies of earlier generations,
or violent factions. There is nothing good in these things,
but it is always best to have respect for the gods.[60]

---

58 A symposium was celebrated by males of noble birth. Women, with the exception of female entertainers, were excluded.

59 *DK* = *Die Fragmente der Vorsokratiker*, 5th to 7th eds., by H. Diels, ed. with additions by W. Krantz.

60 For Xenophanes' skepticism about stories about the gods related in Homer and Hesiod, see 12.8.

5. Divination

5.1 XENOPHON, *SYMPOSIUM* 4.47–49. It is apparent that both Greeks and barbarians believe that the gods know everything, the present and the future. At any rate, all cities and peoples use divination to ask the gods what they should or should not do.

> Divination (*mantike techne*) is the skill or art of interpreting signs thought to be sent by the gods.[1] Xenophon (428–c. 354 BCE) lists different kinds of divination and warns humans to be constant in their regard for the gods in good times as well as bad if they want reliable advice from divination.

5.2 XENOPHON, *THE CAVALRY COMMANDER* 9.9. The gods know all things. By means of sacrifices, birds, voices, and dreams they send signs to whomever they wish. And it is likely that the gods are more willing to advise those who not only ask what they should do when they have a problem, but who also serve the gods to the best of their ability in times of prosperity.[2]

5.3 XENOPHON, *MEMORABILIA* 1.1.3. Believers in divination rely on birds, oracles, signs, and sacrifices. They do not think that the birds or the humans they encounter know what is advantageous for the inquirer, but rather that they are the means by which the gods send signs.

> Such signs were usually interpreted by a specialist or expert, a seer or prophet (*mantis*). An individual or community would consult a seer regarding a situation or problem much in the same way as one consults a doctor. The seer would respond only after he had assessed the social context of the problem and the interests of his client.

> A seer had a responsibility both to his client and to the community at large. There was also the question of his own reputation which depended on his

---

1 On divination, see Flower 2008, especially his chapter on "The Art of the Consultation", and Johnston 2008 with bibliography.

2 *serve the gods*: the Greek *therapeuein* means to attend, pay attention to, respect and thus honor the gods.

advice proving correct and beneficial. These various exigencies could result in a conflict of interest.

When plague afflicts the Greeks, they consult Calchas the seer to discover the cause of Apollo's anger. Calchas specialized in the interpretation of bird signs.

5.4   HOMER, *ILIAD* 1.59–72.

"Son of Atreus, now I think we will have to go home,
driven back from our goal—that's if we escape from death—   60
if plague and warfare combine to overcome the Achaeans;
come, let us ask some prophet or priest, or even a man
who interprets dreams—since dreams are also omens from Zeus—
who may tell us why Phoebus Apollo is now so greatly enraged,
if he blames us because of a vow or a hecatomb unfulfilled;[3]   65
he may be willing to turn the plague aside from us if he
meets with the savory smoke of lambs or unblemished goats.

So speaking he took his seat; and then there stood up among them
Calchas the son of Thestor, by far the best of the bird-
interpreters, he who knew what is, what will be and what   70
has been in the past, who led the Achaeans to Troy with their ships
through the skill in prophecy given to him by Phoebus Apollo.

Calchas reveals that the problem is Agamemnon's refusal to surrender his concubine, the daughter of the Trojan priest Chryses. She must be returned by the Greeks, and a sacrifice made to appease Apollo to whom Chryses had appealed.

5.5   HOMER, *ILIAD* 1.91–100.

Then the splendid prophet took heart and spoke to them in reply:
"He blames you not for a vow or a hecatomb unfulfilled,
but on account of his priest, dishonored by Agamemnon,
when he did not accept the ransom or set his daughter free;   95
for this the far-shooter has given us pain and will give us more;
he will not drive this foul plague back and spare the Danaans
until we restore the glancing-eyed girl to her own dear father,

---

3   *if he blames us*: the implication is that there may have been a flaw in the pronounce-
ment of the vow, or a blemish in a sacrificial victim. In either case, the gods would
be displeased, and so would not accept the sacrifice or vow. *hecatomb*: the sacrificial
offering of a large number of animals. The word literally means one hundred animals, but is not to be taken literally.

without any price or ransom, and take to Chryse a sacred
hecatomb; thus may we propitiate and persuade him."[4]   100

In Sophocles' *Antigone* (first performed in 442/1 BCE), the blind seer Tiresias
is consulted by King Creon who has condemned Antigone, his niece and his
son's fiancée, to death because she has buried her brother's body in defiance
of the king's proclamation. The seer reports the unfavorable results of his
observation of the flight of birds and his burnt sacrifice.

5.6   SOPHOCLES, *ANTIGONE* 998–1014.

Tiresias

You'll find out when you hear the signs from my skilled craft.
As I sat on the ancient seat where I perform
my augury,[5] a haven for all kinds of birds,   1000
I heard the birds give unintelligible voice,
screeching in evil frenzy with a babbling noise.
I sensed them tearing at each other with their bloody
claws—the whirring of their wings was a clear sign.
At once, in fear, I tried to make burnt-sacrifice   1005
upon an altar duly kindled; but Hephaestus
did not blaze forth from the offerings;[6] instead
a putrid liquid from the thighs oozed out upon
the coals, and smoked and spattered, and the gall-bladder
exploded up into the air; the thighs, streaming   1010
with moisture, lay bared of their covering of lard.
I learned about these things—the failure of my rites
of prophecy, which gave no signs—from this boy here.
For just as I lead others onward, he leads me.

---

4 *Chryse*: a location near Troy, where Apollo was worshiped.

5 *augury*: divination by the observation of birds that flocked to a particular place,
probably lured by food.

6 *Hephaestus*: the god of fire. The god's name is here used for the fire itself, indicating
divine rejection of the sacrifice.

Oracles

In Sophocles' *King Oidipous* (first performed between 430 and 425 BCE), Tiresias is summoned by Oedipus to interpret the reply of the oracle of Apollo at Delphi. He tells Oedipus that the cause of the plague is the unsolved murder of Laius, the previous king of Thebes. Laius was also Oedipus' father, though Oedipus is as yet unaware of this relationship.

5.7   SOPHOCLES, *KING OIDIPOUS* 284–315.

Chorus

I know the lord whose vision is the closest to
Lord Phoebus is Tiresias;[7] look into this
with his help, lord, and you'll most clearly learn the truth.

    . . . .

The one who'll show him up is present;[8] for these folk
are leading here the godlike prophet; he's the only
human in whom truth is naturally inborn.

Oedipus

Tiresias, surveyor of all things—those taught   300
and those unspoken, heavenly and walking on
the earth—although you cannot see, you understand
the sickness present in our city; we can find
no champion and no savior from it, but for you.
Phoebus—in case you haven't heard report of this—   305
sent us this answer, when we sent to ask him: that
we'll be released from this great sickness only if
we learn in full who Laius' killers are, and then
kill them or send them forth in exile from the land.
Don't grudge us the prophetic voice of birds or any   310
other road of divination that you have,
rescue yourself, rescue this city, rescue me
from all this taint now emanating from the dead.
We're in your hands; the finest task is for a man
to help with every resource lying in his power.   315

The oracles of Apollo at Delphi were delivered by a priestess, the Pythia, a local woman more than fifty years old, who was appointed for life and was expected to remain chaste throughout her tenure. Before delivering a prophecy, the priestess purified herself in the Castalian spring, and then burned laurel leaves and barley meal on the altar of Apollo's temple. Seated on a tripod (a three-

---

7   *Lord Phoebus*: Apollo, the god of prophecy at Delphi; for his prophecy see below lines 305–309.

8   *him*: the murderer of Laius, the previous king of Thebes.

Figure 5.1. View of Delphi with the remains of the temple of Apollo in the foreground. © istockphoto/Benjamin Lazare.

legged stool) and inspired by the god, she delivered prophecies. She only made prophecies, however, on the seventh day of each month, except for the three months when Apollo was said to be absent from Delphi.[9]

In discussing the behavior of sacrificial animals at Delphi, Plutarch, who was himself a Delphic priest, indicates that the libation poured on a sacrificial animal was to test the victim's vitality and so prove its suitability for sacrifice.[10]

5.8 PLUTARCH, *MORALIA* 435 b–c. What is the significance of pouring libations on sacrificial animals and the refusal to give responses unless the entire victim trembles and shakes from the tips of its hooves when the libation is poured over it? Shaking the head is not enough as in other sacrifices, but the tossing and quivering must extend to all parts of the animal and be accompanied by a sound. Unless this happens, they say that the oracle is not functioning and they do not even bring in the Pythia.

In Euripides' *Ion* (first produced c. 410 BCE), the temple attendant Ion describes Delphi at dawn.

5.9 EURIPIDES, *ION* 86–93.

The untrodden peaks of Parnassus
become light as they receive

---

9   On the Pythia, see Connelly 2007: 72–81 and Johnston 2008: 38–60.

10 See Naiden 2007: 61–73, and also 4.7 and 4.15 with n. 27.

the shield of day for mortals.

The smoke of dry incense

wings up to the roofs of Phoebus.   90

The Delphic woman sits on her holy tripod,

chanting for the Greeks the cries

that Apollo utters.

> Oracles were consulted for advice on a variety of political, religious, and personal problems. Concern about the fertility of both humans and the earth were among the most common enquiries.

5.10 PLUTARCH, *MORALIA* 386 c. [People ask] if they are going to be victorious, if they are going to marry, if it is to their advantage to sail, to farm, or to go abroad.

> The following eight texts, written on lead tablets, are from a small selection the tablets discovered at the oracle of Zeus at Dodona in Epirus in northwest Greece. The tablets record the enquiries made by both political communities and individuals.

5.11 Parke 1967: 260.[11] God. Good Fortune. The Corcyreans enquire of Zeus Naios and Dione,[12] to what god or hero they should sacrifice and pray in order to be of one mind for their good.

5.12 Parke 1967: 262. The community of the ... ask Zeus Naios and Dione whether ... if they join the confederation of the Molossi it will be safe for them.

5.13 Parke 1967: 263. Gods. Good Fortune. Evandros and his wife enquire of Zeus Naios and Dione to which of the gods, heroes, or supernatural powers (*daimones*) they should pray and sacrifice in order that they and their household may have a better and more desirable life both now and for all time.

5.14 Parke 1967: 265. Heracleidas asks Zeus and Dione for good fortune and enquires of the god concerning children, whether there will be any from his wife Aigle whom he has now.

5.15 Parke 1967: 266. God. Good fortune. Anaxippus asks Zeus Naos and Dione about having male offspring from his wife Philiste. To which of the gods should I pray in order that I fare best and most well?

5.16 Parke 1967: 268. Nicocrateia wants to know to which of the gods she should sacrifice in order that she may have a better life and be rid of her illness.

5.17 Parke 1967: 268. Cleotas asks Zeus and Dione if it is better and more profitable for him to keep sheep.

---

11 In an appendix, Parke 1977: 259–273 presents a selection of enquiries made at Dodona, giving the Greek text, a translation, and brief commentary; see also Johnston 2008: 60–75.

12 *Zeus Naios*: Naios (also spelled Naos) is the cultic title of Zeus at Dodona, meaning "the flowing," probably because of the springs in the area. *Dione*: Zeus's consort in this particular cult. Her name is the feminine form of his.

5.18 Parke 1967: 272. Agis asks Zeus Naos and Dione about the blankets and the pillows that he has lost: whether some one from outside may have stolen them.

The responses of the Delphic oracle were highly enigmatic, as the early Greek philosopher Heraclitus (fl. c. 500 BCE) remarks.

5.19 HERACLITUS, *KRS* no. 244. The Lord whose oracle is at Delphi neither speaks out nor conceals, but gives a sign.

In Euripides' *Medea* (first produced in 431 BCE), King Aegeus of Athens, the future father of Theseus, is returning home after consulting the Delphic oracle. He comes to Corinth where he meets Medea, the wife of Jason, and tells her the oracle's response.

5.20 EURIPIDES, *MEDEA* 665–681.

Medea

Greetings to you, too, Aegeus, wise son of Pandion.   665
From where are you coming to this land?

Aegeus

I've come from Delphi, Apollo's ancient oracle.

Medea

What took you to the earth's center of prophecy?

Aegeus

To find out how I might become a father.

Medea

By the gods! You're childless at your time of life?   670

Aegeus

Childless, indeed, by some cruel stroke of fate.

Medea

You're married? You've had experience with women?

Aegeus

Indeed it's not a for lack of a wife or marriage.

Medea

What did Apollo tell you about children?

Aegeus

Words too wise for a man to understand.   675

Medea

Is it right for me to know the god's response?

Aegeus

Certainly, for a clever mind indeed is needed.[13]

---

13 *clever mind*: Medea was famed for her skill with potions and drugs; using her skill she enabled Jason to seize the golden fleece.

Figure 5.2. On an Athenian cup, c. 440 BCE, the goddess Themis is depicted sitting on the tripod as she delivers a prophecy to King Aegeus. In mythology Themis possessed the oracle before Apollo took over Delphi. Themis is shown in the dress of the Pythia, and she is calmly divining from a bowl containing liquid. Art Resource, NY.

Medea

What did he say, then? Speak, if it is allowed.

Aegeus

Not to release the wine-skin's hanging neck[14]—

Medea

Until you do what, come to what place?   680

Aegeus

Until I come to my father's hearth once more.

> Writing in the late first century BCE and early first century CE, Strabo describes the oracular shrine and the vapor that the Pythia inhales; her responses were delivered to the petitioner in verse.

5.21 STRABO, *GEOGRAPHY* 9.3.5. They say that the seat of the oracle is a cavern hollowed deep down in the earth, with a rather narrow mouth, from which a vapor rises that inspires a divine madness. Over the mouth, a high tripod is placed. Mounting this, the Pythia inhales the vapor and then utters oracles

---

14 *Not to release the wine-skin's hanging neck*: to refrain from sexual intercourse.

in both verse and prose, though the latter are put into verse by poets who are temple attendants.[15]

> In his essay "On the decline of oracles," Plutarch (c.50–120 CE) notes that the vapor in the shrine varied in strength.

5.22 PLUTARCH, *MORALIA* 437 c. I think that the exhalation is not always the same, but it periodically abates and then becomes strong again. As for the proof on which I depend, I have as witnesses many strangers and all the attendants of the shrine. It is a fact that the room in which they seat those who come to consult the oracle is filled, not frequently or regularly, but as it happens from time to time, with a delightful fragrance that comes on a current of air from the *adyton*[16] as if from a spring. The fragrance is like the aroma that the most exquisite and costly perfumes exude; it is probable that this phenomenon occurs because of heat or some other force that is engendered there.

> Scientific findings corroborate the accuracy of Plutarch's description. A geological survey has shown that two geological faults intersect exactly under the site of the oracle. Ethylene gas probably rose through fissures created by the faults, perhaps inducing a trace-like state. The lessening of the emission noted by Plutarch may have been increased by an earthquake in the mid-fourth century CE.[17]

> In a discourse on the practice of divination, the Roman author Cicero (106–43 BCE) remarks on the Greeks' custom of consulting an oracle before establishing a new city or starting a war.

5.23 CICERO, *ON DIVINATION* 1.3. What colony did Greece ever send out to Aeolia, Ionia, Asia, Sicily, or Italy without consulting the Pythian or Dodonian oracle, or that of Jupiter Hammon?[18] What war did the Greeks ever undertake without first seeking the advice of the gods?

> The historian Herodotus (writing in the mid-fifth century BCE) reports that a Spartan, Dorieus, set out to found a colony in Libya without consulting the oracle of Apollo at Delphi. The colony failed. When other oracles advised

---

15 Regarding this relatively late testimony of Strabo, note Flower 2008: 215–222, who points out that earlier fifth century BCE evidence indicates the Pythia delivered her own utterances in verse, which suggests that any versification by male attendants was a later development.

16 *adyton*: inner part of the shrine where the Pythia sat on the tripod to deliver the oracles.

17 De Boer, Hale and Chantron 2001: 707–710, and Broad 2006. More recently, however, Flower 2008: 226–227 is skeptical about the alleged effects of ethylene: "Yet if the Pythia was indeed under the influence of ethylene gas, this would have served as a relaxant and mild clarificatory stimulant; she was not what we would call 'high'".

18 *Pythian*: a reference to the oracle of Apollo at Delphi. *Dodonian*: a reference to the oracle of Zeus at Dodona in northwest Greece. *Hammon* or *Ammon*: the hellenized name of Amun, an Egyptian god who was identified with Zeus and later Jupiter. His oracle was in the Libyan desert at Siwa and was consulted by Alexander the Great.

him to establish a colony in Sicily, he safeguarded his second enterprise by checking with the Delphic oracle.

5.24 HERODOTUS, *HISTORIES* 5.42–43. Dorieus asked the Spartans for a group of people and took them off to found a settlement elsewhere, but he did not first consult the Delphic oracle concerning a suitable site, nor did he observe any of the customary formalities; he just sailed to Libya in anger....[19]

Arriving there, he established a colony by the river Cinyps, in an excellent location that belonged to the Libyans. In the third year, however, he was driven out by the Macae (a Libyan tribe) and the Carthaginians, and returned to the Peloponnese. Here, using the oracles collected by Laius, a certain Antichares of Eleon advised him to found the city of Heraclea in Sicily;[20] according to him, all the country of Eryx in western Sicily belonged to the Heraclids, since Heracles himself was its original conqueror.[21] Hearing this, Dorieus went to Delphi to consult the oracle to see whether he should take the land that he sought. The priestess told him that he would take it, whereupon he collected the group of settlers that he had led to Libya and sailed with them along the Italian coast.

> Several reports by Herodotus indicate the oracles' political importance throughout the Mediterranean world in the sixth and fifth centuries BCE.[22] King Croesus of Lydia (ruled c. 560–546 BCE) tested several oracles to see which he could best trust. Impressed by the Delphic oracle, he attempts to win Apollo's favor with grandiose sacrifices and expensive votive offerings.

5.25 HERODOTUS, *HISTORIES* 1.50. Croesus now tried to win the favor of Delphic Apollo by magnificent sacrifices. He slaughtered three thousand sacrificial animals of every kind; he made a huge pile of couches overlaid with gold or silver, golden cups, purple garments, and tunics and burned them, hoping to win the favor of the god by this means. He proclaimed that every Lydian was to offer a sacrifice according to his means. After this sacrifice he melted down an enormous quantity of gold into one hundred and seventeen ingots.

> Croesus asks the oracle if he should attack the Persians and seek some allies. But he fails to realize that the oracle's reply is conditional.

---

19 Dorieus was angry because his older brother Cleomenes, who was said to be slightly mad, became one of the two kings of Sparta. This incident occurred c. 514–512 BCE.

20 *oracles collected by Laius*: the father of Oedipus, who was told by the oracle of Apollo that he would be killed by his son. *Antichares*: probably an oracle monger (a seller of oracles), who was using a collection of oracles apparently attributed to Laius. *Eleon*: a town in Boeotia, home of a legendary seer, Bacis.

21 *Heracles*: the Greek hero, a son of Zeus.

22 Herodotus gives some verse responses directly, whereas others are reported in indirect discourse.

5.26 HERODOTUS, *HISTORIES* 1.53–54. Croesus instructed the Lydians who were going to take the gifts to the temples to ask the oracles if he should undertake a campaign against the Persians and if he should take additional allies. When they arrived at their destination, the Lydians dedicated the votive offerings and consulted the oracle with the following words: "Croesus, King of Lydia and other nations, recognizing these as the only true oracles in the world, has given you gifts worthy of your power of divination, and now asks you if he should march against the Persians and if he should seek some allies."

This was the question, and the answers of both oracles were similar:[23] they foretold that if Croesus attacked the Persians, he would destroy a great empire. They also advised him to find out which of the Greek states was the most powerful and to make a treaty of friendship with it.

Croesus was overjoyed when he learnt the oracles' response. Fully confident that he would overthrow Cyrus' kingdom, he sent further gifts to Delphi, two gold staters for every man, after inquiring the size of its population. In return, the Delphians granted in perpetuity to Croesus and the people of Lydia the right of citizenship for any who wished, exemption from dues, front seats at Delphic events, and priority in consulting the oracle.

Croesus asks the oracle about the length of his reign.

5.27 HERODOTUS, *HISTORIES* 1.55. After these gifts, Croesus consulted the oracle a third time;[24] since he had received the truth from the oracle, he wanted to make the most of it. On this consultation he asked if his reign would be long one. The priestess answered:

"When the day comes that a mule rules over the Medes,

then, soft-footed Lydian, by pebbly Hermus

flee and do not stay, nor be ashamed to be a coward."

Croesus rejoiced most of all in the reply, supposing that a mule would never become king of the Medes in place of a man. This meant that he and his line would remain in power for ever.

After learning that Sparta was the most powerful state in Greece, Croesus makes an alliance with the Spartans and attacks the Persian empire. In the event, however, it is his own kingdom that is destroyed. Defeated, Croesus sends to Delphi to reproach Apollo for his deceit but the Pythia explains that even the gods could not escape Fate. Rather, after receiving the first oracle, Croesus should have asked further questions.

5.28 HERODOTUS, *HISTORIES* 1.91. When the Lydian messengers reached Delphi and asked the questions as instructed, the Pythia is said to have replied that even the god could not avoid what was fated...

---

23 Croesus had also consulted the oracle of Amphiaraus, see Herodotus 1.52 in 6.13 with n. 18.

24 For his first consultation of the oracle, see Herodotus 1.46.

Although Loxias was anxious that the disaster would happen in the time of Croesus' sons rather than that of Croesus, he had not been able to divert the Fates.[25] But he had obtained as much favor for Croesus as the Fates allowed. For he had delayed the capture of Sardis for three years, and so Croesus should realize that he had been captured three years later than was destined for him. Secondly the god had helped him when he was on the funeral pyre.[26]

As for the oracle, Croesus had no right to find fault with what had happened. For Loxias had told him that if he campaigned against the Persians he would destroy a great empire. In response to this, he ought to have sent again and enquired which empire was intended, Cyrus' or his own. But, as he misinterpreted what was said and didn't make a second enquiry, he had to admit that it was his own fault. Moreover, on his last consultation with the oracle, he did not understand what Loxias said about the mule. For the mule was Cyrus, who was the son of parents from different races. He had been born of a nobler mother and a lower-born father. His mother was a Mede and daughter of Astyages, king of Media; but his father was a Persian, a subject of the Medes, and he had married a lady to whom he was in every way inferior. Such was the reply of the Pythia that the messengers took to Sardis and reported to Croesus. He acknowledged that it was his own mistake and not the god's.

> The enigmatic nature of oracular responses is also apparent in Herodotus' account of the Athenians' consultation of the Delphic oracle at the time of the threat of a Persian invasion of Greece in 481 BCE. The oracle told them to flee. However, on the advice of a prominent inhabitant of Delphi, they supplicated the god and asked for a second prophecy, which the Athenian Themistocles interpreted as foretelling an Athenian naval victory at Salamis.

5.29 HERODOTUS, *HISTORIES* 7.141–143. The Athenians were persuaded to do this. "Lord Apollo," they said, "grant us a better oracle concerning our fatherland. Honor these suppliant branches that we bring.[27] Indeed we will not leave your sanctuary, but will remain here in this place until we die." Then the prophetess uttered a second prophecy, as follows:

"Pallas cannot entirely win over Olympian Zeus,

though she prays him with many words and shrewd subtlety.[28]

Yet I will respond to you with this word, having made it as firm
    as adamant:

---

25 *Loxias*: Apollo. *divert the Fates*: see 5.32 for Solon's statement about the inability of seers to ward off Destiny.

26 *helped him*: Apollo had sent a shower of rain to put out the flames of the funeral pyre on which the captured Croesus had been placed (*Histories* 1.87).

27 *branches*: suppliants traditionally carried branches to deposit in the god's shrine.

28 *Pallas*: Pallas Athena, the patron goddess of Athens.

though all else shall be captured within the bounds of Cecrops[29]

and the hollows of the holy mountain of Cithaeron.

Yet in response to Athena, Zeus the loud-voice grants

that only the wooden wall shall not be sacked, benefiting you and
your children.

But do not passively await the onset of the enemy cavalry and foot,

a mighty army from the land.

Turn your back, and withdraw. You will indeed meet him face
to face.

Divine Salamis,[30] you will bring death to the sons of women

when the corn is scattered or the harvest gathered in."

This reply seemed milder that the earlier one and so the envoys wrote it down and returned to Athens. On their arrival they announced it to the people. Of the many different interpretations, as they searched for the meaning of the oracle, the main ones were as follows. Some of the older men said that it seemed to them that the god was foretelling that the acropolis would survive because long ago the acropolis was fenced in with thorn bush. They supposed that this was the wooden wall. But others said that the god meant the ships; so they should prepare ships, abandoning everything else. But those who said that the ships were the wooden walls were baffled by the last two lines spoken by the Pythia:

"Divine Salamis, you will bring death to the sons of women

when the corn is scattered or the harvest gathered in."

These words were not in accordance with the interpretation of those who declared that the ships were the wooden wall. For the oracle-mongers (chresmologoi) took them to mean that if they prepared a fleet they would be defeated off Salamis.[31]

There was a certain Athenian who had recently become prominent; his name was Themistocles, the son of Neocles.[32] He said that the oracle-mongers' suggestion was not correct. For if the word that was spoken really referred to the Athenians, the oracle would not have been expressed so mildly; it would have said, "Wretched Salamis," rather than "Divine Salamis," if the inhabitants were going to die there. The correct interpretation was that the oracle referred to the enemy, not the Athenians. He therefore advised them to fight at sea, because the ships were the wooden wall.

---

29 *Cecrops*: legendary king of Athens, used here for Athens itself.

30 *Salamis*: a large island in the Saronic Gulf, off the coast of Attica.

31 *oracle-mongers*: the Greek *chresmologoi* can mean either collectors, chanters, or interpreters of oracles. The term is generally derogatory and is applied to marginal figures who operated outside the acceptable norms of seercraft (*mantike techne*).

32 Themistocles had earlier persuaded the Athenians to spend the windfall from the silver mines at nearby Laurium to build a navy, as Herodotus 7.144 later notes.

The Athenians judged Themistocles' interpretation preferable to that of the oracle-mongers, who did not want them to prepare for a naval battle and said that they should not take up arms but should leave Attica and settle elsewhere.

> After their overwhelming victory in the bay of Salamis, the Greeks sent magnificent thank-offerings to Delphi.

5.30 HERODOTUS, *HISTORIES* 8.121. The Greeks selected the most choice plunder taken in the battle as a gift for the gods: three Phoenician warships, one to be dedicated at the Isthmus (where it is still to be seen), another at Sunium, and another as an offering to Ajax, in Salamis itself.[33] They then divided up the spoils and sent to Delphi the most choice objects; from these was made the statue of a young man, eighteen feet high, who has the beak of a ship in his hand; this stands beside the gold statue of Alexander of Macedon.[34]

> In the context of the maneuvers before the battle of Salamis in 480 BCE, Herodotus makes his sole authorial statement about prophecies, referring to the interpretation of an oracle of Bacis which Herodotus declares is perfectly clear.[35]

5.31 HERODOTUS, *HISTORIES* 8.77. Now I cannot gainsay that there is no truth in prophecies; nor do I wish to try to discredit them when they are expressed unambiguously. Consider the following:

> When they shall span with ships the sacred coast of
> Artemis of the golden sword to the shore of Cynosura,[36]
> driven mad with hope after sacking shining Athens,
> then shall bright Justice quench mighty Excess, the child
>   of Hybris,[37]
> horrendous in eagerness, thinking to swallow up everything.
> Bronze shall mingle with bronze, and with blood Ares
> will make the sea red; then to Greece loud-voiced Zeus
> and Lady Victory shall bring the day of freedom.

---

33 *Phoenician warships*: the Phoenicians were subject to the Persians and supplied them with a navy. *Sunium*: a promontory at the southernmost part of Attica. The remains of the temple of Poseidon are still to be seen today. *Ajax*: a Homeric hero who came from Salamis.

34 *Alexander of Macedon*: Alexander I (c. 498–454 BCE) who was a benefactor of the Athenians, not Alexander the Great (336–323 BCE).

35 *Bacis*: a seer to whom a collection of oracles collected by King Laius of Thebes were attributed.

36 *sacred coast of Artemis*: Pausanias 1.36 speaks of a shrine of Artemis on Salamis where a victory trophy was set up. *Cynosura*: a promontory on the island of Salamis.

37 *Hybris*: Arrogance, which is followed by Nemesis, Retribution.

With these words of Bacis in mind, so unambiguously uttered, I do not dare to say anything against prophecies, nor will I listen to criticism from others.

> The late seventh–early sixth century BCE Athenian lawgiver Solon remarks that divination will not help humans avoid fate.

5.32 SOLON, Frag.1.53–56 Diehl.

Far-shooting Apollo makes another man a seer,

who recognizes the evil that is coming from afar,

since the gods attend on him. But no divination by birds or sacrificial offering

will ever ward off what is destined to be.

> In discussing the trustworthiness of divination, Cicero notes that Xenophanes of Colophon (c. 570–478 BCE) was the only Greek philosopher to reject divination entirely.[38]

5.33 CICERO, *ON DIVINATION* 1.5. Xenophanes of Colophon, although he asserted the existence of gods, was the only one of the ancient philosophers who utterly rejected divination.

Divination in time of war

> Seers were especially active in times of war. The late fifth century historian Thucydides, who rarely reports religious matters, comments on the prevalence of prophecies and oracles at the beginning of the Peloponnesian War between Athens and Sparta (431–404 BCE).

5.34 THUCYDIDES 2.8. All the rest of Greece was in suspense as the two foremost cities came into conflict. Many were the prophecies that were uttered, and many were those that oracle-mongers (*chresmologoi*) chanted, both to the people who were about to go to war and to the rest of the cities. Moreover, a short time before this, Delos was shaken by an earthquake,[39] although it had not before been hit by an earthquake within the Greeks' memory.

5.35 THUCYDIDES 2.21. Oracle-mongers were chanting oracles of every kind, according as each person was inclined to hear them.

> The biographer Plutarch (late first and early second centuries CE) reports that in 416 BCE priests objected to the decision of the Athenian Assembly to send an expedition to Sicily. One of the generals, Alcibiades, had his own seers who supported the expedition and also suppressed unfavorable prophecies.

5.36 PLUTARCH, *NICIAS* 13. It is said that many objections to the expedition came from the priests. But Alcibiades had other seers (*manteis*) of his

---

38 On Xenophanes, see 12.1–12.8.

39 *Delos*: an island under Athenian domination that was sacred to Apollo.

own and, from a number of supposedly ancient oracles, he quoted one that predicted that the Athenians would win great fame in Sicily.[40] Other messengers, who had been sent to the shrine of Zeus Ammon, came to him with an oracle that the Athenians were going to take all the Syracusans. At the same time, however, they concealed prophecies that suggested anything to the contrary for fear of uttering words of ill omen. Nonetheless, not even the clearest and unmistakable warnings such as the mutilation of the Hermae,[41] could turn the people from their purpose....

> Seers regularly accompanied armies on campaigns to interpret the gods' will. In Sicily, Nicias, one of the Athenian commanders, is so terrified by the dangers portended by an eclipse of the moon that he allows himself to be encircled by the enemy. Plutarch quotes from two experts on divination, indicating the folly of Nicias' decision to delay their retreat.

5.37 PLUTARCH, *NICIAS* 23–24. But when everything was prepared for retreat and none of the enemy were on watch, since they did not expect such a move, there was an eclipse of the moon by night. This greatly terrified Nicias and all those who were ignorant or so superstitious that they were panic-stricken. ... Men thought it [the eclipse] uncanny, a sign from god, foretelling some great disasters. ...

It happened, however, that Nicias did not even have an experienced seer at that point. His former associate, Stilbides, who had done much to rid him of his superstition, had recently died. But, as Philochorus says, the sign was not a bad omen for a retreat, but very favorable: for actions taken in fear need to be concealed, whereas light is hostile to such actions. In addition, as Autoclides writes in his *Exegesis*, men used to be on their guard for three days only in the case of portents of the sun and moon.[42]

But Nicias persuaded the Athenians to wait for another full cycle of the moon, as if he did not see that the moon was restored to pure clarity, once it had passed beyond the area that was darkened and obscured by the earth.

Letting almost everything else go, he was preoccupied with sacrifices and divination. Meanwhile the enemy closed in upon him, surrounding his camp and defenses with their land forces and encircling the harbor with their ships.

> The historian Thucydides, a former general who was exiled because of his own military failure, criticizes Nicias for being delaying the withdrawal from Syracuse because of his dependence on divination.

---

40 *Alcibiades*: one of three commanders of the expedition, who defected to Sparta when charged with polluting the Eleusinian Mysteries; see 12.40–12.42.

41 *Hermae*: sacred pillars surmounted with a head of Hermes, and a model of an erect phallus in the middle, which were displayed outside most houses. On the mutilation of the Hermaes, see 12.40

42 *Philochorus*: c. 340–260 BCE, was not only a historian but also a seer. *Autoclides*: third century BCE? was an expert on the interpretation of omens or portents.

Figure 5.3. A young man holds out the liver of a sacrificial victim for a bearded hoplite (heavy-armed soldier) to inspect. On the left, an old man leans on a staff and seems to be presenting the young man to the hoplite. Black figure amphora, c. 520 BCE. Art Resource, New York.

5.38 THUCYDIDES 7.50. When everything was ready and the Athenians were about to depart, the moon was eclipsed at a time when it happened to be at its fullest. Nicias, who was overly reliant on divination and the like, said he would not even discuss the question of moving until, as the seers (*manteis*) recommended, they had waited "three times nine days." Because of this, the eclipse was the sole reason for their delaying their departure.

5.39 THUCYDIDES 8.1. The Athenians were also angry with the oracle-mongers (*chresmologoi*) and seers (*manteis*) and all who at the time had, by any method of divination, led them to hope that they would conquer Sicily.

Plutarch reports the soldiers' reaction to Nicias' imminent death.

5.40 PLUTARCH, *NICIAS* 26. They were forced to despair of help from the gods when they realized that a man who was as pious as Nicias, who had spared nothing in his observances and devotions to the gods, was suffering a fortune no more fair than the worst and most lowly men in the army.

Military seers generally divined by means of animal sacrifice. Sacrifice before battle (*sphagia*) was performed by cutting the animal's throat and observing its movements and the blood-flow; the flesh of the victim was not eaten. In a non-battle situation, divination was by examination of the victim's liver, after which the meat was consumed.

Several episodes in Xenophon's *Anabasis* illustrate the importance of divination in the military sphere. When Xenophon (c. 430–355 BCE) was thinking of serving as a mercenary in the army of Cyrus, the younger brother of the King of Persia, the philosopher Socrates (469–399 BCE) advised him to consult the oracle of Apollo at Delphi.

5.41 XENOPHON, *ANABASIS* 3.1.5–7. Socrates advised Xenophon to go to Delphi and consult the god about this journey. So Xenophon went and asked Apollo to which of the gods he should sacrifice and pray in order best to make the journey that he had in mind and to do it well and come home safely. In response, Apollo told him the gods to whom he ought to sacrifice. When he returned, he reported the oracle to Socrates. Hearing about it, Socrates criticized him because he had not first asked whether it would be better to make the journey or to remain at home; rather he had decided for himself that he should go and then asked the god how best to make the journey. "Since, however,' Socrates added, you put the question in this way, you must do everything that the god has commanded." And so, after offering sacrifices to the gods that the god had prescribed, Xenophon set sail.

After realizing that the real objective of the expedition was to overthrow the Persian king, Xenophon reports the general concern and his subsequent dream.

5.42 XENOPHON, *ANABASIS* 3.1.11. Xenophon was as distressed as everyone else and was unable to sleep. But at last, getting a little sleep, he had a dream. It seemed to him that there was a clap of thunder and a bolt fell on his father's house, causing the whole house to be ablaze. Thoroughly afraid, he immediately awoke, and judged the dream a good one because in the midst of toil and danger he had seemed to see a great light from Zeus. But on the other hand he was afraid because, although the dream seemed to him to come from Zeus the King, the fire seemed the blaze all around. So he was afraid that he might not be able to escape from the King's territories,[43] but would be enclosed on all sides by considerable difficulties. But the meaning of such a dream can be seen from what happened after the dream.

After the defeat and death of Cyrus, Xenophon became the leader of the Greek mercenaries in their difficult march from Mesopotamia to the Greek colonies on the southern coast of the Black Sea. A soldier's sneeze is interpreted as a sign of their ultimate safety.

5.43 XENOPHON, *ANABASIS* 3.2.8–9. "But if our purpose is to rely on our arms, and not only to make the enemy pay for what they have done and

---

43 *The King's territories*: the King of Persia.

from now on fight total war against them, then — with the gods on our side — we have many glorious hopes of safety." Just as he was saying this, someone sneezed, and when the soldiers heard it, they all with one impulse made obeisance to the god. Xenophon continued, "Since an omen from Zeus the Savior appeared when we mentioned safety,[44] I propose that we make a vow to sacrifice to that god as soon as we reach a friendly land and that we make an additional vow to offer sacrifices to the other gods to the best of our ability."

> This vow was duly fulfilled when they eventually reached the Black Sea, near the Greek colony of Trapezus (Trebizond).

5.44 XENOPHON, *ANABASIS* 4.8.25. Then the Greeks prepared the sacrifice that they had vowed. They had enough cattle for them to sacrifice to Zeus for their safety and to Heracles for his guidance, and to make the offerings they had vowed to the other gods. They also held athletic games on the mountain side where they were encamped.[45]

> Xenophon describes how, when they were midway between the Greek cities of Heraclea and Byzantium, he realized that they would have to continue their journey by land rather than by sea. The army suspected that a series of unfavorable sacrifices was a ruse to keep them there in order to found a colony.

5.45 XENOPHON, *ANABASIS* 6.4.12–22. Xenophon stood up and said: "Fellow soldiers, we must make our journey, so it seems, on foot, for we have no ships. Moreover, we must set out immediately, for there are no provisions if we stay here. Therefore we will make a sacrifice," he continued, "and you must prepare yourselves to fight as you have never fought before; for the enemy have recovered their confidence."

After this the generals began to sacrifice. The seer was Arexion from Arcadia. (Silanus of Ambracia had already hired a boat from Heraclea and fled.)[46] The sacrifice was made in the hope of leaving, but the appearance of the victims was unfavorable, and so they ceased their offerings for that day. Some people dared to say that Xenophon had persuaded the seer to declare that the sacrifices were not favorable for leaving because he wanted to establish a city in that place. Therefore Xenophon proclaimed that anyone who wished should be present next day at the sacrifice, and he announced that if anyone was a seer, he should be there to participate in the inspection of the victims.[47] Xenophon made the sacrifice, and many people attended. But though he sacrificed three times for a departure, the

---

44 *Zeus the Savior*: literally the one who protects and so saves.

45 Athletic games were a regular feature at festivals in honor of the gods.

46 *Silanus*: the previous seer had left the army, after a conflict of interest with Xenophon who wanted to establish a colony rather than return immediately as Silanus advised (Xenophon, *Anabasis* 5.6.15–19, 28–30).

47 *if anyone was a seer*: Xenophon apparently wanted a witness to guarantee that the results of sacrifice were not being manipulated.

omens were against leaving. As a result, the soldiers were angry because the provisions they had brought with them were exhausted and there was no market nearby.

And so they held a meeting, and Xenophon addressed them again, "Men, as you see, the sacrifices are not yet in favor of our journey, and I see that you need provisions. It therefore seems necessary to me that we must sacrifice precisely for this." Then someone got up and said, "It seems to us that there is good reason for the unfavorable sacrifices. I happened to hear from someone who came yesterday on a ship that Cleander, the Spartan governor of Byzantium, intends to come with merchant ships and triremes.[48]

At this news everyone decided to stay, but they still needed to go out in search of provisions. Xenophon again sacrificed, making three attempts without a favorable result. Already men were coming to Xenophon's tent, saying that they didn't have any provisions. But he refused to lead them as long as the sacrifices were unfavorable. On the next day he was beginning to sacrifice again and almost the entire army gathered around the sacrifice because it was a concern to everyone. But there was a shortage of victims. Then the generals did not lead the men off, but called an assembly at which Xenophon said, "Perhaps the enemy have amassed and we will have to fight. Therefore, if we leave our baggage in a defensive place and set out prepared for battle, perhaps the sacrifices will be favorable to us."

On hearing this, however, the soldiers cried out that it was not necessary to go to a fortified position; rather they should sacrifice as quickly as possible. There were no longer any sheep, so they bought a bullock that was yoked to a wagon and sacrificed it. Xenophon begged Cleanor the Arcadian to be on the alert for a good result.[49] But it did not work out that way.

> Of the two thousand men sent out to seek provisions, at least a quarter were killed by the Persian governor's cavalry. Meanwhile, the Greeks had strengthened their camp fortifications and a vessel arrived, bringing barley meal, sacrificial victims, and wine (6.4.23–5.1). After a successful sacrifice, they were finally able to proceed.

5.46 XENOPHON, *ANABASIS* 6.5.2. Xenophon arose early and sacrificed in the hope of departing, and the omens were favorable at the first sacrifice. And then, as the rites were ending, the seer Arexion the Parrhasian saw an auspicious eagle and so he ordered Xenophon to lead the way.[50] The men then crossed the ditch and formed up in order.

---

48 *triremes*: warships. This news proved to be false.

49 *Cleanor*: one of the generals.

50 The eagle was the bird of Zeus.

6. Sanctuaries of the Gods

6.1 HERODOTUS, *HISTORIES* 8.144. Being Greek means having the same blood and language, common shrines of the gods and sacrifices, and the same kinds of customs.

> The Greek word for sanctuary, *temenos*, literally means a cut-off or separate space. This area was sacred (*hieron*) and was generally marked off by pillars or boundary stones or a perimeter wall, thus separating it from the secular world. Within the sanctuary gods were worshiped and rituals enacted. The focal point of the sanctuary was the altar where sacrificial offerings were made.[1]

> The earliest sanctuaries were simple and unpretentious. The eighth century BCE was marked by the emergence of the *polis*, the city state. Homer describes Zeus visiting his sanctuary on Mount Ida near Troy, an open area with springs and an altar. In describing the establishing of a new community, Homer indicates that temples to the gods were among the first essentials.

6.2 HOMER, *ILIAD* 8.47–52.

He came to Ida, gushing with springs, the mother of beasts,
to Gargarus, home of his sanctuary and his smoke-filled altar;
and there the father of men and gods pulled up his horses,
loosed them from the chariot-yoke and shrouded them in dense mist.   50
Then he himself sat down on the peaks and rejoiced in his glory,
as he looked at the Trojan citadel and Achaean ships.

6.3 HOMER, *ODYSSEY* 6.7–10.

Godlike Nausithous had roused them and led them away
from there; he settled them in Scheria, far away from men
who feed on grain; he walled the citadel and built houses,
constructed temples too for the gods and divided the plowland.   10

---

1   On sanctuaries and sacred space, see Pedley 2005.

Sacred space

Sanctuaries constituted sacred space, as did temples and altars. A sanctuary did not necessarily have a temple, particularly in rural areas, where a simple open-air shrine with an altar was common. In contrast, the sanctuaries at Olympia and Delphi each included a number of temples to different gods.

An inscription records a sacred law regulating ritual purity in the sanctuary of Athena Nikephoros (Bringer of Victory) at Pergamum in Asia Minor, enacted by a religious official (*hieronomos*) called Dionysius. Although this inscription dates to the period after 133 BCE when Asia Minor was a Roman province, the regulations reflect long-standing Greek practice.

6.4 *SIG*³ 982. Citizens and all other people who enter the temple of the goddess shall be pure, having washed themselves clean from their own wife or their own husband on the same day, or from another woman or another man for two days; likewise from a death in the family or from a woman in childbirth for two days. But those who have cleansed themselves from a funeral and carrying out of the corpse and have passed back through the gate where the means of purification are placed shall be cleansed on the same day.

At first temples were small buildings constructed of wood or terracotta. Later, by the sixth century BCE, monumental stone temples were constructed in major sanctuaries. The temple was generally rectangular, oriented on an east-west axis, with an altar in front of the steps and the door at the east end. When sacrificing the worshipers did not enter the temple but gathered in front near the altar.

Votive offerings were placed and stored within the temple. Also inside the temple was the cult statue of the god to whom the temple was dedicated. Thus, the god could view the worshipers as they offered sacrifice.

Large panhellenic sanctuaries like Olympia and Delphi with monumental cult buildings developed in the late seventh or early sixth centuries BCE. The geographer Strabo (c. 64 BCE – after 21 CE) describes the location of the sanctuary at Olympia, the temple of Zeus with its famous statue and many votive offerings.[2]

6.5 STRABO, *GEOGRAPHY* 8.3.30. It remains for me to tell about Olympia, and how everything fell under the control of the people of Elis. The temple is in Pisatis, less than three hundred stades from Elis. In front of the temple is a grove of wild olive trees, and the stadium is here. Nearby flows the River Alpheus, which rises in Arcadia and flows into the Triphylian Sea between the west and south.

At first the temple became famous on account of the oracle of Zeus at Olympia. But when the oracle failed, the glory of the temple nonetheless persisted and its fame increased, as we know, because of the festival and

---

2 For illustrations and discussion of the site, see Swaddling 2004 and Pedley 2005: 119–134.

the Olympic games. These were regarded as sacred and the greatest of all games, and the prize was a crown of olive leaves.

The temple was adorned with a mass of votive offerings from all parts of Greece. Among these was the Zeus of beaten gold, an offering from Cypselus the tyrant of Corinth. But the greatest was the statue made by the Athenian Phidias, son of Charmides;[3] it was made of ivory, and it was so large that, despite the size of the temple, the artist apparently lost his sense of symmetry. For he made Zeus seated but almost touching the roof with his head, giving the impression that if he were to stand upright he would take the roof off the temple.

> Pausanias (mid-second century CE) describes the statue of Zeus and the huge altar that had accumulated over the centuries as a result of all the sacrifices that had been made on it.[4]

6.6   PAUSANIAS 5.11.1. The god is made of gold and ivory and is seated on a throne. There is a wreath on his head like twigs and leaves of olive; in his right hand he is holding a statuette of Victory, made of gold and ivory, with a ribbon and a wreath on her head. In the god's left hand is a scepter adorned with every kind of precious metal, and the bird perching on this scepter is an eagle. The god's sandals are gold and so is his cloak, and the cloak is inlaid with small figures and flowering lilies. The throne is finely worked with gold and gems, and with ebony and with ivory; it is painted and carved with figures.

6.7   PAUSANIAS 5.13.8–9. The altar is made from the ash of the thighs of the victims sacrificed to Zeus.... The first stage of the altar at Olympia, which is called the *prothysis*, has a circumference of one hundred and twenty-five feet, and the circumference on the platform of the *prothysis* is thirty-two feet. The total height of the altar is twenty-two feet. It is the custom to sacrifice the victims themselves on the lower stage, the *prothysis*. But the thighs are carried up to the highest part of the altar and burned there.

> Xenophon (428–c. 354 BCE) describes the more modest sanctuary to Artemis that he established on his estate near Olympia. This sanctuary was funded by his share of the booty from the campaign in which he had participated as a mercenary. Xenophon's description, though idealized, gives a vivid picture of a small rural sanctuary on a private estate that served the economy of the surrounding area.

6.8   XENOPHON, *ANABASIS* 5.3.4–13. The generals divided the money received from the sale of the booty, and the tenth-part that they set apart

---

3   *Pheidias*; a famous sculptor who also made the statue of Athena in the Parthenon at Athens.

4   The ashes from the sacrifices were mixed with water from the nearby river Alpheus, and the paste was smeared on the existing pile of ashes to solidify the altar; see Swaddling 2004: 16–18, with drawings of the altar and the statue.

for Apollo and for Artemis of Ephesus, was distributed among the generals, each taking his portion to keep for the gods....[5]

Xenophon bought a plot of land for the goddess in a place that Apollo's oracle had ordained. As it happened, a river called Selinus flows through the plot; and at Ephesus a river Selinus also flows past the temple of Artemis. In both streams, moreover, there are fish and shell-fish, but on the estate at Scillus there is also hunting of all kinds of game.

Here Xenophon built an altar and a temple with the sacred money, and from then on he used to take a tenth of the season's produce of the land and offer sacrifice to the goddess, with all the citizens and men and women from the neighboring districts taking part in the festival. For those who were camping out, the goddess provided barley meal, bread, wine and sweetmeats, as well as a share of both the animals sacrificed from the sacred herds and those taken in hunting....

The place is situated on the road that leads from Sparta to Olympia, about two miles from the temple of Zeus at Olympia. Within the sacred precinct there is meadowland and thickly wooded hills, suitable for rearing pigs, goats, and cattle, as well as horses. And so it is possible to provide fodder for the animals that bring people to the festival.

Surrounding the temple is a grove of cultivated trees that provide all kind of seasonal fruit. The temple itself is a small-scale version of the great temple at Ephesus, and the statue, though made of cypress wood, is like the Ephesian one. A pillar stands by the temple with the following inscription: THIS PLACE IS SACRED TO ARTEMIS. HE WHO OWNS IT AND TAKES ITS PRODUCE MUST OFFER A TENTH PART TO THE GODDESS EVERY YEAR. FROM THE REMAINDER HE MUST KEEP THE TEMPLE IN GOOD REPAIR. IF ANYONE NEGLECTS TO DO THIS, THE GODDESS WILL TAKE CARE OF IT.

> The panhellenic sanctuary at Delphi became the site of the most important oracle in mainland Greece during the seventh century BCE.[6] The site was surrounded by a boundary wall c. 800 BCE, and private houses were removed for the construction of an elaborate temple to Apollo in the late seventh or early sixth century BCE. The original connections of Apollo with the site are difficult to discern. Homer only mentions the sanctuary at Delphi twice, referring to the stone doorsill of the archer Phoebus Apollo in rocky Pytho (*Iliad* 9.404) and to Phoebus Apollo as god of prophecy in sacred Pytho (*Odyssey* 8.79–82).[7]
>
> Strabo describes the site of Delphi, its accessibility, and the *omphalos* or navel stone.

---

5 *Ephesus*: a Greek city on the Aegaean coast of modern Turkey.

6 On the Delphic oracle, see 5.7–5.9 and 5.19–5.29. For a brief history of the sanctuary at Delphi, see Pedley 2005: 135–153.

7 *Pytho*: Delphi.

6.9 STRABO, *GEOGRAPHY* 9.3.6. Although most of the honor paid to this temple was due to its oracle, since of all the oracles it seemed to be the most reliable, the position of the place was an additional advantage. For it is almost at the center of Greece when taken as a whole, between the area inside the Isthmus and that outside it. It was also believed to be the center of the inhabited world.

People called it the navel (*omphalos*) of the earth.[8] In addition they invented a myth, told by Pindar, that two eagles sent by Zeus (though some say crows) met there, one flying from the west and the other from the east. There is also a kind of navel to be seen in the temple; it is draped with ribbons and on it are two likenesses of the mythical birds.

> At the beginning of *Eumenides*, the third play of Aeschylus' *Oresteia*, the deranged Orestes comes as a suppliant to the sanctuary of Apollo at Delphi, pursued by the horrendous Furies (*Erinyes*) who avenge the murder of kinsfolk. He is seeking purification after murdering his mother Clytemnestra, a deed forced on him because she had murdered his father, Agamemnon. The Pythia, the priestess of Apollo, describes the scene inside the temple of Apollo.

6.10 AESCHYLUS, *EUMENIDES* 39–63.

Pythia

I was on my way to the inner shrine with its many garlands,
and I saw upon the navel-stone a man abominated by the gods,   40
seated there, as a suppliant; with blood
his hands and newly drawn sword were dripping,
and he held an olive branch from the top of a tree,
a branch reverently wreathed with a great tuft,
a silvery lock of wool (this is my clear description).[9]   45
And in front of this man slept an awesome troop
of women, seated upon chairs.
Not women, but Gorgons I say;
no, I shall not even compare them to the shape of Gorgons.[10]

….

Such is their dress that it is not right to for them to come   55
near to the gods' statues nor into the houses of humans.[11]

…

---

8 *navel*: see Hesiod, *Theogony* 497–500 in 2.6 with n. 19.

9 Olive branches decorated with interwoven strands of wool were customarily carried by suppliants.

10 *Gorgons*: female monsters, with snakes instead of hair. The most famous gorgon was Medusa, whose gaze turned men to stone.

11 *their dress*: they wore long black robes that were dirty and ragged.

The outcome now must be the concern of the master   60
of this house, the mighty Loxias himself.[12]
He is both healer-seer and prophet,
and for others the purifier of their houses.[13]

Figure 6.1. A red figure mixing bowl (bell-krater) from South Italy (c. 370–360 BCE) depicts Orestes at the Delphic *omphalos* (navel-stone). He is shown clasping the *omphalos* with one hand, and brandishing his sword in the other. His swirling cloak indicates his agitation. On the left is the goddess Athena, helmeted, with a spear in her right hand and her left pointing at Orestes to reassure him that the Furies will be transformed into kindly beings. Two Furies, who have pursued Orestes to Delphi because of his matricide, are depicted in the foreground at the bottom of the scene, sleeping. The one on the left holds a spear; the other, whose spear is resting on the ground, has snakes entwined in her hair and on her arm. Three white ribbons are draped over the *omphalos*, which is circled by two wreathes. To the right of the *omphalos* is Apollo, two arrows in his raised right hand and a laurel branch with berries in the left. Athena wears a robe (*peplos*), and a black aegis or cape, on which is depicted a white gorgon's head and a fringe of snakes. Above on the left, between Athena and Orestes, is a sacrificial bowl; between him and Apollo is a ox-skull decorated with ribbons. Photograph © 2008 Museum of Fine Arts, Boston.

---

12 *Loxias*: Apollo.

13 *purifier of their houses*: on Orestes' purification by means of the blood of a pig, see 4.27.

Figure 6.2. The treasury of the Athenians at Delphi on the Sacred Way leading up to the temple of Apollo. © istockphoto/ Javier García.

In the tragedy *Suppliant Maidens* by Aeschylus (525/4–456/5 BCE), the chorus of suppliant maidens seek asylum under the protection of the gods at an altar within a sanctuary.[14]

6.11 AESCHYLUS, *SUPPLIANT MAIDENS* 83–85.

Even for those who, hard-pressed, flee from war,

there is an altar, offering escape from ruin,

a defense, because of respect for the gods.

> A sanctuary was also a place of safe-keeping. At Delphi several treasuries line the Sacred Way leading to the temple of Apollo. These small temple-like buildings were themselves offerings to the gods, generally from a *polis* or the ruler of a state. Strabo notes the treasuries built by various peoples.

6.12 STRABO, *GEOGRAPHY* 9.3.4. The temple [of Apollo] has been greatly neglected, though it was highly honored in earlier times. Evidence of this are the treasuries, built both by peoples and rulers, in which they deposited not only money which they had dedicated to the god but also works of the best artists.

> Delphi served as an international center not only for the safe-keeping and display of valuable property and works of art donated by various patrons, but also for enhancing the renown of the donor, be it state, ruler, or private individual. Herodotus describes some of the votive offerings made in the temple of Apollo by the non-Greek King Croesus of Lydia.[15]

---

14 English "asylum" is derived from the Greek *asulon* which literally means "a place from which plunder can not be taken".

15 On Croesus' consultation of the Delphic oracle, see 5.25–5.28.

6.13 HERODOTUS, *HISTORIES* 1.50–52. Croesus melted down an enormous quantity of gold into one hundred and seventeen ingots .... He had the image of a lion made of refined gold, in weight some five hundred and seventy pounds. This statue, when the temple of Delphi burned down, fell from the gold block forming its base.[16] Today it is located in the Corinthian treasury.....

Croesus sent all these gifts to Delphi and also the following: two huge-sized mixing-bowls, one of gold that was placed on the right-hand side of the entrance to the temple, the other of silver on the left. ... In addition he sent four silver casks that are in the Corinthian treasury, and two sprinklers for lustral water, one of gold, the other of silver....

There were many other gifts too that were not inscribed including round silver basins, and a gold statue of a woman, four and half feet high, which the Delphians said represented the woman who baked Croesus' bread.[17] Lastly, he sent his own wife's necklaces and adornments. These then were the offerings that Croesus sent to Delphi. He also sent a shield of solid gold and a spear, likewise of solid gold from the shaft to the head, to the shrine of Amphiaraus.[18]

Custom and regulations

Before crossing the boundary into the god's sanctuary, an individual had to purify himself with lustral water. In Euripides' *Ion* (c. 410 BCE) the temple attendant at Delphi orders the other attendants to observe ritual purity.

6.14 EURIPIDES, *ION* 94–108.

Ion

Attendants of Delphic Apollo,

go to the silvery eddies of Castalia;[19]   95

in its purifying waters

cleanse yourselves and proceed to the temples.

Guard your lips in well-omened silence,

offering good words in your private conversation

with those who wish to consult the oracle.   100

The tasks that I have performed

---

16 According to Pausanias (10 5.13), the temple burned down in 548 BCE.

17 Croesus' baker is said to have saved his life when his stepmother tried to poison him.

18 *Amphiaraus*: a seer who was one of the seven who came to Thebes to support Polynices in his struggle against his brother Eteocles for the throne of Thebes after the death of their father Oedipus. Croesus had earlier consulted this oracle (Herodotus 1.46 and 49). Amphiaraus' major sanctuary was at Oropus on the coast of Attica; see 6.25.

19 *Castalia*: a sacred spring near the temple of Apollo.

from childhood, cleansing Phoebus' entrances
with branches of laurel and sacred garlands,
I will perform, while moistening the floor   105
with drops of water. The flocks of birds
that foul the holy dedications
I will put to flight with my arrows.

> Later in the drama, Ion responds to questions from the chorus, a band of
> women visiting the temple.

6.15 EURIPIDES, *ION* 219–232.

Chorus

You there beside the temple,
is it lawful (*themis*) to enter the inmost sanctuary with bare feet?[20]   220

Ion

Strangers, it is not lawful.

Chorus

Then might I ask you a question?

Ion

What do you want to know?

Chorus

Does the house of Phoebus hold the navel (*omphalos*) of the earth?

Ion

Yes, it is hung with garlands, and surrounded by Gorgons.

Chorus

Just as the rumor said!   225

Ion

If you have sacrificed a cake before the temple
and want to make some inquiry of Phoebus,[21]
approach the altar; but do not enter the temple's inner recess
unless you have slaughtered a sheep.

Chorus

I understand. The god's custom
we will not transgress.   230
Our eyes will take delight
in what is outside.

> Sanctuaries were generally administered by a special official, a priest or
> priestess who only served the deity of that shrine or temple, In addition to

---

20 *inmost sanctuary*: the Greek word *guala* is problematic, but seems to refer to the
temple building.

21 *cake*: a sacrificial offering made of meal, honey, and oil.

priests and priestesses, there were attendants like Ion in Euripides' drama and officials responsible for the performance of rites, or the upkeep of temples, accounts, and records. Panhellenic sanctuaries, like those at Delphi and Olympia, would have required a large staff to administer the finances and operation of an organization that in many ways must have resembled that of a large religious organization today. Accommodation and food for visitors would also have been necessary, as well as provision for the large numbers of sacrificial animals.

Most priesthoods were held for a limited period, not for life, notable exceptions being the Pythia and the priestess of Athena Polias.[22] Unlike the latter, the Pythia was chosen from local women who were at least fifty years old and were neither wealthy nor of noble birth. During her tenure of office the Pythia was required to remain celibate.[23]

The gender of the priest did not always correspond to that of the deity served by that priest, as in the case of the Pythia who was the priestess of Apollo at Delphi. Holding a priesthood was regarded as a mark of honor or prestige for the priest's family. Some priesthoods, like that of Athena Polias (Athena of the City), were the prerogative of a particular aristocratic family. Other priests were appointed by lot, by election, or by purchasing the office.

Plato's prescription for the selection of priests, though indicating his preference regarding the use of the lot, reflects general practice, particularly the insistence on the absence of physical defects.

6.16 PLATO, *LAWS* 6.759 c. Regarding priests, we shall entrust it to the god to ensure what is pleasing to him, committing their selection to the divine chance of the lot. But each person who gains the lot will be examined first to see whether he is whole in body and legitimate; secondly, whether he comes from families that are as pure as possible, and is himself clean from murder and all offenses against the gods, and is born of parents who have lived by the same rules.

The following inscription (450–445? BCE) indicates that the priestess of the cult of Athena Nike (Victory) in Athens was to be chosen, presumably by lot, from all Athenian women. Her annual pay and perquisites are listed.

6.17 ML no. 44.[24] the priestess of Athena Nike ... is to be chosen from all Athenian women, and the temple precinct is to be provided with doors as Callicrates

---

22 The Roman writer Pliny the Elder (c. 23/4–79 CE) records that a woman called Lysimache was the priestess of Athena Polias for sixty-four years (Pliny, *Natural History* 34.19.76). Since her name means "the one who stops battle," she may have held her priesthood at the time that Aristophanes wrote his comedy *Lysistrata* (the woman who stops or disbands armies).

23 See Connelly 2007: 43–44 and 73–74.

24 ML no. 44 is the numbering of the inscription in Meiggs and Lewis 1988, a collection of Greek historical inscriptions that is more widely available than earlier publications of these inscriptions. ML provide a full Greek text, often emended, citations of earlier publications, a commentary but no English translation.

shall prescribe.[25] The Official Contractors shall let out the contract during the prytany of the Leontis tribe. The priestess is to receive fifty drachmas [per year] and the legs and skins from public [sacrificial victims]. The temple and stone altar are to be built as Callicrates prescribes.

A fragment from a play by Euripides (produced in the 420s BCE) articulates the prominent role of women in Greek religious life.

6.18 EURIPIDES, *THE CAPTIVE MELANIPPE* Frag. 494 K, lines 12–22.

And where the gods are concerned—I judge this of the first
 importance—
we women play the greatest part. For in the house of Phoebus
it is we women who interpret Apollo's mind. At the holy seat of
 Dodona   15
by the sacred oak the race of women conveys
the thoughts of Zeus to all Greeks who desire it.
As for the rituals performed for the Fates
and the Nameless Goddesses, it is sacrilege for these to be
in men's hands;[26] but in women's hands they flourish,   20
every one of them. Thus in matters that concern the gods
women hold sway.

Since most priesthoods were not a full-time occupation, many male priests also held political office. Like other male citizens, priests were liable for military service. Most priests lived in their own *oikos* (family home), fulfilling their religious obligations on the appointed days when they would wear special robes to mark their priestly office.

An inscription from the island of Chios in the eastern Aegean attests the sale of a priesthood that was to be held for life, on condition that the priest live in the city. The duties and perquisites of the office are listed.

6.19 *LSCG Suppl. 77.* The man who purchases the priesthood shall hold it for life, provided that he continues to live in the city. He is to be exempt from all taxes and receive for himself the first portions from the person who makes a sacrifice, of entrails, shanks, knees, tongue, two double portions of meat, Hermes-cakes, and the offerings of which anyone makes burnt-sacrifices. He will also receive an appropriate share of the feast. If the city holds a feast, he is to receive 1/12 gold stater. If foreigners sacrifice, [he receives the same share as in the case of a Chian, but] the sacrificer [adds in addition ...]

---

25 *all Athenian women*: many traditional priesthoods were restricted to an aristocratic family. *Callicrates*: an Athenian architect.

26 *Dodona*: a location in Epirus, in northwest Greece, where there was an ancient oracle of Zeus. For some questions asked of this oracle, see 5.11–5.18. *Nameless Goddesses*: goddesses that are to be revered, though it is dangerous to name them.

Herodotus comments on the Greek and Egyptian ban on sexual intercourse in temples.

6.20 HERODOTUS, *HISTORIES* 2.64. The Egyptians were the first to forbid men to have intercourse with women within a temple or to enter a temple without washing after having had intercourse. Almost all other peoples except for the Egyptians and Greeks have intercourse in temples and enter temples without washing after intercourse, considering that humans are just the same as the rest of the animals. For they say that they see all the animals and species of birds coupling in the temples of the gods and in the sanctuaries. And if this was not pleasing to the god, so they say, he would not allow it to happen. This is what they say, but I don't approve of it.

It was forbidden to give birth or die within a sanctuary, since such acts would pollute the area. The historian Thucydides describes how the Athenians purified the entire island of Delos, the birthplace of Apollo, during the early years of the Peloponnesian War.

6.21 THUCYDIDES 3.104. During the same winter [426 BCE] the Athenians carried out a purification of Delos in accordance with a certain oracle. The tyrant Pisistratus had purified it earlier, not the whole island, but only that part of it that was visible from the temple.[27] But on this occasion the whole of Delos was purified in the following way. They removed all the burials of the dead that were on Delos and for the future they forbade that anyone should die or give birth on the island, ordering that they should first be carried to Rheneia.[28]

An Athenian law forbade a woman with whom an adulterer is caught from entering a public sanctuary; the punishment for infringement was anything short of death. The aims of the law are described. The authorship of this speech is disputed.

6.22 DEMOSTHENES? *AGAINST NEAERA* 85–86. Women with whom an adulterer is caught are the only women that the law debars from attending our public sacrifices. The laws have granted permission even to foreign women and slave women to enter the sanctuaries in order to see the spectacle and also make supplications. But the laws forbid entry to public sanctuaries to a woman with whom an adulterer is caught. If such a woman does enter and thus transgress the law, any person whatsoever is permitted to inflict upon her any kind of punishment, except death, and to do so with impunity. The law has granted to anyone who encounters her the right to punish her.

The law also provides that such a woman may suffer any outrage short of death without any right to seek redress, so that our sanctuaries be protected from any pollution or profanation. The purpose of the law is to create in women fear sufficient to make them behave temperately, avoid wrong-doing, and manage their households with good judgment. For the law teaches them that, if a woman commits any such error, she will at the

---

27 *Pisistratus*: the tyrant, or ruler, of Athens c. 560–527 BCE.

28 *Rhenaia*: the nearest island to Delos.

same time be expelled from her husband's home and from the sanctuaries of the city.

> An early fourth-century BCE inscription from Chios, an island off the coast of Asia Minor, forbids the dumping of manure or the pasturing of animals within the sacred area.

6.23 *SIG*[3] 986. Resolved by the [state] Council, under the presidency of Tellis: In the sacred groves there is to be no pasturing or dumping of manure.[29] If anyone does pasture sheep, pigs or cattle there, the person who sees it should report it to the authorities if he wishes to remain pure and maintain the god's favor. The fine for a shepherd, swineherd or cowherd shall be 1/12 stater for each animal. If anyone is caught dumping manure, he shall pay five staters if he wishes to become pure and maintain the god's favor. If a person sees such an act and fails to report it, he shall pay five staters, sanctified to the god.

> A late fourth-century BCE inscription from the shrine of Apollo Erisatheus near Athens records a regulation forbidding the cutting of wood within the sanctuary and the removal of any wood from the sacred precinct. The penalties are also listed.

6.24 *SIG*[3] 984. Gods: The priest of Apollo Erisatheus announces, on behalf of himself, the members of the deme, and the Athenian people, that it is forbidden to cut wood in the sanctuary of Apollo, or to carry wood or branches, with or without leaves or dry, out of the sanctuary.[30] If anyone is caught cutting or carrying any of the forbidden things out of the sanctuary and he is a slave, he will be given fifty lashes and the priest shall hand him over to the king-archon and the Council along with the name of his master, in accordance with the decree of the council and the Athenian people. If he is a free person, the priest together with the deme-leader shall fine him fifty drachmas and give his name to the king-archon and the Council, in accordance with the decree of the Council and the Athenian people.

Incubation and healing

> An inscription (386–374 BCE) from the sanctuary of the hero Amphiaraus,[31] near the town of Oropus on the coast of Attica, lists the priests' duties, those of the attendant, the regulations of the sanctuary, and the penalties for infringement. This shrine was a place where people would incubate (sleep overnight) in the hope that they would be healed; it was also the seat of an oracle.

---

29 Pasturing of animals and dumping of manure would cause pollution.

30 *deme*: the local territorial district. *carry ...out of the sanctuary*: trees were integral to the sacred space, and thus no part of them could be removed. Compare the restrictions on taking sacrificial meat out of the sanctuary or city.

31 *Amphiaraus*: see 6.13 with n. 18.

6.25 RO no. 27.[32] Gods: The priest of Amphiaraus is to visit the sanctuary from the end of winter until the season of plowing, with no more than three days between visits, and he shall stay in the sanctuary no less than ten days in each month. He shall require the temple attendant to care for the sanctuary and also for the people who visit the sanctuary, in accordance with the law.

If anyone commits an offence in the sanctuary, either a foreigner or member of the local community, the priest is authorized to fine him up to a maximum of five drachmas, and he shall require security from the person who has been fined. If the offender pays the fine, he is to deposit it in the treasury in the presence of the priest. If anyone suffers some private wrong in the sanctuary, whether foreigner or member of the community, the priest shall give judgment up to a maximum of three drachmas; but, for more serious infractions, the judgments provided in the laws for each case are to be in effect. Any summons arising from an offense in the sanctuary must be issued on the same day. If the defendant does not agree, the trial must be completed on the next day.

Whoever comes to he healed by the god must make an initial offering of at least nine obols of good silver,[33] and deposit it in the treasury in the presence of the temple attendant. [*Lacuna*]. The priest will say prayers over the offerings and place the them on the altar, if he is present; whenever the priest is not present, the person making the sacrifice is to make his own prayers for himself at the sacrifice, but the priest must make the prayers at public sacrifices.

The skin of all animals sacrificed in the sanctuary is sacred. Each person may sacrifice any animal he wishes, but the meat must not be taken outside the precinct. Those who sacrifice must give the priest the shoulder of each sacrificial animal, except when it is the festival. On that occasion, he should receive the shoulder of each of the public sacrificial victims.

Whoever needs to incubate in the sanctuary [—————] obeying the laws. The temple attendant is to record the name of whoever incubates when he deposits his money, and his personal name and the name of his city are to be written on a board displayed in the sanctuary for anyone to see. Men and women are to sleep separately in the sleeping area, men to the east of the altar and women to the west.

---

32 RO no. 27 is number 27 in Rhodes and Osborne 2003, a collection of Greek historical inscriptions more widely available than earlier publications. For each inscription RO provide a full Greek text, often revised on the basis of new evidence, together with citations of earlier publications, an English translation, and commentary.

33 The original fee of one *drachma* (6 obols) was erased, and the higher fee inserted.

Pausanias describes the sanctuary of the healing god Asclepius at Epidaurus;
He also notes that the sacrificial offerings had to be consumed within the
sanctuary.[34]

6.26 PAUSANIAS 2.27.1–3. The sacred grove of Asclepius is surrounded on
all sides by boundary markers. No death or birth takes place within the
enclosure; the same law prevails also on the island of Delos. The offerings,
whether the sacrificer is from Epidaurus or a stranger, are entirely
consumed within the limits of the sanctuary....

The statue of the god is half the size of the statue of Olympian Zeus in
Athens, and it is made of ivory and gold. An inscription attests that the
artist was Thrasymedes of Paros, son of Arignotus. The god is sitting on a
throne, wielding a staff; he holds the other hand above the serpent's head;
a dog lies by his side....[35]

Across from the temple is the place where the god's suppliants sleep. Nearby
there is a circular building of white marble, called the Tholos [Round
House], which is worth seeing....

Within the enclosure there stood slabs; in my time only six are left, but
there were more. On them are the names of men and women who were
healed by Asclepius, the disease from which each suffered, and how it was
cured.

> Four of the inscribed slabs, or stone pillars (*stelae*), described by Pausanias
> have survived. Excerpts (c. 320 BCE) commemorate various acts of healing.
> Although the number of cures recorded for men are greater than those for
> women, about half of the cures for women are for gynecological problems.
> Many of the cures seem fantastic and incredible, but others are more
> realistic.

6.27 RO no. 102.

God [*lacuna*] Good Fortune

Acts of healing (*iamata*) of Apollo and Asclepius.

1. Cleo was pregnant for five years. When she had already been pregnant
for five years, she came as a suppliant to the god and slept in the Sanctuary
(*Abaton*). As soon as she departed from there and was out of the sacred
area, she gave birth to a son who, immediately after he was born, washed
himself in the fountain and crawled around beside his mother. Because of
this good fortune, she put up a votive offering with the inscription: "It is not
the size of the plaque that is a cause for wonder, but the divinity, since Cleo
was pregnant with the burden in her womb for five years until she slept in
the sanctuary and the god made her healthy."

2. A three-year pregnancy: Ithmonica of Pellene came to the Sanctuary in
order to have children. She lay down to sleep and saw a vision. She seemed to

---

34 On the cult of Asclepius, see 14.23–14.27.

35 *serpent*: the snake was the symbol of Asclepius and a distinct species native to
Epidaurus was sacred to him, see 14.24.

be begging the god that she might be pregnant with a daughter, and Asclepius seemed to say that she would become pregnant with a daughter, and that if she were to ask for anything else, he would grant it to her; but she said that she did not need more. She became pregnant and carried a child in her womb for three years until she came to the god as a suppliant, in order to give birth. She lay down to sleep and saw a vision. The god appeared, asking her whether all that she had asked for had not happened and if she had not become pregnant. But she had not asked anything about childbirth, although he had asked her whether she needed anything else and said that he would also grant this. But since she had now come to him as suppliant about this matter, he said that he would also fulfill this for her. After this she hurriedly left the sanctuary and, as soon as she was outside the sacred area, she gave birth to a daughter.

4. Ambrosia from Athens, blind in one eye. She came as a suppliant to the god. As she walked around the temple she laughed at some of the healing records, saying that they were unbelievable and impossible, lame and blind people becoming healthy simply after having a dream. The she lay down to sleep and saw a vision. The god appeared to stand by her, saying that he would make her healthy. In payment, however, she must dedicate a silver pig in the sanctuary in commemoration of her ignorance. With these words, he cut open her diseased eye and poured in a potion. When day came, she departed healthy.

5. A boy who was mute. This boy came to the sanctuary seeking his voice. When he had made the initial sacrifice and performed the customary rites, the attendant who carried fire for the god looked at the boy's father and ordered him to promise to offer a commemorative sacrifice within a year if he obtained what he had come for. Suddenly the boy said, "I promise." Amazed, the father told him to speak again, and he spoke again. From that time on the boy was healthy.

6. Pandarus the Thessalian had marks on his forehead. He slept in the sanctuary and saw a vision. The god appeared to bind his marks with a bandage, ordering him to take off the bandage and dedicate it in the temple when he left the sanctuary. When day came, he stood up, took off the bandage, and saw his forehead free of marks. He dedicated the bandage in the temple; on it were the marks from his forehead.

7. Echedorus received the marks of Pandarus in addition to those he already had. This man took money from Pandarus to make a dedication to the god at Epidaurus, but he did not hand over the money. As he slept he saw a vision. The god appeared, standing by him and asking if he had some money from Pandarus from Euthenai to make a dedication in the sanctuary. He denied that he had taken any such money from him, but said that if [the god] were to make him healthy he would inscribe a statue and dedicate it to him. After this the god bound Pandarus' bandage around the marks, ordering him to leave the sanctuary, wash his face in the fountain, and look at his reflection in the water. When day came, he left the sanctuary and took off the bandage:

Figure 6.3. Votive relief from a healing sanctuary on the Aegean island of Melos, c. 100–200 CE. The inscription reads: "TYCHE [Fortune dedicated this] TO ASCLEPIUS AND HYGIEIA [Health] AS A THANK OFFERING. Art Resource, New York.

it did not have the scars on it. Looking into the water, he saw that his own face had received the scars from Pandarus in addition to his own marks.

11. When the suppliants were asleep, Aeschines climbed a tree and was peering into the Sanctuary. He fell from the tree among some stakes and injured both his eyes. Blind and in distress, he supplicated the god, slept, and became healthy.

12. Euippos had a spearhead in his jaw for six years. When he slept in the Sanctuary, the god removed the spear, placing it in his hands. When day came, he departed healthy, holding the spear in his hands.

> In his comedy *Wealth* (produced **388 BCE**), Aristophanes parodies the ritual of incubation. In this scene, a slave is describing how he took his master, the blind god Wealth, to the sanctuary of Asclepius, hoping that the healing god would cure his master's blindness.

6.28 ARISTOPHANES, *WEALTH* 653–744.

As soon as we approached the god's sanctuary,

leading the fellow who was then most wretched

but is now the happiest and most fortunate in the world,   655

we led him first to the sea and cleansed him.

....

Next we went to the god's sanctuary.

When the cakes and first offerings on the altar   660

were burnt, nourishing Hephaestus' flame,
we bedded Wealth down in the customary manner.
Then each of us arranged our bedding.

….

The temple servant put out the lamps
and told us all to go to sleep,
And, if anyone heard a noise,   670
we were to keep quiet, and so we all lay there properly.

….

I looked up and saw the priest [of Asclepius]
snatching the pastries and the figs
from the sacred table. After that
he went around all the altars,
to see if there were any leftover cakes.   680
Then he consecrated all of them into a sack.

….

Then the god went around, examining
everyone's ailments in due order.
Then his assistant brought him   710
a stone mortar, a pestle, and a box

….

Next he sat beside Wealth,
and first he felt his head,
then he took clean gauze
and wiped around his eyes. Panacea   730
covered his head with a crimson cloth,
and also his entire face.[36] Then the god whistled.
Two snakes darted out of the temple,
extraordinarily large ones….
They slipped silently under the crimson cloth   735
and licked Wealth's eyelids, I guess.
And sooner than you could drink ten goblets of wine
Wealth stood up and could see.
I clapped my hands for joy
and woke my master. The god immediately   740
disappeared into the temple, and the snakes too.
You can imagine how those lying beside him
congratulated him and stayed awake
the whole night long until daylight came.

---

36 *Panacea*: a daughter of Asclepius; her name means "the healer of all."

7. Festivals

7.1 *HOMERIC HYMN TO APOLLO* 146–155.
But you, Phoebus, take the greatest delight in your heart for Delos,[1]
where Ionians with long flowing robes gather
together with their children and their revered wives.
And remembering you with boxing and dancing and song,
they delight you whenever they hold their contest.
….
For he would see the grace of all and would take pleasure in his heart
seeing the men and the women with their beautiful sashes,
and their swift ships, and many possessions.

7.2 ARISTOTLE, *NICOMACHEAN ETHICS* 8.9.5. ...the members of a tribe
or deme come together to perform sacrifices and hold festivals at these
sacrifices, paying honor to the gods and providing a pleasurable respite
for themselves.

> The main function of a festival was to honor and please the gods, who were
> thought to enjoy the same kind of entertainment as humans. A festival
> generally began with a procession and culminated in a sacrifice and a
> communal feast. Also included in many festivals were competitions in music,
> dancing, poetry, performances of tragedies and comedies, and a wide range
> of strenuous athletic contests.[2]

---

1 *Delos*: an island in the Aegean Sea, the birthplace of Apollo.
2 These festivals are often referred to as agonistic, from the Greek *agon*, contest.

Organization and regulation

Organizing a festival involved considerable preparation and expense. A mid-fourth century BCE inscription from Eretria on the island of Euboea gives the regulations for the celebration of the Artemisia, the most important of all Eretrian festivals, in honor of Artemis. Also included is the cost of the various prizes.

7.3   RO no. 73, lines 1–45.[3] Execestus, son of Diodorus, proposed: so that we may celebrate the Artemisia as splendidly as possible and that as many people as possible may participate in the sacrifice, the council and people have passed this resolution. The city is to arrange a competition (*agon*) in music with a budget of 1000 drachmas to the Moderator and Guardian [Artemis] and, for five days before the Artemisia, provide lambs, of which two should be choice animals.

The 27th of the month *Anthesterion* is to be the first day of the music festival, the music competition is to be for rhapsodes, singers to the pipes, lyre players, singers accompanying themselves on the lyre, and singers of parodies.[4] The competitors in the musical contest are also to compete in the processional hymn accompanying the sacrifice in the courtyard, using the performance equipment they employ in the contest.

Prizes are to be given as follows:[5] to the rhapsode 120 [drachmas], to the second 50, to the third 20; to the boy singer to the pipes 50, to the second 30, to the third 20; to the adult-lyre-player 110, to the second 70, to the third 55; to the singer accompanying himself on the lyre 200, to the second 150, to the third 100; to the singer of parodies 50, to the second 10.

Provisions are to be given to the competitors who are present: a drachma a day for each of them, beginning not more than three days before the pre-competition event and continuing until the competition takes place.

Let the demarchs arrange the competition in the fairest way possible, and let them punish according to the law anyone who behaves irregularly.[6]

The districts are to provide choice victims, an ox each year, and the districts are to contribute in regard to the choice victims as at the festival of Hera.

---

3   RO no. 73 is number 73 in Rhodes and Osborne 2003, a collection of Greek historical inscriptions more widely available than earlier publications. For each inscription RO provide a full Greek text, often revised on the basis of new evidence, together with citations of earlier publications, an English translation, and commentary.

4   *Anthesterion*: a month in the Athenian calendar which fell in spring. At this time the Eretrians were under Athenian domination. *rhapsodes*: bards, poetic performers. *parodies*: parodies of Homer that were performed by one individual.

5   *Prizes*: The total of these prizes exceeds the budget stipulated in lines 5–6. Cash prizes were the normal practice, contrasting with the crowns of foliage awarded to the victors at the games held at Olympia, Delphi, Nemea, and the Isthmus.

6   *demarchs*: officials elected by the people (*demos*).

Those who provide the choice victims are to receive the victims' skins.

The officials in charge of the sanctuaries are to judge the victims according to law. If one of the districts does not send its quota, that provision must be put up for bid.

In the sanctuary, any one who wishes may sell whatever he wants, without tax and without paying any duty; the *hieropoioi* are not to tax the sellers.[7]

The demarchs are to draw up the procession in the market-place, where the sacrificial animals are sold: public victims with the most splendid one first, then choice victims, then victims provided by private individuals who wish to take part in the procession.

Let all the competitors in the music contest take part in the procession to ensure that the procession and the sacrifice are as splendid as possible.

The decree shall be written up on a stone stele and stand in the sanctuary of Artemis, to insure that the sacrifice and musical festival for Artemis shall be celebrated in this way for all time, as long as the Eretrian people are free and prosper and have self-government.

> The geographer Strabo (late first century BCE–early first century CE) describes the military display that was part of the procession when the Eretrians were at the height of their power.

7.4   STRABO 10.1.10. The power that the Eretrians once had is indicated by a pillar they set up in the temple of Artemis Amarythia. The inscription said that there were three thousand heavy-armed soldiers, six hundred horsemen, and sixty chariots in the procession.

> An inscription from Magnesia on the Maeander in Asia Minor records regulations for the organization of a festival in honor of Zeus Sosipolis (Protector of the City), instituted after 185/4 BCE. The regulations deal with details of the procession and the duties of the civic official before and after the sacrifice and preparations for the ritual of theoxenia (hosting the gods), in which food was set before the gods' statues.

7.5   *NGSL* pages 97–99, lines 32–64.[8] The current *stephanophoros*, together with the priest and the priestess of Artemis Leucophryne, shall lead the procession on the twelfth of the month Artemision[9] and sacrifice the bull which has been displayed. The *gerousia* (senate), priests, magistrates

---

7   *hieropoioi*: managers of the sacred rites, one of whose tasks was to see that the victims were perfect.

8   *NGSL* is Lupu 2005, a collection of inscriptions recording Greek sacred laws that is more widely available than earlier publications of these inscriptions. *NGSL* provides a full Greek text, often emended, together with citations of earlier publications, an English translation, and commentary. I have used Lupu's Greek text in making my translation.

9   *stephanophoros*: the title of an official who had the right to wear a crown. *the month Artemision*: probably around springtime.

both elected and allotted, ephebes, young men, boys, and winners at the Leucophryena and other crown competitions shall march in the procession. The *stephanophoros* shall lead the procession, carrying the wooden images of all twelve gods in their most beautiful garments; he shall fix a *tholos* in the *agora* (market-place) near the altar of the twelve gods, spread out three couches, as beautiful as possible, and provide for musical entertainment a flute-player, a syrinx-player, and a cithara-player.[10]

On the twelfth of the month Artemision, the *oikonomoi* shall produce three victims,[11] which they will sacrifice to Zeus Sosipolis, Artemis Leukophryene, and Pythian Apollo: a ram as beautiful as possible to [Zeus], a goat to Artemis, and a he-goat to Apollo. They shall sacrifice to Zeus on the altar of Zeus Sosipolis, and to Artemis and Apollo on the altar of Artemis. The priests of these gods shall receive their customary perquisites. When they sacrifice the bull, they shall distribute its meat among the participants in the procession; as for the ram, the goat, and the he-goat, they shall distribute them to the *stephanophoros,* the priestess, the *polemarchoi,* the *prohedroi,* the *neopoiai,* the *euthynoi,* and those performing services. The *oikonomoi* shall make these distributions.[12] When the bull has been consecrated, the *oikonomoi* shall let out a contract for it to be reared by the contractor. The contractor will lead the bull to the market place and obtain what is necessary for its nurture from the grain sellers and the other merchants, and it will preferable if they give [this stuff].

> Most city states had their own distinctive festival calendar, of which the best known is the Athenian, also known as Attic because the various districts or demes of Attica adhered to it. The calendar year began in mid-summer with the month Hekatombaion, in which the Panathenaea, the greatest festival of the year, was celebrated. The twelve Attic months are as follows, noting only those festivals that are mentioned in this book.[13]
>
> *Hekatombaion,* mid-summer (late June–late July): Panathenaea.
> *Metageitnion,* summer (late July–late August)
> *Boedromion,* autumn (late August–late September): Eleusinian Mysteries
> *Pyanepsion,* autumn (late September–late October): Thesmophoria
> *Maimakterion,* winter (late October–late November)
> *Poseideon,* winter (late November–late December): Rural Dionysia
> *Gamelion,* winter (late December–late January): Lenaea
> *Anthesterion,* spring (late January–late February): Anthesteria

---

10 *tholos*: a round or circular building. The verb "fix" suggests the demarcation of an area, perhaps for a tent. *three couches*: for the statues of Zeus, Artemis, and Apollo, the recipients of the sacrifice, as indicated in the next several lines.

11 *oikonomoi*: civic, not religious, officials.

12 *polemarchoi, prohedroi, neopoiai, euthynoi, oikonomoi*: various civic officials.

13 Adapted from Parke 1977: 26–27 and Simon 1983: 5.

Elaphphebolion, spring (late February–late March): City or Great
  Dionysia
Mounychion, spring (late March–late April)
Thargelion, summer (late April–late May): Bendidia
Skiraphorion, summer (late May–late June)

The following excerpt from a local calendar for the Attic deme of Thorikos
(ca. 380–375 BCE) gives specifications for the sacrificial offerings to be made
at local festivals in various months of the Athenian calendar.

7.6   *NGSL* pages 117–119, lines 10–35. [In *Metageitnion*:] for Zeus Kataibates in
the sacred enclosure near the Delphinion a full-grown victim, to be sold.
An oath victim is to be provided for the scrutineers (*euthunai*).[14]

In *Boedromion*: the Prerosia; for Zeus Polieus, a choice sheep, a choice piglet,
at/to Automenai (?) a purchased piglet to be entirely burnt.[15] The priest
shall provide a meal for the attendant; for Cephalus, a choice sheep; for
Procris, a table; for Thorikos, a choice sheep; for the Heroines of Thorikos,
a table; to Sounion, for Poseidon, a choice lamb; for Apollo, a choice young
he-goat; for Kourotrophos, a choice female piglet; for Demeter, a full-grown
victim, for Zeus Herkeios, a full-grown victim, for Kourotrophos a piglet,
for Athena, a sheep, to be sold; at the salt works, for Poseidon, a full-grown
victim, for Apollo, a piglet.[16]

In *Pyanopsion*: for Zeus Kataibates, on the land of the Philomelidae, a full-
grown victim, to be sold, on the sixteenth; (?) for Neanias, a full-grown
victim, at the Pyanopsia...[17]

In *Maimakterion*: for Thorikos, a bovine costing between 40 and 50
drachmas;[18] for the Heroines of Thorikos, a table...

In *Posideion*: the Dionysia.

In *Gamelion*: for Hera, at the *Hieros Gamos*...[19]

---

14 *Pyanopsion.... Pyanopsia*: an alternate spelling of Pyanepsion, the Attic month,
and Pyanepsia, a festival held in that month. *Kataibates*: the one who descends,
with lightning and thunderbolts. Places struck by lightning were dedicated to Zeus
Kataibates. *oath-victim*: a victim sacrificed when an oath was sworn.

15 *Prerosia*: a pre-plowing offering. *Zeus Polieus*: Zeus protector of the city.

16 *Cephalus, Procris*: local heroes who were man and wife. *a table*: for various offerings,
a lesser gift than those offered to the male deities or heroes. *Thorikos*: the eponymous
hero of the deme; little is known of him. *Sounion*: the promontory on the southeast
tip of the Attic coast, where there are the remains of a temple to Poseidon. *Zeus
Herkeios*: Zeus of the enclosure or home. *Kourotrophos*: Nurturer of the Young, an
epithet of Demeter.

17 *Neanias*: Young Man.

18 Parke 1977: 48 estimates the average wage of an Athenian in the mid-fourth century
BCE to be between a one and a half and two drachmas.

19 *Hieros Gamos*: Sacred Marriage, between Zeus and Hera.

In *Anthesterion*: for Dionysus, on the twelfth, a tawny or [black] goat that does not yet have its age-marking teeth; at the Diasia, for Zeus Meilichios,[20] a sheep to be sold.

The Anthesteria

The Anthesteria, one of the earliest attested Greek festivals, was celebrated in communities throughout the Greek world at the beginning of spring in honor of Dionysus as the god of wine.[21]

Most of the meager and often obscure literary sources refer to the Athenian celebration of the Anthesteria in the month of *Anthesterion*, roughly the end of February.[22] The Athenian historian Thucydides notes that this "more ancient Dionysia" was celebrated in the sanctuary of Dionysus of the Marshes, thus distinguishing it from the City Dionysia in *Elaphaboleion* as well as from the Rural Dionysia in *Poseideon*.[23]

7.7   THUCYDIDES 2.15. The sanctuaries that are outside the acropolis are located more in that quarter of the city (at the foot of the acropolis to the south), namely those of Olympian Zeus, of Pythian Apollo, and of Dionysus of the Marshes, in whose honor is celebrated the more ancient Dionysia in the month of *Anthesterion*, on the twelfth day, a custom maintained even today by the Ionian descendants of the Athenians.[24]

The three parts of the Anthesteria were named respectively the *Pithoigia* for the opening of the large clay jars (*pithoi*) containing the new vintage that had been fermenting since the autumn; the *Choes* (Pitchers or Jugs) for the drinking vessels containing wine; and the *Chytroi* (Pots) for the cooking vessels in which were cooked seeds or grains, and vegetable bran flavored with honey.

The first two parts of the festival focused on Dionysus as the god of wine. At the *Pithoigia*, people came together from the vineyards of Attica—farmers, laborers, and slaves alike—bringing large clay jars on carts. The *pithoi* of new wine were probably opened at sundown on the eleventh of Anthesterion. At the same time the temple of Dionysus, which was normally closed

---

20 *Zeus Meilichios*, Zeus the Gentle

21 *Anthesteria*: the name derives from the Greek *anthos*, flower, although what is known of the festival itself seems to have little connection with flowers, beyond the fact that it was held at the beginning of spring.

22 It is generally assumed that the Anthesteria extended over three days, the eleventh through thirteenth. Hamilton 1992: 5-62, however, examines the ancient literary testimony for the Choes festival in detail, questioning its three-day extent and connection with the celebration of a *hieros gamos* with Dionysus.

23 *City Dionysia*: see Athenian drama festivals in Chapter 8.

24 *Dionysus in the Marshes*: the exact location of this temple is problematic, see Parke 1977: 108. *Ionians*: the inhabitants of the Greek cities of the coastal area of Asia Minor, who claimed descent from the legendary Ion, a son of Apollo. The Athenian claim to be the mother-city of all Ionians is false, as Herodotus (1.146) shows.

Figure 7.1. This scene from a large red-figure vase (*stamnos*, c. 450 BCE) depicts women gathered about an image of the god Dionysus that is set up in front of a table. The idol consists of a mask, hung on a pole, with drapery that is held in place with large pins, thus suggesting a makeshift image. On each shoulder is a large disk and the mask is decorated with garlands of ivy. Offerings of cakes or loaves lie on the table between two *stamnoi*. On the far left, a woman plays the double flute. To the right of the table, a woman ladles wine into a cup. The other women move gracefully, holding wine cups. It is disputed which Dionysiac ceremony is depicted. Photograph © 2008 Museum of Fine Arts, Boston.

throughout the year, would have been opened, remaining so until sundown on the following day, the day of the Pitchers.[25]

7.8 PLUTARCH, *MORALIA* 655 e. At Athens, the people start the new wine on the eleventh day of the month *Anthesterion*, calling the day *Pithoigia*.

> A fragment of Phanodemus, an Atthidographer (chronicler of the early history of Athens) who wrote in the fourth century BCE, describes the celebration.[26]

7.9 PHANODEMUS as quoted in ATHENAEUS, *DEIPNOSOPHISTS* 11.465 a. (*FGrHist*. 325 F 12). Phanodemus says that at the temple of Dionysus of the Marshes, the Athenians bring the new wine from the *pithoi* and mix it for the god; then they take it for themselves. Dionysus was called "of the Marshes" because, on that occasion, the new wine was mixed and drunk with water for the first time…. Then, gladdened by the mixture, they celebrate Dionysus with songs and dancing, as they address him with the names Flowery, Dithyrambus, the Frenzied One, and the Roarer.[27]

> A number of late sources, mostly scholia, yield meager information about the festival of the Pitchers (*Choes*). All the temples, with the exception of

---

25 There is confusion in the ancient sources about the precise beginning of each festival day, but it is likely that sundown signaled the end of a day and that the evening and night of that day were reckoned as belonging to the new day.

26 Phanodemus' work only survives in fragments quoted by other authors. The standard reference for these and other fragments from lost works is F. Jacoby, *Die fragmente der griechischen Historiker*. Berlin-Leiden 1923–1958 = *FGrHist*.

27 *Flowery*: decorated with a garland or crown (*stephanos*) of flowers. *Dithyrambos*: an allusion to the dithyramb, a choral song in honor of Dionysus. *the Frenzied One*: an allusion to Dionysus as the god of ritual madness or ecstasy (*mania*). *the Roarer*: another cult name (Greek *Bromios*) of Dionysus that is prominent in Euripides' *Bacchae*.

that of Dionysus of the Marshes, were closed, no sacrifices could be offered, no business conducted. At the beginning of the day, people would chew the leaves of a species of hawthorn that was thought to ward off ghosts, and the doors of the houses were painted with pitch, indicating that this was a day of pollution. Families celebrated the festival inside the house. Children, mainly boys, are depicted in vase paintings with miniature pitchers. The giving of the first pitcher to a child between the age of three and four was a significant event in family life.

The earliest and probably most reliable source for the *Choes* festival comes from Aristophanes' *Acharnians* (425 BCE),[28] where there is a humorous account of a communal feast, followed by an all-male drinking contest with a prize offered by the state for the one who is the first to drain his pitcher.

7.10 ARISTOPHANES, *ACHARNIANS* 1000–1093.

Herald

Attention, people, attention! As our ancestors did, drain your pitchers
(*choes*)   1000
at the sound of the trumpet. The one who is the first
to do this will receive a Ctesiphon-size wine sack.[29]

Dicaeopolis

Slaves! Women! Didn't you hear?
What are you doing? Don't you hear the herald's words?
Boil, roast, and turn the hare-meat,   1005
then quickly take it off the spits, and string the garlands.
Bring the spits so that I can skewer the thrushes.

....

Dicaeopolis

Bring the ladle   1067
so that I can take some wine and pour it for the *Choes* festival.

The messenger summons guests to the feast, telling each guest to bring his own food and wine.

Messenger

Come at once to dinner,   1085

---

28 Hamilton 1992: 14 privileges Aristophanes' testimony over that of Euripides (7.12), and remarks that "The picture presented by the *Acharnians* is of a riotously enjoyable occasion, in which the chugging contest played only a part and perhaps involved only a small portion of the group. It was the main event probably because it was the only public event—one managed by the city at a fixed time under fixed rules. The parties occasioned by the contest, like our present-day football parties, would be private and unregulated."

29 A typical *chous* pitcher had a single handle, a trefoil mouth (with three curves), and contained about two and a half liters. *Ctesiphon*: otherwise unknown, but probably a man notorious for the size of his paunch.

and bring your pitcher (*chous*), and your food-hamper.

The priest of Dionysus invites you.

But be quick; you've long been holding up the meal.

Everything else is ready:

couches, tables, cushions, rugs,   1090

garlands, myrrh, sweetmeats, the whores are there,

cakes, rolls, sesame cakes, wafers,

and beautiful dancing girls....

> After Dicaeopolis has proclaimed that he is the first to drain his pitcher, the comedy ends with him making exaggerated claims about his victory.

7.11 ARISTOPHANES, *ACHARNIANS* 1224–1234.

Dicaeopolis

Take me to the judges. Take me to the king.[30]

Give me the wine-sack.   1225

....

Look, it's empty. Hail the glorious victor!

Chorus

Hail then, if you say so, old man. Hail to the glorious victor.

Dicaeopolis

I filled it with unmixed wine and chugged it, without taking a breath.

Chorus

Hail to the victor now, my noble fellow.

Take the wine-sack and go.   1230

Dicaeopolis

And you must follow and sing "Hail to the glorious victor."

Chorus

Yes, we'll follow for your sake, singing "Hail to the glorious victor"

In honor of you and the wine-sack.   1234

> A different picture of the drinking at the *Choes* is apparent in Euripides' *Iphigeneia in Tauris* (413 BCE), where Orestes tells of his arrival in Athens at the time of the *Choes* festival. Because of the pollution caused by the killing of his mother, he was made to sit at a separate table and so prevented from fully participating in the festival. His experience, he says, has been ritualized in the Athenian celebration of the *Choes*.

---

30 *judges...king:* The reference to judges or umpires indicates that this was a state or public contest. The title of "king," *basileus,* refers to the king archon, the official who carried out the religious duties that had originally been held by kings.

7.12 EURIPIDES, *IPHIGENEIA IN TAURIS* 947–960.

I went there, but at first none of my fellow-guests

willingly received me, saying that I was hated by the gods.[31]

Then those who respected me set my portion as a guest on a separate
table,

because we were under the same roof.   950

By their silence they banned me from speech

so that I was apart from their eating and drinking.

and, filling for each man his own cup

in equal measure, they took their enjoyment.

I did not think it right to blame my hosts,   955

I silently grieved, however, pretending to be unaware,

but deeply lamenting because I was my mother's murderer.

And now, I hear, my misfortunes are a ritual

for the Athenians, and the custom still endures

that Athena's people observe the *Choes* festival.   960

> Phanodemus (fourth century BCE) gives a further version of this aetiological
> story, attributing Orestes' limited welcome to the legendary Athenian King
> Demophon, and noting that he ordered the participants to take their garlands
> to the temple of Dionysus of the Marshes after the drinking contest.

7.13 PHANODEMUS as quoted in ATHENAEUS, *DEIPNOSOPHISTS* 10.
437 c–d, (*FGrHist* 325 F 11). In connection with the Festival of Pitchers
celebrated at Athens, Phanodemus says that King Demophon instituted
it when he wanted to entertain Orestes who had come to Athens. Because
Demophon did not wish Orestes to participate in the sacred rites or share
in the libations since he had not yet been put on trial,[32] he ordered that
the sacred vessels be locked up, and a pitcher of wine to be set before each
participant, saying that a flat cake would be given to the one who was the
first to drain his pitcher.

Because they had been under the same roof with Orestes, Demophon also
ordered that, when they had finished the drinking, they should not place
the garlands they had been wearing on the sacred images. Rather, each
should lay his garland around his pitcher, take the garlands to the priestess
at the temple in the marshes, and complete the ritual in the precinct. Since
that time, the festival has been called the "Pitchers."

---

31 *fellow-guests*: the Greek is *xenoi*, and *xenia* is guest-friendship, a contract whereby
each individual will assist or protect the other when needed. *hated by the gods*: an
allusion to the pollution caused by his murder of his mother Clytemnestra.

32 *he had not yet been put on trial*: Apollo had ordered Orestes to go to Athens to be
tried for matricide. Orestes' trial is the subject of Aeschylus' *Eumenides*. Although
Orestes had been purified at Delphi, concern about pollution evidently still lingered.
See 4.27 and 9.28.

The western Greek historian Timaeus of Tauromenium in Sicily (c. 350-260 BCE) notes that Dionysius, a Sicilian ruler, offered a prize for the man who was the first to drain his *chous*.

7. 14 TIMAEUS as quoted in ATHENAEUS, *DEIPNOSOPHISTS* 10.437 b. Timaeus says that the tyrant Dionysius set up a golden crown as a prize at the festival of the *Choes* for the one who was the first to drain his *chous* and that Xenocrates the philosopher finished first. Xenocrates took the golden crown and, as he departed, placed it on the herm set up in his courtyard, the one on which he usually place crowns of flowers when he returned home in the evening.[33] He was admired for this deed.

In Aristophanes' *Frogs* (405 BCE) the chorus of frogs that inhabit the precinct of Dionysus in the Marshes describe the coming of drunken revelers.

7.15 ARISTOPHANES, *FROGS* 209–220.

Brekekekex koax, koax,

Brekekekex koax, koax!   210

Children of the marsh and streams,

let's voice a cry, along with the pipes,

our own fair-sounding song

— koax koax —

that once we voiced for the Nysaean son of Zeus,[34]   215

Dionysus in the Marshes,

when the mob of drunken revelers,

came to my precinct

on the festival of the Pots (*Chytroi*).[35]

Brekekekex koax, koax.   220

A scholion to Aristophanes' *Acharnians* 1076 notes that Theopompus, a Greek historian of the fourth century BCE, explains the origin of the name of the festival of the Pots.

7.16 SCHOLION TO ARISTOPHANES, *ACHARNIANS* 1076. Theopompus says that those saved from the flood boiled a pot of panspermia, from which the festival takes its name.[36] They sacrificed on the *Choes* to Hermes Chthonios, but no one tasted from the pot. Those who were saved [from the flood] did this, as they prayed to Hermes for those that had died.

---

33 *herm*: a sacred pillar surmounted with a head of Hermes, and a model of an erect phallus in the middle, which was displayed outside most houses.

34 *Nysaean*: Nysa was a mountain, said to be the birthplace of Dionysus.

35 *on the festival of the Pots*: probably in the early morning hours of that day.

36 *the flood*: in the myth of the five ages, Zeus sent a flood to destroy the people of the age of bronze because he was angry at their decadence. *panspermia*: a concoction of seeds, grains and honey. *Hermes Chthonios*: Hermes is called "of the underworld" because he escorted the souls of the dead to that place.

A scholion to Aristophanes' *Frogs* 218 also quotes from Theopompus' explanation of the name of the festival of the Pots.

7.17 SCHOLION TO ARISTOPHANES, *FROGS* 218. For the festival of the Pots. *Chytroi* is an Athenian festival. It is celebrated for the following reason which Theopompus explains thus. "Therefore the people who had been saved [from the flood] called the whole festival by the name of the day on which they took heart." Then he says, "they have the custom of sacrificing to them and to no one of Olympians at all but to Hermes Chthonios" and (he says) "No one of the priests tastes from the pot that everyone throughout the city boils. This they do in the day." (He also says) "The people then present prayed to Hermes on behalf of the dead." Contests were held there, called Chytrine, as Philochorus says in the sixth book of his *Atthis*."[37]

> Two ancient sources are often cited as evidence that on the evening of the festival of the Pitchers a ceremony of sacred marriage (*hieros gamos*) was enacted between the *basilinna*, the wife of the king, and the god Dionysus.[38] Neither passage, however, specifically connects the ceremony with the Anthesteria.[39]

7.18 ARISTOTLE?, *CONSTITUTION OF THE ATHENIANS* 3.5. The king occupied what is now called the Boukoleion, near the *prytaneion*.[40] This is indicated by the fact that even now the union (*symmeixis*) and marriage (*gamos*) of the king's wife (*basilinna*) with the god Dionysus takes place there.

> In a speech attributed to Demosthenes, the prosecution alleges that the stipulations regarding the religious ceremonies performed by the wife of the king had been broken by the king's wife, the daughter of the defendant Neaera who was not an Athenian citizen.

7.19 DEMOSTHENES?, *AGAINST NEAERA* 73. On behalf of this city, this woman [the daughter of Neaera] performed the sacred rites that must not be spoken of;[41] she also saw what it was not fitting for her, a foreigner, to see. And, despite her lack of status, she entered where no other of the numerous Athenian citizens enters, except the wife of the king. She administered the sacred oath to the venerable priestesses who preside over the rites and she

---

37 *Philochorus*: 340–260 BCE, a historian who wrote a history of Attica that has only survived in fragments quoted by later authors.

38 The authorship of both these works is disputed.

39 *king*: see 7.11 n. 36. *ceremony of sacred marriage*: Most modern scholars think that this ceremony was part of the Anthesteria and that it took place on the night of transition from the Day of the Pitchers to that of the Pots but Hamilton 1992: 53–57 concludes that the connection with the Anthesteria is "without firm basis."

40 *prytaneion*: this building was the symbolic center of the *polis*; it contained the *hestia* (hearth) of the city and was the place where distinguished citizens and foreign dignitaries were entertained with honor.

41 *must not be spoken of*: literally "the unspeakable things," i.e., the secret rites.

was given to Dionysus as his wife.[42] She performed on the city's behalf the rites that our ancestors handed down for the service of the gods, the rites that are many, sacred, and not to be spoken of. How is it in accordance with piety for an ordinary woman to perform the things that is not possible for all to hear, especially a woman like this who has done such things?

7.20 DEMOSTHENES?, *AGAINST NEAERA* 74–76. In ancient times, men of Athens, there was sovereignty in our state.... The king offered all the sacrifices, and those that were most sacred and must not be spoken of were performed, as was natural, by his wife, the *basilinna*. They established a law that the king's wife was to be a citizen and that she should not have had sexual intercourse with any other man, in order that, in accordance with our ancestral customs, the sacred rites that must not be spoken of be celebrated on the city's behalf and that the customary rituals be properly performed, without omission or innovation.

This law was engraved on a stone marker that was set up near the altar in the sanctuary of Dionysus in the Marshes .... In this way, the people testified their piety to the god and left a pledge for posterity to show the kind of woman that we require to perform the rites and to be given in marriage to the god. This is why they set up the marker in the most ancient and sacred sanctuary of Dionysus in the Marshes in order that only a few have knowledge of what was written. For the sanctuary is only opened once a year, on the twelfth day of the month of Anthesterion.[43]

The Thesmophoria

> The festival of the Thesmophoria in honor of Demeter was celebrated by Greek communities in the autumn, before the time of sowing the winter crop. Unlike most Greek festivals, men were excluded from participating in or having knowledge of these rites. The name of the festival literally means "the carrying of the *thesmoi*." *Thesmos* literally means "what is laid or put down," and is also used to denote customs or laws.

> Writing in the late first century BCE, Diodorus reports two traditions about Demeter: she told humans how to cultivate grain and gave them laws (*thesmoi*).

7.21 DIODORUS 5.68. When the grain still grew haphazardly among the other plants and was yet unknown to humans, Demeter was the first to gather it, to realize how to prepare and preserve it, and to show humans how to sow....

Some people say that it was she who also introduced laws through which humans have become accustomed to deal justly with each other, and they

---

42 *venerable priestesses*: fourteen women who were appointed by the king to be responsible for the temple in the Marshes.

43 i.e., probably at sundown on the eleventh day.

called this goddess Thesmophoros [Law Bringer] after the laws that she gave them.

> In Athens, the Thesmophoria was celebrated in the month of *Pyanepsion* (September–October) over a period of three days: the *Anodos*, or Way Up took place on the eleventh of that month; the *Nesteia*, or Fast, on the twelfth; and the *Kalligeneia* or She of the Beautiful Birth on the thirteenth. The three-day festival was preceded by two other all-female festivals: the Stenia on the ninth, when women gathered together, blaspheming and verbally abusing each other, and the Thesmophoria in the deme of Halimous where the leading women of Athens went on the tenth of *Pyanepsion*. At the conclusion of the festival, there was a great feast, after which the women returned to their homes, probably after two nights of sexual abstinence.[44]

> Aristophanes' *Women at the Thesmophoria* (411 BCE), tells us very little about the actual rites. The audience merely learns that the rites were secret, restricted to women, held at night, and that slaves were not admitted once the ceremonies began.[45] In a parody of the invocation at the beginning of the Athenian assembly, Aristophanes substitutes the names of female deities for the masculine gods customarily invoked.

7.22 ARISTOPHANES, *WOMEN AT THE THESMOPHORIA* 295–305.

Ritual silence, please; ritual silence. Pray to the Two Thesmophorian
 Goddesses,

also to Wealth, to Kalligeneia, to the Nurse of the Young,   300

to Hermes, and to the Graces,[46] that this assembly and today's meeting

may be conducted in the finest and best manner, to the great benefit of
 the city of the Athenians,

and also with good fortune for you yourselves. May the woman whose
 actions   305

and words best serve the Commonwealth of the Athenians

and the Commonwealth of Women be victorious.

Let this be your prayer, and for yourselves all good things. Hail,
 Paion,   310

hail! Paion, hail Paion! [47] Let us rejoice!

> The women invite Demeter and Persephone to the sacred precinct.

---

44 See Dillon 2002: 110–120.

45 On slaves, see Aristophanes, *Women at the Thesmophoria* 293–294.

46 *the Two Thesmophorian Goddesses*: Demeter and Persephone. *Kalligeneia*: the bearer of fair offspring, a cultic epithet of Demeter.

47 *Paion*: also addressed as Paian, who was originally a healing god often identified with Apollo and Asclepius, but later came to mean a song that was addressed to the gods in political, military, and personal situations.

7.23 ARISTOPHANES, *WOMEN AT THE THESMOPHORIA* 1148–1159.

Come also, propitious and gracious

Ladies, to your own precinct

where men are forbidden to behold

the sacred rites that by torchlight

you illumine, an immortal sight.

Come, enter, we pray,

all powerful Thesmophorian goddesses.

> Two late sources yield problematic accounts of the rites. Marginal notes
> by a thirteenth century CE scoliast profess to explain a passage from
> Lucian's *Dialogues of the Hetaerae* (second century CE). An excerpt from the
> *Protrepticus* of the Christian writer Clement of Alexandria, (c. 190 CE), tells
> a story to account for the women's ritual of throwing piglets into a pit.[48]

> Modern scholars have generally explained the Thesmophoria as a fertility
> festival. Lowe, however, suggests that the piglets and the pine branches are
> fecundity symbols offered, not in the hope of future fecundity, but rather as
> thank offerings to Demeter for her gift of grain which "civilized the human
> race." Lowe also notes the scholiast's use of "they believe" and "they say,"
> which distances the scholiast from the beliefs that are attributed to the
> participants in the ritual.[49]

7.24 SCHOLION TO LUCIAN, *DIALOGUES OF THE HETAERAE* 2.1.

Thesmophoria: a festival of the Greeks involving mysteries, also known
as Skirophoria. The more mythological explanation for the celebration of
this festival is that when Kore [the Maid] was carried of by Pluto,[50] as she
was picking flowers, a swineherd Eubouleus was grazing his pigs on that
spot and they were swallowed up together by Kore's chasm. Therefore, in
honor of Eubouleus, piglets are thrown into the chasms of Demeter and
Kore.

Women called "dredgers" bring up the putrified remains of what was
thrown into the pits (*megara*). After maintaining a state of sexual purity
for a period of three days, these women then go down into the inmost
sanctuaries; they bring up the remains and place them on the altars. They
believe that anyone who takes some and sows it with the seed will have a
good crop.

They say that there are also snakes down below in the chasms, which eat
most of what is thrown down. And so noise is made whenever the women

---

48 For relevant passages from Lucian's *Dialogues* and Clement of Alexandria and other
   related Greek texts, with translations, see Lowe in Blundell and Williamson 1998:
   165–170.

49 Lowe in Blundell and Williamson 1998: 149–173.

50 *Pluto*: Hades, god of the underworld.

dredge and whenever they set those models down again, so that the snakes they believe are guarding the shrines will go away.

They bring up sacred objects that are not to be spoken of, things made of dough, models of snakes and of male genitalia. They also take pine branches because of that plant's fertility. These are also thrown into the *megara* (this is the name of the shrines) and also piglets, as mentioned above—the latter because of their fecundity as a symbol of vegetable and human generation, as thank offerings to Demeter; because, in providing the fruits of Demeter, she civilized the human race....

It is called Thesmophoria because Demeter is given the epithet "Lawgiver" because she set down customs (*nomoi*), that is, laws (*thesmoi*) under which humans have to provide and work for their food.

7.25 CLEMENT OF ALEXANDRIA, *EXHORTATION TO THE GREEKS* 17.1. Do you also want me to explain to you Pherephatta's flower-picking and her rape by Aidoneus, the opening of the earth and Eubouleus' pigs that were swallowed up with the Two Goddesses [*sic*], as a result of which the "megarizing" women throw in pigs at the Thesmophoria?[51] The women variously celebrate this myth at festivals throughout the city, the Thesmophoria, Skirophoria, Arretophoria, as they act out the rape of Pherephatta in many ways.[52]

> The third century BCE poet Callimachus describes the Procession of the Basket, which likely contained mystical objects—a celebration probably modelled on a ritual at the Athenian Thesmophoria.

7.26 CALLIMACHUS, *HYMN* 6.118–138.

Sing, virgins, mothers add your voices:
"Demeter, all hail, nurturer of many, giver of good measures."
And as four white horses pull the Basket,   120
so will the great goddess, the wide-ruler, come to us
bringing the white spring, white summer, winter,
and the season of withering. She will protect us for another year.
When, without sandals and with unbound hair, we walk through the city,
so shall we have our feet and heads unharmed forever.   125
And as the basket-bearers bring baskets full of gold,
so may we taste unlimited gold.
The uninitiated may follow as far as the city hall;
the initiated right to the goddess's temple
—all who are younger than sixty. But women who are pregnant,   130

---

51 *Pherephatta*: Persephone. *Aidoneus*: Hades or Pluto. *megarizing*: going down into the *megara*, pits mentioned in the scholion above.

52 *Arretophoria*: this reading is problematic, and apparently does not refer to the Arrephoria.

Figure 7.2. A scene from the east frieze of the Parthenon depicting the priestess of Athena Polias facing two *Arrephoroi* carrying their secret bundles and, on the right, a male figure, perhaps the king (*basileus*) archon, receiving a *peplos* from a girl. Art Resource, New York.

and those who stretch their hands to Eileithyia[53] or are in pain,
it's enough that they go as far as their knees allow them. To them Deo[54]
shall give everything in abundance, just as if they came into her temple.

Hail goddess, and keep this city safe in harmony
and prosperity. And in the fields grant all things in abundance.   135
Nourish the cattle, bring us sheep, bring us grain, bring in the harvest,
nourish peace also, so that he who sows may reap.
Be gracious to me, thrice-invoked, great queen of goddesses.

The Panathenaea

The Athenian festival of the Panathenaea was celebrated annually in the month of Hekatombaion in honor of the birth of Athena, the patron goddess of Athens.[55] This festival probably dates from at least the seventh century BCE and was originally celebrated simply by the gift of a new robe (*peplos*) for the statue of Athena Polias in the Erechtheum. Each year, aided by older women, a *peplos* was woven by two young girls between the ages of seven

---

53 *Eileithyia*: goddess of childbirth.

54 *Deo*: Demeter.

55 On the Panathenaea, see Neils 1992.

and eleven, the *arrephoroi* who spent a year on the acropolis serving Athena.[56] The presentation ceremony was preceded by a procession across the Agora to the Acropolis where the robe was presented and sacrifice made.

Sometime in the 560s, probably in emulation of he panhellenic festivals to be discussed in the next chapter, athletic contests including the *pentathon*, running, and boxing were introduced. These contests which were also open to non-Athenian competitors were held every four years and this quadrennial festival is known as the Great Panathenaea . Given what we know about the various contests, the Great Panathenaea probably lasted about eight days. Later the program included musical competitions, recitations of Homer's epic poetry, athletic and equestrian contests, dancing in armor, racing with torches, dismounting from a chariot, and also a boat race in the harbor.

Victors in the contests at the Great Panathenaea were awarded an amphora, a large two-handled vessel, containing olive-oil that came from olive trees sacred to Athena. The best products of Athenian potters and painters, these prizes were taken home to Greek cities ranging from Marseilles to the Black Sea. Most Panathenaic amphoras are inscribed with the legend "OF THE CONTESTS FROM ATHENS" (TON ATHENETHEN ATHLON). The black figure technique was retained for the Panathenaic amphoras, despite the ubiquity of red-figure vases after the late sixth century BCE, and the imagery also remained virtually unchanged. On the reverse there is usually a representation of the athletic or equestrian contest for which the prize was awarded.

In an epinician ode in honor of an athlete from Argos who was a victor in the wrestling contest at the Panathenaea, Pindar (518–c. 446 BCE) alludes to a Panathenaic amphora.

7.27 PINDAR, *NEMEAN* 10.31–36.

The god knows the subject of my song, as does anyone who strives
for the heights of the ultimate contests. For most high
is the institution of Heracles that Pisa won.[57] Yet, as a prelude,
twice before in the rites of the Athenians
sweet voices have acclaimed him and, in earth burnt by fire,
the fruit of the olive has come to the brave people of Hera   35
in the confines of richly decorated jars.[58]

Probably the most spectacular feature of the Panathenaea was the procession in which the representatives of different segments of Athenian society, including metics (resident aliens), walked or rode along the Panathenaic Way from the Ceramicus, or Potters' Quarter, through the agora to the Acropolis. The procession is represented/depicted in a series of relief sculptures on the Parthenon, the temple to Athena built 437–432 BCE,

---

56 On the *arrephoroi*, see 3.13 with note.

57 *Heracles...Pisa*: an allusion to the Olympic games.

58 *people of Hera*: the people of Argos, where Hera was the preeminent deity.

Figure 7.3. Panathenaic amphora, 530–520 BCE (damaged and somewhat restored). Photographs © 2008 Museum of Fine Arts, Boston.

Side A. Athena is depicted in silhouette striding to the left, armed with a shield and spear; she wears the distinctive aegis, a snake-fringed cloak that she is said to have received from Zeus: on the shield is depicted in white the head and forepart of a leopard. The goddess is framed by two columns surmounted by cocks. The inscription "of the contests from Athens" is on the right of the left-hand column.

Side B. A race with five runners. The sharply bent position of their arms indicates the race is long distance.

in the hey-day of Periclean Athens. The scenes on this famous frieze, like other stone sculptural reliefs and statues, was originally painted in bright colors and is arguably the best known visual representation of one of the most essential features of a festival.

After the Persian Wars, a ship drawn on a cart became part of the procession. The ship's sail was a larger version of the *peplos* woven for Athena. In two plays of Euripides, reference is made to a *peplos* depicting the story of the battle of the Olympian gods against the Titans that was woven for the goddess.[59] In the first excerpt, Hecuba, the enslaved Trojan queen, imagines herself in Athens weaving a *peplos*. In the second, Iphigenia, living in Tauris in the Black Sea area, doubts whether she will ever return to her native Greece.

7.28 EURIPIDES, *HECUBA* 466–474.

In the city of Pallas,
shall I yoke colts to
the beautiful Athenian chariots
on the saffron-colored robe,
embroidering it with intricate

59 On the weaving of the *peplos* see Barber in Neils 1992: 112–114.

Figure 7.4. The Parthenon on the Athenian Acropolis, 448–432 BCE. ©
istockphoto/.

brightly colored flowers,

or the race of Titans

that Zeus the son of Cronus

lays low with a fiery bolt?

7.29 EURIPIDES, *IPHIGENIA IN TAURIS* 222–224.

Nor to the sound of my loom,

shall I weave the image of Athenian Pallas

and the Titans.

> The following excerpt from an Athenian inscription (c. 335 BCE) gives some
> idea of the expenses incurred in mounting the annual Panathenaic festival
> (sometimes referred to as the Lesser or Little Panathenaea). Two fragments
> of this inscription give the beginning of a law and part of an attached decree
> concerning income from "Nea," a tract of land that was to be used to purchase
> animals for sacrifice at the annual celebration of the Panathenaea. On the
> first fragment (Side A not given here), the moving of the law is described,
> whereas Side B gives details of the disposition of the income.

7.30 RO no. 81, side B 1–35.[60] ... in order that - - - piously - - - annually, and the
sacrifice in honor of Athena takes place every year on behalf of the Athenian

---

60 For the Greek text of sides A and B with a translation and commentary, see Rhodes
and Osborne 2003: 396–402. On side A the income is estimated at only two talents
(1200 drachmas), but on side B it is apparent that 41 *minae*, the equivalent of 4100
drachmas, was realized, thus suggesting that the second side is a later addition. Parke
1977: 48 estimates the average day-wage of an Athenian at this period to be between
one and a half to two drachmas.

Figure 7.5. View from the Acropolis across the Agora to the temple of Hephaestus. © istockphoto/Styve Reineck.

people, as well prepared as possible, and that all the other things required for the goddess' festival are well managed by the *hieropoioi* forever, let it be decreed by the people, and the rest in accordance with the council.[61]

The *hieropoioi* are to sacrifice two sacrifices, the sacrifice to Athena Goddess of Health (*Hygeia*) and the sacrifice made in the old sanctuary as in the past.[62] They are to distribute five portions of meat to the *prytaneis* and three to the nine archons and one to the Treasurers of Athena and one to the *hieropoioi* and three to the Generals and taxiarchs and the customary distribution to the Athenians who walk in the procession and to the *kanephoroi*.[63] Then they are to divide the rest of the meat among the Athenians.

---

61 *hieropoioi*: a group of ten men, one from each Athenian tribe, who managed the sacred rites. One of their duties was to ensure that the victims were perfect.

62 *old sanctuary*: the restoration of the text at the point is disputed, see Rhodes and Osborne 2003: 401.

63 *archons*: nine annually elected magistrates. They are to receive three portions between them, thus getting more than the *prytanneis* who only received a tenth of one portion. The ten *hieropoioi* and ten treasurers had to share one portion. *kannephoi*: basket carriers. Carrying the baskets with the sacrificial implements was a highly honored task, usually given to young girls; see 3.13.

The *hieropoioi* together with the cattle-buyers, when they have purchased the cows using the 41 minas [4100 drachmas] rent from the Nea and dispatched the procession for the goddess, must sacrifice all these cows on the great altar of Athena, except for one that they have pre-selected from the best quality cows; this they must sacrifice on the altar of Nike.[64] After they have sacrificed them to Athena Polias and Athena Nike, they should then distribute the meat from all the cows purchased using the 41 minas to the Athenian people in the Ceramicus as in the other distributions of meat.[65] They should distribute the portions to each deme according to the number of participants in the procession that each deme sends.

For the expenses of the procession, the butchering, the decoration of the great altar, and all the other necessary expenditures for the festival and the all-night celebration, 50 drachmas are to be provided. The *hieropoioi* who administer the annual Panathenaea are to make the all-night celebration as splendid as possible for the goddess. They should dispatch the procession at sunrise, punishing those who do not obey orders with punishments according to the laws.

---

64 The temple of Nike (Victory) is to the right of the Propylaea (the entrance to the acropolis) as one approaches the Parthenon.

65 *Ceramicus*: the Potters' Quarter which is located at some distance from the acropolis, across the agora and beyond the temple of Hephaestus.

8. Competitions in Honor of the Gods

8.1 THUCYDIDES 5.18. With regard to the common sanctuaries, anyone who wishes may, without fear, offer sacrifices, consult the oracles, and attend as a spectator according to the ancestral customs, both by land and sea.

> This religious stipulation, reaffirming the sacred truce (*ekechairia*), was the very first clause in the Peace of Nicias between Athens and Sparta in 421 BCE. The sacred truce, a temporary cessation of hostilities among warring Greek states, allowed safe travel to a common sanctuary for celebration of a panhellenic festival.
>
> The four most famous panhellenic festivals were the Olympic, Pythian, Isthmian, and Nemean Games.[1] There were athletic and sporting contests at all four festivals, and musical contests at all except the Olympic games. The games at Olympia were celebrated in honor of Zeus. The Pythian games held at Delphi were in honor of Apollo, the Isthmian at the isthmus near Corinth were in honor of Poseidon, and the Nemean at Nemea between Corinth and Argos were also in honor of Zeus.
>
> From the eighth century BCE onward people came together at fixed times to such sanctuaries from cities throughout the Greek world, mainland Greece itself, Asia Minor, the Black Sea area, Italy, and Sicily, and also from Egypt and Cyrene to offer sacrifices and either compete in "games" or contests honoring a particular god, or to be spectators.
>
> Festivals involving contests are often referred to as "agonistic," from the Greek *agon*, struggle or contest. These competitions were for prizes offered for races, boxing, wrestling and many other strenuous physical contests but also music, poetry, and drama which involved both music and dance.
>
> The traditional date of the foundation of the Olympic games is 776 BCE, the date from which the Greeks reckoned their calendar. Events were said

---

1   On Olympia and the games, see Swaddling 2004. For discussion of all four sites and games, see Miller 2004 a. Both works include illustrations.

to have occurred in a specified year of a specified Olympiad, each Olympiad consisting of four years. Likewise the Pythian games were held every four years, in the third year of an Olympiad. The Isthmian and Nemean games were celebrated every two years.[2] In the first year of an Olympiad, the Isthmian festival was held in April/May, followed by the Olympic festival in July/August. In the second year, the Nemean festival was celebrated in July/August. In the third year, the Isthmian festival in April/May was followed by the Pythian in July/August, and the Nemean festival was celebrated in July/August of the fourth year. These four festivals were known as "crown games," since the victorious contestants were awarded crowns, that is, garlands or wreathes made from branches or plants.[3]

Statues commemorating the victors were set up on the site of the games, and also in the native cities of the victors to commemorate their triumphal return. References in Pausanias and a list of Olympic victors indicate that the competitors came from Greek cities throughout the Mediterranean world. Some of the more illustrious victors had special victory (epinician) odes composed as a further memorial. These odes were sung at the festival itself and/or later in the victor's home town. Pindar (c. 518–c. 446 BCE) and Bacchylides (c. 520–450 BCE) composed victory odes commemorating the victories of Hiero, the ruler of Syracuse, at both Olympia and Delphi.[4]

The Olympic games

Herodotus tells how Tritantaechmes, who belonged to the Persian army which had just defeated the Spartans at the battle of Thermopylae in 480 BCE, was surprised to learn from some deserters that the Greeks were celebrating the Olympic games and the prize was a mere olive wreath, not money.

8.2   HERODOTUS 8.26. A few deserters came, men who had nothing to live on and wanted to work. When they were brought before the king, the Persians asked what the Greeks were doing. One individual asked the question on behalf of them all. The deserters told them that the Greeks were celebrating the Olympic games and watching athletic contests and chariot races. He then asked what was the prize for which they were competing. They replied that the gift was a crown of olive-leaves.... When Tritantaechmes learned that the prize was a crown, not money, he could not keep silent but said before everyone, "O dear! What kind of men have you brought us to fight

---

2   The Pythian games were established in 586 BCE, the Isthmian in 580 BCE, and the Nemean in 573 BCE.

3   The prize at Olympia was a wreath of wild olive; that at Delphi, of laurel (a plant sacred to Apollo); at the Isthmian Games, pine branches; at the Nemean, wild celery. In most other contests monetary prizes were awarded.

4   Pindar, *Olympian* 1 and Bacchylides 5 both celebrate Hiero's victory in the chariot race at Olympia in 476 BCE; likewise Pindar's *Pythian* 1 and Bacchylides 4 celebrate his victory in the chariot race at Delphi in 470 BCE.

against, Mardonius, men who compete not for material things but for excellence?" [5]

> In contrast to foreigners, the Greeks exercised naked, although this was not the original practice.[6]

8.3   THUCYDIDES 1.6. The Spartans were the first to bare their bodies, strip openly, and rub themselves down with oil after exercising. In early times, even in the Olympic games, they wore *diazomata* around their genitals in the contests;[7] and it is not many years since they stopped this practice. Even today many non-Greeks, especially in Asia, wear *diazomata* in boxing and wrestling contests. Indeed one could show that the early Greeks had many other customs that are like those of the non-Greeks of the present day.

> Two later sources, one writing in the late first century BCE and the other in the late second century CE, agree on a date for stopping use of the *diazoma*, but attribute the innovation to different men. The dating of this innovation, however, is considerably earlier than Thucydides' statement that it was not long before his own time.

8.4   DIONYSIUS OF HALICARNASSUS 7.72. The first Greek to strip and run naked was Acanthus the Spartan in the fifteenth Olympiad [720 BCE]. Before then all the Greeks were ashamed to appear at the games with their bodies entirely naked, as is clear in Homer, the most reliable and earliest of witnesses, when he has the heroes girding up.

8.5   PAUSANIAS 1.44.1. Near the tomb of Coroebus is buried Orsippus who won the *stadion* at Olympia [720 BCE]. While the other athletes in the competition wore *perizomata* in accordance with the ancient practice, he ran naked... I think that he deliberately let the *perizoma* slip off at Olympia, realizing that a nude man can run more easily than one who is girt.

> Pausanias notes the re-establishing of the Olympic festival after consultation with the Delphic oracle and the institution of the sacred truce (776 BCE). He also reports traditions that the gods held contests with each other at Olympia. Finally he reports the beginning of the documented Olympic festivals and the introduction of the various contests.

8.6   PAUSANIAS 5.4.5–6. Later Iphitus, who was descended from Oxylus, and a contemporary of Lycurgus who wrote the laws of the Spartans, arranged the games at Olympia and re-established the Olympic festival and instituted the sacred truce.[8]....

---

5   *Mardonius*: commander of the Persian infantry who was defeated and killed at the battle of Plataea in 479 BCE.

6   The word "gymnastics" derives from the Greek *gymnos*, naked.

7   *diazomata*: the word *diazoma* and its variant *perizoma* are generally translated as loin cloth or girdle.

8   *Lycurgus*: the traditional founder of the Spartan constitution. *sacred truce*: the Greek *ekecheiria,* literally a holding of hands, symbolized an agreement for all Greeks to cease hostilities for a certain period. For the crown games a truce was declared for a period of one month before the games to ensure safe travel for athletes and their entourage.

At this time Greece was being destroyed by tribal strife and by plague. It occurred to Iphitus to ask the god at Delphi for a cure for these troubles, and they say that the Pythian priestess said that Iphitus himself and the people of Elis should restore the Olympic games.[9]

8.7 PAUSANIAS 5.7.10. Some sources say that Zeus wrestled here for the throne with Cronus himself,[10] whereas others say that he celebrated the games in honor of his victory. Among the victors, Apollo is said to have outrun Hermes and beaten Ares in boxing. Because of this, they say, the Pythian flute is played for the jumping in the *pentathlon*,[11] since the flute is sacred to Apollo, and Apollo won Olympic victories.

8.8 PAUSANIAS 5.8.6–9. When the unbroken recorded tradition of the Olympiads began, there was first the foot-race (*stadion*), and Coroebus of Elis was the victor [776 BCE]. There is no statue of Coroebus at Olympia, but his grave is on the borders of Elis. Later, at the fourteenth festival, the double foot-race was added [724 BCE].…. At the eighteenth, the pentathlon and wrestling are recorded. … At the twenty-third festival, they restored the prizes for boxing. … At the twenty-fifth they admitted the race of full-grown horses.… At the eighth festival after this they acknowledged the men's *pancration* and the horse-race.

> There were thirteen contests for males, held over a period of five days, ten for adults and three for youths. The oldest and most prestigious contest was the *stadion*, a foot race over the distance of a stade (approximately 600 feet). The winner of this race received the title *Olympionikes* (Olympic victor), and the entire Olympiad was identified by his name. Two of the most grueling contests were the *pentathlon*, and the *pancration*, a form of all-out wrestling in which virtually no holds were barred.

> Writing in the mid-third century CE, Philostratus describes the dangers of the *pancration*.

8.9 PHILOSTRATUS, *PICTURES IN A GALLERY* 2.6. Pancratiasts practice a dangerous kind of wrestling. They have to suffer backward falls which are not safe for the wrestler, and learn holds by which one can still win even if one has fallen. They must have skill in various methods of strangling; they bend an opponent's ankle and twist his arm, throwing punches and jumping on him. All these practices are permitted in the *pancration*, except for biting and gouging.

8.10 PAUSANIAS 6.4.1. There is a statue of a man from Sicyon, a pancratiast, named Sostratus. His nickname was Acrochersites [Fingerman], because he would grab his opponent by the fingers, bending them and not letting

---

9   *Elis*: a city-state some 22 miles northwest of Olympia; its citizens presided over the Olympic games.

10 *wrestled here for the throne*: an allusion to Zeus' overthrow of Cronus; see Hesiod's *Theogony* lines 492–506 (2.6).

11 *pentathlon*: a contest comprising five different events: the discus, standing jump, javelin, *stadion*, and wrestling.

go until he knew his opponent had surrendered. He won twelve victories at Isthmia and Nemea combined, three at Olympia, and two at Delphi.

Epictetus, the mid-first to second century CE philosopher, describes the rigors and risks involved in training for the Olympic games.

8.11 EPICTETUS, *DISCOURSES* 3.15.2–5. You say, "I want to win at Olympia." Well, consider the preliminaries and the sequel. When you have done that, set to work if is it's good for you. You must submit to discipline, follow a strict diet, keep away from desserts, train under compulsion, at a fixed time, in heat or in cold. You must not drink cold water or wine whenever you want. You must hand yourself over to a trainer exactly as you would to a doctor. Then, in the contest, you have to dig in beside your opponent.[12] Sometimes you will dislocate your wrist, sprain your ankle, swallow mouthfuls of sand, and be flogged. And, after all, that there are times when you will be defeated. After you have thought about all this, enter the games if you want.

The Olympic contests were under the jurisdiction of *Hellanodikai* (male judges or umpires of the Greeks). These *Hellenodikai* lived at Elis for ten months in a special building in the marketplace where they were instructed by the *nomophylarchoi* (guardians of the law).[13]

Two days before the Olympic festival began, a procession set out from Elis for Olympia. The procession was led by the *Hellanodikai* and other officials including the Sixteen Women, followed by the athletes and their trainers, then horses and chariots along with their owners, jockeys, and charioteers. After stopping overnight, they paused as they crossed the boundary between Elis and Olympia to sacrifice a pig and perform purification rites at the fountain of Pieria.

8.12 PAUSANIAS 5.16.8. Whatever ritual is established for the Sixteen Women or the *Hellenodikai* to perform, is only performed after they have purified themselves with a pig that is suitable for purification and with water.[14] The purification takes place at the spring of Piera which is on the road as you come along the level road from Olympia to Elis.

Before entering the contest, the athletes, their fathers, brothers, and trainers swore a solemn oath before a statue of Zeus Horkios, the oath god.

8.13 PAUSANIAS 5.24.9–11. Of all the images of Zeus, the Zeus in the Bouleuterion [Council house] is most likely to strike terror into the hearts of wrongdoers. He is named Horkios and in each hand he holds a thunderbolt. Beside this image it is the custom for athletes, their fathers and their brothers, as well as their trainers, to swear an oath upon slices of boar's

---

12 *dig in*: a technical term that probably refers to the preliminary exercising in sand or mud.

13 Pausanias 6.24.3.

14 The Sixteen Women were a board of elderly women from Elis who supervised an Olympic festival in honor of Hera, see 8.24.

flesh that in no way will they commit a violation of the Olympic Games. The athletes in the men's category also swear that they have kept strictly to their training for ten successive months. Those who judge the ages of the boys and the foals that are entering the race also take an oath that they will judge fairly and without taking bribes, and that they will protect and not divulge what they learn about the candidate, whether accepted or not.

I forgot to ask what they customarily do with the boar after the athletes have taken the oath. The ancient custom of dealing with victims was that humans should not eat the flesh on which on which an oath had been sworn. Homer makes this quite clear. For the boar, from which slices were taken for Agamemnon to swear that he had not slept with Briseis, was thrown into the sea by the herald.[15] ...

Such was the ancient custom. In front of the feet of Zeus Horkios is a bronze plate inscribed with elegaic verses, the intent being to strike terror into the those who foreswear themselves.

> Thucydides tells how a Spartan competitor falsely identified himself as a Boeotian and was publicly whipped because Spartan competitors were debarred in that year.[16]

8.14 THUCYDIDES 5.50. The Spartan Lichas, the son of Arcesilaus, was given a beating on the course by the attendants of the umpires. When his chariot and pair won, it was announced that Lichas belonged to the Boeotian people, since he had no right to enter the contest. He had then come onto the course and put a headband on the charioteer in order to show that the chariot belonged to him.

> Pausanias records two Olympic victories of Euthymus of Locri. One was awarded after the judges disqualified the victory of Theagenes, his opponent, who was given a heavy fine because of his spitefulness.

8.15 PAUSANIAS 6.6.4–6. Euthymus was born in the land of the Locrians in Italy; they live near the Zephyrian cape. His father was called Astyles, but the locals say that Euthymus was the son, not of this man, but of the river Caecinus, which divides the territory of Locris from that of Rhegium....[17]

Although Euthymus won the victory in boxing in the 74th Olympiad [484 BCE], he did not win at the next Olympiad. For Theagenes of Thasus wanted to win both the boxing and the *pancration* at the same Olympiad. He beat Euthymus in the boxing but did not have enough strength to win the olive crown in the *pancration* because he was already exhausted by his fight with Euthymus. The umpires penalized Theagenes with a fine of one talent to

---

15 Homer, *Iliad* 19.266–268.

16 The Spartans were debarred from the Olympic games of 420 BCE because they had not paid a fine that had been imposed on them according to Olympic law; see Thucydides 5.49–50.

17 *son...of the Caecinus river*: a legend that probably developed after his heroization, see 8.16 with note.

be paid to Zeus, and another talent to be paid to Euthymus for the harm done to him.[18] They judged that Theagenes had entered the boxing contest merely to spite Euthymus. Because of this, they condemned him to pay the extra fine privately to Euthymus. At the 76th Olympiad [476 BCE] Theagenes paid in full the fine to Zeus... and, as compensation to Euthymus, he did not enter the boxing. Euthymus won the crown for boxing at this festival and at the following one.

> An inscription on the base of his statue at Olympia indicates that Euthymus was posthumously heroized.

8.16 *INSCRIFTEN VON OLYMPIA* 144.

Euthymus of Locri, son of Astycles, after winning three times at
   Olympia,
set up this statue to be admired by mortals.[19]
Euthymus of Locri Epizephyri dedicated it.
Pythagoras of Samos made it.

> Despite his disqualification in the games of 484 BCE, Theagenes went on to win several victories and was later heroized by his fellow citizens. Pausanias tells the story of how his statue was thrown into the sea and the Delphi oracle ordered the people of Thasus to worship the athlete as a god.

8.17 PAUSANIAS 6.11.5–9. The total number of crowns that Theagenes won was one thousand four hundred. After he died, one of his enemies came every night to his statue in Thasus, and whipped the bronze image as if he were flogging Theagenes himself. The statue stopped this outrage by falling upon the man and killing him; whereupon the sons of the dead man prosecuted the statue for murder. The people of Thasus threw the statue into the sea, in accordance with the laws of Draco, who, when he wrote the homicide laws for the Athenians, imposed banishment even upon inanimate objects that fell and killed a person.

In time, however, when the earth did not yield the Thasians' crops, they sent envoys to Delphi, where Apollo instructed them to recall their exiles. Obeying his word, they restored the exiles, but this did not cure the famine. They went to the Pythia a second time, saying that although they had followed the instructions, the anger of the gods was still remained. The Pythia replied: "You do not remember your great Theagenes."

The Thasians were at a loss, unable to think how to recover the statue of Theagenes. They say that fishermen who had put to sea in search of fish happened to catch the statue in their nets and brought it back to land. The Thasians put the statue back in its original position and now they sacrifice to Theagenes as if he were a god. I know of many places, both among the

---

18 *talent*: a large sum of money that was equal to 6000 drachmas.

19 *admired by mortals*: Miller 2004 a: 162–164 notes that these words are a later addition to the inscription, suggesting that Euthymus' heroization was posthumous.

Greeks and barbarians, where statues of Theagenes have been set up and the natives worship and honor him as a healing power.

> A daughter of King Archidamus of Sparta (ruled ?469–427 BCE) was heroized in her home town asthe first woman to own racehorses and win the chariot race at Olympia.[20] Her statue was also set up at Olympia; the inscribed statue base has survived.

8.18 PAUSANIAS 3.15.1. Cynisca, the daughter of King Archidamus of Sparta, has a hero's shrine in the Plane-tree Grove. She was the first woman to raise horses and the first to win a chariot race at Olympia.

8.19 PAUSANIAS 6.1.6. At Olympia, beside the statue of Troilus, is a stone ledge with a chariot and team and a driver and a statue of Cynisca herself by Apelles,[21] and there is an inscription about Cynisca.

8.20 *INSCRIFTEN VON OLYMPIA* 160.

Kings of Sparta were my fathers and brothers.

I, Cynisca, won with a team of fast horses

and erected this statue. I proclaim that I am the only woman in all Greece

to win this crown.

> Although women were forbidden to attend the Olympic games on certain days, *parthenoi* (virgins, as opposed to married women) were permitted as spectators and a priestess watched the games from her seat on an altar.[22]

8.21 PAUSANIAS 5.6.7. Along the road from Scillus to Olympia, before you cross the river Alpheus, there is a precipitous mountain with high cliffs. it is called Mount Typeion. From here it is the law of the Eleans to hurl down any woman whose presence is discovered at the Olympic games, or even on the other side of the river Alpheus, on the forbidden days.

8.22 PAUSANIAS 6.20.8–9. At the end of the row of statues made from the fines imposed on the athletes, there is an entrance called the Hidden Entrance. Through it the umpires and also the competitors enter the stadium. The stadium is a bank of earth, and on it is seating for the presidents. Opposite the umpires is a white marble altar; on this a woman sits and watches the Olympic games, the priestess of Demeter of the Ground, an office awarded by Elis from time to time to different women. Virgins are not barred from watching the games.

> On days that were not forbidden, virgins and women were allowed to sacrifice on the lower level (*prothysis*) of the altar of Zeus.[23]

---

20 As in the case of Lichas (8.14), the owner of the equestrian team was honored, not the driver of the chariot.

21 *Apelles*: famous artist of the late fourth century BCE.

22 On women and athletics, see Dillon 2002: 131–32 and Miller 2004 a: 150–159.

23 On this altar, see 6.7.

8.23 PAUSANIAS 5.13.10. There are stone steps leading from either side to the lower levels, but those going from the lower to the upper part of the altar are composed of ash. Virgins and married women are permitted to go as far as the lower level at times when they are not excluded from Olympia; but only men are permitted to climb from here to the top of the altar.

At the Heraea, a festival in honor of the goddess Hera that was supervised by the Sixteen Women, virgin girls competed in footraces.

8.24 PAUSANIAS 5.16.2–3. Every four years the Sixteen Women weave a robe for Hera, and the same women hold the games that are called Heraea. The games are foot-races for virgin girls. These girls are of different ages: the youngest are the first to run, after them come the next youngest, and the last to run are the oldest maidens. They run with their hair loose and their tunics a little above their knees; their right shoulder is bared as far as the breast. The course for the race is the track of the Olympic stadium, less about a sixth of its length. They give the winners crowns made of olive-branches and a share of the cow sacrificed to Hera; and the girls are permitted to dedicate statues inscribed with their names.

Athenian drama festivals

Each year the Athenians celebrated three drama festivals: the City or Great Dionysia, the Rural Dionysia, and the Lenaea, each in honor of the god Dionysus. By the early fifth century BCE, there were annual competitions for the performance of tragedies, satyr plays, dithyrambs and, after 487/6 BCE, comedies.[24] Drama competitions, like the athletic and musical contests that we have examined, were enacted in a religious context.

The most important of these festivals, the City or Great Dionysia, was celebrated in the month *Elaphoboleion*, at the end of winter and the beginning of the sailing season when a large number of people would have been free

---

24 *dithyrambs*: special hymns in honor of Dionysus performed by two choruses, one of fifty men and the other of fifty boys. *satyr plays*: in the fifth and early fourth centuries BCE, a satyr play followed the performance of three tragedies, all four plays being written by the same author. The chorus consisted of satyrs, legendary wild men displaying animal features (horse's ears and tail) and a phallus, whose wanton and often lascivious behavior was in sharp contrast to that of the tragic chorus. Two satyr plays have survived, Euripides' *Cyclops* and part of Sophocles' *Ichneutae* (Trackers), together with numerous fragments. Since Aristotle, *Poetics* 4.17, reports that tragedy developed from the *saturikon* (some kind of performance by satyrs), it is suggested that satyr plays were introduced into the festival when tragedies included non-Dionysiac material; see OCD entry on satyr plays.

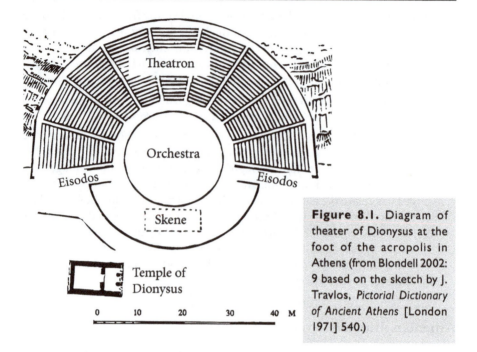

Figure 8.1. Diagram of theater of Dionysus at the foot of the acropolis in Athens (from Blondell 2002: 9 based on the sketch by J. Travlos, *Pictorial Dictionary of Ancient Athens* [London 1971] 540.)

to attend.[25] This festival is generally considered to have been established, or at least elaborated, during the rule of the tyrant Pisistratus (c. 560-527 BCE). Like the Panathenaea, it became an occasion for the city to showcase itself to the Greek world.

After c. 500 BCE dramatic performances were held in the open-air theater of Dionysus that was located within the god's precinct at the foot of the acropolis. The audience was seated on the slopes of the *theatron*, probably originally on the ground, looking down on the *orchestra*, the dancing area where the chorus performed the choral odes. At the front of the *theatron*, on a level with the *orchestra*, were carved stone seats for the judges, the priest of Dionysus, other religious and civic dignitaries, public benefactors, and distinguished foreign visitors. The chorus entered and exited via the two *eisodoi*. The action took place on the *skene* (usually translated as "stage," though it literally means "tent" or "hut") in front of a backdrop that usually represented a palace or house with one or two doors through which the actors entered and exited.

---

25 Scholars have long been divided on the question of whether women were spectators at the plays. The arguments for their presence of Henderson 1991: 133–147 are
   opposed by Goldhill 1994: 347–369. Sourvinou-Inwood 2003: 177–184 maintains that
   "respectable Athenian women" were present at the theatrical performances and that
   they participated in all parts of the City Dionysia, except for the *komos*.

At the Great Dionysia the performances took place over three or more days. Three tragedians were chosen to compete, each offering three tragedies and a satyr play. Most tragic dramas were based on well known myths. Five comic poets each offered a single play. The ten tribes competed with each other, offering two dithyrambs.

The Chief Magistrate (Eponymous Archon) was in charge of the organization of the festival. He selected the playwrights whose plays were to be performed and appointed the citizens who were to be financially responsible for the production of these plays. The *choregus*, or impresario, was a wealthy citizen who undertook the expense of equipping and training both the chorus and actors. This task, known as a "liturgy," was viewed as a civic duty and a mark of honor for the *choregus* and his deme. Since the producers were competing with each other, it was in the interest of the *choregus* to do the best possible job, regardless of expense, for the deme, himself and, of course, the god.

The orator and politician Demosthenes was acting as *choregus* for the performance of a dithyrambic chorus of fifty men. He brought a prosecution against Meidias who, he alleged, had tried to ruin his preparations. Demosthenes emphasizes the desecration of the equipment he had commissioned.

8.25 DEMOSTHENES, *AGAINST MEIDIAS* 16. The sacred garment—indeed, I regard as sacred everything that is being prepared for the festival until after it has been used—that garment and the gold crowns that I was having made for the chorus to wear, he plotted to destroy, gentlemen of Athens, by a night raid on my goldsmith. And he did destroy them, but not completely.

A few days before the festival, the archaic cult statue was taken in a procession from Dionysus' temple near the theater and placed in a small shrine in preparation for the procession into the city.

8.26 PAUSANIAS 1.29.2. Outside the city ...near the Academy[26]... there is a small temple, into which every year on fixed days they carry the image of Dionysus Eleuthereus.

This ritual reflects the story of the initial rejection of the cult, the god's revenge, and his eventual acceptance on the recommendation of the Delphic oracle.

8.27 SCHOLION TO ARISTOPHANES, *ACHARNIANS* 243. Pegasus of Eleutherae (Eleutherae is a *polis* in Boeotia) came to Attica, bringing the statue of Dionysus. The Athenians did not receive the god with honor, but he did not depart from those who took this decision without exacting a price. For the god became enraged and struck the male sexual organs with an incurable disease. Exhausted by the disease, which proved stronger than any human magic and skill, sacred ambassadors were sent to consult

---

26 *Academy*: the public gymnasium in Athens, from which derives the name of the school established there by Plato. It was outside the city, near the Dipylon Gate and the small hill of Colonus.

Apollo. When they returned, they said that the only cure was to introduce the god with all honor. Persuaded by these reports, the Athenians made phalluses privately and publicly, and with these they venerated the god in commemoration of the disease.[27]

> The statue of Dionysus was taken from the temple near the Academy to the altar of the Twelve Gods in the Agora where a *xenismos*, a ritual reception and entertaining a guest or foreigner, was celebrated. An escort of ephebes, accompanied by revellers, then took the statue to the theater probably by night.[28] The statue was placed in the orchestra, the circular space in which the choruses danced as they sang the choral odes.
>
> On the following day, 10 Elaphobolion, there was a public procession to the sanctuary. The myth of Dionysus' revenge for his initial rejection was represented by men carrying models of giant phalluses. Marching in the procession were civic officials, representatives from the different areas of the city, metics (resident aliens) dressed in purple, the producers or impresarios of the plays (*choregoi*), bearers of sacrificial offerings, a young maiden carrying a basket (*kanephoros parthenos*) with the first fruits (*aparchai*), and attendants bringing the sacrificial victims, which would have included at least a bull and cattle probably led by ephebes. The procession was followed by a great sacrifice and a banquet, with the sacrificial meat being distributed to all. The drama competitions took place in the following days, with the statue of Dionysus in place as a spectator at the performances held in his honor.

---

27 *phallus*: an image of the penis, often as erect, that was displayed in rituals generally associated with fertility.

28 See Sourvinou-Inwood 2003: 69–100 for full details of this reconstruction of the ancient evidence.

9. The Gods and Justice from Homer to Aeschylus

9.1 HOMER, *ILIAD* 24.524–533.

> There is no gain to be had from chilling lamentation;
> this is how the gods have spun the thread of fate for us wretched   525
> mortals, to live in grief; but they do not know any sorrow.[1]
> Two storage-jars stand full of gifts in the storeroom of Zeus,
> one of them holding the evils he gives and the other one blessings.
> If Zeus who hurls the thunder-bolt gives someone a mixture
> of both he sometimes meets with evil and sometimes with good.   530
> But if he gives someone only woeful gifts he degrades him;
> evil starvation drives him over the splendid earth,
> and he wanders deprived of honor from gods and mortals alike.

> > At the end of the *Iliad*, Achilles attributes to Zeus the ultimate responsibility
> > for the allocation of good and evil to mortals. At the beginning of the *Odyssey*,
> > however, the poet emphasizes the gods' support for retribution or justified
> > revenge, a concept that becomes a unifying theme of the poem.[2] Zeus
> > deplores the way in which mortals blame the gods for sending evil, remarking
> > that mortals make their troubles worse through their own criminal folly.

9.2 HOMER, *ODYSSEY* 1.26–47.

> While he sat there enjoying the feast, the rest of the gods
> were assembled together within the halls of Olympian Zeus.
> The father of men and gods was the first to speak among them;
> for in his heart he thought of what happened to splendid Aegisthus,

---

1   *spun the thread of fate*: an allusion to Klotho, one of the three Fates; see 1.19.

2   On the different moral climate between the *Iliad* and *Odyssey*, see Lloyd-Jones 1983:
    28–32.

killed by Orestes, Agamemnon's glorious son.[3]   30
Thinking of him he spoke these words among the immortals:
"Oh no! Those mortals are making the gods responsible, saying
all evils come from us, yet they bring pain on themselves
as well, beyond due measure, by their own criminal folly,[4]
like Aegisthus, who recently passed due measure and took to his bed 35
the wedded wife of Atreus' son, whom he killed when he came home,
though he knew it meant sheer doom for him, for we told him ourselves
in advance, sending sharp-eyed Hermes Argeiphontes to tell him
not to kill the man and not to go courting his wife,[5]
for there would be payment to come for Atreus' son from Orestes,   40
when he grew up and desired to return to the land of his birth.
So Hermes spoke, but for all his good intentions he failed
to persuade the mind of Aegisthus; and now he has paid for it all."
   Then grey-eyed Athena, answering him, addressed him in turn:
"Son of Cronus, our father, who rule supreme among rulers,   45
Aegisthus indeed lies dead in a fitting act of destruction;
so too may anyone else be destroyed who does such deeds."

> After killing his wife's suitors, Odysseus tells his aged nurse Eurycleia not
> to exult, saying that their deaths were caused by Destiny and their own
> wicked deeds.

9.3   HOMER, *ODYSSEY* 22.411–416.

"Keep your joy in your heart, old woman; restrain your cries;
it is not pious for us to exult so over the slain.
Destiny sent by the gods overcame these men, and their own
wicked deeds; they treated with honor no human being
upon this earth who crossed their path, whether evil or good;   415
through their own criminal folly they met with this foul fate."[6]

> The gods of the *Odyssey* are not concerned only with justified revenge.
> Zeus is also represented as the protector of strangers and suppliants.
> When Nausicaa, the daughter of King Alcinous of Phaeacia, discovers a

---

3 *Aegisthus*: the lover of Agamemnon's wife, Clytemnestra. Here Aegisthus is held
   responsible for Agamemnon's murder; later, however, the ghost of Agamemnon
   blames Zeus for devising his destruction when, on his return home, he was killed by
   his wife and Aegisthus (*Odyssey* 24.96–97).

4 *criminal folly*: the Greek *atasthalia* means folly or recklessness that we would consider a crime requiring punishment by the state, not a blood relative.

5 *Hermes Argeiphontes*: Hermes, the messenger of the gods, who killed the multiple-
   eyed monster Argos, hence the epithet Argeiphontes (Argos-slayer).

6 *their own criminal folly*: the same Greek word is used much earlier by Zeus (9.2) in
   the context of the killing of Aegisthus. See n. 4 above.

ship-wrecked man who, unbeknownst to her, is Odysseus, she reminds her attendants of the rights of strangers.

9.4   HOMER, *ODYSSEY* 6.206–209.

This miserable wretch has come here to us as a wanderer,
whom we should care for, since all strangers and beggars are sent
by Zeus, and a gift that is small to the giver is friendly to them.
Come, my attendants, and give both food and drink to the stranger.

> Helped by Nausicaa and clothed in a mist of invisibility by the goddess Athena, Odysseus makes his way to the palace, where he supplicates Queen Arete, begging her and Alcinous to help him return to his homeland.

9.5   HOMER, *ODYSSEY* 7.139–171.

But splendid much-enduring Odysseus went through the palace
concealed in the dense mist poured on him by the hand of Athena,[7]   140
until he reached Arete where she sat with king Alcinous
Odysseus threw his arms round the knees of queen Arete,[8]
and that moment the mist supplied by the god flowed from him.
When they saw him everyone in the house fell silent
and looked on him in wonder. Odysseus made his entreaty: 145
"Arete, daughter of Rexanor like to the gods, I am here
having suffered many hardships to supplicate your husband
and you, by your knees, and the guests at your feast here—may the gods
give them
prosperity during their lives, and may each one leave to his children
possessions within his halls and due reward from the people.   150
Arrange an urgent escort to take me home to my fatherland
quickly, for I have long been suffering far from my dear ones."
So speaking he sat down at the hearth in the dust and the ashes
beside the fire.[9] The company all fell silent and still.
At last an old man spoke in their midst, Echeneus the hero;   155
he was an elder among the Phaeacian men and surpassed
the others in speaking, since he knew many ancient traditions;
with good sense he addressed the company, speaking among them:
"Alcinous, it is neither a fine nor a fitting thing

---

7   Throughout the *Odyssey*, Athena is Odysseus' protecting deity; she intervenes in various guises, thus enabling him to overcome all the problems that beset his home-coming.

8   *threw his arms…*: a ritual mode of declaring oneself a suppliant.

9   Odysseus debases himself, as befits a suppliant, by sitting in the ashes of the hearth and thereby placing himself at the focal point of the *oikos*.

for a stranger to sit on the ground at the hearth in the dust and the
   ashes.   160
The others are holding back while they wait to receive your word.
Come, raise up the stranger, seat him upon a chair well wrought
with silver nails, and order the heralds to mix more wine,
to pour in libation to Zeus, the lord of the thunder-bolt,
the god who attends on suppliants, who should be respected;   165
let a housekeeper give him supper too from her stores within."
   When Alcinous, sacred of strength, heard this he took by the hand
intelligent much-devising intricate-minded Odysseus,
raised him from the hearth and had him sit on a gleaming chair
in place of his son, the kindly-hearted Laodamas, who   170
was sitting closest to him, the one that he loved the most.

> After hosting Odysseus, Alcinous offers him gifts and an escort home, though
> he is still ignorant of Odysseus' identity. The offer and acceptance of gifts
> symbolized and affirmed the bond of guest-friendship that would continue
> and be passed on to the descendants of both guest and host.[10]

9.6   HOMER, *ODYSSEY* 8.544–547.

This has all been arranged for the sake of the stranger, who should be
   respected,
the send-off and friendly gifts for him that we give out of friendship.   545
A suppliant stranger's the same as a brother, at least to a man
who has even a little grasp on wisdom within his breast.[11]

> After revealing his identity, Odysseus relates how he supplicated the
> monstrous Cyclops Polyphemus and was repudiated.

9.7   HOMER, *ODYSSEY* 9.266–276.

"But as for us, having reached here we fall at your knees
as suppliants, hoping that you will provide us with guest-friend gifts
or other kinds of gifts, as it's right to do for a stranger.
Respect the gods, most mighty one! We are suppliants;
strangers and suppliants both have their honor protected by Zeus,   270
Zeus Xenios who attends on strangers, who should be respected."
So I spoke; he replied at once, relentless of heart:
"How naive you are, stranger, or else you have come here from far away,
you who urge me to dread the gods or avoid their wrath;

---

10 *guest-friendship*: Greek *xenia*, a bond of hospitality, a relationship between two
   people who are not related by blood but come from different cities or countries.

11 *the same as a brother*: equating guest-friendship with such close kinship indicates the
   importance of the *xenia* concept in the Greek world for both strangers and suppliants.

we Cyclops pay no attention to Zeus who carries the aegis,   275
or the rest of the blessed gods, since we are stronger by far." [12]

> After blinding Polyphemus, Odysseus tells him that this is Zeus' punishment for not respecting the rights of strangers, and for killing and eating several of his companions.

9.8   HOMER, *ODYSSEY* 9.475–479.

"Cyclops, he turned out not to be lacking in strength, the man
whose comrades you ate with mighty force in your hollow cave.   476
Your evil deeds were certainly going to catch up with you,
you stubborn fool, without the reverence to keep you from eating
strangers in your house; so Zeus and the other gods have repaid you."

> In *Works and Days*, a didactic poem addressed to his brother Perses, Hesiod invokes the Muses, the daughters of Zeus. In contrast to Zeus as portrayed in Homer's *Iliad* but consistent with Homer's *Odyssey*, Hesiod's Zeus is concerned with the justice (*dike*) of human actions.

9.9   HESIOD, *WORKS AND DAYS* 1–9.

Muses of Pieria who glorify with song,
come tell of your father Zeus in song;[13]
thanks to him mortal men are both famous and obscure,
known and unknown, by the will of great Zeus.[14]
easily he makes one strong, easily he crushes the strong,   5
easily he lowers the high and raises the lowly,
easily straightens the crooked and withers the proud,
high-thundering Zeus whose home is most high.
Hear me, see and listen, straighten decrees with justice [*dike*].

> The earliest meaning of *dike* is custom, usage, or way, and so it came to mean " the right way," and hence justice. In Hesiod's *Theogony*, Dike (Justice) is the daughter of Zeus by his second wife Themis, whose name means "Right" or "Established Custom." Themis' other children are also listed, including the three Moirae or Fates.

---

12 *pay no attention to Zeus...*: by scorning the gods Polyphemus puts himself outside the norms of civilized behavior, thus justifying Odysseus' subsequent blinding of the monster who imprisons him and his comrades in his cave, killing and eating them one by one. Nonetheless, he incurs the anger of Poseidon, Polyphemus' father, who further delays Odysseus' homecoming.

13 *Pieria*: the area to the north of Mount Olympus that was famous for the cult of the Muses.

14 *by the will of great Zeus*: compare Homer, *Iliad* 1.5, "and the will of Zeus was accomplished."

9.10 HESIOD, *THEOGONY* 901–906.

Second, he married sleek Themis, who bore the Horae,

Eunomia and Dike and blooming Eirene,[15]

who tend the works of mortal men, and the

Moirae, to whom wise Zeus gave most honor,

Klotho and Lachesis and Atropos,[16] who give   905

mortal men to have both good and evil.

> In *Works and Days*, Hesiod personifies Justice as he warns of the dangers
> of doing violence to her.

9.11 HESIOD, *WORKS AND DAYS* 213–219.

Perses, listen to justice and do not foster violence;

for violence is bad for the poor. Even the prosperous

cannot easily bear its burden; they too are weighed down by it,   215

when they encounter disaster.[17] The better path is to go by the other
  route

in the direction of justice. For Justice triumphs over violence

in the end; it is only by suffering that the fool gains understanding.[18]

9.12 HESIOD, *WORKS AND DAYS* 219–231.

For Oath runs quickly alongside crooked judgments (*skoliai dikai*).

There is an uproar when Justice (*Dike*) is dragged to wherever she
  is led   220

by bribe-devouring men as they make judgments with crooked justice.

Weeping, Justice follows to the city and abodes of the people,

clothed in mist, and bringing evil to mortals

who would drive her out since they were not straight with her.

But those who give straight judgments (*itheiai dikai*) to strangers   225

and their own people, without exceeding what is just,

their city blooms, and the people in it flourish.

Peace that nurtures young men exists throughout the land,

and loud-voiced Zeus never decrees cruel war against them.

Those who make straight judgments (*ithudikai*) are not pursued by
  famine   230

or disaster (*ate*). But easily they tend the fields that are their concern.

---

15 *Horae*: the Seasons. *Eunomia*: Lawfulness, abiding by the laws, having good laws.
   Dike: Justice. *Eirene*: Peace.

16 *Klotho*: the Spinner who spins the thread of life. *Lachesis* : the Allotter, who measures
   the thread. *Atropos*: the Unbending One who determines and terminates that thread,
   often by cutting it.

17 *disaster*: *ate*, ruin.

18 *only by suffering…*: cf. below Aeschylus, *Agamemnon* line 178 in 9.19.

9.13 HESIOD, *WORKS AND DAYS* 238–247.

But for those who practice wicked violence and cruel deeds,
Zeus the loud-voiced decrees justice (*dike*).
For often even an entire city suffers because of an evil man   240
who commits an offence and devises criminal acts (*atalastha*).
The son of Cronus sends from heaven great trouble,
famine together with a plague. Then the people perish;
their women do not bear children and their houses dwindle
because of Zeus' contriving. And again, at another time,   245
the son of Cronus destroys their wide army or their wall,
or he robs them of their ships on the sea.

> Hesiod advises rulers to be just because Zeus is the overseer of the
> omnipresent, immortal guardians of justice, including Justice herself.

9.14 HESIOD, *WORKS AND DAYS* 248–269.

You rulers, also mark well for yourselves
this justice; for the immortals are nearby
among human beings, taking note of all who, with crooked
   judgments,   250
oppress one another and disregard the anger of the gods.
For on the bounteous earth Zeus has thirty thousand immortals
watching over human beings;
they keep watch on judgments and cruel deeds.
Clothed in mist, they wander everywhere over the earth.   255
There is also the maiden Justice, daughter of Zeus,
revered and respected among the gods who dwell on Olympus;
whenever anyone harms her with crooked slander,
immediately she sits beside her father Zeus, the son of Cronus,
and tells him of men's unjust intent so that   260
the people pay for the criminal folly (*atalasthia*) of the princes who,
   with evil intent,
give perverted judgments by speaking crookedly.

Guard against this, you princes, give straight judgments,
you who devour bribes; forget completely crooked judgments.
The one who does evil to another does evil to himself,   265
and an evil plan proves most evil for the planner.
The eye of Zeus, seeing and understanding all things,
observes these things too, if he so wills. Nor does it escape his notice
what sort of justice it is that the city keeps within itself.[19]

---

19 Cf. Hesiod, *Works and Days* 105: It is not possible to escape the mind of Zeus, and
Theogony 613: It is not possible to deceive or surpass the mind of Zeus.

Solon, the late seventh to early sixth century BCE Athenian poet and lawgiver, examines the ways in which Zeus enforces justice, concluding that sooner or later retribution will come. As Lloyd-Jones notes, "Solon takes an Odyssean and not an Iliadic view of divine motivation; he denies that the gods put evil thoughts into men's minds, and puts the responsibility for action fairly and squarely on the human agent."[20]

9.15 SOLON, Frag. 1.1–43 Diehl.

Radiant daughters of Mnemosyne (Memory) and Olympian Zeus,

Muses of Pieria, hear my prayer.[21]

Grant me prosperity from the blessed gods and

from all mortals a good reputation.

Make me pleasing to my friends, but fearsome to my enemies;   5

to the former one to be respected, but to the latter one who is terrible to behold.

Wealth I long to have, but am unwilling to obtain it unjustly.

For Justice always comes afterward.

The riches that the gods give to a man remain firmly his,

from the deepest root to the highest peak.   10

But wealth that is sought with violence comes all disordered;

persuaded by unjust deeds, it follows

unwillingly. Ruin (*ate*) is soon a part of the mix.

The beginning comes from a small thing, like a fire

— a trifle at first, it ends in disaster.   15

Human deeds of violence do not endure for long.

But Zeus looks to the end of everything, and this happens suddenly.

Just as a spring gale quickly scatters the clouds,

stirring up the depths of the billowing unwearied sea,

and ravaging the fair-worked fields throughout the grain-bearing land;   20

then it reaches the high heavens, the seat of the gods,

making the air clear again.

Then the goodly strength of the sun shines on the fertile earth,

and not a cloud is to be seen.

Such is the retribution of Zeus. He is not,   25

like a mortal, quick to anger at each and every thing;

but always and unceasingly, he is aware of the one

who has evil in his heart. That individual is found out in the end.

One pays immediately, another later; some, indeed, escape,

---

20 Lloyd-Jones 1983: 44.

21 *Muses of Pieria*: cf. the invocation at the beginning of Hesiod's *Works and Days*, 9.9.

and they themselves do not suffer what the gods have destined
   for them.   30
Still, it does arrive: the innocent pay for their deeds,
either their children or their posterity.
This is the way that we mortals are minded, whether we are good or bad.
Each of us thinks the way he always has
until he experiences some trouble. Then he immediately laments.   35
Before that, we rejoice in vain hopes, open-mouthed.
A man who oppressed by a grievous illness
believes that he will become healthy.
Another who is a coward thinks himself brave.
One who is ugly thinks himself handsome.   40
One who has no money and is constrained by poverty
always seems to be on the point of having much wealth.
Everyone has his own agenda.

> At the conclusion of the poem, Solon declares that Moira, Fate or Destiny, brings both good and evil and, like other gifts of the gods, cannot be avoided.

9.16 SOLON, Frag. 1. 63–76 Diehl.

Indeed Fate brings to mortals both evil and good,
and the gifts of the immortal gods are inescapable.
There is danger in every kind of business, nor does anyone know   65
at the beginning of a project how it is going to turn out.
Sometimes a man who strives to do well falls
unawares into great and terrible ruin (*ate*),
whereas to one who does evil god gives in all things
good fortune to deliver him from folly.   70
No stated end is prescribed for wealth.
Those of us who have the greatest life today
are doubly eager; who could satisfy everyone?
The immortals give possessions to mortals,
but from these appears Ruin (*ate*), coming now to one   75
then to another, whenever Zeus sends it in retribution.

> Herodotus attributes another reflection to Solon.

9.17 SOLON (as cited in Herodotus, *Histories* 1.32). Where human affairs are concerned, I know that the divine (*to theion*) is envious of human prosperity and likes to cause trouble....

But whoever has the greatest number of advantages that I have mentioned, keeps them to the end, and dies a good death, that man, in my opinion, deserves to be called happy. In every matter, one must look to the end to see how it will turn out. For often god (*theos*) gives a man a glimpse of prosperity before utterly ruining him.

> As we saw at the end of the previous chapter, the Athenians annually celebrated the City or Great Dionysia, a drama festival in honor of Dionysus at which the god's statue was prominently displayed. Three authors competed for a prize, each offering three tragedies that were usually based on well known myths. However, as Sourvinou-Inwood argues, for the fifth-century BCE audience these tragedies were not a "purely theatrical experience" but rather a "ritual performance." Greek tragedy, moreover, was a "discourse of religious exploration" that was "intimately connected with the ritual context in which tragedies were performed, and within which tragedy had been generated."[22]

> One basic part of that ritual and religious exploration was performed by the chorus, a group of twelve or fifteen male actors. They performed as a unit, dancing in the orchestra as they sang odes to the accompaniment of appropriate musical instruments.

> The poet Aeschylus (c. 525–456 BCE) is said to have called his tragedies "rich slices from the banquet of Homer."[23] In the *Oresteia*, a trilogy that won first prize at the Great Dionysia of 458 BCE, Aeschylus explores the story of the murder of Agamemnon by his wife Clytemnestra and the avenging of their father's death by Orestes who thereby commits the crime of matricide. Underlying these murders is the ancestral curse on Agamemnon's family. In the previous generation Thyestes had seduced the wife of Atreus, the father of Agamemnon. Atreus invited his brother to a feast where Thyestes dined off the flesh of his own children who had been killed by Atreus. In the next generation, Agamemnon had sacrificed his daughter Iphigenia before he could sail to Troy. While Agamemnon was besieging Troy, Clytemnestra was seduced by Aegisthus, Thyestes' son.

> At the beginning of *Agamemnon*, before Agamemnon's return from Troy, the chorus of Greek elders foreshadow the gods' retribution, especially that of Zeus.

9.18   AESCHYLUS, *AGAMEMNON* 55–71.

Chorus

On high Apollo, or Pan, or Zeus   55
hears the shrill bird-cry
of their fellow sky-dwellers, and sends on
the transgressors the Erinys,
the one who brings punishment, though late.[24]

---

22 Sourvinou-Inwood 2003: 1 and 4.

23 Athenaeus, *Deipnosophists* 347e.

24 *Pan*: a minor god, who originated in Arcadia; he was represented as half man and half goat. His shrine in Athens was in a cave at the base of the acropolis: see 14.7. *Erinys*: the avenging Fury, who punishes those who have murdered their own kin.

And so the sons of Atreus are sent   60
against Alexander by the one who is more powerful,
Zeus Xenios.²⁵ Because of a woman of many men,
he will ordain many struggles that weary the limbs,
as the knee is brought low in the dust and the spear-shaft shattered
in the preliminaries before the sacrificial offering.²⁶   65
This he will ordain for Greeks and Trojans alike. The matter
is wherever it is now; and it will be fulfilled to its destined end.
Not by burnt sacrifices, nor by libations
nor offerings that know no fire   70
will he assuage the inexorable anger.²⁷

The chorus reflect on the mystery and power of Zeus.

9.19 AESCHYLUS, *AGAMEMNON* 160–183.

Chorus

Zeus, whoever he is, if this name   160
pleases him when invoked,
by this name I invoke him.
I am unable to compare him—
though I've pondered all things—
to anyone but Zeus, if this fruitless burden   165
may truly be cast from my mind.²⁸

...

But the one who eagerly sings of Zeus' triumph
will hit the target of complete understanding.   175
For it was Zeus who put men on the road to understanding
by ordaining that understanding
comes through suffering.²⁹
In place of sleep, pain flows into the heart,

---

25 *sons of Atreus*: Agamemnon and Menelaus. *Alexander*: also known as Paris, the son of King Priam of Troy. Paris abducted Helen, the wife of King Menelaus of Sparta. *Zeus Xenios*: in the context of revenge for the abduction of Helen by Alexander/Paris, Zeus is appropriately styled as Xenios, the guardian and protector of hosts and guests.

26 *woman of many men*: Helen. *sacrificial offering*: a metaphor for the destruction of Troy.

27 *he…*: Alexander/Paris will not be able to appease the anger of the gods who have determined that Troy will be destroyed.

28 *fruitless burden*: Zeus is the only means of relief from the fears that the Chorus has expressed.

29 Cf. Hesiod, *Works and Days* 218, in 9.11.

bringing the remembrance of woes.   180
And discretion comes,[30] even to those who are unwilling.
There is a violent grace that comes from the gods
sitting on the dread helmsman's bench.[31]

> Immediately before Agamemnon's triumphant return from Troy, the chorus
> again sings of retribution.

9.20 AESCHYLUS, *AGAMEMNON* 750–781.

Chorus

Among mortals there has long been an ancient saying   750
that a man's prosperity,
when it grows to greatness,
produces offspring and does not die childless.
From good fortune there springs   755
insatiable grief for a family.
I am apart from others in my thinking.
The impious deed
breeds greater ones as its progeny,
each like its own stock.[32]   760
It is ever the destiny of just and upright households
to produce fair offspring.

Ancient excess (*hybris*) tends to produce
excess that renews itself
in the evil deeds of mortals,   765
sooner or later,
whenever the appointed time for birth arrives;
an incontestable, invincible spirit
is produced, unholy recklessness
that is black ruin (*ate*) for the house,   770
in the image of its parents.

But Justice shines
in smoke-filled houses,
honoring the righteous life.   775
Halls that are bedecked with gold

---

30 *discretion*: the Greek verb *sophronein* means to think moderately or safely.

31 *helmsman's bench*: a metaphor for the seat of ultimate power.

32 An allusion to the curse upon the family of Agamemnon as a result of his father
Atreus' punishment of his brother Thyestes by killing the latter's children and feast-
ing him on their flesh.

by unclean hands she abandons with averted eyes,

as she goes to what is holy.[33]

She does not respect the power of wealth

that is falsely stamped by praise.   780

And she guides all things to their end.

> The chorus laments the murder of Agamemnon, recognizing while also
> questioning that this is Zeus' will.

9.21 AESCHYLUS, *AGAMEMNON* 1485–1488.

Chorus

Woe, woe, for the action of Zeus

who is responsible for all things.

For what is fulfilled for mortals without Zeus?

Which of these things is not brought about by the gods?

> In an earlier play, *Suppliant Maidens* (precise date unknown, but probably
> produced after 467 BCE), the chorus sing of the desire (*himeros*) of Zeus.

9.22 AESCHYLUS, *SUPPLIANT MAIDENS* 86–100.[34]

Chorus

May the desire of Zeus, if it is truly of Zeus,

dispose well; for it is not easy to track.[35]

Dim and shadowy stretch   93

the pathways of his mind,

beyond understanding to perceive.   95

It falls safely, not on its back,   91

if matters are decreed to fulfillment by the nod of Zeus.

It flares everywhere,   88

even in the darkness with black fortune for the race of mortals.   90

He hurls mortals utterly   96

from their high towered hopes,

but uses no violence.

Everything of the gods is effortless.   100

Sitting where he is, from his sacred throne

he somehow causes his purpose to be accomplished completely.

---

33 *unclean hands*: an allusion to Atreus' murder of his brother's sons and probably also
   to Agamemnon's murder of Iphigenia.

34 Teubner text, edited by Martin L. West 1998, kindly translated by Shirley Barlow.

35 *desire of Zeus*: the Greek *himeros* denotes a stronger force than that of Zeus' will
   (*boule*) that determined the fate of Troy (Homer, *Iliad* 1.5).

In the second part of the *Oresteia*, Agamemnon's children Electra and Orestes are reunited. On recognizing her brother, Electra cries out for vengeance.

9.23 AESCHYLUS, *LIBATION BEARERS* 244–245.

Electra

Only may Power and Justice, together with Zeus

as the third and mightiest of all, be on your side!

Orestes trusts in the power of Apollo and the oracle ordering him to avenge Agamemnon's murder.

9.24 AESCHYLUS, *LIBATION BEARERS* 269–284.

Orestes

Loxias' mighty oracle, which bids me pass through this danger,

will never betray me.[36]   270

With many loud cries, Loxias named chilling plagues

to freeze my warm heart,

if I do not take vengeance on those guilty of my father's murder.

In the same way it tells me to take life for life,

enraged by loss of my possessions.   275

With my own dear life, he said,

I would pay this debt, suffering many terrible evils,

For he spoke revealing to mortals the anger

of the malignant powers from beneath the earth, and telling of plagues:

ulcers assaulting the flesh with savage jaws,   280

a canker devouring its original nature.

And upon this disease a white hairs would grow.

And he spoke of other assaults of the Erinyes,

caused by the shedding of my father's blood.[37]

For the dark arrows of the infernal powers,   285

who seek vengeance for those who were slain by their family,

madness, and groundless fears in the night disturb and torment

the man who sees clearly, though he moves his eyebrows in the dark.

And so he is pursued out of the city, his body maimed by the bronze

    whip.   290

Such a person shall have no share in the festal bowl

in the pouring of libations.

The unseen anger of his father bars him from the altar.[38]

No one may receive or stay with such a person,

---

36 *Loxias*: Delphic Apollo.

37 *Erinyes*: avenging furies.

38 Cf. the curse on the polluted murderer of Laius, 4.26.

but he shall die friendless, dishonored by all, 295
terribly shriveled by a death that wastes him.
These were the oracles and surely I must trust them.
Even if I do not trust them, the deed must still be done.

> The Chorus, Orestes and Electra unite to make contact with the ghost of Agamemnon.

9.25 AESCHYLUS, *LIBATION BEARERS* 306–337.

Chorus

Come, mighty Fates, through Zeus
grant fulfilment,
even as now Justice turns!
"For hateful words let hateful words
be fulfilled." As she demands her due, 310
the voice of Justice cries aloud.
"For murderous blow let murderous blow atone."
"Let the doer suffer."
Such is the thrice-aged story that proclaims these words.

Orestes

Father, o unhappy father, 315
what word or deed
can I send to you on the breezes from above,
there where you lie in your resting place,
a light opposing the darkness.
Yet a funeral lament that brings them honor 320
is nonetheless welcome
to the sons of Atreus who lie before this house.

Chorus

My son, the mind
of the dead man is not subdued
by the ravening jaws of the fire. 325
Though late, he makes his anger clear.
The dead man is bewailed,
the punisher is revealed.
The lament due to fathers
and parents makes its search 330
when loudly raised.

Electra

Hear then, father, as we mourn
with copious tears.

Your two children bewail you
with a dirge at your tomb.   335
As suppliants and exiles alike,
your tomb has received them.

> After killing Clytemnestra and Aegisthus, Orestes accepts responsibility for
> matricide, but declares that it was authorized by Apollo.

9.26 AESCHYLUS, *LIBATION BEARERS* 1026–1039.

Orestes

While I am still in my right mind, I proclaim to my friends
and declare that not without justice did I kill my mother,
the polluted killer of my father, an object of hatred to the gods.
And I count as the author of the spell that produced this boldness
the prophet of Pytho, Loxias, whose oracle told me   1030
that if I did this deed I should be free of guilt,
but if I failed to do this—I will not utter the penalty;
for no man's arrow will reach such woes.
And now behold me, and see how, armed
with this branch and garland, I shall approach   1035
the shrine at earth's navel, the domain of Loxias,
and the light of the fire that is called everlasting,
a fugitive because of the shedding of the blood of my kin. To no other
  hearth
did Loxias bid me turn.

> In the opening scene of *Eumenides,* the third part of the trilogy, Orestes,
> pursued by his mother's Furies, has taken refuge in the temple of Apollo
> at Delphi.[39]

9.27 AESCHYLUS, *EUMENIDES* 64–93.

Apollo

I will not betray you; your guardian to the end,
whether by your side or far away,   65
I shall not be gentle to your enemies.

...

Do not grow weary as you struggle
in this ordeal; but go the city of Pallas.
Sit there, and take her ancient image in your arms.[40]   80
There we will have judges of your case and words
to charm them, and we will find the means

---

39 See Figure 6.1 for illustration of Orestes at Delphi.

40 *city of Pallas*: Athens where there was an ancient wooden statue of Pallas Athena.

to release you completely from this suffering.

For I am the one who persuaded you to kill your mother.

Orestes

Lord Apollo, you know how to be just;   85

but since you have that understanding, learn also not to be neglectful!

Your strength to do good is your surety.

Apollo

Remember, do not let fear overcome your mind.

You, Hermes, my brother and son of the same father,

guard him; be true to your title,   90

be his escort and guide this suppliant of mine.[41]

For Zeus respects the sanctity of outlaws

that comes to mortals with an auspicious escort.[42]

> Orestes is acquitted by the casting vote of Athena, who addresses the Furies.

9.28 AESCHYLUS, *EUMENIDES* 794–799.

Athena: Trust me, and do not bear ill-will!

For you are not defeated, but in equal votes   795

the trial resulted in the truth, and did not dishonor you.[43]

There was clear testimony from Zeus,

and he who gave the oracle was himself a witness,[44]

so that Orestes should not be harmed because of his deed.

---

41 *your title*: Hermes was known as *Pompaios*, the one who escorted or guided travellers.

42 *outlaws*: an allusion to Zeus as the protector of suppliants and strangers.

43 *dishonor*: the word *atimia* also means a loss of civic rights. Thus Athena is declaring that Orestes is no longer an outlaw.

44 *he who gave the oracle*: Apollo

10. The Gods in Sophocles and Euripides

10.1 SOPHOCLES, *ANTIGONE* 450–457.

It was not Zeus who made this proclamation;
nor was it Justice dwelling with the gods below
who set in place such laws for humankind,
nor did I think your proclamations had such strength
that, mortal as you are, you could outrun those laws
that are the gods', unwritten and unshakable.
Their laws are not for now or yesterday, but live
forever; no one knows when first they came to light.

> In the above excerpt from Sophocles' *Antigone* (first produced 442/1 BCE), Oedipus' daughter Antigone is addressing King Creon, whose proclamation she has defied when she buried the body of her slain brother Polynices. In *Women of Trachis* (first produced possibly 438–432 BCE), Hercules, the son of Zeus and Alcmena, is dying in agony as a result of a poisoned garment innocently given him by his wife. In his delirium, he has ordered that he be burned alive on a funeral pyre. At the end of the play, Heracles' son Hyllus blames Zeus for these terrible events.

10.2 SOPHOCLES, *WOMEN OF TRACHIS* 1264–1278.

Hyllus

Attendants, lift him.[1] Grant to me
great compassion in what I now do.   1265
For you see how little compassion the gods
have for what has happened.
They begot us and are called our fathers,

---

1 *lift him*: Hyllus is asking the attendants to lift the dying Hercules onto the pyre.

yet they bear the sight of such suffering.

No one foresees what is to come.   1270

What is happening now is pitiful for us,

and shameful for the gods.

But of all men it is hardest for him

who has suffered this ruin.

Do not be left behind at the house, maiden.[2]   1275

You have seen strange and mighty deaths

and sufferings, many and terrible.

And there is none of it that is not Zeus.

> In Sophocles' *King Oidipous* (first produced probably between 430 and 428
> BCE), Oedipus is brought to the realization that he has fulfilled his destiny
> by killing his father Laius and marrying his mother Jocasta. The underlying
> theme of the play is the awful and inexorable power of destiny or fate.
> Despite his best intentions, Oedipus was bound to fulfill this terrible fate
> that Apollo's oracle had revealed to his parents even before his conception.
> The chorus invokes the gods when they hear the news that the oracle of
> Apollo has declared that the cause of the plague afflicting the city is the
> pollution caused by the presence of the murderer of King Laius.

10.3   SOPHOCLES, *KING OIDIPOUS* 151–215.

Chorus

O sweet-spoken Voice of Zeus,

with what meaning have you come

from gold-rich Pytho to gleaming Thebes?[3]

Mind racked with fear, I quiver with dread,

Delian Paian to whom we cry aloud,[4] in awe at you.   155

What debt will you ordain—something new,

or one that returns as the seasons revolve?

Tell me, child of golden Hope, immortal Voice!

I call first on you, daughter of Zeus,

   immortal Athena.

I beseech too your sister Artemis, our land's support,   160

who sits on her glorious circular throne

in the market-place, and far-shooting Apollo.

---

2   *maiden*: Hyllus addresses the leader of the chorus, in preparation for their exit and
   the end of the play.

3   *Pytho*: Delphi.

4   *Delian Paian*: a healing god who is closely associated and often identified with
   Apollo. Delos was the place of the birth of Apollo and Artemis. Apollo is invoked
   here as the god of healing, not as the oracular god of Delphi.

Appear to me as three-fold protectors from doom,
if you banished the flames of disaster
When doom rushed over our city   165
in the past, come now as well!

....

Grant that raging Ares, who flames at me now,
attacking without the bronze of shields,[5]   191
surrounded by screaming,
turn his back on my fatherland
and run rushing in retreat.

....

Oh you who wield the power
of fire-bearing lightning,   200
oh father Zeus, destroy him
with your thunderbolt!
Lycian lord, I also wish
the invincible arrows
from your gold-spun bowstring   205
to spread out, stationed in our defense,[6]
and the fire-bearing gleam of Artemis' torches,
with which she darts through the Lycian mountains;[7]
and I call on the god of the golden head-dress,
who shares his name with this land,   210
Bacchus, face flushed with wine,
companion of the Maenads,
whose worshipers cry aloud, Euoi,[8]
to approach us flaming with gleaming pine-torch
and attack the god dishonored among gods.[9]   215

---

5 *raging Ares, who flames...*: Ares, the god of war, is (mistakenly) envisaged by the
   chorus as the god who has sent the plague.

6 *Lycian lord*: Apollo.

7 *Lycia*: a region in the southwest of modern Turkey that is often associated with
   Apollo and Artemis.

8 *who shares his name...*: an allusion to Dionysus'/Bacchus' birth in Thebes; thus, the
   god is called Theban, and Thebes "Bacchic." *Maenads*: frenzied women, devotees of
   Dionysus. *Euoi*: the ritual cry of bacchic worshipers.

9 *the god dishonored...*: as god of war, Ares was hated by the other gods.

After the blind seer Tiresias has declared that Oedipus is the killer of Laius,[10] the chorus is torn between believing the prophet and their trust in Oedipus, their king.

10.4   SOPHOCLES, *KING OIDIPOUS* 498–506.

Chorus

Zeus and Apollo have understanding
and knowledge of mortal affairs;
among men, though, there's no true way to judge   500
if a prophet's worth more than I am.
A man may outstrip cleverness
with cleverness of his own.
But I for one will never assent
to his critics before I see   505
their words prove to be right.[11]

As Oedipus begins to realize that there may be some truth in Tiresias' declaration that he is the murderer of Laius, his wife Jocasta (the widow of Laius and also his mother) tries to alleviate his fears but, in so doing, she reveals several clues that only confirm the truth of the prophet's words.

10.5   SOPHOCLES, *KING OIDIPOUS* 707–725.

Jocasta

Release yourself from fear about the matters that
you're speaking of. Listen to me and learn that there's
no mortal creature sharing in prophetic skill.
I shall reveal to you brief evidence of this: 710
an oracle once came to Laius—I won't say
from Phoebus, but from Phoebus' servants—saying that
his destiny would be to perish at the hand[12]
of any child that would be born to him and me.
And yet, the story goes, some foreign robbers killed   715
him one day at a junction where three highways meet;
as for our child, three days had not passed since his birth
when Laius yoked his feet and threw him out, at someone
else's hand, on the untrodden mountainside.
So Phoebus did not bring to pass that he should be   720
his father's murderer, or Laius suffer at
his own child's hand—the awful thing he feared; yet this

---

10 On Oedipus' appeal to Tiresias, see 5.7.

11 *his critics*: those who believe the words of Tiresias that Oedipus is the murderer of Laius.

12 *his destiny would be to perish*: note the inevitability of this prophecy.

is what the words of prophecy marked out for them.
So pay them no attention; if a god seeks what
he needs, he'll easily uncover it himself.[13]   725

Jocasta declares her contempt for prophecy.

10.6   SOPHOCLES, *KING OIDIPOUS* 848–858.

Jocasta

Know well this *is* the story that he brought to light;[14]
it is impossible that he disown it now,
since all the city heard these things, not I alone.   850
But even if he deviates from what he said
back then, he never will reveal that it is true,
my lord, that Laius' murder was predicted right,
For Loxias expressly said that he must die
at my son's hands; yet it was never my unhappy   855
child that killed him, since the infant perished first.[15]
Therefore, as far as prophecy's concerned, I would
in future not look this way as opposed to that.

The chorus express their piety and reflect on *hybris* and injustice.[16]

10.7   SOPHOCLES, *KING OIDIPOUS* 863–910.

Chorus

May destiny be at my side
as I bear reverence and purity
in all my words and deeds,   865
under those laws set up, lofty of foot,
born in heaven's bright air,
which have no father but Olympus;
the mortal nature of men did not
give them their birth, nor shall   870
forgetfulness ever put them to sleep;
the god in them is great and untouched by age.[17]

---

13 *he'll easily uncover it*: ironically Jocasta herself has already begun the revelation of
   the truth by mentioning the murder of Laius at a place where three roads meet, and
   the exposed child's yoked feet.

14 *the story that he brought to light*: a house-slave escaped the scene of Laius' murder
   and reported it in Thebes. Oedipus has sent for this man.

15 *Loxias*: Apollo.

16 *hybris*: excessive, outrageous behavior.

17 Cf. the divine laws described in Sophocles, *Antigone* 450–457, in 10.1.

Outrage (*hybris*) gives birth to kings;[18]
surfeited in futile folly
with much that is inopportune,   875
disadvantageous, outrage mounts
to the topmost pinnacle and plunges
down necessity's precipice,
where feet are useless.
Yet I pray that god may never break up   880
the contest that's good for the city;
never shall I cease to have god as my champion.

But if someone travels
haughtily in hand or word,
unfearful of Justice, not revering   885
the seats of divinities,
may an evil destiny seize him
for his ill-destined decadence,
unless his profits are reaped justly
and he abstains from irreverence,   890
or if he clings in wicked folly
to that which is untouchable.[19]
What man in that case will succeed
in warding off the arrows of rage from his life?
For if such deeds are held in honor   895
why should I dance for the gods?[20]

I will no longer reverently go
to earth's untouchable navel,
or to the temple at Abae,
or that of Olympia,[21]   900

---

18 In the following lines, Sophocles personifies *hybris*, imagining her climbing to the top of a mountain, overbalancing and being thrown down by the momentous effort of her ascent.

19 *untouchable*: unholy, impious.

20 *why should I dance for the gods?*: with this question the chorus express their doubts about continuing to honor gods who sanction such impious deeds as those that Oedipus seems to have committed. Dance is part of the ritual and, as they utter these words, the chorus members are dancing as well as singing.

21 *earth's untouchable navel*: an allusion to the *omphalos* at Delphi. *Abae*: a town near Delphi, where there was also an oracle of Apollo. *Olympia*: the site of an oracle of Zeus, in addition to being the venue for the Olympic games.

if these prophecies don't fit together
for every mortal hand to point to.
Rather, oh Zeus ruling in power,
if you are rightly so addressed, lord of all,
may you and your immortal rule   905
not rest unaware of this.
For people are already dismissing
the oracles about Laius—they decay;
Apollo no longer stands conspicuous in honor;
and godliness has vanished.[22]   910

> The chorus reflects on the futility of human life.

10.8   SOPHOCLES, *KING OIDIPOUS* 1186–1195.

Chorus

Ah, generations of mortals,
how I count your lives
as equal to nothingness!
For who, what man gains more of happiness
than just enough to think he's so,   1190
then sink like the setting sun?
Taking your fate from god,
yours, as my exemplar,
yours, poor wretched Oedipus,
I count no mortal thing as blessed.   1195

> In Euripides' *Hippolytus*, one of his earlier plays (428 BCE), the action is
> driven by Aphrodite and her anger because Hippolytus, the bastard son
> of the King Theseus, reviles her and will only acknowledge the power of
> Artemis, goddess of virginity. In Homer's *Iliad* we saw the awesome power
> of Aphrodite when Helen tried to disobey the goddess.[23] In Euripides' play,
> Aphrodite will cause Hippolytus' death and that of the innocent Phaedra,
> Theseus' wife, by causing her to fall in love with her stepson and ultimately
> commit suicide.
>
> At the beginning of the play, Aphrodite, goddess of procreation, reveals
> the entire plot.

---

22 *godliness*: *ta theia*, literally divine things, the things of the gods. On the chorus'
  outburst, Flower 2008: 19 remarks, "The chorus is so psychologically invested in
  its system of religious beliefs and practices that it would rather that Laius had been
  killed by his own son, as Apollo had long predicted..., than by a stranger."

23 See 2.15.

10.9 EURIPIDES, *HIPPOLYTUS* 1–23.

Aphrodite

I am powerful and not without a name among mortals
and within the heavens. I am called the goddess Cypris.[24]
Of those who dwell within Pontus
and the boundaries of Atlas and see the light of the sun,[25]
I treat well those who revere my power,   5
but I trip up those who are proud towards me.[26]
For this principle holds among the race of the gods also:
they enjoy being honored by mortals.
I shall now show the truth of these words:
Theseus' son Hippolytus, the Amazon's offspring,   10
reared by pure Pittheus—
he alone of the citizens of this land of Trozen
says that I am by nature the most vile of divinities.
He spurns the bed and doesn't touch marriage,[27]
but honors Apollo's sister, Artemis, the daughter of Zeus,   15
considering her the greatest of divinities.
Always consorting with the virgin through the green wood,
he rids the land of beasts with swift dogs,[28]
having come upon a more than mortal companionship.
I don't begrudge them these things; why should I?[29]   20
But I will punish Hippolytus this day
for the wrongs he has done me. I won't need much toil,
since long before this I prepared most of what has to be done.

10.10 EURIPIDES, *HIPPOLYTUS* 38–50.

Aphrodite

And now the poor woman [Phaedra], moaning and overwhelmed
by the goads of passion, is dying

---

24 *Cypris*: a common name of Aphrodite, reflecting her connection with the island of Cyprus.

25 *Pontus*: the Black Sea area. *boundaries of Atlas*: the straits of Gibraltar ...thus including the entire Mediterranean world.

26 *proud*: the Greek *phronousi mega* implies hybris, arrogance because Hippolytus refuses to acknowledge Aphrodite's power.

27 Worship of Aphodite involves not only ritual observance but also participation in her realm.

28 Artemis is associated with hunting and the wild.

29 *I don't begrudge them...*: Hippolytus can worship Artemis if he wishes, but Aphrodite also demands recognition of her divine power.

in silence—none of the household knows her disease.   40
But not like this is this love destined to turn out;
I will reveal the matter to Theseus and it will be brought[30]
to light. As for the young man who wars against me,
his father will kill him with the curses the lord of the sea,
Poseidon, gave to Theseus as a gift,   45
that he could pray to the god three times not in vain.
Phaedra will keep her good reputation,
but still she will die. For I do not value her suffering more
than my enemy's paying me
such a penalty that I am satisfied.   50

> On entering, Hippolytus immediately invokes Artemis.

10.11 EURIPIDES, *HIPPOLYTUS* 59–71.

Hippolytus

Follow me, follow, hymning
the child of Zeus, heavenly Artemis, who cares for us.   60

Hippolytus and Attendants

Lady, lady, most revered,
offspring of Zeus,
hail, I say, hail, daughter
of Leto and Zeus, Artemis,   65
most beautiful by far of maidens,
you who in the expanse of heaven
dwell in the hall of your great father,
in the gold-rich house of Zeus.
Hail, I say, most beautiful,   70
most beautiful of those on Olympus.

> One of the servants, a slave in Theseus' house, begs Aphrodite to ignore Hippolytus' parting remark, "But to that Cypris of yours I say good riddance."

10.12 EURIPIDES, *HIPPOLYTUS* 114–120.

Servant

The young when they think that way
should not be imitated. But I, as is fitting for slaves to speak,   115
will pray to your statue,
mistress Cypris; and you should be forgiving.

---

30 *reveal the matter to Theseus*: Phaedra commits suicide, leaving a note in which she alleges that Hippolytus violated her. Theseus believes this and curses his son, invoking Poseidon.

If someone because of his youth has an intense spirit
and speaks rashly about you, pretend not to hear him;
for gods ought to be wiser than mortals.[31]   120

> The chorus sings of the destructive power of Eros (physical desire).

10.13 EURIPIDES, *HIPPOLYTUS* 525–532.

Chorus

Eros, Eros, you who drip desire   525
down into the eyes as you lead sweet delight
into the souls of those you war against,
never may you appear to me with harm
or come out of measure.
For the shaft neither of fire nor of the stars is superior   530
to Aphrodite's, which Eros, the son of Zeus,
sends forth from his hands.

> Near the end of the play, when news is brought that Hippolytus is dying,
> the chorus sing of Aphrodite's power.

10.14 EURIPIDES, *HIPPOLYTUS* 1268–1281.

Chorus

You lead the unbending mind of gods and of mortals captive,
Cypris, and along with you is
the one with many-colored wings,[32] encompassing them   1270
with his very swift wing;
Eros flies over the earth
and over the sweet-echoing briny sea,
and he bewitches anyone whose maddened heart
he rushes against, winged and gold-shining—   1275
the young of the mountains and those of the sea,
whatever the earth nourished
and the blazing sun looks upon,
and men; over all of these, Cypris,
you alone hold sway in royal power.   1280

> The goddess Artemis appears on the roof of the stage building (*skene*) in front
> of which the human drama is being enacted. She is suspended by a *mechane*,
> a crane-like device, hence the expression "the god from the machine" (*deus
> ex machina*). The goddess addresses Theseus.

---

31 *for gods ought to be wiser …*: cf. the remark of Cadmus at the end of *Bacchae* line
1348 in 10.32: "Gods ought not to be like mortals in their passions."

32 *the one with many-colored wings*: Eros.

10.15 EURIPIDES, *HIPPOLYTUS* 1325–1341.

Artemis

You did terrible things, but even so	1325
it is still possible for you to obtain forgiveness even of them;	
for Cypris wanted these things to happen,	
sating her desire.[33] This is the custom of the gods:	
no one is willing to oppose the desire	
of whoever wants something, but we always stand aloof.	1330
For—I know this well—if I hadn't feared Zeus	
I would never have come to this degree of disgrace,[34]	
to allow the dearest to me of all mortals	
to die. But first of all your not knowing	
frees your error from wickedness;	1335
and then your wife in dying did away with	
the refutation of her words, so that she persuaded your mind.	
These evils then have burst upon you especially,	
but it is painful for me too; for the gods do not enjoy it	
when the pious die, but we destroy	1340
the base along with their children and houses.[35]	

> Artemis promises the dying Hippolytus that he will be worshiped as a hero.

10.16 EURIPIDES, *HIPPOLYTUS* 1423–1430.

Artemis

But to you, o miserable one, in return for these ills,	
I will give the greatest honors in the city	
of Trozen: unyoked maidens before marriage	1425
will cut of locks of their hair for you,[36] who over a long time	
will enjoy the fruits of their tears' deepest mourning.	
Always the maidens will be inspired to sing songs	
about you, and Phaedra's love for you will not	
fall away nameless and be kept silent.	

---

33 *terrible things*: Theseus believed Phaedra's suicide note that Hippolytus had violated her, despite the latter's denial. In response to Theseus' invocation of Poseidon, a bull appeared from the sea, startling Hippolytus' horses, causing his chariot to crash and fatally injure him.

34 *If I hadn't feared Zeus*: Zeus' will prevails over the wishes of Aphrodite and Artemis.

35 *but we destroy…*: Artemis shows the same lack of compassion for Phaedra as does Aphrodite; see lines 48–50 in 10.10.

36 On dedications by a girl before marriage, see 3.18.

The apparent injustice of Zeus is the theme of Euripides' *Heracles* (possibly 417 BCE). In Heracles' absence, his mortal father Amphitryon is forced to leave the altar of Zeus Soter (the Rescuer or Savior) where he has taken refuge.

10.17 EURIPIDES, *HERACLES* 339–347.

Amphitryon

Zeus, in vain I got you as a sharer of my wife,

in vain I called you partner in my child.[37]   340

You were after all less of a friend than you seemed.

I, a mortal, defeat you, a great god, in excellence,

for I did not betray Heracles' children.[38]

But you knew how to go secretly into beds,

taking others' wives when no one offered,[39]   345

but you do not know how to save your friends.

You are some ignorant god or by nature unjust.[40]

The goddess Iris, messenger of the gods, appears above the stage and explains to the chorus that Hera, Zeus' wife, has sent her with Lyssa (Madness) to cause Heracles to kill his wife Megara and their children in a fit of madness.

10.18 EURIPIDES, *HERACLES* 822–842.

Iris

Don't be afraid, old men, in seeing this offspring of Night,

Lyssa and me, the servant of the gods,

Iris: for we come with no harm to the city,

but against one man's house we wage war,   825

who they say is from Zeus and Alcmena.[41]

Until he completed fully his bitter trials

necessity was keeping him safe, nor would his father Zeus

allow either me or Hera to harm him at any time.

---

37 *sharer of my wife*: an allusion to the story that Zeus disguised himself as Amphitryon during the latter's absence on military campaign. Zeus slept with Amphitryon's wife Alcmena, begetting Heracles.

38 *I did not betray…*: Amphitryon is asserting his moral superiority over Zeus, since he has done all he can to protect Heracles' children, whereas Zeus has made no effort on their behalf, even though they are his grandchildren.

39 *go secretly into beds…*: an allusion to Zeus' seduction of the unsuspecting Alcmena. *when no one offered*: that is, uninvited.

40 *ignorant*: the Greek *amathes* also suggests "stupid" or the more colloquial "dumb." The implication is that Zeus is incapable of learning or understanding.

41 *from Zeus and Alcmena*: Heracles; note Iris' implied skepticism about Heracles' paternity.

But since he's gone through the toils of Eurystheus,[42]   830
Hera wishes to attach to him kindred blood
by his killing of the children, and I wish the same.
But come then, pull together your implacable heart,
unmarried maiden of dark Night,[43]
and against this man drive, stir up   835
fits of madness, disturbances of mind to kill his children,
and leapings of his feet; let out the murderous cable
so that conveying through Acheron's strait
his crown of beautiful children,[44] killed in familial murder,
he may recognize what sort is Hera's anger against him   840
and learn mine. Otherwise the gods are nowhere
and mortal things will be great, if he doesn't pay the penalty.

> After committing the murders and recovering his senses, Heracles asks Theseus, king of Athens, why he should go on living and why anyone should pray to a goddess like Hera.

10.19 EURIPIDES, *HERACLES* 1301–1310.

Heracles

Why then should I live? What gain shall I have
in possession of a worthless, unholy life?
Let the famous wife of Zeus dance,
striking Olympus' sparkling floor with her shoes.
For she has achieved the purpose she wished,   1305
turning upside down the first man of Greece
from the foundations. Who would pray
to such a goddess? One who because of a woman,
in jealousy over Zeus' union, destroyed
Greece's benefactor, who was not at all blameworthy.   1310

> Theseus dissuades Heracles from committing suicide; since the gods behave badly and live with the consequences of their actions, mortals should do likewise.

---

42 *toils of Eurystheus*: the twelve labors that Heracles had to perform for Eurystheus, the son of Alcmena and Amphitryon, who was born shortly before Heracles. Hera was angry because Heracles is Zeus' bastard son, and so she tricked Zeus into making Heracles the slave of Eurystheus until these labors were completed.

43 *unmarried maiden of dark Night*: Lyssa, the personification of madness who has accompanied Iris.

44 *Acheron's strait*: Acheron was a river of the underworld.

10.20 EURIPIDES, *HERACLES* 1313–1321.

Theseus

<If you were going to be the only person defined by misfortune>
I would advise you <to kill yourself> rather than suffer ills.[45]
But no one of mortals is untouched by fortune,
nor of the gods, if, as I assume, the stories of poets aren't false.   1315
Have they not joined in illicit unions
with one another? Have they not defiled their fathers
with bonds for the sake of ruling? But nevertheless they dwell
on Olympus and endure their errors.[46]
And yet what will you say if, a mortal, you   1320
take these fortunes too much to heart, when the gods do not?

> Heracles dismisses Theseus' arguments based on poetic stories of the gods
> but acknowledges that he must submit to fortune.

10.21 EURIPIDES, *HERACLES* 1340–1357.

Heracles

Oimoi! These things are incidental to my ills;   1340
For I don't believe that the gods put up with
illicit unions and binding hands with chains—
neither did I think this proper nor will I be persuaded—
nor that one is by nature master of another.
For god, if he is truly god, lacks   1345
nothing; these are the wretched stories of poets.[47]
But I take care, even in these ills,
that I not, by leaving the light, incur a charge of cowardice.
For anyone who cannot withstand the blows of fortune
would not be able to withstand a man's weapon.   1350
I will brave death; and I will go to your
city and owe you a thousand thanks for your gifts.[48]
But indeed I tasted a thousand labors,
none of which I refused, nor did I let fall

---

45 See Esposito 2002: viii notes that Halleran provides supplemental translations
(marked < >) to fill gaps in the Greek text.

46 *illicit unions*: an allusion to the adulterous behavior of Zeus and other Olympians.
defiled their fathers with bonds: an allusion to the overthrow of Ouranos by Cronus
and of Cronus by Zeus; see 2.5 and 2.6.

47 For further challenges to traditional religion, see 12.1–12.30. For the association of
poetry with lying, see Hesiod, *Theogony* 27–28 in 2.2.

48 *I will go to your city*: Theseus has offered to purify Heracles from the pollution caused
by the murder of his wife and children and to give him a home in Athens.

streams from my eyes, nor would I ever have thought   1355

that I would come to this—to shed tears from my eyes.

But as things are now, as it seems, I must be a slave to fortune.

> In Euripides' *Trojan Women* (415 BCE), Hecuba, the Queen of Troy, is about
> to be taken into slavery by the Greeks. Seeing no end to her suffering, she
> calls on the gods, while also doubting their willingness to help.

10.22 EURIPIDES, *TROJAN WOMEN* 467–471.

Hecuba

It is not surprising

I should faint at what I suffer and have suffered and will continue to
  suffer.

Oh, you gods! They make poor allies for me to call on,

yet there's something to be said for invoking them   470

whenever one of us is in trouble.

> Hecuba questions the existence of the gods, as she laments over the body
> of her grandson Astyanax, Hector's son, whom the Greeks had flung from
> the battlements of Troy. She makes the ironic comment that, had it not
> been for the divinely ordained destruction of Troy, her family would not
> have achieved the fame bestowed by epic poetry.

10.23 EURIPIDES, *TROJAN WOMEN* 1240–1250.

Hecuba

So the gods amounted to nothing after all! There was only my
  suffering   1240

and their discriminating hatred of Troy.

My sacrifices were useless. And yet had not god (*theos*)

turned the world upside down,

we should have acquired no significance, and should have remained
  unsung,

instead of giving themes of song for future generations.[49]   1245

Go now and bury the body in its poor tomb.

For it has such garlands as befit the dead.

I think it makes little difference to the dead

if a person is richly bedecked.

This is merely an empty pretension for the living.   1250

> At the end of the play, in utter despair, Hecuba deplores the futility of
> invoking the gods.

---

49 *giving themes of song for future generations*: a bitter echo of the epic hero's ideal,
  which was to win glory and be a role model for posterity; see Homer, *Iliad* 6.357,
  22.305, and *Odyssey* 8.579–580.

10.24 EURIPIDES, *TROJAN WOMEN* 1277–1283.

Hecuba

O Troy, who once breathed forth your greatness among barbarian
   peoples,

you will now be robbed of your glorious name.

They are burning you and they are already dragging us from the land

as slaves. O Gods! Yet why do I call upon the gods?   1280

They did not listen when they were appealed to before.

Come let us rush into the pyre. Best for me

to die with this country of mine as it burns.

> In Euripides' *Ion* (c. 410 BCE), Ion, a temple attendant at Delphi, has just
> heard of the wrong done to Creusa, a woman who has borne a child to
> Apollo and has come to discover the child's whereabouts. Unaware that she
> is his mother, Ion muses about the immorality of the gods.

10.25 EURIPIDES, *ION* 436–451.

Ion.

I must admonish Phoebus

for his action. Does he take maidens by force

and then betray them? Does he beget children in secret

and is not concerned when they die? But not you, Apollo! In your
   strength,

you pursue virtue. For any human who   440

is evil by nature, is punished by the gods.

How then is it just for you to write laws for mortals,

when you yourselves act lawlessly?

But if—for it will not be, and I'm merely making an argument—

you paid a fine to mortals for violating their women,   445

you, Apollo, Poseidon, and Zeus who rules over heaven

the payment for your injustice would see the temples empty.

For you put pleasure before prudence

in your haste to commit injustice. No longer is it just to call mortals evil

if they imitate the famed deeds of the gods.   450

Rather we should censure those who teach such things.

> Creusa denounces Apollo.

10.26 EURIPIDES, *ION* 906–922.

Creusa

I call on you, the son of Leto,

you who dispense the oracular voice

near the golden throne

and the earth's center.   910

I will proclaim my voice in your ears.

You are a cowardly adulterer.

For no previous favor

to my husband,

you set a son in his house.   915

But my son, and your's too, was left, unknowing,

a prey for the birds,

deprived of his mother's swaddling clothes.

Delos hates you, and the young laurel

that grows by the palm with the delicate leaves   920

where Leto brought forth her divine children,

the fruit of her union with Zeus.[50]

> Euripides again portrays the inexorable power of a god in his last play, *Bacchae*. Dionysus, god of theater, mask, ecstasy, madness, wine, and illusion,[51] is the central figure of this drama that was performed in the Theater of Dionysus in Athens at the Great Dionysia of 406/5 BCE, though the playwright himself had gone into exile and recently died. This play is an invaluable source of information about three elements of Dionysiac, or Bacchic, ritual: going to the mountain to dance (*oreibasia*); tearing in pieces (*sparagmos*) an animal's body—a goat, fawn, or a bull—and devouring the animal's raw flesh (*omophagia*).
>
> At the beginning of the play Dionysus, in mortal guise as a stranger from Lydia (western Turkey), speaks the prologue, declaring to the audience his determination to be recognized by the people of Thebes as a god, the son of Zeus and the mortal Semele.

10.27 EURIPIDES, *BACCHAE* 1–5.

Dionysus (disguised as a "Stranger.")[52]

I have come to this land of Thebes as the son of Zeus.

Dionysus is my name. Semele, the daughter of Cadmus,[53]

gave me birth after being forced into labor by fiery lightning.

Exchanging my divinity for human form I have arrived

at Dirce's streams and the waters of Ismenus.[54]   5

---

50 *Delos*: an island, sacred to Apollo, in the center of the Aegean where Leto is said to have given birth to Apollo and Artemis, children of Zeus. *divine children*: Apollo and Artemis.

51 See Henrichs *OCD* 3 entry *Dionysus*.

52 Until almost the end of the play Dionysus remains in this disguise.

53 *Cadmus*: the former king of Thebes, who has handed his power to his grandson Pentheus.

54 *Dirce and Ismenus*: two small rivers of Thebes.

10.28 EURIPIDES, *BACCHAE* 20–54.

Dionysus

I first came to this Greek city	20

only after I had roused to dancing all those Asian lands

and established my rites there so that I might be seen by mortals as a
    god.[55]

  It was this very Thebes, of all the Greek lands, that I first incited

to female shrieks of ecstasy, wrapping her in fawnskins,

putting into her hands the thyrsus, my ivy javelin.[56]   25

I did this because my mother's sisters,[57] of all people,

denied that I, Dionysus, was begotten from Zeus. Semele, they say,

was seduced by some mortal but then, by Cadmus' clever contrivance,

she charged the error of her bed to Zeus. For this reason,

because Semele had lied about her union with the god,   30

her three sisters sneered that Zeus had killed her.

To punish that slander I myself stung those same sisters,

hounding them from their homes with fits of frenzy so that now,

knocked out of their senses, they make their homes on Mount
    Cithaeron.[58]

I forced them to wear the vestments of my mysteries   35

and the entire female seed of Cadmeians, all who were women,

I drove from their homes in madness. Mingled together

with Cadmus' daughters, the women of Thebes sit beneath green firs

on roofless rocks. For this city must learn well,

even if it doesn't want to learn, that it is still uninitiated in my bacchic
    rites.   40

I must vindicate my mother Semele

by revealing myself to mortals as the god whom she bore to Zeus.

Cadmus, then, has passed the power and privileges of his monarchy

to the son of his daughter Agave. But that one, Pentheus,

---

55 *roused to dancing*: dancing was an essential part of the ritual; see above Sophocles,
King Oidipous 896, "why should I dance for the gods?" (10.7 with note). Dionysus'
devotees performed ecstatic dances to the music of the flute, cymbals, tambourines,
drums, or a stringed instrument (*barbiton*). Such worship is frequently represented
on Greek vases. *Asian lands*: Dionysus has previously described his progress from
the east to the coast of Asia Minor (in modern Turkey).

56 *ecstasy*: Greek *ekstasis*, literally a stepping out of oneself, hence the English "ecstasy."
fawnskins: the ritual dress of Bacchic worshipers. *thyrsus*: a long pole, topped with a
pine-cone, entwined with ivy and/or snakes, and carried by the devotees of Dionysus.

57 Semele's sisters were Agave (the mother of Pentheus), Autonoe, and Ino.

58 *Cithaeron*: a mountain, ten miles south of Thebes.

fights against the gods by fighting against me.[59] He thrusts me away   45
from his libations and mentions me nowhere in his prayers.
For this reason I shall show him and all Thebans
that I am a god. After setting matters here in order
I will move on to another land, revealing myself there too.
But if the city of Thebans, with wrath and weapons,   50
seeks to drive the Bacchae down from the mountain
I will wage war on the city, marshalling my army of maenads.[60]
For this reason I have changed my appearance to a mortal one
and transformed my shape into the nature of a man.

> The chorus of fifteen bacchants (devotees of Dionysus) describe the rites
> that they celebrate in the mountains with the god as they sing and dance
> in his honor.

10.29 EURIPIDES, *BACCHAE* 135–168.

Chorus

Sweet is the pleasure the god brings us in the mountains   135
when from the running revelers
he falls to the ground clad in his sacred fawnskin.
Hunting the blood of slaughtered goats for the joy of devouring raw flesh
he rushes through the mountains of Lydia, of Phrygia.
Hail to the Roaring God, Bromios our leader! Euoi![61]   140
The ground flows with milk,
flows with wine,
flows with the nectar of bees.
The Bacchic One,[62] lifting high
the bright-burning flame of the pine-torch,   145
like the smoke of Syrian frankincense,
springs up and rushes along with his wand of fennel.
Running and dancing he incites any wanderers,
shakes them with shouts of joy
tossing his luxuriant locks to the wind.[63]   150
Amidst the cries of "euoi" he roars out:
   "Onward you Bacchae,

---

59 *Pentheus*: the new king of Thebes, who is also Dionysus' cousin.

60 *Bacchae*: female devotees of Dionysus. *maenads*: frenzied worshipers of the god.

61 *Bromios*: another name of Dionysus. *Euoi*: a ritual cry of ecstasy invoking Dionysus.

62 *The Bacchic One*: Dionysus himself.

63 *luxuriant locks*: long, flowing hair was a distinctive feature of Dionysus, in contrast
   to the other male Olympian gods.

Onward Bacchae,
glittering pride of gold-flowing Mt. Tmolus.[64]
Sing and dance for Dionysus   155
as the rumbling drums roar!
Glorify him joyously!
"Euoi, euoi!" Yes, sing out
your Phrygian incantations.
As the holy flute   160
roars holy hymns,
glorify him, maenads,
as you climb
to the mountain,
to the mountain!"   165
Secretly rejoicing, then,
like a filly grazing with her mother,
the bacchant leaps
swift and nimble on her feet.

> The chorus extols the blessings that Dionysus brings to humans; they also
> warn against excess, advising moderation.

10.30 EURIPIDES, *BACCHAE* 416–431.

Chorus

The god who is the son of Zeus
delights in festivities
and loves Peace, the goddess
who bestows bliss and nourishes youths.
In equal measure he has given   420
to the rich and the humble
so that mankind now possesses wine,
bringer of joy, banisher of care.
He hates the man whose concern is not this—
by day and by friendly night[65]   425
to live to the end a life of blessedness.
It is wise to keep one's heart and mind
at a distance from men of excess.
whatever beliefs the common folk
have come to adopt and still practice,   430
these I would accept.

---

64 *gold-flowing Mt. Tmolus*: a reference to the gold dust carried from the mountain by
the River Pactolus, in Lydia.

65 *friendly night*: Dionysus' rituals were mostly celebrated at night.

Figure 10.1. Sicilian skyphos cup, c. 400 BCE, depicting Agave holding the head of Pentheus and a sword; she rushes to the right preceded by a maenad holding a vine branch. This maenad has her head thrown back in the typical posture of Bacchic ecstasy. Photograph © Museum of Fine Arts, Boston.

> The disguised Dionysus tells the chorus that he will lead Pentheus dressed as a female bacchant to join the bacchants on the mountain, where he will be killed by his mother.

10.31 EURIPIDES, *BACCHAE* 847–861.

Stranger

Women, the man stands within the cast of our net.

He will come to the Bacchae and pay the penalty of death!

Dionysus, now the deed is yours—for you are not far off.

Let us punish him! First put him outside his mind.   850

Instill a light-headed frenzy. Since, if he reasons well,

he definitely won't be willing to dress in a woman's costume.

But if he drives off the road of reason, he will dress up. [66]

I want the Thebans to mock him

as we parade him through the city in his dainty disguise,   855

after those terrifying threats of his.

I'll go and dress Pentheus up in the very adornments

---

66 Cross-dressing is a familiar feature of initiation rites, signifying the assumption of a new identity.

he'll wear to Hades after being slain by his mother's hands.

He will come to know Dionysus, the son of Zeus,

that he is, in the ritual of initiation, a god most terrifying,[67]   860

but for mankind a god most gentle.

> At the end of the play, after Cadmus has brought his daughter Agave to the realization that she has killed her son, Dionysus appears on top of the building at the back of the stage.

10.32 EURIPIDES, *BACCHAE* 1340–1351.

Dionysus

I say these things as Dionysus, born not from a mortal father   1340

but from Zeus. If you had known how to behave wisely

when you chose otherwise, you would now be happy

and have the son of Zeus as an ally.

Cadmus

Dionysus, we beg you, we have wronged you.

Dionysus

You were late to understand us. When you ought to have known us,

  you did not.   1345

Cadmus

We have recognized our mistakes now. But your punishment is too

  severe.

Dionysus

Yes, but I am a god and was treated with hybris by you.

Cadmus

Gods ought not to be like mortals in their passions.[68]

Dionysus

Long ago Zeus, my father, assented to these things.

Agave

Alas, old man, it has been decreed—miserable exile.   1350

Dionysus

Why, then, do you delay what necessity mandates?

---

67 *a god most terrifying*: a reference to the terrors of the ritual death experienced by an individual before his rebirth on initiation into the mysteries of Dionysus.

68 Compare the servant's plea to Aphrodite in *Hippolytus* 120 in 10.12: "The gods ought to be wiser than mortals." Both pleas are in vain; the gods do not forgive.

11. Mystery Cults and Initiation

11.1 PLATO, *PHAEDO* 69 c. It is possible that those who established the initiation rites (*teletai*) were not being trivial. They may really have had a hidden meaning when they said long ago that whoever goes to the house of Hades uninitiated and unenlightened will lie in the mire,[1] whereas the person who arrives there purified and initiated will dwell with the gods.

11.2 PINDAR, Frag. 131 a.
Blessed are all those with the rites (*teletai*) that relieve one from distress.

11.3 SOPHOCLES, Frag. 837.
Three times blessed
are those mortals who, after seeing these rites
go to the realm of Hades. They are the only ones
who have life there, the rest have every kind of evil.

11.4 EURIPIDES, *BACCHAE* 72–77.
O blessed is he who, happy in his heart,
knows the initiation rites of the gods,
purifies his life and
joins his soul to the cult group,   75
dancing on the mountains, with holy purifications
celebrating the Bacchic rituals.

> Greek mystery cults contrast with the various cults of the *polis*, since the individual was regarded as a member of a religious group, as distinct from his civic community. Such groups shared the common experience of initiation, wearing a distinctive and identical form of dress when participating in ritual activity. At the height of the initiation ceremony, the "mysteries"

---

1   *Hades*: the god of the underworld. Pindar, *Olympian* 2.57–78 (3.37) contrasts the punishment of the wicked in the underworld with the blessed afterlife of those who have lived righteously.

were revealed—the sacred things (*ta hiera*) that were not to be divulged to the uninitiated.

In Euripides' *Bacchae*, the disguised Dionysus refuses to give Pentheus details about the rites.

11.5   EURIPIDES, *BACCHAE* 465–474.

Pentheus

And from what source do you bring these rites to Greece?

Stranger (Dionysus in disguise)

Dionysus, the son of Zeus, sent me.

....

Pentheus

And was it in a dream or face to face in daylight that he forced you into his service?

Stranger

It was face to face. He looked at me, I at him. And he gave me his
sacred rites freely.   470

Pentheus

And those rites—in your view, what form do they take?

Stranger

That is forbidden knowledge for any mortals who are not Bacchae.

Pentheus

And what benefit does it hold for those who sacrifice?

Stranger

It is unlawful for you to hear but the benefit is worth knowing.

The English term "mysteries" derives from the Greek noun *mystes*, an "initiate." Initiation involved purification followed by a communion with the divine that was thought to set the individual apart from non-initiates, giving the initiate a feeling of blessedness that made provision for "personal needs in this life and after death."[2]

11.6   PLATO, *REPUBLIC* 330 d–e. When a man is near to the realization that he going to die, he becomes fearful and anxious about matters that had never occurred to him before. He may have laughed earlier at the stories told about people in the realm of Hades that those who commit crimes on earth must pay for them in the underworld; but now these stories begin to disturb his soul with the possibility that they might be true.

Plutarch (c. 50–120 CE) reports several lines by Pindar (518–446 BCE) about the pious in Hades.[3]

11.7   PINDAR, Frag. 129.

For them shines the strength of the sun

---

2   On mystery cults, see Burkert 1987.

3   Plutarch, *Consolation to Apollonius* 35.120 c.

below when it is nighttime up here,

and in meadows of red roses their country place

teems with...shady frankincense trees

and bushes of golden fruit.   5

Some delight in horses and exercises, others in checkers,

and others in lyres. Among them complete blessedness blooms and
flourishes.

A fragrance spreads through the beloved land,

as they continually mingle offerings of every kind

with far-gleaming fire on the gods' altars.   10

> Plutarch describes initiates' hopes of a blissful afterlife.

11.8 PLUTARCH, *MORALIA* 1105 b. Yet such tales as these [about the terrors of the underworld] are not feared by very many people because they are the teachings and fable stories of mothers and nurses. Even those who fear them think that some sort of initiations and purifications will help. Once purified, they believe they will continue to play and dance in Hades in places where there is brightness, a sweet breeze, and a sound of voices.

> Plutarch reports the reaction of Diogenes the Cynic philosopher (c. 412/403–c. 324/321 BCE) to such expectations.

11.9 PLUTARCH, *MORALIA* 21 f. What! Do you mean that Pataikion the thief will have a better lot after death than Epaminondas because he has been initiated?[4]

> Mysteries range from the older mysteries of Demeter at Eleusis to the rituals associated with Dionysus and those attributed to Orpheus, a legendary singer and poet. The ancient literary sources tell us very little about what took place at these ceremonies, beyond descriptions of various processions of initiates and initiands (candidates for initiation) before and after a secret ceremony, and vague allusions to "things that must not be spoken of" and "unspeakable things" that were revealed at the initiation itself. Although some later ancient sources profess to know the ultimate revelation of Demeter at Eleusis, their accounts differ. Secrecy has generally prevailed, giving rise to much speculation over the centuries.

> Plato mentions the peddling of books said to have been written by two legendary figures, Musaeus and Orpheus, prescribing rituals that professed to grant release from the evils in the afterlife.

11.10 PLATO, *REPUBLIC* 364 b–365 a. Begging priests and seers come to the doors of the rich and persuade them that they have the god-given power to cure with sacrifices and incantations, accompanied by pleasurable festivals, whatever misdeeds have been committed by themselves or their ancestors.

---

4 *Epaminondas*: a famous general of Thebes who briefly established the predominance of his city, 379–362 BCE. Plutarch (late first to early second century CE) came from a city near Thebes.

If someone wants to injure an enemy, for a small fee he can harm a just or an unjust person alike, since they persuade the gods to do their bidding, so they say, by certain charms and binding spells....[5]

They offer a bundle of books by Musaeus and Orpheus—descendants of the Muses and the Moon, so they say—in which rituals are prescribed.[6] With these rituals, they persuade not only individuals but whole cities that there is release and purification from misdeeds through sacrifices and pleasurable entertainment, both for the living and for the dead; these they call *teletai* (rites) which deliver us from evils in the afterlife, where terrible things await those who neglect to sacrifice.

> Aristophanes refers to the gifts of Orpheus and Musaeus.

11.11 ARISTOPHANES, *FROGS* 1030–1033.

Consider, from the beginning,

How helpful the noble poets have been.

Orpheus revealed to us initiations and abstention from slaughter,[7]

Musaeus gave us oracles and ways to cure diseases.

> A reference in Euripides' *Hippolytus* alludes to a connection between Orphism and Dionysiac worship, as Theseus charges his son Hippolytus with engaging in Orphic and Bacchic behavior.

11.12 EURIPIDES, *HIPPOLYTUS* 952–957.

Now pride yourself, and through your vegetarian diet

be a huckster with your food,[8] and with Orpheus as lord

play the bacchant and honor many vaporous writings[9]—

for you're caught. I proclaim to everyone   955

to flee such men as these; for they hunt you down

with their solemn words, while they devise disgraceful deeds.

> In discussing the resemblances between the customs of the Greeks and Egyptians, the historian Herodotus mentions Orphic and Bacchic rites in the context of a taboo on the wearing of wool.

11.13 HERODOTUS, *HISTORIES* 2.81. Woolen articles are never taken into temples, nor are the Egyptians buried with them; for it is unholy. These practices are very like the rituals (*orgia*) known as Orphic and Bacchic which are actually Egyptian and Pythagorean. For it is unholy for anyone

---

5 *charms and binding spells*: see 13.3-13.25.

6 *Musaeus*: a mythical singer, whose name means "He of the Muses."

7 *abstention from slaughter*: Orphics refrained from the consumption of flesh and animal sacrifice.

8 *vegetarian diet*: abstention from meat was typical of the ascetic doctrines attributed to Orpheus.

9 *vaporous writings*: an allusion to the cryptic nature of the Orphic texts; see 11.15-11.21.

initiated into these rites to be buried in a woolen garment. There is a sacred story that is told about the matter.

> The Orphic myth of Dionysus probably developed between the late sixth and early fifth century BCE. By the end of the fifth century BCE, written texts attributed to Orpheus were apparently wide spread, but the myth to which they refer probably had developed earlier. Orpheus figures in several myths and is variously portrayed as a foreigner, singer, magician, initiator. He is also the human who is said to have gone down to the underworld to bring back his wife Eurydice.[10]

> The story can be partially reconstructed from a number of different literary sources ranging from a Pindar (fifth century BCE) to Olympiodorus (Neoplatonic philosopher of the sixth century CE). The result is a strange combination of elements from traditional myths with other elements strikingly at variance with Hesiodic theogony.

> Zeus raped his mother Rhea-Demeter who produced Persephone. In the form of a snake, he raped Persephone who produced Dionysus. Zeus surrendered the rule of the world to the infant Dionysus. The Titans, perhaps at the instigation of Hera, kidnapped Dionysus, tearing him in pieces, boiling, and roasting him. Zeus then killed the Titans with lightning and from their ashes the human race was born. By some means or other Dionysus was recreated.[11] In humans there are elements of the Titans and also of Dionysus. Therefore humans must perform rituals in honor of Dionysus and his mother Persephone, and also expiate the crime of the Titans.

> Plato (*Meno* 81 b8–c4) quotes the following fragment of Pindar (518–c.446 BCE) and then goes on to note that Pindar and others say that the a human's soul is immortal. Consequently, it is necessary to live one's entire life as piously (*hosiotata*) as possible.

11.14 PINDAR, Frag. 133.

But for those from whom Persephone accepts retribution
for her ancient grief,[12] in the ninth year she restores their souls
to the upper sunlight. From them come proud kings
and men who are swift in strength
and greatest in wisdom, and for the rest of time   5
they are called sacred heroes by mortals.

---

10 On the dating and problematic identity of Orpheus, see Graf and Johnston 2007: 66–93 and 165–184.

11 The concept of the death and resurrection of a god is at variance with the Homeric concept of divine immortality.

12 *her ancient grief*: the loss of her child Dionysus.

Orphic and Bacchic texts

Our knowledge of Orphic ritual derives mainly from archaeological finds that underscore the limitations of the extant literary sources. A small number of gold tablets with ritual texts for the afterlife have been discovered in burial locations extending from southern Italy and Sicily to Greece itself and Asia Minor. These texts refer to both Orphic and Bacchic/Dionysiac ritual.[13]

Several inscribed bone tablets discovered in Olbia on the northern shore of the Black Sea indicate Orphism in a Dionysiac context, one of which lists "life," "death," "life," truth," in combination with Dionysus' name.[14] References to Orphic poetry are also found in a carbonized papyrus scroll (probably fourth century BCE) that was discovered among the remains of a funeral pyre on the covering slabs of two tombs excavated at Derveni in Macedonia in 1962.[15]

Inscribed on the gold tablets are terse, and often enigmatic, mnemonic devices giving instructions, advice, passwords, and directions for the descent into the underworld.[16] The longer texts are metrical. A rectangular gold tablet (c. 400 BCE) was discovered in the grave of a woman at Hipponium, a small Greek colony in Calabria in southern Italy. Folded several times, the tablet was lying on the upper chest of the skeleton.

11.15 Graf and Johnston, no. 1.

This is the work of Memory, when you are about to die
down to the well-built house of Hades. There is a spring at the right side,
and standing by it a white cypress.[17]
Descending to it, the souls of the dead refresh themselves.
Do not even go near this spring!
Ahead you will find from the Lake of Memory, [18]
cold water pouring forth; there are guards before it.
They will ask you, with astute wisdom,
what you are seeking in the darkness of murky Hades.

---

13 For an edition and translation of thirty-nine texts, with a map indicating their find-spots, and a history of scholarship on the tablets, see Graf and Johnston 2007: 1–65.

14 See Graf and Johnston 2007: 64–93, and also 185–187.

15 For the fragmentary Greek text with a translation, see Betegh 2004: 4–55.

16 For discussion of the eschatology described on the tablets, see Graf and Johston 2007: 94–136.

17 *spring*: the desire for water is a common theme in the tablets, as is also the insistence on keeping to the right of the house of Hades.

18 *Lake of Memory*: Graf and Johnston 2007: 120 conclude that "the Waters of Memory ... probably guarantee simply that they [the initiates] will arrive in paradise with their recollections intact, unlike those who drink from the Waters of Forgetfulness, and that they therefore will be able to enjoy their rewards fully."

Say, "I am a son of Earth and starry Sky,[19]

I (masculine) am parched with thirst and am dying: but quickly grant me

cold water from the Lake of Memory to drink."

And they will announce you to the Chthonian King,[20]

and they will grant you to drink from the Lake of Memory.

And you, too, having drunk, will go along the sacred road on which other

glorious initiates and *bacchoi* travel.[21]

> One of several gold tablets found near Thurii in Lucania in southern Italy, fourth century BCE:

11.16 Graf and Johnston, no. 5.

1. I come from the pure, Queen of the Chthonian Ones,

2. Eucles, Euboleus and the other immortal gods.[22]

3. For I also claim to be of your happy race.

4. But Moira overcame me and the other immortal gods   4a

and the star-flinger with lightning.[23]   4b

5. I have flown out of the heavy difficult circle,

6. I have approached the longed-for crown with swift feet,

7. I have sunk beneath the breast of the Lady, the Chthonian Queen,

8. I have approached the longed-for crown with swift feet.

9. "Happy and blessed, you will be a god instead of a mortal."[24]

10. A kid I fell into milk.[25]

---

19 *son of Earth and starry Sky*: Graf and Johnston 2007: 116 consider that this declaration is "another way for the soul to establish that it has been initiated and thereby has earned a special relationship with the gods."

20 *Chthonian King*: Hades.

21 *initiates*: possibly initiates of the Eleusinian mysteries, rather than synonymous with the *bacchoi*; see Graf and Johnston 2007: 120–121. *bacchoi*: apparently a select band of Bacchic devotees; see Plato, *Phaedo* 69 c, who quotes a saying from the mysteries: "Many are the *thyrsus* bearers, but few are the *bacchoi*." See also Graf and Johnston 2007: 143.

22 *Queen of the Chthonian Ones*: Persephone. *Eucles, Euboleus*: probably Hades and Dionysus, see Graf and Johnston 2007: 123.

23 *Moira*: Fate or Destiny. *star-flinger with lightning*: Zeus, see Graf and Johnston 2007: 125.

24 *god instead of a mortal*: see Graf and Johnston 2007: 114–116.

25 *a kid I fell into milk*: see Graf and Johnston 2007: 128–129: "The best theory understands the phrase as a proverb expressing happiness.... to be in the midst of abundance, or to make a new beginning."

Two ivy-shaped gold leaf tablets,[26] late fourth century BCE, were discovered in a woman's sarcophagus in Pelinna in Thessaly in northwest Greece.

11.17 Graf and Johnston, no. 26 a, b.

Now you have died and now you have come into being, O thrice happy one, on this same day.

Tell Persephone that the Bacchic One himself released you.[27]

Bull, you jumped into milk.

Quickly you jumped into milk. [This line is missing from b]

Ram, you fell into milk.

You have wine as your fortunate honor.

And below the earth there are ready for you the same prizes [or rites] as for the other blessed ones. [This line is missing from b]

In an unknown location in Thessaly, a rectangular gold tablet, mid-fourth century BCE, was found in a bronze vase used as crematory urn.

11.18 Graf and Johnston, no. 29.

I (masculine) am parched with thirst and am dying; but grant me to drink

from the ever-flowing spring. On the right is a white cypress.

"Who are you? Where are you from?" I am a son of Earth and starry Sky. But my race is heavenly.

The author of the Derveni Papyrus comments on Orphic rites.

11.19 The Derveni Papyrus, column 6.[28] Prayers and sacrifices appease the souls, and the incantation of the magi has the power to remove the *daimones* when they obstruct. Obstructing *daimones* are avenging souls. This is why the magi perform the sacrifice, as if they were paying a penalty.[29] They pour water and milk on the sacred offerings, and with these liquids they also make the libations. They sacrifice countless many-knobbed cakes, because the souls are also innumerable. Initiates [*mustai*] make a preliminary sacrifice to the Eumenides, in the same way as the magi. For the Eumenides are souls.[30]

11.20 The Derveni Papyrus, column 7. For it is not possible to state at the same time the meaning of the words and what is being said. Orpheus' poetry is something strange and enigmatic for people. For he did not want to tell them contentious riddles, but rather important things by means of riddles.

---

26 Ivy is one of the adornments worn by Bacchic devotees.

27 *The Bacchic One*: Dionysus Lysios, the one who frees or releases. In Orphic mythology, Dionysus was the son of Persephone, queen of the underworld.

28 For the entire fragmentary Greek text with a translation, see Betegh 2004: 4–55. I used Betegh's Greek text for my translation.

29 *magi*: itinerant sorcerers or magicians.

30 *Eumenides*: spirits, whose name literally means "The Kindly Ones."

Indeed, he is telling a sacred discourse (*hieros logos*) from the first to the last word. As he makes clear in the well-chosen verse: for after ordering them to put doors to their ears, he says that he is [?not legislating] for the many... [?but only for] those pure in hearing....

The author criticizes the practice of taking money under false pretences.[31]

11.21 The Derveni Papyrus, column 20. ... all those people who have performed rites in the cities have seen the sacred things. I am less surprised that these people do not have knowledge. For it is not possible to listen to and, at the same time, comprehend what is being said. But all those people who seek understanding from one who practices the sacred as his craft should be wondered at and pitied.

"Wondered at" because they think they will receive knowledge before they perform their rites, but they depart after performing them, before they have any knowledge and without having made any further enquiry; they simply suppose that they know something of what they have seen or learned. They are "to be pitied" because it is not sufficient for them to have spent their money prematurely, but they also depart deprived of their judgment. Before they perform the sacred rites, they hope that they will achieve knowledge; when they have performed them, they depart, deprived even of hope.

The Mysteries of Demeter at Eleusis

The mysteries of Demeter at Eleusis in Attica are the most famous of the mystery cults in the Greek world and probably the most ancient.[32] The sanctuary at Eleusis, some 22 km. from Athens, was absorbed by Athens in late seventh or early sixth century. Although two local families, the Eumolpids and Kerykes, retained their priestly prerogatives, the Athenian state maintained strict control over the cult which became open to all Greek-speaking peoples, including women and slaves. Only murderers, the polluted, and those not speaking Greek were barred from initiation.

The mysteries were held in honor of the goddess Demeter, her daughter Persephone the Maid (Kore) and Iacchus who was invoked as the patron god of the initiates in their procession to Eleusis.[33] Although the cult was basically associated with agriculture and the fertility of the earth, it also offered initiates hope of a better afterlife—a feature that probably accounts for its appeal and popularity for more than a thousand years during which people came from all over the Mediterranean world to be initiated.

---

31 Cf. the peddling of the writings attributed to Orpheus and Musaeus mentioned by Plato in 11.10.

32 On Eleusis and the Eleusinian festivals, see Parker 2005: 327–368. On the iconography of the mysteries, see Clinton 1992.

33 For the procession in honor of Iacchus, see 11.31.

Writing in the mid-fourth century BCE, Isocrates tells of Demeter's two great gifts to Attica, the fruits of the earth and the initiation rites.

11.22 ISOCRATES, *PANEGYRICUS* 28–29. The first necessity for our human nature was provided by our city. For even though the story has become legendary, nevertheless it deserves to be told again. Demeter came to our land in her wanderings after Kore was carried off. As result of the good services, which only initiates are allowed to hear, Demeter was kindly disposed to our ancestors, and she gave them two gifts that are the greatest in the world: the fruits of the earth that make it possible for us to rise above the life of beasts, and the initiation rites which offer sweeter hopes about the end of life and all eternity to those who are initiated. Our city was not only beloved of the gods but also devoted to humankind, and so, when it possessed so many blessings, it did not begrudge them to others but gave to all a share of what it received. And we continue even now to reveal the rites each year.

The Roman author Cicero (106–43 BCE) comments on the benefits of initiation into the Eleusinian mysteries. Pausanias (second century CE) mentions writings inside the sanctuary at Eleusis.

11.23 CICERO, *LAWS* 2.36. We have learned the beginnings of life, how to live in joy, and how to die with better hope.

11.24 PAUSANIAS 1.38.7. My dream forbade me to write a description of the things within the wall of the sanctuary; the uninitiated, of course, have no right to learn the things that they are prevented from seeing.

The Homeric *Hymn to Demeter* is the earliest surviving literary source to mention these mysteries. Composed c. 675–625 BCE, probably before the Athenian takeover of the cult, the hymn relates the story of the institution of the mysteries by Demeter in her search for her daughter Persephone (*Kore*, the Maid) who had been carried off to the underworld by the god Hades. Because of the loss of her daughter, Demeter hid the grain to prevent it from germinating.

11.25 *HOMERIC HYMN TO DEMETER* 452–453.

For the white barley was hidden

by the designs of fair-ankled Demeter.

Apparent in this poem are explanations of some of the rituals that are attested in later sources.

11.26 *HOMERIC HYMN TO DEMETER* 38–58.

But the mountain peaks and the depths of the sea rang

with her [Persephone's] immortal voice, and her queenly mother heard her.

And a sharp grief took hold of Demeter in her heart, and with both hands   40

she tore the veil on her immortal hair,

and she cast her dark cloak down from both her shoulders,

and she rushed like a bird over the nourishing land and sea
searching. But no one either of gods or mortal men
was willing to tell her the truth, nor   45
did any of the birds come to her as a true messenger.

For nine days, then, over the earth queenly Deo[34]
roamed about, holding blazing torches in her hands,
and she never tasted ambrosia or the sweet drink, nectar,[35]
as she grieved, nor did she wash her skin with water.   50
But when indeed the tenth Dawn came bringing light,
Hecate,[36] holding a torch in her hands, met her
and spoke to her, telling her the news,

"Mistress Demeter, bringer of seasons, giver of splendid gifts,
who of the heavenly gods or mortal men   55
seized Persephone and grieved your dear heart?
For I heard her voice but did not see with my eyes
who it was. I am telling swiftly the whole truth."

> Demeter learns from the Sun (Helios) that, at Zeus' bidding, her daughter has
> been abducted by Hades, the god of the underworld, to be his wife. Disguised
> as an old woman, Demeter comes to the house of Celeus of Eleusis.

11.27 *HOMERIC HYMN TO DEMETER* 90–104.

But a more terrible and savage grief came into Demeter's heart.   90
Then, angered at the dark-clouded son of Cronus,[37]
she avoided the assembly of the gods and lofty Olympus,
and went among the cities of men and their rich fields
softening her form for a long while.[38] No one of men
and of deep-girded women recognized her when they looked at her, 95
until she came to the house of the thoughtful Celeus,
who at that time was a lord of fragrant Eleusis.

….

She looked like a very old woman, one excluded from   101
childbearing and the gifts of garland-loving Aphrodite,
as are the nurses for the children of law giving-kings
and the housekeepers in their echoing homes.

---

34 *Deo*: probably a shortened form of Demeter.

35 Ambrosia and nectar are the food and drink of the gods.

36 *Hecate*: underworld goddess, often associated with magic.

37 *dark-clouded son of Cronus*: Hades.

38 *softening her form*: disguising her divine form to avoid recognition by mortals.

Celeus' wife, Metaneira offers the disguised goddess hospitality. This part of the hymn is generally thought to offer a mythic explanation of the ritual silence, fasting and abstention from food, abusive and obscene jesting, and the drinking of a potion, the *kykeon* , all of which were part of the initiation into the Eleusinian mysteries.

11.28 *HOMERIC HYMN TO DEMETER* 190–210.

Reverence and awe and pale fear seized Metaneira.   190

And she yielded her chair and bade her sit.

But Demeter, bringer of seasons, giver of splendid gifts,

was unwilling to sit on the shining chair.

She stayed silent, her beautiful eyes downcast,

until devoted Iambe set out for her   195

a well-placed seat and threw over it a silver-white fleece.[39]

Then sitting down, she held her veil before her with her hands.[40]

For a long time she sat on the chair speechless in her grief,

nor did she greet anyone by word or gesture,

but unsmiling, tasting no food or drink,   200

she sat wasting away with longing for her deep-girded daughter,

until devoted Iambe, intervening with jokes

and many jests, moved the holy lady

to smile and laugh and have a propitious heart;

indeed in later times too she used to please her in her moods.[41]   205

Metaneira offered her a cup filled with honey-sweet wine,

but she refused it, for she said it was not right

to drink the red wine. But she bid Metaneira to give her

a drink of barley-meal and water mixed with fresh pennyroyal.

And she, having made the potion,[42] gave it to the goddess as she had asked.

---

39 *Iambe*: the personification, or eponym, of the iambic meter, which was the regular rhythm used for comic jesting or insults.

40 *sitting down*: see Shelmerdine 1995: 44: "Both written and pictorial evidence indicates that a preliminary ceremony in which the veiled initiate sat on a skin-covered stool was a regular part of the ritual. In the hymn Demeter takes the part of the initiate in this *thronosis* (sitting ceremony)."

41 Iambe's jesting probably involved buffoonery and obscenity; sexual jesting was a typical feature of festivals connected with fertility, intended to avert evil and bad luck.

42 *the potion*: Greek *kykeon*, which the preceding line indicates was a simple mixture of barley-meal, water, and a herb, pennyroyal; this potion was drunk by the initiates after breaking their fast.

Taking it to show respect, the great mistress Deo   210

......[43]

> Demeter reveals her divinity, and demands that a temple and altar be established for her at Eleusis.

11.29 *HOMERIC HYMN TO DEMETER* 268–313.

"I am Demeter, holder of honor, who is the greatest
help and joy to immortals and mortals.
But come, let all the people build me a great temple   270
and below it an altar, beneath the acropolis and its sheer wall
overlooking Kallichoron on a jutting hill.
I myself will teach my rites, so that hereafter
you may propitiate my heart by performing them reverently."
So speaking, the goddess changed her size and form,   275
thrusting away old age. Beauty breathed around and about her.
and a lovely scent spread from her fragrant
robes, and from the goddess' immortal skin a light
shone far off, and her golden hair spread down over her shoulders,
and the well-built house was filled with a bright light, as if from
   lightning.   280

....

Then he [Celeus] called the people from all districts to an assembly
and ordered them to build a rich temple to fair-haired Demeter
and an altar on a jutting hill.

They obeyed at once and heeded his words,
and they built it as he had ordered, and it grew by the decree of the
   goddess.   300
When they had finished and quit from their toil,
each man went home. But golden-haired Demeter
remained sitting there, apart from all the blessed ones,
wasting away with longing for her deep-girded daughter.
And she caused a most terrible and savage year for men   305
on the much-nourishing land, and the earth did not sprout
any seed, for fair-wreathed Demeter buried it.
Many curved ploughs did the oxen drag in the soil in vain,
and much white barley fell to no avail on the earth.

---

43 At this critical point, two lines are evidently missing from the text, leaving the sentence incomplete. *to show respect*: thus Shelmerdine 1995: 45 interprets this phrase to imply Demeter's respect for the hospitality offered to her, although her grief still forbids her to drink. Others think it means "for the sake of the ritual" that will ultimately be established.

And now she would have destroyed the whole race of mortal men   310
with painful famine, and she would have deprived
the Olympians of the splendid honor of gifts and sacrifices
if Zeus had not noticed and pondered in his heart.

> Zeus intercedes with his brother Hades, and Persephone is returned to
> her mother, though only for part of the year. Zeus sends Rhea to convey
> his intent to Demeter. The conclusion of the hymn articulates the benefits
> for initiates.

11.30 *HOMERIC HYMN TO DEMETER* 463–482.

"And he [Zeus] has agreed that your daughter would [spend]
the third part of the circling year beneath the misty gloom,
but two parts with you and the other immortals.   465
He said it would be accomplished thus, and with his head he nodded
    assent.
But come, child, and obey me, and do not rage too much
without end at the dark-clouded son of Cronus.
But make the life-giving seed grow for men at once."

So she [Rhea] spoke and fair-wreathed Demeter did not disobey,   470
But at once made the seed rise up from the fertile soil.
All the wide earth was laden with leaves and flowers.
Then, going to the kings who give laws,
she revealed to Triptolemus and Diocles, driver of horses,
and mighty Eumolpus and Celeus, leader of the people,[44]   475
the performance of her sacred mysteries and taught her rites to all—
holy rites (*semna*) that are not to be transgressed, or asked about,
or discussed; for a great reverence (*sebas*) for the gods restrains one's
    speech.
Blessed is he of men on earth who has seen these things,   480
but whoever is uninitiated in the mysteries, whoever has no part in
    them, never
has a share of the same joys when he is dead below the dank gloom.

> The Eleusinian Mysteries were celebrated annually in spring and autumn.
> The Little or Lesser Mysteries were held in the month of *Anthesterion*
> (February/March) and formed the first grade of initiation, involving a ritual
> purification and probably fasting. The Greater Mysteries took place over a

---

44 *Triptolemus*: an important hero in later Athenian legend. He is said to have received
   the gift of grain from Demeter and to have taught humans the art of agriculture.
   Diocles: a hero of Megara to the west of Eleusis. This reference suggests that Megara
   had control over Eleusis before the Athenians took over. *Eumolpus*: the father of
   the family of priests, the Eumolpidae, who retained control of the right to utter the
   sacred words of the ritual.

period of ten days in late September, in the Athenian month of *Boedromion*, and involved two stages: the ritual of initiation (*teletai*) of initiands, and the higher initiation (*epopteia*) of those who had already been initiated.

At the beginning of the Greater Mysteries, a group of ephebes went from Athens to Eleusis to bring the *hiera* (sacred objects) to the Eleusinion, a shrine at the foot of the acropolis. The boxes or chests containing the sacred objects were transported on a wagon escorted by the Eleusinian priestesses. The Mysteries began officially on 15 *Boedromion* when, in the presence of the hierophant (the one who revealed the *hiera*) and the sacred torch bearer, the sacred herald made a proclamation which barred non-Greek speakers and those who were polluted from participation.

The second day was known as "*Halade Mustai*," literally "to the sea, initiates!" The participants went down to the sea at Phaleron, where a piglet was sacrificed as a scapegoat by each would-be initiate.[45] To cleanse them from pollution, the ashes of the sacrifice were scattered. Those undergoing initiation probably also purified themselves in the sea, after which they dressed in new robes and their heads were crowned with myrtle-wreaths. They then returned in a procession to Athens for another sacrifice of purification. The events of the third and fourth days of the festival are uncertain.

On 19 *Boedromion*, the *hiera* were taken back to Eleusis, escorted by the ephebes and Eleusinian priestesses, to the Telesterion. a large hall with a capacity to seat 3000, where the initiation proper would take place.[46] The procession was headed by a statue of Iacchus, followed by the wagon containing the *hiera*. Then came the priests, the initiands, members of Areopagus and Council of Five Hundred, Athenian magistrates, the citizens according to their tribe and deme, followed by the initiates and also spectators. The emblem of the initiates was a bundle of branches which they carried and waved as the progressed on their way to Eleusis. This procession, mainly on foot, probably took the entire day.

In Aristophanes' comedy *Frogs* (first performed in 405 BCE), a chorus of Eleusinian initiates makes its entrance, as they invoke Iacchus.

11.31 ARISTOPHANES, *FROGS* 316–356.[47]

Chorus (off stage)

Iacchus, o Iacchus!

Iacchus, o Iacchus!

....

Iacchus, dwelling here most honored in your abode,

Iacchus, o Iacchus,   325

---

45 Since the initiates came from all classes of society, a piglet would not be an excessive economic burden.

46 For a description of the Telesterion, see Mylonas 1961.

47 I have followed the line numbering of Henderson's 2002 Loeb translation.

come to this meadow to dance
with your reverent band of followers,
tossing about your brow
a fruitful, a luxuriant
crown of myrtle, and with bold foot   330.1
stamping in our licentious,
sportive worship,
that owes its greatest share to the Graces, a dance   334/5
pure and sacred to holy initiates.

.....

Raise the blazing torches, brandish them in your hands,
Iacchus, o Iacchus,   342
light-bringing star of our nighttime rite!
See, the meadow blazes with fire,
 and the knees of the aged are leaping.   345
They shake off their cares
and the long seasons of their many years,   347/8
as they perform the sacred rite.
With your torch light up the way forward,   350
and lead to the blossoming meadow
our dancing youth, o blessed one!

Chorus leader

Observe reverent speech, and the following shall stand apart from our
   dances:
whoever is unfamiliar with utterances like this, or has not purified his
   thoughts,   355
or has never seen or danced in the rites of the noble Muses,[48]

> As the procession crossed one of the bridges on the way to Eleusis,
> prominent Athenians were subjected to ritual insults and mockery, a device
> to ward off evil and prevent *hybris*. The jesting recalls that of Iambe in the
> *Homeric Hymn to Demeter*, as she made the grieving Demeter smile and break
> her silence.[49] On arrival at Eleusis, the initiates and those about to be initiated
> probably rested during the day, 20 *Boedromion*, fasting like Demeter,[50] in
> preparation for the initiation ceremony at night inside the Telesterion.
>
> Three Christian authors writing in the late second and third centuries CE
> make a variety of assertions about the ultimate revelation. Hippolytus of

---

48 At this point the list of those who are to be barred from the rites becomes less serious.

49 See *Homeric Hymn to Demeter* and 198–205 in 11.28.

50 See *Homeric Hymn to Demeter*, 49–50 in 11.26.

Rome claims that the *hierophant* displayed an ear of cut wheat at the climax of the initiation ceremony, whereas Tertullian declares that it was an image of a penis or phallus.[51] Clement of Alexandria (late second century CE) alleges that murder, sex, and criminal acts were a part of the ritual of initiation. Nonetheless, his diatribe may preserve part of the Eleusinian *synthema* — the sacred words uttered by the initiates as part of their initiation.

11.32 CLEMENT OF ALEXANDRIA, *EXHORTATION TO THE GREEKS* 2.18. The formula of the Eleusinian mysteries is as follows: "I have fasted, I have drunk the *kykeon*.[52] I have taken from the box (*kiste*), having done my task, deposited into the basket and out of the basket into the box."

51 Hippolytus, *Refutation of all heresies* 5.8.39–40; Tertullian, *Against the Valentinians* 1.

52 See *Homeric Hymn to Demeter,* 209 in 11.28 with note.

12. Challenges to Traditional Religion

The Presocratics

12.1   XENOPHANES, *KRS* no. 170.[1]

[There is] one god, greatest among gods and mortals,
in no way similar to mortals either in body or in thought.

12.2   XENOPHANES, *KRS* no. 171.

Always he remains in one place, absolutely motionless,
nor is it fitting for him to go to different places at different times,
but without effort he shakes all things by the thought of his mind.

12.3   XENOPHANES, *KRS* no. 172.

All of him thinks, sees and hears.

> For Thales (first half of the sixth century BCE), "All things are full of gods." By contrast, Xenophanes (c. 570–478 BCE) posited a single, non-anthropomorphic deity. These two men are among the group of thinkers generally known as the presocratic philosophers. In three more fragments, Xenophanes comments on the anthropomorphism of traditional Greek religion.

12.4   XENOPHANES, *KRS* no. 167.

Mortals consider that the gods are born;
they have clothes and speech and bodies like their own.

---

1   The fragments of authors whose works have mostly been lost are collected in *KRS* = Kirk, G. S., Raven, J., and Schofield, M.,*The Presocratic Philosophers*, 2nd edition, Cambridge 1983. The fragments are individually numbered, and KRS provide a Greek text, an English translation, commentary and notes. I have used the KRS Greek text in making my translation.

12.5 XENOPHANES, *KRS* no. 168.

The Ethiopians say that their gods are snub-nosed and black,

the Thracians that theirs have light blue eyes and red hair.

12.6 XENOPHANES, *KRS* no. 169.

But if cattle and horses or lions had hands

that enabled them to draw and paint pictures as humans do,

they would portray their gods as having bodies like their own:

horses would portray them as horses, and oxen as oxen.

> Xenophanes declares that there is no certainty about the gods, and he criticizes the amorality of the gods as portrayed by Homer and Hesiod.

12.7 XENOPHANES, *KRS* no. 186.

No human knows, or ever will know,

the certainty about the gods and about everything I say.

Even if anyone happened to say the complete truth,

he would not know it. For everything is fashioned by its appearance.

12.8 XENOPHANES, *KRS* no. 166.

Homer and Hesiod have attributed to the gods

everything that is a disgrace and reproach among humans:

stealing, committing adultery, and deceiving each other.

> The later philosopher Plato (c. 429–347 BCE) has his ideal state censor amoral stories about the gods.

12.9 PLATO, *REPUBLIC* 377b–378a.

First it seems the makers of tales must be controlled. If they make a fine tale, it must be approved, but if not, it is to be rejected. ….Most of the current stories must be rejected…. The ones that Hesiod and Homer told us, and also the other poets, who composed false tales and used to tell them to humans and still do so….

For example, when Ouranos did what Hesiod says he did, and how Cronus took revenge upon him; and then Cronus' deeds and his sufferings at the hands of his son. Not even if they were true, would I think that they should lightly be told to thoughtless young people.[2]

> A presocratic philosopher, Anaximander of Miletus (died c. 547 BCE), wrote a treatise "On the Nature of Things," in which he posited the infinite (*to apeiron*) as the beginning of all things, declaring it to be "the divine."

12.10 ANAXIMANDER, *KRS* no. 108. Of the infinite there is no beginning…. But this seems to be the beginning of the other things, and to enfold all things and direct all things…. And this is the divine (*to theion*); for it is immortal and indestructible, as Anaximander and most of the physical speculators say.

---

2 Cronus castrated his father Ouranos (Sky) and was later overthrown by his son Zeus; see 2.5 and 2.6.

Heraclitus of Ephesus, who was active c. 500 BCE, makes several statements about "the god" (*ho theos*) and religious matters, but repudiates the rituals of purification and initiation.

12.11 HERACLITUS, *KRS* no. 204. God is day night, winter summer, war peace, satiety hunger [all the opposites, this is the meaning]; but he becomes different in the way that fire, when it is mixed with spices, is named according to the scent of each of them.

12.12 HERACLITUS, *KRS* no. 206. To god all things are beautiful and good and just, but humans have supposed some things to be unjust, others just.

12.13 HERACLITUS, *KRS* no. 250. Those who speak with sense must rely on what is common to all, as a city must rely on its law, and with much greater reliance. For all the laws of humans are nourished by one law, the divine law; for it has as much power as it wishes and is sufficient for all and still prevails.

12.14 HERACLITUS, *KRS* no. 247. The character of a human being is his *daimon* (spirit).

12.15 HERACLITUS, *KRS* no. 241. Humans vainly purify themselves of blood-guilt by defiling themselves with blood, as though one who had stepped into mud were to wash with mud; he would seem to be mad, if someone noticed him doing this. They pray to these statues, as if they were talking to houses; for they do not recognize the true nature of gods or heroes.

12.16 HERACLITUS, *KRS* no. 242. The mysteries celebrated by humans are practised in an unholy manner.

Anaxagoras of Clazomenae in Asia Minor (500–428 BCE) settled in Athens until he was threatened with prosecution for impiety, probably in 437/6 BCE, and was forced to leave. He maintained that Mind (*Nous*) had initiated the whole cosmic process.

12.17 ANAXAGORAS, *KRS* no. 476. All other things have a portion of everything, but Mind is infinite and self-ruled, and is mixed with nothing but is all alone by itself....

Mind controls all things, both the greater and the smaller, that have life. Mind controlled also the whole rotation, so that it began to rotate in the beginning. And it began to rotate first from a small area, but it now rotates over a wider and will rotate over a wider area still.

And all the things that are mingled and separated and divided off, all are known by Mind. And all things that were to be—those that were and those that are now and those that shall be— Mind arranged them all, including this rotation.

12.18 PLUTARCH, *PERICLES* 32. A decree was introduced by Diopeithes, announcing that anybody who did not recognize the gods or taught theories relating to the heavens was liable to prosecution; the aim was to cast suspicion on Pericles through Anaxagoras.[3] ... Pericles so feared for Anaxagoras that he sent him away from the city.

The Sophists

The Sophists were teachers or professors who traveled throughout the Greek world, making their living by giving lectures and instruction on a variety of subjects. These teachers "were not a school, nor even a single movement, having neither a common set of doctrines nor any shared organization."[4] There was a high demand for their services, especially teachers offering rhetorical training to would-be politicians. In the middle of the fifth century BCE, under the leadership of Pericles, Athens became the cultural center of the Greek world, attracting intellectuals and artists who enhanced the life of the city. But the professors of such skills frequently disturbed the more conservative members of society by questioning traditional values, especially those concerning religion.

Protagoras of Abdera,[5] (c. 490–420 BCE) spent considerable time in Athens, where he became a friend of Pericles.

12.19   PROTAGORAS, *DK* 80 Frag. B 1. Man is the measure of all things, of things that are that they are, and of things that are not that they are not.[6]

12.20   PROTAGORAS, *DK* 80 Frag. B 4. Concerning the gods I am unable to discover whether they exist or not, or what they are like in form. For there are many obstacles to knowledge, the obscurity of the subject and the brevity of human life.

Plato describes Protagoras' popularity and the deference shown by his followers.

12.21   PLATO, *PROTAGORAS* 315 a–b. Those who followed behind listening to their conversation seemed mostly to be foreigners—Protagoras draws them from every city that he passes through, charming them with his voice like Orpheus,[7] and they follow his voice, spellbound—but there were some Athenians in the group as well. As I looked at the group, I was delighted to notice what care they took never to get in front or to be in Protagoras' way. Whenever he and those with him turned round, the listeners divided this

---

3   *recognize the gods*: the Greek verb *nomizein* is often translated as "to believe [in the gods]" but, more literally and correctly, it means to consider, acknowledge, or respect the gods *as* gods and, so, accord them worship. *Pericles*: a prominent Athenian politician (c. 490–429 BCE). Diopeithes' decree is generally dated to the late 430s BCE.

4   See *OCD* 3 entry *sophists*.

5   *Abdera*: a Greek colony in Thrace.

6   Cf. Aristotle, *Metaphysics* 1062 b13: Protagoras said that man is the measure of all things, meaning simply and solely that what appears to each man assuredly also *is*.

7   *Orpheus*: the legendary singer, son of Apollo and a muse.

way and that in an orderly manner. Then, executing a circular movement, they always formed up in perfect order behind him.

> The Roman writer Cicero (106–43 BCE) reports a tradition that Protagoras was exiled from Athens and his works burned.[8]

12.22 CICERO, *ON THE NATURE OF THE GODS* 1.63. Protagoras of Abdera, the greatest sophist of his age... was sentenced by a decree of the Athenian assembly to be banished from the city and from the country because he began a book with the words, "Concerning the gods, I am unable to affirm either how they exist or how they do not exist." By a decree of the Athenian assembly, he was banished from the city and from its territory, and his books were burned in the market-place. I can well believe that this example has discouraged many people from professing such an opinion, since an expression of doubt could not escape punishment.

> Cicero and Diodorus (late first century BCE) report the expulsion from Athens of Diagoras of Melos, a lyric poet who was active in the last decades of the fifth century.[9]

12.23 CICERO, *ON THE NATURE OF THE GODS* 1.63. Again did not Diagoras, who was called the Atheist,...openly deny the existence of the gods?

12.24 DIODORUS 13.6.7. While these events were taking place,[10] Diagoras, who was called the Atheist, was accused of impiety. Fearing the people, he fled from Athens. The Athenians announced the reward of a silver talent for the man who should kill Diagoras.

> In 431 BCE war broke out between Athens and Sparta, the former controlling a maritime empire and the latter being a land-based power that controlled a league of the Peloponnesian states through its military strength. This struggle, generally known as the Peloponnesian War, lasted until 404 BCE, when Athens was defeated and forced to surrender to the Spartans. In 399 BCE, the philosopher Socrates (b. 470/69 BCE), who had been satirized as the central figure in Aristophanes' *Clouds*, was condemned to death because he refused to recognize the gods that were recognized by the state and because he introduced other new divinities.

> Prodicus of Ceos, a small island near Athens, was a contemporary of Socrates, but little is known of his life and works beyond a few references that were written several centuries later.[11]

---

8 The date of Protagoras' departure from Athens is unknown. Plato, however, makes no mention of this decree nor of his departure, but says that he had "never ceased to be held in high esteem;" see 12.32.

9 *Melos*: a small island in the southern island that was brutally subjugated by the Athenians in 416 BCE because the inhabitants tried to remain neutral in the war between Athens and Sparta.

10 *these events*: the arrival of the Athenian expedition in Sicily in 415 BCE.

11 Sextus Empiricus, a philosopher, who probably wrote at the end of the second century CE, is a late source for our knowledge of the lost works of several philosophers.

12.25 PRODICUS, *DK* 84 B5. Prodicus of Ceos says, "The ancients considered that the sun and moon, rivers, springs, and in general all the things that sustain life were gods, because of their usefulness; for example, the Egyptians considered the Nile a god." And so bread is called Demeter, wine Dionysus, water Poseidon, fire Hephaestus, and so on with everything that is useful to humans.

12.26 PRODICUS, *DK* 84 B5. Those who are charged with being atheists say that there is no god at all, for example, Euhemerus[12]... and Diagoras of Melos, and Prodicus of Ceos .... Prodicus says that anything that benefits life is assumed to be a god, such as the sun and moon, rivers and lakes, meadows and fruits, and everything of that sort.

12.27 CICERO, *ON THE NATURE OF THE GODS* 1.118. But what of this? Prodicus of Ceos said that the gods were personifications of things that were beneficial to life—and so, what has he left us of religion?

> Critias (c.460–403 BCE) was a wealthy aristocrat and long-time associate of Socrates. A lost play entitled *Sisyphus* is attributed to Critias by Sextus Empiricus (end of second century CE), but Aetius, a late first century CE writer, attributes the play to Euripides.[13] In a fragment from this play, the main character, Sisyphus, gives a rational account of the origin of human belief in the gods.[14]

12.28 CRITIAS? *DK* 88. B 25. And Critias, one of those who held tyrannical power at Athens,[15] seems to come from the brigade of atheists, since he says that ancient lawgivers fabricated the deity as an overseer of men's successes and failures so that no one should get away with doing his neighbor an injustice, watching out for the retribution of the gods....

[The speaker is Sisyphus]

There was a time when the life of humans was unruly, uncivilized
and beastlike, the slave of brute force,
when there was no reward for the good
nor punishment for the wicked.
Then, I believe, men established laws   5
to chastise, so that justice be the sole ruler

---

12 *Euhemerus*: late third–early second century writer who claimed that Ouranos, Cronus, and Zeus had originally been great kings who were later worshiped as gods by their grateful subjects.

13 Aetius 1.17.2.

14 *Sisyphus*: a trickster who was condemned in the underworld forever to roll a rock up a hill; as soon as he neared the summit, the rock rolled back to the bottom of the hill.

15 *held tyrannical power*: Critias was one of the Thirty Tyrants, a group of Athenian oligarchs who were appointed by the Spartans to govern Athens and restore the ancestral constitution after Athens' defeat in the Peloponnesian War in 404 BCE.

and make insolence (*hubris*) its slave,
and whoever committed an error was punished.

Then, since laws prevented them
from obvious deeds of violence   10
but they were still committing them in secret, it seems to me
that a man of shrewd and subtle mind
invented for mortals the fear of the gods, so that
there might be something to frighten the wicked even if
they acted, spoke or thought in secret.   15

This was why he introduced the conception of divinity (*to theion*).
There is, he said, a spirit (*daimon*) enjoying unending life,
hearing and seeing with his mind, exceedingly wise
and all-observing, possessor of a divine nature.
He will hear everything spoken among mortals   20
and can see everything that is done.
If in silence you are devising evil,
it will not escape the notice of the gods,
so wise are they. With these words
he presented the most seductive of teachings,   25
concealing the truth with lying words.
He said that the gods live in a place, the mention
of which especially terrorizes humans.
In this way, as he knew, fears come to mortals
and help for their wretched lives,   30
from the vault on high, where he saw
lightnings and terrible roars
of thunder...
. ...

With such fears did he surround mankind,
and so by his story gave
the divine a beautiful home in a fitting place
and, by his laws, he extinguished lawlessness.   40
. ...

And so, I think, someone first persuaded
mortals to believe that there exists a race of gods.

Of the three Athenian tragedians, Euripides was most influenced by the Sophists, as is apparent in several excerpts in the previous chapter. In a fragment from a lost play (*Bellerephon*), a character questions the existence of the gods.

12.29 EURIPIDES, Frag. 286.

Does anyone then say that there are gods in heaven?

No, there are none, if anyone is willing

not to be foolish enough to believe the old story.

Look at matters for yourselves, if you don't

believe my words. I say that tyranny   5

kills many people and strips them of their property;

men break their oaths and sack cities.

And in so doing they are more prosperous

than those who remain pious and inactive day after day.

I know of small cities that honor the gods   10

that are subject to others more powerful and more impious than they;

For they have been overwhelmed in battle by numerous spears.

In Euripides' *Helen* (412 BCE), a messenger remarks on the futility of seercraft, but the chorus responds with traditional piety.

12.30 EURIPIDES, *HELEN* 744–760.

Messenger

But as for seercraft

I see how worthless it is, and full of lies.

There is no help in the flames of sacrifice

or the cries of winged creatures. It's folly

to think that the birds can help humankind.

.....

Why then do we resort to seers? We should sacrifice   753

to the gods and ask for blessings, and leave prophecy alone.

.....

Good sense and good advice are the best prophets.

Chorus

As far as seers are concerned we agree

with the old man. If someone has the gods

as friends, he has the best seer in his home.   760

The Roman writer Cicero comments on the attitude to divination of several of the more prominent Greek philosophers.

12.31 CICERO, *ON DIVINATION* 1.5. In my opinion, the ancients were influenced more by results than convinced by reason. Indeed some very subtle arguments have been put together by philosophers to prove the trustworthiness of divination. To mention the most ancient of these,

Xenophanes of Colophon was the only one who admitted the existence of gods but rejected divination entirely.

But all the rest, with the exception of Epicurus who babbled about the nature of the gods,[16] approved of divination, though not in the same way. For example, Socrates and all the Socratic school, and Zeno and his followers continued to follow the opinions of the ancient philosophers, agreeing with the Old Academy and with the Peripatetics.[17] Earlier Pythagoras gave weight to the practice of divination, since he himself wanted to be a seer.[18]

> In Plato's dialogue *Meno*, Anytus, who was one of Socrates' accusers, deplores the pernicious influence of the Sophists but Socrates responds by citing the excellent reputation of Protagoras.[19]

12.32 PLATO, *MENO* 91 c–e.

Anytus: I hope no relative of mine or any of my friends, Athenian or foreign, would be so mad as to go and let himself be ruined by those people [the Sophists]. For they are clearly the ruin and corruption of any one they associate with.

Socrates: What do you mean, Anytus? How can you say such a thing?...

It is surely unbelievable that Protagoras deceived the whole of Greece for more than forty years, corrupting his pupils and sending them away worse than they were before; and all that time—to this very day—he has never ceased to be held in high esteem. For I believe that he died when he was almost seventy, and that he was practicing for forty years. And not only Protagoras, but there are many others, some before his time, and others even today. Are we therefore to suppose from your remark that they knowingly

---

16 Epicurus (341–270 BCE) taught that the cosmos is the result of accident, a chance conglomeration of atoms. The gods, though they exist, are compounds of atoms like everything else in the universe, but they have no concern with the affairs of men. They live an ideal life, remaining forever undisturbed, and do not dispense favors or punishments.

17 Zeno (335–263 BCE) was the founder of Stoicism. *Old Academy*: the school of philosophy founded by Plato in the early fourth century BCE. The name derives from the area that was sacred to the hero Academus, where the public *gymnasium*, or exercise ground, was located. *Peripatetics*: a school of philosophers who met in a sanctuary dedicated to Apollo, the Lyceum, which was outside the city wall. A formal school was established there by Aristotle in 336 BCE. In the late fifth century a gymnasium was built there, as it had become a meeting place for Athenian young men with Socrates and for visiting Sophists.

18 *Pythagoras*: born in Samos, an large island off the coast of modern Turkey, in the mid-sixth century BCE. He migrated to Croton, a Greek colony in southern Italy, c. 530 BCE, where he founded a sect or society that had initiation rites, special dietary laws, secret doctrines and burial rites. To him is attributed the doctrine of the transmigration of souls; see 3.34.

19 The dramatic date of this dialogue is early 402 BCE, after the defeat of Athens and the imposition of Spartan rule, but it was probably written c. 386/5 BCE. On Protagoras, see 12.19–12.22.

deceive and ruin their pupils, or are they unaware of what they are doing? Are we to deem these men mad, men whom some people consider are the wisest of men?

Anytus: Far from it, Socrates. They aren't the ones who are mad, but rather those of the young men who give them money; and even worse are those who entrust them to the Sophists. Worst of all are the cities who allow them in and do not expel them, whether it be a foreigner or a fellow inhabitant who tries such a thing.

> During the second half of the fifth century BCE, Socrates was the leading intellectual figure in Athens. In 423 BCE Aristophanes' *Clouds* satirized Socrates and the theories of several other intellectuals who had come to Athens in the years before the Peloponnesian War. In the early years of the war the freedom of speech that was an integral part of Greek Old Comedy aroused considerable animosity, causing Aristophanes to revise the play a few years later. More than twenty years after the original production, when Athens had been defeated, Aristophanes' portrayal of Socrates in *Clouds* was cited in Plato's *Apology* as one of the factors that contributed to Socrates' trial and condemnation.
>
> The surviving version of *Clouds* is the revision that was never staged. In commenting on the modern reactions to this version, Price notes, "The play, often seen as merely comic, in fact articulates a set of profound objections to free thinkers."[20]
>
> In *Clouds*, a conservative father Strepsiades (Twister) urges his spendthrift son Pheidippides to go to Socrates' Thinkery (*Phrontisterion*), in order to learn how to talk his way out of his debts. The son refuses, and so the father goes instead, thus creating a comic reversal, with the elderly uneducated Strepsiades being confronted with caricatures of the intellectual ideas of the Sophists. As with any caricature or parody, some part of the representation must have a basis of familiarity, if not fact. As Henderson has observed, "In Aristophanes' plays, the world depicted by the plot and the characters on the stage was the world of the spectators in their civic roles: as heads of families and participants in governing the state. ... This depiction of public life was designed both to arouse laughter and to encourage reflection about people and events not possible in other public contexts. Thus it was at once a distorted and an accurate depiction of public life, like a modern political cartoon."[21]
>
> When Strepsiades enters the Thinkery, he sees Socrates suspended in a basket, contemplating the heavens.

---

20 Price 1999: 85.

21 Henderson 1992: 5.

12.33 ARISTOPHANES, *CLOUDS* 224–253.

Strepsiades

First tell me, pray, just what you're doing up there.

Socrates

I tread the air and contemplate the sun.   225

Strepsiades

You're spying on the gods from a wicker basket?

Why can't you do that, if you must, down here?

Socrates

                                                              Never

could I make correct celestial discoveries

except by thus suspending my mind, and mixing

my subtle head with the air it's kindred with.   230

If down below I contemplate what's up,

I'd never find aught; for the earth by natural force

draws unto itself the quickening moisture of thought.

The very same process is observable in lettuce.

Strepsiades

How's that?   235

It's thought that draws the moisture into lettuce?

Come down, Socratikins, come down here to me,

so that you can teach me what I've come to learn.

Socrates

And what might that be?

Strepsiades

                              I want to learn oratory.

By debts and interest payments and rapacious creditors   240

I'm assailed and assaulted and stand to lose my property.

Socrates

So how did you manage to slip into this condition?

Strepsiades

It's an equine ailment that's eating me up alive.[22]

No matter. Teach me one of your Arguments,

the one that pays no debts. Whatever your fee,   245

I'll pay it, I swear by all the gods, in cash.

Socrates

What do you mean, 'the gods'? In the first place, gods

---

22 *equine ailment*: Pheidippides' debts had been incurred because of his obsession with
chariot-racing and an aristocratic lifestyle.

aren't legal tender here.[23]

Strepsiades

Then how do you swear?

With iron coins, as in Byzantium?

Socrates

You want to know the truth about the gods,   250

what they really are?

Strepsiades

By God I do, if it's really possible.

Socrates

And to enter into communion with the Clouds,

who are our deities.[24]

Strepsiades

I'd like to very much.

In a mock initiation ceremony, Socrates makes the following prayer for Strepsiades who has been wreathed and sprinkled with meal, like a sacrificial victim.

12.34 ARISTOPHANES, *CLOUDS* 263–268.

Socrates

Let the oldster speak with reverence.

let him hear our pious prayer.

Mighty Master, Air unbounded,

thou who hold the floating earth,[25]

Ether bright, and Clouds so awesome,[26]

goddesses of thunder loud!   265

Rise on high, o mistresses,

appear to him who thinks on you!

---

23 On "recognizing" the gods, see 12.18 with note.

24 Henderson 1992: 31 n. 1 remarks: "No Greek would think of worshipping the clouds; they are 'goddesses' suitable only for the comic Thinkery of Socrates, who teaches men how to obscure reality by making it as changeable and evanescent as the clouds."

25 *Air...floating earth*: see Henderson 1992: 32 n. 2: "Ionian philosophers as early as Anaximenes held that the earth was a disc supported by air (one of the four 'elements', along with earth, water and fire); for Aristophanes air (empty and insubstantial) symbolizes the emptiness and insubstantiality of Socratic theories and values."

26 *Ether*; see Henderson 1992: 32 n. 3: "The 'ether' was thought to lie between the air and the sky; though it was popularly considered to be divine because of its proximity to the gods, the philosophers speculated about its relationship (if any) to the four elements of the biosphere."

After the Chorus of Clouds enter, Socrates declares that they are the only gods.

12.35 ARISTOPHANES, *CLOUDS* 364–381.

Socrates

These [the Clouds] are the only gods my man; and
   All the rest are fantasies.   365

Strepsiades

Come now, don't you all consider
Zeus on high to be a god?

Socrates

Zeus, you say? Don't kid me! There's no
Zeus at all.

Strepsiades

        What's that you say?
Who makes rain, then? That's what I would
like to know right off the bat.

Socrates

Clouds, of course! I'll prove it so by
arguments irrefutable.

   ....

Socrates

Clouds fill up with lots of water,   376
   then they're forced to move about,
sagging suddenly with rain, then
   getting heavier perforce,
collide with one another, breaking
   up and making crashing sounds.

Strepsiades

Who is it, though, that starts them [the clouds] moving?
   Isn't that the work of Zeus?

Socrates

Hardly. It's cosmic Vertigo.[27]

Strepsiades

          What?
Vertigo? I never realized   380
Zeus is gone and in his place this
Vertigo's become the king

---

27 *cosmic Vertigo*: Greek *dinos* 'rotation' or 'whirling' was an essential part of Democritus' atomic theory of the universe.

Socrates has Strepsiades promise to recognize the new gods of the Thinkery.

12.36 ARISTOPHANES, *CLOUDS* 423–426.

Socrates

Promise that you'll recognize no
  god but those *we* recognize,
Emptiness and Clouds and Tongue, the
  one and only Trinity?

Strepsiades

Even if I met the other
  gods I wouldn't speak to them,   425
or sacrifice or pour libations
  or burn the incense on their altars.

> At the end of the play Strepsiades blames the Clouds for his misfortunes, but they react as the upholders of traditional religion.

12.37 ARISTOPHANES, *CLOUDS* 1452–1464.

Strepsiades

You Clouds, it's all your fault I suffer this!
I trusted you to handle my affairs.

Chorus Leader

No, you're responsible for doing it to yourself:
you took the twisting road that leads toward evil.   1455

Strepsiades

Why didn't you tell me that at the very start,
instead of leading a poor old clod astray?

Chorus Leader

We do the same thing every time we see
a man who's fallen in love with what is wrong;
we cast him down in sheer calamity   1460
until he learns devotion to the gods.

Strepsiades

Alas, O Clouds, a lesson hard but fair!
I shouldn't have tried to cheat my creditors
of their money.

> Strepsiades utters words that would ultimately prove most damaging to the reputation of the historical Socrates.

12.38 ARISTOPHANES, *CLOUDS* 1476–1477.

Strepsiades

What lunacy! Damn, I must have been insane,
to drop the gods because of Socrates!

The play ends with Strepsiades attempting to burn down the Thinkery and urging the chorus to pursue Socrates and his pupils because of their impiety.

12.39 ARISTOPHANES, *CLOUDS* 1513–1514.

Strepsiades

Pursue them, hit them, stone them for many crimes,

but most of all for injustice toward the gods![28]

The mutilation of the Herms and the profanation of the Mysteries

The public criticism of Aristophanes' production of *Clouds* in 423 BCE, the decree of Diopeithes, the flight from Athens of Anaxagoras, Diagoras, and probably also Protagoras are all indicative of a perceived threat to traditional religion. Similar fears were aroused in 415 BCE when the mutilation of the herms and allegations that the Eleusinian mysteries had been profaned coincided with the imminent departure of an Athenian expedition to Sicily to open a new theater of war against the Spartans and their allies. The herms were sacred pillars, rectangular blocks surmounted with a head of the god Hermes and, in the middle, a model of an erect phallus. These pillars were located outside houses and shrines throughout the city.

Thucydides reports that the mutilation was deemed an impiety, an omen jeopardizing the expedition, and a conspiracy to overthrow the democracy. Alcibiades, a former pupil of Socrates and one of three generals appointed to command the Sicilian expedition, was charged with being involved in both the mutilation and the profanation of the Mysteries. He offered to stand trial before leaving Athens.

12.40 THUCYDIDES 6.27–29. Meanwhile the stone statues of Hermes in the city of Athens—these are rectangular pillars that customarily stand in great numbers both in the entrances to private homes and in sacred shrines—almost all had the faces mutilated in a single night. No one knew who had done it, but large rewards were offered by the state for the detection of the perpetrators. A decree was also passed that, if anyone, citizen or stranger or slave, knew of any other occurrence of a profanation (*asebema*), he should not be afraid to come forward and reveal the information. They took the matter very seriously; for it seemed to be an omen for the expedition and, at the same time, to be a conspiracy to cause a revolt and overthrow the democracy.

Information was given by some metics and their attendants.[29] They knew nothing about the herms, but they said that earlier there had been some

---

28 *injustice toward the gods*: the Greek *tous theous edikoun* literally means "they were wronging the gods."

29 *metics*: resident aliens.

mutilation of other statues by drunken young men who were fooling around; also a mockery (*hybris*) of the mysteries was being performed in private houses. Among the accused was Alcibiades.

The charges were taken up by those who were especially opposed to Alcibiades because his was an obstacle to their maintaining firm control of the people. For they thought that, if they could get rid of him, they would be supreme. So, they exaggerated the matter, shouting that the mockery of the mysteries and the mutilation of the herms were aimed at the overthrow of the democracy; and Alcibiades had been involved in all of these things. As further proof they cited his general unconventional and undemocratic behavior.

Immediately Alcibiades defended himself against the informers' charges. He was ready to stand trial before sailing—the preparations had already been completed—in order to determine whether he had done any of these things. If he had done any such thing, he would pay he penalty. But if he were acquitted, he would keep his command. Before witnesses he declared that they should not accept slanderous allegations about him in his absence, but that they should kill him at once, if he had done wrong. For he said that it was wiser not to send him on such an important expedition with an accusation of this sort still undecided.[30]

> The biographer Plutarch (c. 46–after 120 CE) reports that Alcibiades was ordered to sail and had some initial success. His enemies, however, linked the mutilation of the herms with the profanation of the Mysteries and initiated prosecutions.

12.41 PLUTARCH, *ALCIBIADES* 20. Alcibiades failed to convince the Athenians, but he was ordered to sail; and so he put to sea with his fellow generals.... After reaching Italy and taking Rhegium, he proposed a plan for the conduct of the war. Nicias opposed it, but Lamachus approved, and so he sailed to Sicily. He won over Catana but achieved nothing more, because he was soon recalled by the Athenians to stand trial.

At first, as I have said, nothing more than vague suspicions and slanders were made against Alcibiades by a number of slaves and resident aliens. Then, once he was out of the way, his enemies worked against him more vigorously. They linked the outrages committed against the herms with the affair of the mysteries, alleging that they were part of a conspiracy to overthrow the government. Therefore anyone accused of any connection with either episode was imprisoned without trial. The people now felt angry with themselves for not bringing Alcibiades to trial and securing judgment against him on such serious charges at the time of the offence. Any relative, or friend, or associate of his who encountered their anger experienced exceedingly harsh treatment.

---

30 *an accusation of this sort still undecided*: if he were guilty of *asebeia* (impiety), the anger of the gods would put the expedition in jeopardy.

Summoned to return to Athens, Alcibiades anticipated arrest by defecting to Sparta. Plutarch reports the impeachment, noting that he was condemned by default.

12.42 PLUTARCH, *ALCIABIADES* 22. The impeachment against him is still on record and is as follows:

"Thessalus, the son of Cimon, of the deme Laciadae, accuses Alcibiades, the son of Cleinias, of the deme Scambonidae, of committing sacrilege against the goddesses of Eleusis, Demeter, and Kore, by making a mockery of the Mysteries; revealing them to his companions in his own house, wearing a robe such as the hierophant wears,[31] when he reveals the rites to the initiates; calling himself hierophant, Pulytion Torch-bearer, and Theodorus, of the deme Phegaea, Herald, addressing the rest of his companions as *Mustae* and *Epoptae*,[32] contrary to the laws and institutions established by the Eumolpidae, Heralds, and priests of Eleusis."

Alcibiades was condemned by default, his property was confiscated, and it was further decreed that his name should be publicly cursed by all priests and priestesses. It is said that Theano, the daughter of Menon of the deme Agraule, was the only one who refused to obey this decree; she declared that she was a priestess of prayers, not curses.

The enormity of the profanation is articulated by the speech writer Lysias arguing for the prosecution in the later trial of Andocides in 400 or 399 BCE. Lysias contrasts Andocides' impiety with the atheism of the non-Athenian Diagoras.[33]

12.43 LYSIAS, *AGAINST ANDOCIDES FOR IMPIETY* 17–19. Observe how much more impious this man [Andocides] has been than Diagoras the Melian. For the latter was impious in speaking about the sacred rites and festivals of a city that was foreign to him, whereas Andocides' impiety was an act concerning the sanctities of his own city. Where these sacred things are concerned, you should be angry at your own citizens rather than strangers…. Andocides has made it clear to the Greeks that he does not recognize the gods.

Lysias describes Andocides' acts of impiety.

12.44 LYSIAS, *AGAINST ANDOCIDES FOR IMPIETY* 51. For this man [Andocides] put on a ceremonial robe and, in imitation of the rites, he revealed the sacred things to the uninitiated, and gave voice to the forbidden words. Those deities whom we recognize and acknowledge, to whom we sacrifice and pray with our devotions and purifications—these he mutilated. And for such deeds priestesses and priests stood up and cursed him, facing

---

31 *hierophant*: the one who reveals the sacred rites, the chief priest of the mysteries.

32 *Mustae and Epoptae*: Mustae were initiates, but *Epoptae* were initiates who had undergone a higher form of initiation.

33 On Diagoras, see 12.23 and 12.24.

west and shaking out the purple robes according to the ancient and time-honored custom.

> After his defection, Alcibiades gave the Spartans strategic advice that contributed to several Spartan successes in the ensuing years. Then he abandoned the Spartan cause, gained the support of a Persian governor, and negotiated with the Athenians in the fleet. The Athenians won several naval victories over the Spartans, thus restoring him to favor in Athens.

> On his return, Alcibiades addressed the Athenian assembly, attributing his misdeeds to evil fortune and a jealous divinity. He was elected as general with absolute powers, his property was restored, and the curses against him annulled (Plutarch, *Alcibiades* 33). To affirm his piety, Alcibiades provided a military escort for the procession to Eleusis.

12.45 PLUTARCH, *ALCIABIADES* 34. Ever since Decalea had been fortified,[34] Spartan forces had controlled the approaches to Eleusis, and so the festal procession had been celebrated without elaboration, going by sea. The customary sacrifices, dances, and many of the sacred rites enacted on the road as Iacchus is escorted to Eleusis had, of necessity, been omitted.

Alcibiades realized that it would be a splendid gesture, both for his respect for the gods and his reputation in the eyes of men, if he could restore the festival to its traditional form by having the infantry escort the procession by land as they marched with their spears past the enemy.

In this way he would either frustrate and humiliate Agis if the king made no move,[35] or, if attacked, he would fight a battle that was sacred and approved by the gods in defense of the highest and most sacred interests, in full view of his native city and with all his fellow citizens as witnesses of his valor.

…

He posted sentries on the heights and sent out an advance guard at daybreak. Then, taking the priests, the initiates, and the initiators, he placed them in the center of his column and conducted them along the road to Eleusis in solemn order and complete silence. So imposing and awesome was the spectacle that those who were not jealous of him declared that he had proved himself not merely a general but a high priest and initiator of the mysteries. None of the enemy dared to attack, and he brought the procession safely back to Athens.

> After some minor Athenian victories, Alcibiades lost the generalship when one of his subordinates was defeated and killed by the Spartans. He remained in Asia Minor and did not return to Athens. When the Athenians were finally defeated he was killed on the order of the Spartan authorities.

---

34 *Decalea*: a location in the foothills of Mount Parnes, overlooking the Attic plain, garrisoned by the Spartans in 413 BCE on the advice of Alcibiades.

35 *Agis*: the Spartan king.

The trial and death of Socrates

Four years after the end of the Peloponnesian War, Socrates (470/69–399 BCE) was tried by a jury and condemned to death on charges of impiety.[36] Although he could have avoided prosecution by leaving Athens, he remained to face trial and drank the fatal hemlock a few days after his condemnation.

Unlike the Sophists, Socrates left no writings, nor do we have the speech for the prosecution. Three contemporary sources, however, yield information about his teachings and methods: Aristophanes' *Clouds*, and the writings of two of his former pupils, Plato (c. 429–347 BCE) and Xenophon (c. 430–after 362 BCE). Many scholars have privileged the testimony of Plato's *Apology* over that of Xenophon and Aristophanes (b. in the 450s, died c. 386 BCE), but each author should be considered in his own literary and historical context.

Parker's observations are more perspicacious: "Religious resentment against Socrates was, however, not necessarily the less acute for being misdirected. The portrait of 'Socrates' in Aristophanes' *Clouds* becomes, therefore, a document of prime importance. For our purpose, it does not matter at all whether 'Socrates' bears much relation to the historical figure. What is important is that the play is treated in Plato's *Apology* as a typical expression of the popular prejudices against him. For many jurors, therefore, 'Socrates' was, in caricature, Socrates.... Popular fears of impiety are here [in *Clouds*] displayed, much more fully and clearly than in any other source." [37]

Although the charges against Socrates were primarily religious, the intent of the trial was also political. Among Socrates' earlier students and associates were not only Alcibiades but Critias, a friend of Alcibiades and admirer of Spartan ways who had also been implicated in the mutilation of the herms.[38] After the defeat of Athens in 404 BCE, Critias was one of the Thirty Tyrants; he was killed in the civil strife that resulted in their overthrow in 403 BCE. Socrates' connection with these two men who achieved such notoriety during the Peloponnesian War can only have contributed to his unpopularity in the aftermath of that war.

Diogenes Laertius (probably third century CE), who wrote on the lives and doctrines of ancient Greek philosophers, gives the deposition and charge against Socrates:

---

36 On the technical question of whether Socrates was impeached under Diopeithes' decree (see 12.18) or indicted for misdemeanors, see Parker 1996: 208–210.

37 Parker 1996: 203.

38 On Critias, see 12.28.

12.46 DIOGENES LAERTIUS 2.40. The deposition in the case, which, according to Favorinus,[39] was still preserved in the Metroön, was as follows: "This indictment and deposition is sworn by Meletus, the son of Meletus of the deme of Pitthos, against Socrates, the son of Sophroniscus of the deme of Alopece. Socrates has done wrong because he does not recognize the gods that the city recognizes.[40] He also does wrong because he corrupts the youth. The penalty demanded is death.

> In Plato's *Euthyphro*, Euthyphro is discussing Meletus' charges with Socrates. He points out the problems created by Socrates' claim to have a personal *daimonion* or spirit.

12.47 PLATO, *EUTHYPHRO* 3 b.

Socrates. He [Meletus] says that I make gods, and that in making new gods I do not recognize the old gods.[41] And he says that it is for the sake of the old ones that he is indicting me.

Euthyphro. I understand, Socrates. But it's because you say that the *daimonion* comes upon you from time to time. On the grounds, therefore, that you are making religious innovations,[42] Meletus has laid this charge against you and is going to court in order to arouse prejudice against you. For he well knows that such matters are easy to misrepresent where the majority is concerned.

> In his *Apology*, Plato attributes to Socrates an analysis of the charges, pointing out to the jury that the slanders date back to the previous generation.

12.48 PLATO, *APOLOGY* 18 a–c. First of all, gentlemen of the jury, it is just that I defend myself against the earliest charges that have been falsely laid against me, and against my earliest accusers;[43] and then the later accusations and accusers. For a great many people have made accusations against me for a great many years, though there's no truth in what they say. And I am more afraid of those people than I am of Anytus and his colleagues, although they are dangerous enough.

More dangerous, however, are those who won your trust, since they got hold of most of you when you were children. Without any truth they accused me, saying, "There is a certain wise man (*sophos*) called Socrates who has

---

39 *Favorinus*: c. 85–155 CE, a philosopher, sophist, man of letters, and friend of Plutarch.

40 *done wrong*: the Greek verb is *adikein*—to do wrong, commit an injustice. *recognize the gods*: on the Greek verb *nomizein*, to recognize, acknowledge, accept, and thus worship, see above 12.18 with n. 3.

41 *new gods*: the Greek word *kainos* which means "new" or "strange," recurs in the different accounts of the charges.

42 *making religious innovations*: the Greek *kainotomountos peri ta theia* literally means "making innovations concerning divine matters."

43 *my earliest accusers*: those whose hostility to Socrates derived from his portrayal in Aristophanes' *Clouds*.

theories about the heavens and has investigated everything below the earth, and makes the weaker argument prevail over the stronger." These are the people, gentlemen, who have spread these rumors, who are my dangerous accusers. For those who hear them suppose that anyone who inquires into such matters does not recognize the gods.

> Socrates reads the charges and refers to his portrayal in Aristophanes' *Clouds*.

12.49 PLATO, *APOLOGY* 19 a–c. Let us go back to the beginning and consider what the charge is that has given rise to this prejudice against me, encouraging Meletus to bring this indictment. Very well. What did those who did the slandering say when they uttered their slanders?

I must read out their affidavit, as though they were my criminal accusers. "Socrates is a wrongdoer and a busybody,[44] in that he inquires into things below the earth and in the heavens, makes the weaker argument prevail over the stronger,[45] and teaches these same things to others." It goes something like that. You have seen it for yourselves in Aristophanes' comedy where a certain Socrates is transported around up there, proclaiming that he is walking on air, and uttering a great deal of other nonsense about things of which I know nothing, be they great or small.

> Socrates suggests that the charge of corrupting the youth derives from his method of cross-examination, which was notorious for exposing an individual's ignorance.

12.50 PLATO, *APOLOGY* 23 c–d. A number of young men, especially those who have the leisure and are sons of wealthy fathers, follow me of their own accord because they enjoy hearing people being cross-examined. These often copy my method and attempt to question other persons. And then, I suppose, they find an abundance of people who think that they know something, whereas they really know little or nothing. Consequently those who are cross-examined become annoyed with me, though not with themselves. And so they complain that there is an abominable individual called Socrates who is corrupting the youth.

Whenever anyone asks them what it is that Socrates does, and what he teaches, they have no answer, not knowing what to say; rather, to avoid appearing to be confused, they resort to the stock charges against all philosophers: teaching about things in the heavens and below the earth, a failure to recognize the gods, and making the weaker argument prevail over the stronger. They would be unwilling, I think, to admit the truth: which is that they are clearly pretending to knowledge when they know nothing at all.

---

44 *wrongdoer*: see above 12.46 with n. 40.

45 *weaker argument appear the stronger*: see Aristophanes, *Clouds* 112–118.

Socrates names his three accusers and the professions of the men on whose behalf they are acting, thus implying that the trial is political. He summarizes three charges.

12.51 PLATO, *APOLOGY* 23 e–24 b. Among my accusers were Meletus, Anytus, and Lycon. Meletus was angered on account of the poets, Anytus on account of the artisans and politicians, and Lycon on account of the orators. And so, as I said in the beginning, I would be amazed if I were able to rid your minds of this prejudice in the short time that I have because it has become so big....

Let us take up the deposition. It goes something like this: it is alleged that Socrates is a wrongdoer because he corrupts the youth and does not recognize the gods that the state recognizes, but recognizes other new divinities (*daimonia kaina*).

Socrates addresses the charges of atheism and failure to recognize the traditional gods.

12.52 PLATO, *APOLOGY* 26 c–e.

Socrates: I can't understand whether you claim that I teach that I recognize the existence of some gods — that is, that I myself recognize that gods exist, I am not a complete atheist, and I am not a wrongdoer in this respect; that these gods, however, are not the ones that the state recognizes, but other ones, and that this is what you charge me with; namely that I recognize other ones. Or do you allege that I do not recognize gods at all and that I teach this to others?

Meletus: This is what I say: you do not recognize gods at all.

Socrates: You surprise me, Meletus; what is your object in saying that? Are you suggesting that I don't consider that the sun and moon are gods, as humans generally do?[46]

Meletus: By Zeus, he certainly does not, gentlemen of the jury, since he says that the sun is a stone and moon a mass of earth.

Socrates: My dear Meletus, do you imagine that you're prosecuting Anaxagoras?[47] Do you so despise these gentlemen, and assume them to be so ignorant as not to know that the writings of Anaxagoras of Clazomenae are full of such theories? And do you seriously think that the young men get these ideas from me when they can buy them in the orchestra for a drachma at most,[48] and so make fun of Socrates if he tries to pass them off as his own?.... By Zeus, Meletus, is that your opinion of me? Do I recognize no god?

Meletus: No, none at all, by Zeus, in no way whatsoever.

---

46 The argument is that the sun and moon were not deities that received public worship. People might think of the Sun and Moon as gods, but they could not be expected to worship them.

47 *Anaxagoras*: see 12.17 and 12.18.

48 *orchestra*: the dancing place in the theater which would be vacant for much of the year and so could accommodate bookstalls.

Socrates discusses his personal *daimonion*.

12.53 PLATO, *APOLOGY* 31 d. A certain divine or daimonic something comes upon me, the very thing that Meletus ridicules in the indictment. It began in my early childhood—a certain voice that comes to me; and when it comes it always holds me back from what I am intending to do, and never urges me on. It is this that turns me against public life, and a very good thing too, in my opinion. Be assured, gentlemen, had I undertaken to engage in politics, I should long ago have lost my life, without being of any benefit either to you or to myself.

Xenophon, who was not in Athens at the time of Socrates' death, gives his version of Socrates' defense.

12.54 XENOPHON, *APOLOGY* 10–13.

Hermogenes says that Socrates had this resolve [to die] when he came before the jury after his adversaries had charged him with not recognizing the gods worshiped by the state, introducing new divinities, and corrupting the youth.[49] In response Socrates said, "The main thing that amazes me in Meletus, gentlemen, is what may be the basis for his assertion that I don't recognize the gods. For everyone who happened to be nearby saw me sacrificing at the communal festivals and the public altars, even Meletus himself, if he had so wished.

As for introducing "new divinities," how could I be guilty of that merely because I say that a voice of god signals to me what I should do? Surely those who take omens from the cries of birds and utterances of men take their proof from "voices"? And will anyone dispute that thunder utters its "voice," or that it is an omen of the greatest importance? Doesn't the priestess who sits on the tripod announce the god's will through a "voice"? Moreover, doesn't everyone use and recognize these terms when speaking of god's foreknowledge of the future and his forewarnings given to those he wishes?

The only difference is that they call the sources of their signs "birds," "utterances," "omens," or "seers;" whereas I call mine "a divine thing." And I think that in using such a term I am speaking with more truth and religious feeling than those who ascribe the gods' power to birds.

As for the charge that I do not utter falsehoods against the god, I offer the following proof: I have revealed the god's advice to many of my friends and on no occasion has it been proved false.[50]

---

49 *Hermogenes*: one of the Socratic circle who, as Plato attests (*Phaedo* 59 b), was among the witnesses. *this resolve*: to accept the death penalty rather than be forced to beg for a longer life and experience the troubles of old age.

50 On Socrates' advice to Xenophon to consult the Delphic oracle before embarking on Cyrus' expedition, see 5.41.

12.55 XENOPHON, *MEMORABILIA* 1.1.2–3. The general talk was that Socrates claimed that a *daimonion* gave him signs. And this, in my opinion, was the principal reason that he was charged with introducing new divinities (*kaina daimonia*). He was doing nothing "newer" than believers in divination who rely on birds, oracles, signs, and sacrifices.

> Diogenes Laertius reports Socrates' condemnation, death, and the aftermath.

12.56 DIOGENES LAERTIUS 2.42. Socrates was condemned to death by a plurality of eighty votes. He was put in prison, and a few days later drank the hemlock, after much noble discourse recorded in Plato's *Phaedo*....

So he was taken from humankind, and not long afterwards the Athenians underwent such a change of mind that they closed the wrestling grounds and the gymnasia. They banished all the other accusers but put Meletus to death, and they honored Socrates with a bronze statue.

13. Magic, Sorcery, and Witchcraft

13.1   PLATO, *REPUBLIC* 364 b–c. Begging priests (*agyrtai*) and seers (*manteis*) come to the doors of the wealthy and persuade them that they have the god-given power to cure by means of sacrifices and incantations (*epoidais*) that are accompanied by pleasurable feasts whatever misdeeds they or their ancestors have committed. If someone wants to injure an enemy, for a small fee he can harm a just or an unjust person alike, since they persuade the gods to do their bidding, so they say, by certain charms and binding spells.[1]

> Plato comments on the prevalence of incantations (*epoidai*), charms (*epagogoai*), and binding spells (*katadesmoi*) that were peddled by itinerant beggar priests (*agurtae*) and seers (*manteis*). The distinction between such charlatans or quacks and the true seer or diviner who has official status within a state is implicit in an excerpt from Sophocles' *King Oidipous*.[2] After the seer Tiresias has reluctantly divulged that Oedipus is the murderer of Laius, Oedipus supposes that his brother-in-law Creon is using Tiresias as a tool to depose him.

13.2   SOPHOCLES, *KING OIDIPOUS* 385–389.

[T]he trusty Creon, he who always was my friend,
has crept against me secretly desiring to
depose me, sneaking in this conjuror (*magos*), this scheme-
weaving deceptive beggar-priest (*agyrtes*) with eyes only
for profit, blind in using his prophetic skill.

---

1   *binding spells*: the Greek word *katadesmos* derives from the verb *katadein* to tie fast, bind, and thus immobilize. Graf 1997: 120 notes that "The usual objective of ritual binding is, thus, to subject another human being to one's will, to make the person unable to act according to his or her own wishes."

2   For confidence in Tiresias as a true seer, see 5.7.

Binding spells

Archaeological finds offer concrete evidence of the use of binding spells. These spells are written on lead tablets and on papyrus scrolls.

Lead tablets, often pierced by one or more nails and inscribed with curses, were placed in graves, sanctuaries of chthonic deities, and underground bodies of water in order to make contact with the powers of the underworld. Lead, perhaps because of its color or weight, may have been viewed as particularly appropriate to the underworld. Such objects are particularly significant because, unlike much literary evidence, they reflect the rituals and beliefs of people whose lives would otherwise be unrecorded by history. These magic rites were undertaken by an individual on his own behalf, often with the intent to harm, and usually with the help of a *magos*, wizard, witch, or sorceress acting as a sort of priest , though one lacking sanction of the community or *polis*.

Papyri, generally known as the Greek magical papyri, date from the second century BCE to the fifth century CE. These texts, discovered in the sands of Egypt, offer a variety of magical spells, formulae, chants, and rituals. Although many of the papyri are of a later date than the period covered by this book, they nevertheless offer valuable information about practices that had long been in prevalent in the Greek world.[3]

One of the earliest binding spells (late sixth or early fifth century BCE) was discovered in a necropolis near Selinus in Sicily. The curse names the tongue, the particular organ of the intended victims that most threatens the maker of the curse, and is probably in the context of a legal dispute.

13.3   Lopez Jimeno 1991 no. 3 (O no. 168)[4]

(Side A) The tongue of Eucles and the tongue of Aristophanis and the tongue of Angeilis and the tongue of Alciphron and the tongue of Hagestratos. The tongues of the advocates of Eucles and Aristophanis. The tongue of … [lacuna]

(Side B) And the tongue of Oinotheos and the tongue of …[lacuna]

An Attic lead binding-curse tablet against an individual's opponents and against any future binding curses dates to the early fourth century BCE. On side A, the targets of the curse are specified as precisely as possible. Side B identifies a dispute at law as the context of the curse.

---

3   See Betz 1996, for translations of a large number of the magical papyri and also the demotic spells.

4   (O no. 168) equals passage number 168 in Ogden 2002, a collection of translations of Greek texts on magic, ghosts and witchcraft; there is a brief commentary on each text, but no Greek texts are given. Some selections in this current chapter correspond at least partially to passages translated with commentary by Ogden. Because the primary sources for magic and the occult can be especially inaccessible, references to a numbered Ogden passage are provided where available, so that the reader can readily find additional examples.

13.4   Jordan 1999 no. 1 (O no. 169)

(Side A) If anyone puts a binding spell on me, be it man or woman, slave or free, alien or citizen, from my household or from outside it, whether through envy toward my work or my actions; if anyone puts a binding spell on me invoking Hermes, be it Hermes *Eriounios* or Hermes the Restrainer or Hermes the Trickster, or some other power, I bind in return all my enemies.[5]

(Side B) I bind my opponents in court Dion and Granicus.

> A second- to first-century BCE legal-curse tablet, found in Megara or Arcadia in Greece, is addressed to Pasianax, probably the ghost of the man buried in the tomb in which the tablet was found.[6] The intent is to forestall lawsuits by making the would-be prosecutors as speechless as the ghost.

13.5   DTAud 43, 44 (O no. 170)

A. Whenever you, O Pasianax, read this text, —but you will never read this text, O Pasianax, nor will Neophanes ever bring a case against Agasibalus. But just as you, O Pasianax, lie here ineffectual, so too may Neophanes become ineffectual and nothing.

B. Whenever you, O Pasianax, read this text—but you will never read this, nor will Acestor or Timandrias ever bring a case against Eratomenes. But just as you lie here ineffectual and nothing, so may Acestor and Timandridas be ineffectual and nothing.

> A fourth-century Attic lead curse tablet against pimps, bawds, and prostitutes. Binding the speech of these individuals was presumably to prevent them soliciting customers.

13.6   DTAud 52 (O no. 177) Cercis, Blastus, Nicenader, Glycera. I bind Cercis and the speech and actions of Cercis and his/her tongue before bachelors and whenever they read this, only then may Cercis have the power to speak.[7]

I bind Theon, himself and his girls and his trade and his resources and his work and his speech and his deeds. Underworld Hermes, perform this act of restraint and keep reading this so long as these people live.

> In *Laws* Plato lists various magic practices sold by corrupt individuals who reject traditional religion and declares that such individuals should be punished.

13.7   PLATO, *LAWS* 10.909 a–b. As for those who, like wild beasts, declare that the gods do not care and are open to bribes, and those who, in contempt for men, charm the souls of many of the living, claiming that they charm the dead, and promise to persuade the gods, bewitching them, as it were, with

---

5   *Hermes*: he is invoked as the god who conducts the dead to the underworld. *the Restrainer*: this epithet suggests that Hermes is to perform the binding.

6   Ogden 2002: 211 notes a 1999 suggestion of E. Voutiras that Pasianax, which means "Lord of all," is an underworld spirit (*daimon*).

7   The gender of Cercis is disputed.

sacrifices, prayers, and incantations—in this way, for the sake of money, they attempt utterly to destroy individuals, entire families, and cities. The court should punish one judged guilty of these things according to the law...

> Plato addresses the problem of willful and deliberate poisoning caused by potions, foods, and ointments prepared by sorcerers or witches, and binding spells that cause physical injury. Those convicted of such practices should be executed.

13.8   PLATO, *LAWS* 11.933 a–b and e. [This kind of] poisoning operates through sorceries, incantations, and so-called binding spells by convincing those who are bold enough to cause injury that they can indeed do so, and by also convincing their victims that they are certainly being harmed by those who have the power of bewitchment.

With things like this, it is neither easy to know what is the truth, nor, if one does know it, to convince others. It is not worthwhile to try to tell the souls of men who are suspicious of each other to ignore all such things, whenever they happen to see molded wax figures in doorways or at crossroads or in some cases on the tombs of their ancestors, if we do not ourselves have a clear opinion about such matters....

And if a person is judged to be causing injury by binding spells or charms or certain incantations or poisoning of any sort, whether he is a seer or interpreter of portents, he must be put to death.

> Evidence for actual legislation against harmful magic and its repression is scanty. The following clauses from an inscription (c. 470 BCE) from Teos, a city on the coast of Asia Minor near Ephesus, record a series of measures to protect the welfare of the state, prescribing either the death penalty or a curse on the offender and his family.

13.9   ML no. 30[8] (O no. 278)

1. If anyone makes harmful spells/poisons against the Teian state or against its individuals, he is to die, both himself and his family.[9]

2. If anyone obstructs the importation of grain into Teian territory by any means, be it by land or sea, or sends it back once it has been imported, he is to die, himself and his family.

.....

6. Those officials who do not perform this curse at the statue of Dynamis (Power) when the games begin at the Anthesteria or the festival of Heracles or that of Zeus, are to be the object of the curse.

---

8   ML no. 30 is the numbering of the inscription in Meiggs and Lewis 1988, a collection of Greek historical inscriptions that is more widely available than earlier publications of these inscriptions. ML provide a full Greek text, often emended, citations of earlier publications, a commentary, but no translation.

9   *harmful spells/ poisons*: *pharmaka deleteria*. The Greek word *pharmakon* can mean poison or spell.

7. If anyone breaks the inscription on which this curse has been written, or chips off the letters, or makes them disappear, he is to die, both himself and his family.

> An inscription, probably written in the fourth century BCE, is the recreation of an earlier oath enacted by the Spartan settlers on the island of Thera, c. 630 BCE. Many of these settlers were forced to resettle in Libya because of famine.[10] The oath was accompanied by the ritual burning of wax dolls, with the prayer that those who broke the oath would experience the same fate as the dolls.

13.10 ML no. 5, lines 40—51 (O no. 236). Oaths were sworn to this agreement both by those who remained in Thera and those who sailed as colonists. They invoked curses on those who should break these terms and fail to abide by their oath, whether they were among those settling in Libya or those remaining behind in Thera. They modeled wax dolls and burned them as they invoked the curse, all of them coming together, men, women, and girls.

They prayed that the one who did not abide by these oaths but transgressed them should melt and dissolve just like the dolls, he himself, his descendants, and his property; but that those that did abide by these oaths, whether among those sailing to Libya or those remaining behind in Thera, should have many good things, both they themselves and their descendants.

> The following extracts from the beginning of a long list of instructions for making a doll to attract the love of a woman comes from a fourth-century CE papyrus discovered in Egypt.

13.11 *PGM* IV 296–355 (O no. 239). Amazing binding love spell (*philtrokatadesmos*). Take some wax or clay from a potter's wheel and mold two figures, male and female. Arm the male like Ares, wielding a sword in his left hand and striking the female's neck on her right side. Put the female doll's hands behind her back and make her kneel. Smear the stuff on her head or on her neck. Then write on the doll of the woman being attracted. On her head, write: "ISEE IAO ITHI OUNE BRIDOLOTHION NEBOUTOSOUALETH;" on her right ear, "OUER MECHAN;" on her left ear, "LIBABA OIMATHOTHO;" on her face, "AMOUNABREO"....

Take thirteen bronze needles and insert one of them into the brain while intoning: "I pierce your brain," (insert her name); insert two into her ears, two more into her eyes, one into her mouth, two below her rib cage, one into her hands, two into her vulva and anus, and two into the soles of her feet, saying once each time: "I pierce the (insert name of part) of (insert her name), so that she may think of no one except me alone (insert your name)."

Take a lead tablet, inscribe the same spell on it and recite it. Bind the tablet to the figures as you take a thread from a loom and make 365 knots, while

---

10 For more, but different, details about this incident, see Herodotus 4.150–158.

intoning, as you know how to, "Abrasax, constrain her." Place it at sunset by the grave by one who has died prematurely or violently and lay alongside it flowers of the season. The following is the inscribed and recited spell.

"I deposit with you this binding spell (katadesmos), chthonic gods and UESEMIGADON, maiden Persphone Ereschigal, and Adonis the BARBARITHA;[11] underworld Hermes, THOOUTH PHOKENTAZEPSEU AERCHTHATHOU MISONKTAI KALBANACHAMBRE; powerful Anubis PSIRINTH,[12] holder of the keys to Hades; gods and demons of the underworld, men and women who have died prematurely, boys and maidens, year after year, month after month, day after day, hour after hour. I adjure all demons in this place to assist this demon. Rouse yourself for me, whoever you are, whether male or female, and go to every district, every block, and every house.

Bring her and bind her. Bring her (insert her name), the daughter of (insert her mother's name) whose essence you have. Make her be in love with me (insert your name) whom (insert your mother's name) bore. Let her not fornicate, let her not be buggered, and do not allow her to do anything that brings pleasure with another man, except with me alone (insert your name) so that she is unable either to drink or eat....[13]

> In a late fourth or early third century BCE lead tablet from Acanthus in Macedonia, a man casts an attraction spell on two women, imposing restrictions on them until they favor him.

13.12 Jordan 1999 no. 3 (O no. 205)

A. Pausanias binds Sime, daughter of Amphitritus (may no one but Pausanias undo this spell) until she does for Pausanias everything Pausanias wants. May she not be able to get hold of a sacrificial victim of Athena, nor may Aphrodite look kindly upon her, before Sime holds Pausanias tight.

B. Of Melissa of Apollonia.[14] Pausanias binds Aenis. May she not be able to get hold of a sacrificial victim or achieve any other good thing before Aenis looks kindly on Pausanias. May no one but Pausanias undo this spell.

> Erotic curse tablets can be divided into two categories, separation or attraction. A fourth-century BCE separation lead curse tablet from Attica probably comes from a grave. The invoker of the curse hopes to destroy relations between Theodora and her lover, Charias.[15]

---

11 *Adonis*: a divine figure of eastern origin; a beautiful youth with whom, according to the Greeks, Aphrodite fell in love. She entrusted him to Persephone who also fell in love with him, refusing to give him back. Zeus decreed that he should spend four months with Aphrodite, four with Persephone and four doing as he wished.

12 Anubis: an Egyptian god.

13 For an entire translation of this long spell see Ogden 2002: 247–250 with commentary.

14 *Of Melissa*: this reference to a third woman is puzzling.

15 For discussion, see Gager 1992: 90.

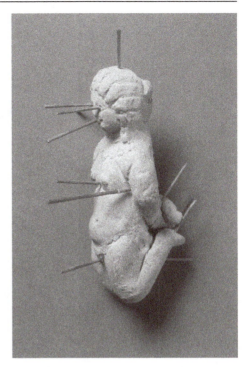

Figure 13.1. Female execration figure pierced with needles, for ritual cursing. Terracotta, Roman period from Egypt. Louvre, Paris. Art Resource, New York.

13.13 DTAud 68.

(Side A) I bind Theodora in the presence of the female one at Persephone's side,[16] and in the presence of those who are unmarried. May she be unmarried and whenever she is about to talk with Callias and with Charias—whenever she is about to discuss deeds and words and business … words, whatever he indeed says. I bind Theodora to remain unmarried to Charias and (I bind) Charias to forget Theodora, and (I bind) Charias to forget… Theodora and sex with Theodora.

(Side B) [And just as] this corpse lies unfulfilled, [so] may all the words and deeds of Theodora be unfulfilled with regard to Charias and to the other people. I bind Theodora before Hermes of the underworld and before the unmarried and before Tethys.[17] (I bind) everything, both (her) words and deeds toward Charias and other people, and (her) sex with Charias. And may Charias forget sex. May Charias forget the girl, Theodora, the very one whom he loves.

16 *the female one at Persephone's side*: Hecate, a goddess associated with magic and witchcraft.

17 *Tethys*: the wife of Oceanus, the sea god.

A fourth century BCE tablet from Nemea near Corinth is intended to separate two male lovers, without invoking any deity.[18]

13.14 *SEG* 30.353.

I turn Euboles away

from Aineas,

from his face,

from his eyes,

from his mouth,

from his breasts,

from his soul (*psyche*),

from his belly,

from his penis,

from his anus.

from his whole body.

I turn Euboles away

from Aineas.

Three binding spells for scorpions.

13.15 *PGM* XXVIII a. OR OR[19] PHOR PHOR SABAOTH ADONE SALAMA TARCHEI ABRASAX, I bind you, scorpion of Artemisia, three hundred and fifteen times, on the fifteenth day of Pachon...

13.16 *PGM* XXVIII b. HOR HOR PHOR PHOR IAO ADONAEI SABAOTH SALAMAN TARCHCHEI, I bind you, scorpion of Artemisios, on the 13th.

13.17 *PGM* XXVIII c. HOR HOR PHOR PHOR ADONAI SALAMA RTHACHI, I bind you, Artemisian scorpion, on the fourth day of Phanenoth, PHOR OR OR OSOA DDD RRR.

Four recommendations for amulets to be worn as a contraceptive.[20]

13.18 *PGM* LXIII 25 (O no. 255). A contraceptive: Take a bean that has a small insect in it, and wear it as an amulet.

13.19 *PGM* LXIII 26. A contraceptive: Take a bean, that has been pierced, tie it up it in a piece of mule skin, and wear it as an amulet.[21]

13.20 *PGM* XXII a 11–14 (O no. 235). The following verse if carried with a magnetic stone or even recited, acts as a contraceptive: "You should never

---

18 For discussion, see Gager 1992: 92.

19 Betz 1996: 265 notes that the name OR should probably be pronounced, HOR, i.e., Horus, an Egyptian god who is often involved in Egyptian scorpion spells.

20 *amulet*: an object worn on the person to ward off evil, disease or other undesirable happenings; sometimes applied to the skin as protection against infection or disease.

21 *mule skin*: mules are sterile.

have been born and should have perished unmarried."[22] Write this on a new piece of papyrus and tie it with the hairs of a mule.

13.21 *PGM* XXXVI 321–332. A contraceptive, the only one in the world: Take as many bitter vetch seeds as you want for however many years you want to remain sterile.[23] Soak them in the menses of a menstruating woman. Let her soak them in her own genitals. And take a living frog and throw the bitter vetch seeds into its mouth so that the frog swallows them; then release the frog alive at the place where you captured him. And take a seed of henbane,[24] steep it in mare's milk; and take the nasal mucus of an ox, with grains of barley, put these into the skin of a fawn and bind it up on the outside with a piece of mule skin, and attach it to an amulet at the time of the moon's waning [which is] in a female sign of the zodiac on a day of Cronos or Hermes. Mix in also with the barley grains wax from the ear of a mule.

Instructions for an amulet against spells.

13.22 *PGM* XXXVI 256–261 (O no. 270). Take a triangular piece of pottery from a place where three roads meet.[25] Take it in your left hand, and inscribe it with myrrh ink and then hide it. Write "ASSTRAELOS CHRAELOS, destroy every spell that is cast against me (insert your name), because I adjure you by the great and terrifying names, the names at which the winds shudder and rocks are shattered when they hear them." [seven characters or signs follow]

A prayer for justice by a mother, Artemisia, because her daughter has been deprived of full burial rites, allegedly by the girl's father whom she curses. The oldest of the Greek Magical Papyri, it was deposited in the main temple of Oserapis in the Serapeium at Memphis in Egypt (fourth century BCE).

13.23 *PGM* XL 1–18 (O no. 190) O master Oserapis and gods sitting with Oserapis, I, Artemisia, daughter of Amasis, pray to you, against the father of my daughter, because he deprived her of funeral gifts and a tomb. So if he acted justly to me and his own children likewise—and in fact he has acted unjustly to me and his own children likewise—may Oserapis and gods grant that he should receive no tomb from his children, and that he should not bury his own parents. As long as my cry for help is deposited here, may he and all his possessions be destroyed miserably on land and sea, by Oserapis and the gods that sit in attendance on him, and may he not find propitiation with Oserapis, nor with the gods that sit with Oserapis.

Artemisia has deposited this supplication, supplicating Oserapis and the gods that sit with Oserapis to administer justice. And so long as this supplication lies here, may the father of my little girl find the gods in no way

---

22 Homer, *Iliad* 3.40; these words are addressed to Paris by his brother Hector.

23 *bitter vetch*: a grain legume, said to have medicinal value.

24 *henbane*: a poisonous plant.

25 *a place where three roads meet*: Hecate, a goddess of the underworld, was thought to frequent crossroads.

propitious. If anyone picks up this text and does an injustice to Artemisia, may the god punish him....[26]

> The second column of a sacred law (c. 460 BCE) discovered near Selinus in Sicily gives directions for dealing with an *elasteros*, an avenging spirit or attacking ghost.[27]

13.24 Jameson, Jordan, and Kotansky 1993: 16, column B (O no.123). If a person wants to purify himself from *elasteroi*, he is to make a proclamation wherever he wants and at whatever point in the year he wants and in whatever month he wants and on whatever day he wants and facing in whatever direction he wants. Then let him purify himself.

He is to welcome it (the *elasteros*) and give it water for washing the hands, a meal and wine, and he is to give salt to this same one.[28] He is to sacrifice a piglet to Zeus, to go out [from the sanctuary] and turn around.[29] He may then be addressed. He may eat and he may sleep wherever he wishes.[30] If someone wants to be purified of the *elasteros* of someone outside his family or of a member of his family, one that has been heard or one that has been seen, or any (*elasteros*) at all, he is to be purified in the same way as a murderer, when he is purified of his *elasteros*. Once he has sacrificed a full-grown (sheep) on the public altar, he is to be pure.[31] He is to mark off a boundary with salt, sprinkle water from a gold cup, and go away. Whenever someone needs to make sacrifice to an *elasteros*, he is to sacrifice as he does to the immortal gods. He is to slaughter the victim so that the blood flows into the earth.

Sorcery and witchcraft in the literary sources

> In Aeschylus' *Eumenides* (458 BCE) the chorus of Erinyes (Avenging Furies) cast a binding spell on Orestes before his trial for murdering his mother.

13.25 AESCHYLUS, *EUMENIDES*, 305–306 and 341–346.

You will not be slaughtered on an altar, but we will feast on your living flesh,

and you will hear our song as it binds you.

---

26 At this point the text has several gaps, making it unintelligible.

27 Ogden, 2002 no. 123 translates *elasteroi* as "attacking ghosts," whereas Jameson, Jordan, and Kotansky 1993: 40 define an *elasteros* as "an angry spirit that haunts the killer on behalf of the victim."

28 *welcome*: the common term for receiving and providing the customary hospitality to a stranger—ritual gifts of water, food, wine, and salt.

29 *piglet*: a young pig is the standard victim in purification rites; see Aeschylus, *Eumenides* 283 in 4.27. *turn around*: probably a magical ritual, in which the sacrificer turned around and did not look back, or was himself turned around, or made a circular movement; see Jameson, Jordan, and Kotansky 1993: 43.

30 *He may then be addressed...*: at this point the sacrificer apparently returns to normal life after a period of isolation.

31 This sacrifice at the public altar of Zeus concludes the ritual.

….

Over our sacrificial victim

this is our song: insanity,

mind-ruining derangement,

a hymn of the Erinyes to bind the mind,   345

unaccompanied by the lyre,[32] withering to mortals.

> Theocritus (early third century BCE), who worked in Alexandria at the court
> of Ptolemy Philadelphus, wrote an elegant poem entitled "The Sorceress"
> (*Pharmakeutria*). Several magical devices or tools are mentioned in his poem,
> most notably the *iunx* or *iynx*, a small wheel-like device, usually made of metal
> and pierced by two holes at the center, through which a looped thread was
> passed. When spun, it emitted "a sound that was seductive and persuasive
> but that also—like so many seductive and persuasive sounds—was possibly
> deceptive, spelling ruin for its listener."[33] The name is thought to derive
> from the *iunx*, the wryneck bird that can twist its head round without
> moving the rest of its body. This movement of the bird was interpreted as
> an erotic mating dance.
>
> A woman called Simaetha enlists the help of her slave-girl Thestylis as she
> employs magic to bring back Delphis, her lover.

13.26 THEOCRITUS, *IDYLL* 2.1–62.[34]

> Where are my bay leaves? Fetch them Thestylis. Where are my love
>   potions (*philtra*)?
>
> Garland the bowl with the crimson wool of a sheep,
>
> so that I may bind my unkind lover.[35]
>
> The cruel man has not come near me for eleven days,
>
> and does not know whether I am dead or alive.
>
> Nor has the unfeeling man knocked on my door.
>
> Eros and Aphrodite have gone elsewhere, taking his fickle mind with
>   them.[36]
>
> Tomorrow I shall go to Timagetus' wrestling school
>
> to see him, and I'll reproach him for the way he is treating me.
>
> But now I will bind him with sacrifices. Come, Moon,   10
>
> shine brightly. For I shall sing quietly to you, goddess,

---

32 *lyre*: a stringed instrument often used to soothe or charm.

33 Johnston 1995: 178.

34 For a translation of this entire poem, see Ogden 2002 no. 89.

35 *bay leaves…. crimson wool*: these are intended to act as apotropaic devices that protected the woman from the magic spell she is invoking.

36 *Eros*: god of Love, who often accompanies Aphrodite.

and to you chthonian Hecate,[37] before whom even dogs tremble
as you come across the tombs and black blood of the dead.
Hail, dread Hecate, and be with me to the end of my task,
making my potions (*pharmaka*) no less potent than those of Circe
Medea, or golden-haired Perimede.[38]

    Magic wheel (*iunx*), draw this man to my house.
First barley grains are consumed in the fire. Come scatter them,
Thestylis. Wretched woman, is your mind wandering?
Or do you think I'm ridiculous, you stupid girl?
Scatter this and at the same time say: "These are Delphis' bones, I
    scatter."   20

    Magic wheel (*iunx*), draw this man to my house.
Delphis caused me pain; so, thinking of Delphis,
I burn this bay leaf. And as this bay leaf catches fire and crackles loudly,
suddenly flaring up and leaving no ash for us to see,
so too may Delphis' flesh shrivel in the flames.

    Magic wheel (*iunx*), draw this man to my house.
Now, I will burn the bran. You, Artemis, can move
even the adamant in Hades' realm,[39] and anything less difficult.
Thestylis, the dogs are howling throughout the city.   30
The goddess is at the crossroads. Sound the bronze gong as quickly as
    possible.[40]

    Magic wheel (*iunx*), draw this man to my house.
See! The sea is silent, silent the breezes,
only the pain within my breast is not silent.
But I am ablaze for the man who took my virginity, causing me misery
and destroying my good name, instead of making me his wife.

    Magic wheel (*iunx*), draw this man to my house.
As I now melt this wax with the goddess' help,
so may Delphis of Myndos be melted with sudden love.[41]

---

37 *chthonian Hecate*: goddess of the underworld, to whom dogs were sacrificed; she was
    worshiped at crossroads.

38 *Circe*: famous enchantress in the *Odyssey*; her magic turned Odysseus' men into pigs.
    Medea: probably the most famous mythical witch, best known from Euripides' *Medea*.
    Perimede: otherwise unknown, unless she is to be identified with "Agamede of the golden
    hair," mentioned by Homer, *Iliad* 11.740–741 for her knowledge of magical drugs.

39 *Artemis*: in post-classical times Artemis was often identified with Hecate. *adamant*:
    one of the toughest, hardest and impermeable metals.

40 *bronze gong*: this gong was sounded to protect the magician from the evil powers he
    has aroused.

41 *Myndos*: a town on the southern coast of Asia Minor, used here to identify Delphis.

And as this *rhombos* whirls around with Aphrodite's help,[42]   40
so may he whirl round to my door.
 Magic wheel (*iunx*), draw this man to my house.
Three times I pour a libation and, Lady, three times I say these words.[43]
If another woman lies with him, or a man,
may he forget this person as completely as they say Theseus
forgot fair-haired Ariadne on Dia.[44]
 Magic wheel (*iunx*), draw this man to my house.
Hippomanes[45] is a plant from Arcadia, which drives to madness
all the swift mares and the foals on the mountains.
May I see Delphis in this condition, coming to my house   50
from the sleek wrestling school,[46] driven like them into madness.
 Magic wheel (*iunx*), draw this man to my house.
Here is a bit of cloth that Delphis lost from his cloak.
I tear it up and throw it into the fierce fire.
Alas, cruel Eros, why have you drunk all the black blood
from me, clinging to me like a leech from the marshes?
 Magic wheel (*iunx*), draw this man to my house.
Tomorrow I will I grind up a lizard, making an evil potion for him.
But now, Thestylis, take these herbs and smear them
above his threshold while it is still night.   60
And murmur all the while, saying, "These are the bones of Delphis that
 I smear."
 Magic wheel (*iunx*), draw this man to my house.

 An earlier reference to the *iunx* occurs in Pindar's fourth *Pythian Ode* (c.
 462 BCE), where Jason uses the *iunx* to cause the Colchian princess Medea
 to fall in love with him and help him steal the golden fleece.

13.27 PINDAR, *PYTHIAN* 4.213–223.

The Cyprus-born mistress of the sharpest arrows
bought from Olympus the variegated *iunx*,[47] binding it

---

42 *rhombos*: a "bull-roarer," a metal or wooden disc that emits an increasing moan as it
   is whirled faster and faster; or possibly a variant on the *iunx*; see Ogden 2002: 240.

43 *Lady*: Hecate.

44 *Theseus*: the Athenian hero is said to have abandoned his bride, Ariadne, on the island
   of Dia (Naxos) after she had helped him kill the Minotaur and escape from Crete.

45 *Hippomanes*: a love potion that is variously said to derive from a plant (as here), a
   growth on the forehead of a new-born foal, a discharge secreted by the mare, or the
   semen of a stallion.

46 *sleek wrestling school*: "sleek" because athletes smeared olive oil on their bodies.

47 *Cyprus-born mistress*: Aphrodite.

to a four-spoked wheel,   215

bringing the bird of madness to mortals

for the first time. Prayers and charms

she taught to the wise son of Aeson,[48]

so that he might take away Medea's respect for her parents,

so that desire for Greece might burn in her heart

and drive her with the whip of Persuasion.

And quickly she showed him how to succeed in the contest set by her
   father.   220

She blended drugs [*pharmakosaisa*]with olive oil as a protection against
   harsh pains

and gave them to him to anoint himself.

They agreed to be joined with each other in sweet marriage.

> Medea is probably the best known witch described in the literary sources.
> In mythology she is the granddaughter of Helios (Sun), and the daughter of
> Aeetes, the king of Aia in Colchis, in the Black Sea area. Another famous
> witch, Circe who appears in Homer's *Odyssey*, is a daughter of Helios, and
> thus the aunt of Medea.[49] The third century BCE poet, Apollonius of Rhodes,
> wrote an epic poem, the *Argonautica*, in which he describes Jason's quest
> for the golden fleece. In the following two excerpts, the speaker is Argus,
> companion of Jason and the builder of the Argo, the ship in which Jason and
> the Argonauts sailed to the land of Colchis.

13.28 APOLLONIUS RHODIUS, *ARGONAUTICA* 3.475–480.

Son of Aeson, you will despise the advice I'm going to give you.

But it's not a good idea to give up your endeavor because of a bad
   situation.

In the past you heard me speak of a girl

who practices witchcraft under the guidance of Hecate, daughter of
   Perses.[50]

If we can persuade her to help, I think you no longer need fear

defeat in the contest.   480

13.29 APOLLONIUS RHODIUS, *ARGONAUTICA* 3.528–533.

There is a girl, reared in the house of Aeetes

whom the goddess Hecate taught to handle with exceeding skill

all the potions [*pharmaka*] that the dry land and the full-flowing waters
   produce.

---

48 *son of Aeson*: Jason.

49 For a good selection of the literary sources referring to Circe, Medea and other
   related witches, see Ogden 2002: 78–101.

50 *practices witchcraft*: the Greek is *pharmassein*, a word that means both the casting of
   spells and the use of potions or drugs.

With these potions the blast of the unwearied flame is quenched,

with these she immediately stays the roaring course of rivers,

checking the stars and the paths of the sacred moon.

> Medea goes with her attendants to the shrine of Hecate, goddess of
> the underworld, with her box of potions, to invoke the powers of the
> underworld to help her in her task. The poet describes the origin of the
> potion (*pharmakon*) that will make Jason invulnerable.

13.30 APOLLONIUS RHODIUS, *ARGONAUTICA* 3.844–869.

Medea took from the hollow casket

a potion, which they say is called Prometheum.

If a man should smear his body with this potion,

after first appeasing the Maiden, the only begotten, with a sacrifice made
  by night,

then that man will not be wounded by the blows of bronze,

nor would he give way when confronted with blazing fire. But on that
  day

he would be superior in courage and might.   850

It was first produced when the ravening eagle

on the ridges of the Caucasian mountains let drip to earth

the ichor of tortured Prometheus.[51]

From this a flower sprang forth, its size was the length of the forearm,

  its color like a Corycian crocus,   855

and it rose up on twin stalks. But in the earth

its root was like newly-cut flesh.

Medea had gathered its dark moisture, like the sap of a mountain oak,

in a Caspian shell to make the potion.

But first she bathed in seven ever-flowing waters,   860

calling seven times on Brimo, nurturer of youth,

Brimo who wanders by night, she of the underworld, queen among the
  dead.[52]

This she did, in the gloom of night, wearing dark garments.

With a roar the dark earth shook from below

when the Titan's root was cut. And the son of Iapetus   865

himself groaned, his heart distraught with pain.[53]

---

51 *ichor*: the liquid that flowed in veins of the immortals. *tortured Prometheus*: a Titan
and thus immortal; he was condemned by Zeus to be have his liver, which continually renewed itself, torn out by an eagle, because he had given humans the gift of fire
(Hesiod, *Theogony* 506–616).

52 *Brimo*: an underworld goddess often identified with Persephone.

53 *son of Iapetus*: Prometheus.

And she took out the charm and placed it in her fragrant band,
just below her ambrosial breast.
Going forth, she mounted on her swift chariot.

Medea spellbinds the monstrous serpent that guards the golden fleece.

13.31 APOLLONIUS RHODIUS, *ARGONAUTICA* 4.123–166.

Jason and Medea came down the pathway to the sacred grove,
looking for the huge oak tree, on which the fleece
was hung, like a cloud that blushes red   125
in the blazing rays of the rising sun.
But right in front the serpent, watching with his sharp sleepless eyes,
stretched out his long neck to meet their advance,
letting out a hideous hiss.
All around them the long river banks echoed and the boundless grove.

….

And as above smouldering wood countless eddies of smoke
spiral upwards mingling with soot,   140
and one quickly springs up on top of another,
rising upward from below in spirals;
so then did that monster roll his countless coils,
covered with horny dry scales.
As it writhed, the girl came before its eyes;   145
in a sweet voice, she summoned to her aid Sleep,
the highest of the gods, to bewitch the monster. She cried to the queen
of the underworld, the night-wanderer, to look kindly upon her
  undertaking.
Fearful, the son of Aeson followed her, but the serpent,
already bewitched by her song, relaxed its long spiraling spine,   150
straightening out it countless coils,
like a dark wave, rolling in a calm sea,
silent and without sound. But still
it raised aloft its terrifying head, eager
to envelop them both in its deadly jaws.   155
But she, with a freshly cut sprig of juniper,
dipped unmixed potions from her brew, as she chanted her song,
sprinkling them over his eyes. And all around the immense fragrance
of the spell cast sleep. On the very spot, it let its jaw sink down
and rested, its countless coils extending far behind   160
throughout the wood with its many trees.
Then, he seized the golden fleece from the oak,

as the girl ordered him. And she, standing firm,
smeared the beast's head with her potion, until
Jason himself ordered her to turn back to the ship.   165
And so she left the shady grove of Ares.

> Spells and potions were also used for healing purposes. In describing the
> healing skills of Asclepius, Pindar (518–c. 446 BCE) mentions the use of
> potions [*pharmaka*], the application of external remedies, possibly amulets,
> and surgery.[54]

13.32 PINDAR, *PYTHIAN* 3.47–53.

All who came to him afflicted by festering sores,
or with limbs wounded by gleaming bronze
or by a far-hurled rock,
or with bodies that were wasting from the scorching summer   50
or chill of winter, he relieved of their various ills,
restoring them. Some he tended with soothing incantations,
while others drank comforting potions, or he wrapped remedies around
  their limbs,
others he restored by surgery.[55]

> Plutarch reports a story that the dying Pericles was given an amulet.

13.33 PLUTARCH, *PERICLES* 38. At that time, as seems likely, the plague attacked
Pericles, not violently, as happened to others, or acutely, but by gradually
weakening him. It went through various phases, slowly exhausting his body
and undermining his noble spirit.... Theophrastus tells the story that when
Pericles was sick he showed one of his visiting friends the amulet that the
women had fastened round his neck, thus implying that he was in a very
bad way if he was allowing himself to be subjected to such foolishness.[56]

> A reference in Plato's *Charmides* mentions the use of a leaf as an amulet that
> only worked as a cure for a headache if an incantation was also performed.
> Potions, surgery, charms, and amulets are futile, however, if one indulges
> in an excessive lifestyle.

13.34 PLATO, *CHARMIDES*, 155 e. 5–8. There is a certain leaf, but there is also an
incantation (*epoide*) to go with the remedy (*pharmakon*). If one intones the
charm (*epoide*) at the same time as the leaf is applied, the remedy produces
a complete cure. But without the incantation, the leaf is ineffective.

13.35 PLATO, *REPUBLIC* 426 b. 1–2. Until people give up eating and drinking too
much, and idleness, and debauchery, no medicines [*pharmaka*], or surgery,
no charms [*epoidai*] or amulets [*periapt*a] will do them any good.

---

54 On Asclepius, see 6.25–6.27 and 14.23–14.27.

55 *potions...remedies*: here the same word, *pharmaka*, is used.

56 *Theophrastus*: c. 371–c. 278 BCE, an associate and pupil of Aristotle.

Much of the evidence for the practice of magic that we have examined so far dates to the classical and post-classical periods.The Roman writer Pliny the Elder (23/24–79 CE) comments on Homer's silence on magic in the *Iliad* as opposed the *Odyssey* .

13.36 PLINY, *NATURAL HISTORY* 30.2.5–6. It is particularly surprising that Homer is so silent about magic in his poem on the Trojan War, and yet so much of his work in the wanderings of Ulysses (Odysseus) to the extent that the entire work depends on it, if one interprets as magic the episode of Proteus and the songs of the Sirens, and especially the episode of Circe and the summoning of the dead from the underworld, where magic is the sole theme.[57]

Homer describes the ritual enacted by Odysseus in order to commune with the dead of the underworld. The ritual of necromancy is an inversion of that performed to the Olympian gods. Black rather then white victims are sacrificed, and the meat is not consumed but is burned in honor of the chthonic gods.

13.37 HOMER, *ODYSSEY* 11.20–50.

We went to that place, and pulled our ship up onto the shore;	20
we brought out the sheep, then walked by the side of Ocean's stream	
until we came to the spot that Circe had told us about.	
Eurylochus and Perimedes then took hold of the sacred	
victims; drawing the sharpened blade from beside my thigh	
I dug a pit that measured a cubit in each direction,	25
and poured in liquid offerings for all of the dead,	
first honey mixed together with milk, and then sweet wine,	
and thirdly water, and then I sprinkled white barley in.	
I supplicated at length the strengthless forms of the dead,	
vowing to slaughter an uncalved heifer in my halls—	30
the best that I had—if I got to Ithaca,[58] heap good gifts	
up high on a pyre, and sacrifice to Tiresias	

---

57 *Proteus*: a minor sea god whom Menelaus meets near Egypt. Proteus avoids answering Menelaus' questions by continually changing his shape until Menelaus finally holds him fast (*Odyssey* 4.349–570). *Sirens*: enchantresses who live on islands between the rock on which the monster Scylla lives and the whirlpool Charybdis. The Sirens' singing entices sailors to draw near to the rocks, where they perish (*Odyssey* 12.39–54 and 158–200). On the advice of Circe, Odysseus blocks his men's ears with wax, but has them tie him to the ship's mast so that he can hear their song. *Circe*: the sorceress who turned Odysseus' men into pigs. He, however, resisted her magic and, with the help of Hermes, rescued his companions; see *Odyssey* 10.210–409.

58 *uncalved heifer*: probably a yearling, see *Odyssey*. 3.421, in 4.8 with n. 21. *Ithaca*: Odysseus' home.

alone a ram,[59] all black, outstanding among my flocks.
After beseeching them, the tribes of the dead, with vows
and prayers, I took the sheep and holding them over the pit   35
I cut their throats, and the cloud-dark blood flowed into it;
the spirits of those who had died came gathering then from Erebus:
brides and unmarried youths; old men who alive had endured
much hardship; childish unmarried girls, grief fresh in their hearts;
great numbers of men who had once been wounded with spears of
  bronze,   40
slain in warfare, still with their blood-stained armor upon them;
The spirits approached my pit from every side in a swarm
with unearthly outcry, and sallow fear took me in its grip.
But then I urged on my comrades, ordering them to skin
the sheep that were lying there slaughtered by the relentless bronze,   45
consume them completely with fire, and offer up prayers to the gods,
to stalwart Hades and terrifying Persephone;[60]
meanwhile I drew the sharpened sword from beside my thigh
and sat there, and would not let the strengthless forms of the dead
come near to the blood until I had heard Tiresias speak.   50

---

59 *Teiresias*: the blind seer whom Circe had ordered Odysseus to consult concerning
   his return to his home in Ithaca (*Odyssey* 10.490–541). *a ram, all black*: black victims
   were sacrificed to the gods in the underworld.

60 *Hades*: here the god of the underworld, though elsewhere used of the underworld
   itself. *Persephone*: wife of Hades, and daughter of Demeter.

14. New Cults and New Gods

14.1 LYSIAS? *AGAINST NICOMACHUS* 18. By making the sacrifices prescribed in Solon's code,[1] our ancestors have handed down to us a city superior in greatness and prosperity to any in Greece. And so we ought to perform the same sacrifices as they did, if for no other reason, than for the good fortune that resulted from these rituals.

14.2 ISOCRATES, *AREOPAGITICUS* 29–30. [Our ancestors] did not worship the gods or celebrate their rites irregularly or erratically. They did not send three hundred oxen to be sacrificed whenever they wanted, nor did they omit the ancestral sacrifices whenever it suited them. Nor did they celebrate imported festivals that included a banquet in an extravagant manner whenever it occurred to them....

Rather their sole concern was not to destroy any of the ancestral practices and not to add anything that was not traditional. For they thought that piety (*eusebeia*) consists, not in paying out large sums of money, but in not disturbing any of the rites that their ancestors had handed down to them.

> The speech generally attributed to Lysias (459/8–380 BCE) and that of Isocrates (436–338 BCE) articulate the essential conservatism of Greek religion. Isocrates also recognizes the possibility of change provided that the ancestral rites were not affected. The evidence for the introduction of new gods and cults, however, is sparse, deriving mostly from fifth century BCE Athens. The actual arrival or even the establishing of a new cult has left little trace in either the archaeological or literary record. Thus, the likelihood that a cult may have already entered an area before its official adoption should not be overlooked. Evidence for the official sanctioning of new cults in Athens, moreover, is scanty and even paradoxical.[2]

---

1 *Solon*: the late seventh and sixth century law-giver.

2 Parker 1996: 214–217.

Establishing a new cult, whether public or private, required considerable planning and resources on the part of the state or the individual. Land had to be purchased and consecrated as a sanctuary (*temenos*) where an altar could be set up for sacrifice. A temple and cult statue were common but not essential. Provision was also advisable for buildings to accommodate offices, dining rooms, and sacred vessels. In addition, funds were necessary for the administration and maintenance of the sanctuary, and for the cost of future sacrifices.

The expense and process involved in organizing cultic worship are apparent in Plutarch's description of Nicias' reorganization of the festival of Apollo on the island of Delos and his purchase of a small estate that he dedicated to Apollo to provide revenue for future festivals.[3]

14.3   PLUTARCH, *NICIAS* 3–4. It is on record how outstanding and worthy of the god were Nicias' devotional offerings on Delos and his demonstration of generosity. For the choruses that cities used to send to sing the praises of the god were generally landed on the island in a very disorderly manner… But when Nicias took charge of sacred mission, he first landed the chorus, sacrificial victims, and other equipment on the island of Rheneia. Then, by night, he spanned the strait between Rheneia and Delos (which is not very wide) with a bridge of boats that he had brought with him from Athens, which had been made to the required size, magnificently gilded, painted, and hung with garlands and tapestries. At daybreak he led the procession in honor of the god, with his chorus lavishly adorned and singing as it marched, across the bridge to land.

When the sacrifices, choral contests, and banquets were finished, Nicias set up the famous palm tree of bronze as a thank offering to the god, and also consecrated a small estate, which he had bought for 10,000 drachmae. The revenue from this was to be used by the islanders on sacrifices and providing a banquet, at which they would pray for blessings for Nicias from the gods. These instructions were engraved on a column which he left on Delos, as it were to guard his benefaction….

In all this it is clear that there is a certain ostentation and vulgarity aimed at increasing Nicias' prestige and gratifying his ambition. But to judge from his other qualities and his general character, one should trust that his love of display was the result of his piety, and that courting popularity and thereby influencing the masses were secondary. He was the sort of man who was excessively overawed by the supernatural and particularly subject, as Thucydides tells us, to the influence of divination.[4]

Shortly after the naval victory of Salamis in **480 BCE**, Themistocles set up a sanctuary to Artemis Aristoboule (Giver of the Best Advice) in his

---

3   On Nicias (c. 470–413 BCE), one of the wealthiest men in Athens, and his excessive piety, see 5.37–5.38, 5.40. For a brief description of the festival on Delos, see 7.1.

4   Thucydides 7.50; see 5.38.

own deme. Unlike Nicias' later dedications on Delos, the people found his appropriation of this new cult offensive.[5]

14.4 PLUTARCH, *MORALIA* 869 d. If, as some people say, there are any Antipodaeans living beneath the earth, I imagine that not even they have failed to hear of Themistocles and his advice. For he advised the Greeks to fight at sea before Salamis and, when the enemy had been defeated, established a temple to Artemis Aristoboule in the deme of Melite.

14.5 PLUTARCH, *THEMISTOCLES* 22.1. Themistocles offended the people by building a temple of Artemis whom he styled Aristoboule, thus implying that he had given the best advice to the Athenians and the Greeks. He located the temple near his own house in the deme of Melite. ...A small statue of Themistocles used to stand in this temple of Artemis Aristoboule even in my own day, from which he seems to have been a man not only of heroic spirit but also heroic presence.

> Stories were invented to account for the arrival or establishing of a cult in a particular place. In explaining the reason for the presence of phalluses in Dionysiac ritual, a scholiast on Aristophanes' *Acharnians* tells of the Athenians' initial opposition to the cult of Dionysus and the god's reprisal.

14.6 SCHOLION TO ARISTOPHANES, *ACHARNIANS* 243. Pegasus of Eleutherae (Eleutherae is a *polis* in Boeotia) came to Attica, bringing the statue of Dionysus. The Athenians did not receive the god with honor, but he did not depart from those who took this decision without exacting a price. For the god became enraged and struck the male sexual organs with an incurable disease. Exhausted by the disease, which proved stronger than any human magic and skill, sacred ambassadors were sent to consult Apollo. When they returned, they said that the only cure was to introduce the god with all honor. Persuaded by these reports, the Athenians made phalluses privately and publicly, and with these they venerated the god in commemoration of the disease.

> Claiming an epiphany or visitation from a god or hero is a recurrent theme in the introduction of new cults and rituals In the *Homeric Hymn to Demeter*, the goddess casts off her disguise as an old woman and proclaims her divinity, ordering that a temple be built to her at Eleusis and giving instructions about the sacred rites of the Eleusinian Mysteries.[6] In the fifth century BCE, the historian Herodotus tells the story of the Athenians' adoption of the cult of Pan, a minor rustic deity who is represented as half man and half goat. The god appeared to the Athenian messenger Philippides, when he was going to Sparta to ask for help against the impending Persian invasion. Unlike the example from the Homeric hymn, this story derives from a period in which the historical context is verifiable.

---

5 On Themistocles' advice at Salamis, see 5.29. In 471/0 BCE Themistocles was exiled for ten years, and died in Asia Minor c. 464 BCE.

6 *Homeric Hymn to Demeter* 268–299 in 11.29.

14.7   HERODOTUS 6.105. The generals sent Philippides as a herald to Sparta. He was an Athenian and a trained long-distance runner. As Philippides himself said and announced to the Athenians, Pan met him near Mount Parthenium above Tegea.[7] Calling out Philippides' name, the god ordered him to ask the Athenians why they did not pay attention to him even though he was well-disposed to them, and had many times already been useful to them and would continue to be so in the future. The Athenians believed that this was true and, when their affairs were restored to prosperity,[8] they built a shrine to Pan at the foot of the Acropolis. From the time of the god's message, they have worshiped him with annual sacrifices and a torch race.

> Plutarch reports a story that the Athenian hero Theseus appeared at the battle of Marathon.

14.8   PLUTARCH, *THESEUS* 35. In later times, the Athenians decided to honor Theseus as a hero especially because many of the men who fought the Persians at Marathon believed that they saw the apparition of Theseus clad in full armor and rushing ahead of them against the barbarians.

> Shortly after the Persian Wars, the Athenian general Cimon recovered bones that were reputed to be those of Theseus from the island of Scyros in the Aegean, brought them to Athens, and established a hero-cult in his honor. In this incident the manipulation of religion for political purposes is apparent.

14.9   PLUTARCH, *THESEUS* 36. After the Persian wars... the Athenians consulted the oracle at Delphi and were instructed by the Pythian priestess to take up the bones of Theseus, give them honorable burial in Athens, and protect them. It was difficult to find the grave and remove the remains because of the inhospitable and savage nature of the Dolopians, the inhabitants of Scyros. Nevertheless, Cimon captured the island... Ambitious to find the place where Theseus was buried, he caught sight of an eagle, at a place resembling a mound, pecking at the ground with its beak, so they say, and tearing it up with its talons. By some divine inspiration he understood that they should dig at this place. There they found a coffin of a man of huge size with a bronze spear and a sword lying beside it.

When Cimon brought these relics home on board his trireme, the Athenians rejoiced, welcoming them with magnificent processions and sacrifices, as though Theseus himself were returning to his city. He lies buried in the center of Athens near the present Gymnasium,[9] and his tomb is a sanctuary for runaway slaves and all those who are down-trodden and fear the powerful. For Theseus was the champion and helper of the distressed and always gave a kindly ear to the petitions of the downtrodden.

---

7   *Tegea*: a town in Arcadia, a desolate mountainous region inhabited mainly by sheep and goats.

8   *restored to prosperity*: i.e., after their victory over the Persians at Marathon.

9   The exact site of the tomb is unknown.

In the mid-sixth century BCE, when the Spartans were having no success in the war against Tegea, their northern neighbor, they asked the advice of the Delphic oracle, which advised them to bring back the bones of Orestes, son of Agamemnon, from Tegea. A Spartan named Lichas solved the riddle of the oracle and discovered a larger than life-sized corpse in a smithy. After reporting his discovery in Sparta, he returned to Tegea, leased the smith's land, and retrieved the bones. From that time most of the Peloponnese was under Spartan control.

14.10   HERODOTUS 1.67–68. In their earlier war with Tegea, the Spartans had continually had the worst of it, but by the time of Croesus,... they had gained the upper hand.[10] This is the story of their success: after a long series of defeats in the war they sent to Delphi and asked which of the gods they should propitiate in order to prevail over the Tegeans. The priestess responded that they should bring home the bones of Orestes, the son of Agamemnon.

When they were unable to find the tomb of Orestes, they sent again to ask the god where the body of Orestes lay. To their enquiries the priestess replied:

> In Arcadia lies Tegea in a level place,
>
> two winds blow there under strong restraint,
>
> striking and counter-striking, and trouble upon trouble;
>
> there life-producing earth holds Agamemnon's son.
>
> If you bring him home, you will prevail over Tegea.

When the Spartans heard this, they were no nearer to finding the body. They searched everywhere, until Lichas... solved the problem... He went to Tegea and entered a forge where he saw some iron being hammered out; he watched this process in amazement. Seeing his astonishment, the smith stopped working and said: "Your present astonishment at seeing me work in iron would be nothing, my Spartan friend, if you had seen what I saw. I wanted to make a well in the courtyard here; as I was digging I came upon a burial mound seven cubits long.[11] Not believing that men were taller than they are today, I opened the mound and saw a corpse the same size as its length. I measured it and shoveled the earth back."

After pondering the smith's account of what he had seen, Lichas concluded that this was the body of Orestes, as the oracle had foretold. He guessed that the two winds were the smith's two pairs of bellows, the striking and counter-striking were the hammer and the anvil, and the trouble upon

---

10 *Croesus*: the king of Lydia, c. 560–546 BCE.

11 *burial mound*: earth heaped up over a corpse, the typical burial accorded to a hero; see 3.41 for Homer's description of the burial of Hector (*Iliad* 798–801). Such burials began in the tenth century BCE, but became widespread in the eighth century BCE. Evidently the cult at Tegea was no longer active since, according to the story, the smith had been unaware of the existence of the burial.

trouble was the beaten iron. For he also guessed that the discovery of iron was a source of trouble for humans.

Having reached these conclusions, he went back to Sparta and recounted the whole story to the Spartans. The Spartans pretended that he was guilty of a crime and exiled him. And so he went back to Tegea, told the smith of his misfortune, and leased the courtyard because the smith refused to sell it. Eventually, after persuading the smith, Lichas took up residence there and dug up the grave. Collecting the bones, he took them to Sparta. And from that time, in any trial of strength, the Spartans were by far superior in warfare. They had now conquered most of the Peloponnese.

Pausanias notes the location of Orestes' tomb in Sparta.

14.11 PAUSANIAS 3.11.10. The Spartans also have a sanctuary of the Fates, and the tomb of Agamemnon's son Orestes is beside it. When his bones were brought from Tegea in accordance with an oracle, this is where they buried him.

During the late seventh and sixth centuries BCE, an exotic foreign goddess arrived in the Greek world, one who has no mythological connection with the Olympian gods. She is variously known as "Meter" (the Mother), "the Mother of the Gods," Cybele," or "Cybebe."

This goddess came from Anatolia (modern Turkey), where she was represented as living among the rocks of the high mountains. She was a matronal, nurturing goddess and was portrayed as accompanied by wild animals, usually lions. The Greek cities of Ionia (west coast of modern Turkey) were probably intermediaries in the spread of the goddess' cult to mainland Greece. By the end of the sixth century BCE, visual representations of the Mother had become Hellenized. She is portrayed seated on a throne, wearing Greek garments, a *chiton* or tunic,with a *himation* or cloak draped over her lap. She wears a crown on her head and carries a *tympanum* (small drum or tambourine) in her left hand and a dish for offerings in her right. Lions are also frequently depicted.

The ecstatic nature of the Mother's worship is described in the following brief *Homeric Hymn*.

14.12 *HOMERIC HYMN TO THE MOTHER OF THE GODS* 1–5.

Sing to me, Muse, clear-voiced daughter of great Zeus,

about the Mother of all gods and of all men,

to whom the sound of castanets and drums along with the piercing
      sound of flutes

Is a delight, and the howling of wolves and flashing-eyed lions,

and echoing mountains and wooded glens.

In a chorus from Euripides' *Helen* (first produced in 412 BC), references to the Mother of the gods and her entourage are intertwined with the story of a goddess searching for her daughter.

14.13 EURIPIDES, *HELEN* 1301–1311.

Chorus

The mountain goddess with swift feet,

the Mother of the gods, speeds

through the wooded glens,

by the cataracts of rivers,

by the resounding wave of the sea,   1305

in anguish for the loss

of her daughter, whose name is unspoken.[12]

Her resounding cymbals

send forth a piercing din,

as the goddess drives her chariot,   1310

drawn by beasts of the wild.

> In Euripides' *Bacchae*, the chorus of bacchants sings of the blessings bestowed on Cybele's devotees.

14.14 EURIPIDES, *BACCHAE* 78–79.

Chorus

O blessed the man who dutifully observes

the mysteries (*orgia*) of the Great Mother, Cybele.

> Private sanctuaries of the Mother were established by Themistocles and the poet Pindar (518–c. 446 BCE). When Themistocles was exiled in Asia Minor, some Persians plotted to assassinate him in a village called the Lion's Head, but the goddess appeared and warned him of the danger.

14.15 PLUTARCH, *THEMISTOCLES* 30. It is said that at noon on that day, as Themistocles slept, the Mother of the Gods appeared to him in a dream and said: "Themistocles, avoid a head of lions, or else you may encounter a lion. In return for this service, you must make your daughter Mnesiptolema my priestess." Greatly disturbed, Themistocles offered a prayer to the goddess and left the main road. Taking a roundabout way, he by-passed that place...

In this way Themistocles escaped the danger and he was so struck by this epiphany of the goddess that he built a temple in Magnesia in honor of Dindymene and appointed his daughter, Mnesiptolema, to be her priestess.[13]

14.16 PINDAR, *PYTHIAN* 3.77—79.

But I want to pray

to the Mother. For to her, along with Pan, before my door

the maidens often sing at night;

she is a goddess to be revered.

---

12 *daughter*: Persephone, queen of the underworld, whose name must not be spoken.

13 *Dindymene*: another name for Cybele, deriving from a mountain where she was worshiped.

14.17 PAUSANIAS 9.25.3. Across the river Dirce are the ruins of Pindar's house and a sanctuary of Mother Dindymene. Pindar dedicated statue that was made by Aristomedes and Socrates of Thebes.[14] The custom is to open the sanctuary on one day in the year and no more, but I happened to arrive on that day and I saw the marble statue and the throne.

> Exactly when the cult of Meter was officially established in Athens is uncertain. The goddess received private cult offerings in the sixth century BCE, and it has been suggested that she had a public sanctuary in the Agora at the end of the sixth century. If so, the temple would have been destroyed during the Persian invasion of 480 BCE and probably restored around 460 BCE.[15] The goddess' temple, the Metroön, was located near, if not within, the Bouleuterion or Council Chamber, and also served as the public archive. A statement of Demosthenes (*Proemia* 44) that it was the practice of the presiding council members (*prytaneis*) to sacrifice to the Mother of the gods, and also to Zeus, Athena, Apollo, and the other gods, further indicates the importance of the of the cult in Athenian civic life.[16]

> Our sources for the aetiology of the Athenian cult of the Mother are extremely late. The Roman emperor Julian (361–363 CE) relates that the Athenians expelled a *gallus*, a priest of the Mother, "since he was introducing new gods." On the advice of the Delphic oracle, the goddess was appeased by the establishing of the Metroön.[17]

14.18 JULIAN, *ORATIONS* 5.159 a. The Athenians learned by experience that it was not good to mock one who was celebrating the rites (*orgia*) of the Mother. The story is that they treated the *gallus* contemptuously and drove him out since he was introducing new gods. They did not understand the nature of the goddess, and that she was honored by them under the name of Deo, Rhea, and Demeter.[18]

Then followed the wrath of the goddess and the appeasing of it. The priestess of the Pythian god … ordered them to propitiate the wrath of the Mother of the Gods. And so, as the story goes, the Metroön was established, a place where the Athenians used to keep all their state records.

> Photius, a Byzantine lexicographer who wrote in the ninth century CE, tells the story of a *metragyrtes*, a priest of the Mother of the gods, who

---

14 *Aristomedes and Socrates*: these artists are otherwise unknown.

15 Parker 1996: 188 with bibliography.

16 Roller 1999: 163: "Taken as a whole, the evidence implies a close integration of Meter with the respected cults of the Athenian democracy."

17 *gallus*: the *galli*, eunuch priests of the goddess, are not mentioned in the sources until the Hellenistic period. For discussion of the late sources and of the *galli*, see Roller 1999: 163–169 and 229–231.

18 *Deo*: another name for Demeter. On the ultimate conflation of the Anatolian Meter with the mother goddesses Gaia (Earth), Rhea, and Demeter, see Roller 1999: 169–177.

came to Athens and was killed because he initiated the women into the
goddess' rites.[19]

14.19   PHOTIUS. *Metragyrtes*: an individual came to Attica and initiated the
women into the mysteries of the Mother of the gods, as the story goes.
The Athenians killed him by throwing him on his head into a pit. When
a plague occurred, they received an oracle ordering them to propitiate
the murdered man. And because of this they built the Bouleuterion, [in
the place] where they killed the *metragyrtes*. They made a fence around
it, and consecrated it to the Mother of the Gods, setting up a statue of the
metragyrtes. They used the Metröon for an archive and repository of law,
and filled up the pit.

> A scholiast on Aristophanes' Wealth (Plutus) gives a different explanation of
> the priest's murder, connecting Meter with the goddess Demeter and her
> search for Persephone.[20]

14.20   SCHOLION TO ARISTOPHANES, *WEALTH* 431. [the Athenians] threw
the Phrygian [priest] of the Mother of the gods [into the pit] because they
thought he was mad, since he proclaimed that the Mother was coming in
search of Kore.[21]

> In the context of the Peloponnesian War (431–404 BCE), there are several
> references to the worship of other new or foreign gods in Athens. The
> Roman writer Cicero refers to a comedy of Aristophanes that is no longer
> extant in which Sabazius, a Phrygian god, and other foreign gods were
> satirized and put on trial.

14.21   CICERO, *ON THE LAWS* 2.37. Aristophanes, the wittiest poet of Old
Comedy, so attacks new gods and all night festivals that were a part of
their worship that he represents Sabazius and other foreign gods as being
brought to trial and expelled from the city.

> The worship of Bendis, a Thracian goddess who is represented as a booted
> huntress, somewhat resembling Artemis, probably came first to the Piraeus,
> where she was worshiped by foreign residents in that area. The date of the
> arrival of the cult is difficult to discern, but it was well established by the
> last decades of the fifth century BCE. The best known reference to Bendis
> occurs at the beginning of Plato's Republic, the dramatic date of which is
> c. 410 BCE.

14.22   PLATO, *REPUBLIC* 327a–328a. I went down to the Piraeus yesterday with
Glaucon, the son of Ariston. I intended to pray to the goddess [Bendis] and,
at the same time, I wanted to see how they would handle the festival since
they were celebrating it for the first time. I thought that our own Athenian

---

19 *metragyrtes*: the word literally means a collector or begging priest (*agyrt-*) for the
Mother (*Meter*). These priests went around begging for funds for the cult; see Plato,
Republic 364 b–c in 13.1.

20 Cf. Euripides, *Helen* 1306–1307 in 14.13.

21 *Kore*: the Maid, Persephone.

procession was fine, and no less outstanding was that of the Thracians. After making a prayer and watching the procession, we were setting out for the city. ...

Adeimantus intervened: "Don't you know that there is going to be a torch-race on horseback this evening, in honor of the goddess?"

"On horseback?" said I, "that is a novelty. Are they going to hand on the torches in relays, as they race on horseback? Is that what you mean?"

"Exactly," said Polemarchus. "And there will also be an all night festival that will be worth seeing.[22] We intend to watch it after dinner. We will be joined by many of our young men here and talk with them. So please stay."

> The cult of Asclepius as healer is first attested at Epidaurus in the northwest Peloponnese in the early fifth century BCE. From there it spread to other parts of the Greek world.[23] Asclepius differs from most other gods of the Greek pantheon, in that he was a mortal who, after death, was worshiped both as a hero and as a god. In Homer he appears as a mortal, the father of two distinguished practitioners of healing, Podalareius and Machaon (Iliad 2.731–732). The earliest version of his birth and death is in Pindar's Pythian Ode 3, where he is said to be a son of Apollo, who is also associated with healing, and a mortal woman, Coronis. Pregnant with Apollo's child, she married a mortal; a raven informed Apollo, whereupon the god killed her but rescued the unborn child from her funeral pyre.
>
> Pindar (518–c.446 BCE) tells how Asclepius was struck by a thunderbolt from Zeus because he had restored a dead man to life.[24]

14.23 PINDAR, *PYTHIAN* 3.54–60.

But even wisdom is ensnared by gain.

Appearing in his hands with its overpowering reward,   55
gold prompted even him [Asclepius] to bring back from death
a man who had already been taken. But then, with his hands,
Cronus' son took the breath from both men's chests,
swiftly, as the lightning flash hurled doom upon them.
It is necessary to seek what is proper from the gods with our mortal
  minds,
recognizing what is before our feet, and the nature of our destiny.   60

> In describing the sanctuary of Asclepius at Epidaurus, Pausanias remarks on the peculiar color of the snakes in that area. He also reports that Asclepius was believed to have been taken to Sicyon, a city west of Corinth, in the form of a snake.

---

22 All-night festivals were commonly associated with orgiastic cults.

23 See 6.27 for some of the cures attributed to Asclepius at Epidaurus.

24 See 13.32 for the preceding lines of this ode, in which Pindar describes the healing skills of the adult Asclepius.

14.24 PAUSANIAS, 2.28.1. The snakes, including a distinct species of yellowish color, are regarded as sacred to Asclepius, and are tame with humans. These are peculiar to the area of Epidaurus.

14.25 PAUSANIAS, 2.10.3. The people of Sicyon say that the god was brought to them from Epidaurus on a carriage drawn by two mules and that he was in the likeness of a snake.

> The cult of Asclepius as healer was established in Athens c. 420 BCE by an otherwise unknown individual, Telemachus; the motive for importing the cult is disputed.[25] Unlike Bendis, Asclepius was a near neighbor. In Aristophanes' *Wasps* (lines 122–123), produced in 422 BCE, there is a reference to a temple of Asclepius and the practice of incubation on the island of Aegina in the Saronic Gulf. Although the Athenian cult was established first by a private individual, it had become public by the middle of the fourth century BCE.
>
> The establishing of Asclepius' cult in Athens was commemorated by an inscription, now fragmentary, that recorded the stages by which the god came to city of Athens via the port of Zea in the Piraeus and the Eleusinion. This inscription was set up by Telemachus, together with an elaborate sculpted relief depicting the cult, which probably included a representation of the incubation chamber and the god himself with his daughter Hygeia (Health). After residing in the Piraeus for about a year, the god was taken to the upper city, accompanied by a snake and Health, probably in a wagon belonging to Telemachus.[26]

14.26 *IG* II² 4960. ...coming up from Zea? during the Great Mysteries, he lodged? [in the Eleusinion] and summoning a snake? from its home brought it here on [a wagon]... At the same time came Health? And so this whole shrine was founded in the archonship of Astyphilos of Kydantidae [420/419 BCE].

> Another early sanctuary of Asclepius was in the southeastern Aegean on the island of Kos, which became the medical center of the Greek world in the fifth century BCE with the development of Hippocratic medicine. During the fourth century BCE a network of sanctuaries originating from Epidaurus developed. By the early third century BCE there were probably almost two hundred sanctuaries dedicated to him throughout the Greek world. This cult had a special appeal to individuals in a period when people's concerns were increasingly removed from the religion of the *polis* as a result of the defeat of the Greeks by Philip II of Macedon in 338 BCE. The sanctuary at Epidaurus continued to function as a healing center until Christianity was officially recognized by the Roman emperors in the fourth century CE.
>
> The Roman historian Livy (c. 59 BCE–17 CE) reports the bringing of Aesclepius to Rome in 292 BCE.

---

25 Also problematic are late sources indicating a connection of the poet Sophocles with the coming of Asclepius.

26 Neither the inscription nor relief have survived in their entirety; for reconstruction, see Garland 1992: 118–121 and Parker 1996: 177–178 with bibliography. The question marks in the translation indicate where the stone is broken.

14.27 LIVY, BOOK 11, *PERIOCHA*. When the state was troubled by a plague, envoys were sent to bring the image of Asclepius from Epidaurus to Rome. They brought back a snake which had crawled into their ship. It was generally believed that the god himself was present in this snake. When the snake went ashore on the Tiber island, a temple was built there to Asclepius.

> We have seen several examples of the worship or heroizing of a legendary or historic figure after death. One further innovation should be considered: that of a general or ruler becoming the object of worship during his lifetime. The first Greek to receive such honors is said to have been the Spartan Lysander, who was instrumental in the defeat of Athens in 404 BCE.

14.28 PLUTARCH, *LYSANDER* 18. At this time [after his victory over the Athenian fleet] Lysander was more powerful than any Greek before him, and he gave the impression that his ambition and conceit exceeded his power. He was the first Greek, so Duris tells us,[27] in whose honor Greek cities erected altars and offered sacrifices as though he were a god, the first for whom songs of triumph were sung…. The people of Samos decreed that their festival in honor of Hera should be called Lysandreia.

> When Alexander the Great (356–323 BCE) overthrew the Persian Empire, the conquered peoples expected him to accept the divine honors that they traditionally accorded their rulers. After Alexander had taken possession of Egypt, he went to consult the oracle of Zeus Ammon. Plutarch gives two versions of Alexander's consultation of the oracle, in one of which the oracle greeted Alexander as Zeus' son.[28]

14.29 PLUTARCH, *ALEXANDER* 27. When Alexander had crossed the desert and arrived at the shrine, the prophet of Ammon welcomed him on the god's behalf as a father greeting his son….This is the account that most writers have given of the oracles pronounced by the god…

Others say that the prophet wished as a mark of courtesy to address him with the Greek phrase "O, paidion," [o, my son]; but, because of his foreign pronunciation, the priest ended the words with "s" instead of "n," saying "o, paidios." Alexander is said to have been delighted at this slip of pronunciation, and so the legend grew up that the god had addressed him as "O, pai Dios" [i.e., son of Zeus].

14.30 PLUTARCH, *ALEXANDER* 28. Alexander generally conducted himself haughtily towards the barbarians, like a man fully persuaded of his divine birth and parentage, but with the Greeks it was within limits and somewhat rare that he assumed his own divinity … But it is clear that Alexander himself was not conceited or puffed up by the belief in his divinity, but used it for the subjugation of others.

---

27 *Duris*: a historian (c. 340–260 BCE) whose work only survives in quotations by later authors.

28 See the coin depicting a statue of Zeus with the legend, "Of Alexander," Figure 1.4.

In 307 BCE, sixteen years after Alexander's death, the Athenians voted divine honors to a Macedonian, Demetrius the Besieger of Cities, who had freed Athens from its autocratic governor.

14.31 PLUTARCH, *DEMETRIUS* 10. Demetrius' benefactions had made his name glorious and great, but the Athenians now made it obnoxious and annoying because of the extravagance of the honors that they voted him. For example, they were the first people in the world to confer upon Antigonus and Demetrius the title of king.[29] Both men had previously made it a matter of piety to decline this title, for they regarded it as the one royal honor that was still left for the descendants of Philip and Alexander; and so it should not be assumed or shared by others.

The Athenians, moreover, were also the only people who gave them the title of Savior-Gods.[30] They stopped the ancient custom of designating the year by the name of the chief magistrate, instead, they annually elected a priest of the Savior-Gods, prefixing his name to public edicts and private contracts.

They also decreed that likenesses of Demetrius and Antigonus should be woven into the sacred robe of Athena, together with those of the other gods.[31] They consecrated the spot where Demetrius had first stepped from his chariot and built an altar there, which they called the altar of the Descending Demetrius.

> The conquests of Alexander and the establishing of the three great Hellenistic kingdoms by Alexander's successors resulted in a more cosmopolitan society throughout the Mediterranean world. People traveled more freely from city to city, taking their own gods with them while also adopting new ones, such as the Egyptian deities Isis and Serapis. The old festivals were continued with new ones being added. For example, the Ptolemaea was added to the Athenian calendar in 224 BCE, honoring Ptolemy III Euergetes of Egypt. This festival was celebrated with the customary processions and athletic contests for all Athenian males.

> In the second and first centuries BCE, the Romans conquered Greece and the Greek cities of Asia Minor, overthrowing the Hellenistic monarchies. Traditional religious practices were generally maintained but adapted to the new political exigencies. After the Roman general Flamininus had defeated Philip V of Macedon in 196 BCE, he was hailed as "Savior" and granted rituals in the Greek city of Chalcis that were still performed in Plutarch's own time, three hundred years later.

14.32 PLUTARCH, *FLAMININUS* 16. Even in our own day a priest of Titus [Flamininus] is elected and appointed and, after sacrifice and libations in his honor, they sing a set hymn. Because of its length I shall not quote it

---

29 *Antigonus*: father of Demetrius.

30 *Savior-Gods*: the title "Savior" (*Soter*) refers to protection, well-being and safety in this life.

31 *sacred robe*: the *peplos* for Athena, see commentary at Figure 7.2.

in its entirety, but only the closing words of the song: "we revere the trust (*pistis*) of the Romans, cherished by our solemn vows. Sing, maidens, to Zeus the great, to Roma, Titus, and the trust of the Romans. Hail Paean Apollo.[32] Hail Titus our savior."

> The Greek historian Dio, writing in the early third century CE, notes the promotion of ruler cult in the Greek cities in Asia Minor and Bithynia in the time of the emperor Augustus (27 BCE–14 CE). In Rome and Italy, however, emperors were only granted divine honors after death.

14.33   DIO 51.20.6–8. Augustus meanwhile, among other business, allowed sanctuaries in Ephesus and Nicaea to Roma and to his father, Caesar, naming him the *Hero Julius*.[33] These were the leading cities of Asia [Minor] and Bithynia at this time. He ordered the Romans living there to honor these divinities. But he permitted foreigners (whom he styled "Greeks") to consecrate sanctuaries to himself—the Asians in Pergamon and Bithynians at Nicomedia. That is where this practice started and it has been continued under other emperors, not only among Greek nations, but among all others subject to Roman rule. In Rome itself and the rest of Italy, no emperor, no matter how worthy of renown, has dared to do this. However, when they die, even there those that ruled with integrity are granted various divine honors and *heroa* (hero's shrines) are built to them.

> The readiness of a pluralistic society to proclaim the appearance of a god is illustrated by the account in *Acts of the Apostles* of the visit of the Christian apostle Paul and his disciple Barnabas in the mid-first century CE to the Greek city of Lystra in southwestern Asia Minor. When Paul healed a man who had been lame from birth, the people thought that he and Barnabas were gods who had come down from heaven.

14.34   *ACTS OF THE APOSTLES* 14.10–18. The man leaped up and began to walk. There was a crowd watching what Paul did, and these people called out in the local language: "The gods have come down to us in the likeness of humans." So they called Barnabas Zeus and Paul Hermes since he was the chief speaker.[34]

And the priest of Zeus, whose temple was outside the city, brought bulls and garlands to the gates, wanting to hold a sacrifice with the crowd. But when Barnabas and Paul heard this, they tore their clothes and rushed out into the crowd, saying: "Why are you doing this? We are human beings too, with a nature like your own. We bring the good news that you should turn away from these empty ways to the living god.... " But despite these words,

---

32 *Roma*: the cult of the goddess Roma originated in Smyrna (modern Izmir in Turkey) in 195 BCE and became widespread in the Roman provinces. *Paean Apollo*: Apollo is here addressed as healer and thus savior.

33 *his father, Caesar*: Octavian, later known as Augustus, had been adopted by his great-uncle Julius Caesar in the latter's will.

34 *Hermes*: the messenger of the gods.

they had difficulty in stopping the crowds from performing a sacrifice in their honor.

> This selection of sources for the religious practices of the Greeks is perhaps best concluded with an excerpt on traditional piety from a work by Porphyry, the late third-century CE scholar, philosopher, and student of religions, who maintained that simple offerings of the fruits of the earth are just as acceptable to the gods as expensive animal sacrifices.

14.35 PORPHYRY, *ON ABSTINENCE FROM KILLING ANIMALS* 2.13–15.

Everything belongs to the gods, but the crops are thought to be ours, for we sow them, plant them and make them grow with other kinds of care. Therefore, we should sacrifice from what is ours, not from what belongs to others.

Something that is inexpensive and easy to procure is more sacred and pleasing to the gods than something that is difficult to procure, and that which is easiest for sacrificers is readily available, a source of constant piety. But something that is neither sacred nor inexpensive should not be sacrificed at all, even if it is available....

In the first place, many peoples do not possess any sacrificial animals, unless you count those that are unworthy. Secondly, the majority of people who live in cities do not have animals. Moreover, if someone says that they do not have cultivated crops, this does not apply to other produce of the earth; nor is it so difficult to get produce as it is to get animals. An inexpensive thing that is easy to get contributes to continual piety, and to the piety of everyone.

Experience indicates that the gods are more pleased by this than by great expense. Otherwise the Pythia would not have said that the god was better pleased with the man from Hermione, who sacrificed three finger-breadths of ground grain from his pouch, than with the Thessalian who brought cattle with gilded horns and hecatombs to Pythian Apollo. Therefore, inexpensive things are dear to the gods, and the divinity considers the character of the sacrificers rather than the amount of the sacrifice.

Gods[1]

Aphrodite: goddess of sexual desire and procreation. According to Hesiod, born from the foam created by Cronus' castration of Ouranos. In Homer, she is the daughter of Zeus and Dione. She is often addressed as "Cypris," the Cyprian.

Apollo: son of Zeus and Leto; god of prophecy, music, healing and medicine, often addressed as Phoebus (Phoibos) Apollo, or Loxias.

Ares: son of Zeus and Hera, god of war

Artemis: virgin daughter of Zeus and Leto. She presided over important aspects of life, including the transition from girlhood to marriage and thence to childbirth. She was also a death-bringing goddess, responsible for the deaths of women, especially in childbirth. As a huntress she protected wild beasts and their young.

Asclepius (Asklepios): god of healing, a son of Apollo and the mortal woman Coronis.

Athena (Athene): virgin daughter of Zeus and Metis, goddess of handicrafts, especially those of women, patron goddess of Athens.

Bacchus: see Dionysus.

Bendis: a Thracian goddess who resembled Artemis the huntress.

Castor: son of Leda and Tydareus (a mortal), and the twin brother of Pollux (Greek Polydeuces), who was Zeus' son. Pollux shared his immortality with his brother; they spent half their time on earth near Sparta and the other half in Olympus.

Cronus: son of Ouranos (Sky) and Gaia (Earth), husband of Rhea and father of Zeus. Cronus castrated his father Ouranos.

Cybele or Cybebe: the great Anatolian mother goddess, who was also known as Meter. Her cult came to mainland Greece in the late seventh and early sixth centuries BCE.

---

1 For the major Greek gods and their relationship to each other, see Figure 1.3, The Family of Zeus.

Demeter: daughter of Cronus and Rhea, and sister of Zeus with whom she produced Persephone. She was the goddess of grain who controlled all crops and vegetation.

Dionysus (also known as Bacchus): son of Zeus and Semele; god of wine, ecstasy, the mask, impersonation, and the theater.

Gaia: the goddess Earth, wife of Ouranos (Sky), also knows as Ge or Gaea.

Hades (Pluto): brother of Zeus, god of the underworld, who abducted Persephone, the daughter of Zeus and Demeter.

Hecate: a sinister goddess associated with magic and witchcraft, the moon, creatures of the night, dog sacrifices, and crossroads.

Hephaestus (Hephaistos): son of Hera, god of fire.

Hera: sister and wife of Zeus; goddess of marriage and women's life.

Hermes: son of Zeus and Maia; messenger of the gods, who guided people, especially travelers, and escorted the souls of the dead to the underworld.

Hestia: daughter of Cronus and Rhea, and thus sister of Zeus, Hera, etc.; goddess of the hearth.

Iris: minor goddess and messenger of the gods.

Kore: see Persephone.

Mother of the Gods: see Cybele.

Pan: minor god, who originated in Arcadia; he was represented as half man and half goat.

Persephone: daughter of Demeter and Zeus; she was carried off by Hades to be his wife in the underworld; she is also known as Kore, the Maid.

Poseidon: son of Cronus and Rhea, and brother of Zeus and Hades; god of the sea and earthquakes.

Rhea: daughter of Ouranos (Sky) and Gaia (Earth); married her brother Cronus.

Sabazius: a foreign god, of Phrygian or Thracian origin.

Zeus: son of Cronus and Rhea, king of gods and of men.

GLOSSARY

Names, places, institutions, and terms

Achilles (Greek, Akhilleus): Greece's greatest fighter at Troy, son of the mortal Peleus and the sea nymph Thetis.

acropolis: usually the highest spot in a city where temples and final defenses were built. In Athens, it was where the old temple of Athena and the Parthenon were situated.

Aegisthus (Greek, Aigisthos): lover of Clytemnestra wife of Agamemnon. The lovers were murdered by her son Orestes to avenge the death of Agamemnon.

Agamemnon: son of Atreus and brother of Menelaus. He was the leader of the Greek expedition to Troy and was murdered on his return home by his wife Clytemnestra and her lover Aegisthus. His son Orestes avenged his death by killing the lovers.

Agave: daughter of Cadmus of Thebes and mother of Pentheus.

agora: literally a "gathering place," it came to mean the marketplace and was the civic center of any city or town.

Alcibiades (Greek, Alkibiades): c. 450–404 BCE. Athenian general and politician, accused of complicity in the profanation of the Eleusinian mysteries. He defected to Sparta, but later returned to Athens. After winning several victories, he again fell out of favor and was killed in Asia Minor.

Alcmena: a mortal woman who was deceived by Zeus into believing that he was her husband Amphitryo; from this union she gave birth to Heracles.

Alexander the Great: king of Macedon, ruled 336–323 BCE. He conquered the Persian empire and extended his empire as far as the Punjab. He founded the city of Alexandria and died in Babylon, leaving no clear successor.

Alexander/Alexandros: see Paris.

Amphitryo: husband of Alcmena who bore Heracles to Zeus.

amulet: an object worn on the person to ward off evil, disease or other undesirable happenings; sometimes applied directly against the skin.

Andocides (c. 440–390 BCE): an Athenian who was implicated in the profanation of the Eleusinian mysteries; he later delivered a speech in his own defense.

Andromache: wife of the Trojan warrior Hector.

Antigone: daughter of Oedipus and Jocasta, who buried her brother Polynices, thus defying the edict of King Creon. Condemned to death by Creon, she was led to a tomb where she was left to die. Warned by Tiresias, Creon reversed his decision only to hear that Antigone had hanged herself.

Anthesteria: a festival in honor of Dionysus.

aulos: a pipe whose sound was produced by means of a double reed (rather like an oboe); it provided accompaniment for the chorus at dramatic performances, and for personal poetry; it was also used to keep soldiers in step.

bacchant: worshiper of Dionysus/Bacchus.

bouleuterion: council chamber.

Cadmus: founder of the city of Thebes, father of Agave and Semele, the mothers of Pentheus and Dionysus.

Calchas: Greek seer or prophet.

chorus: a group of originally twelve and later fifteen male actors who performed as a unit, dancing in the orchestra as they sang choral odes to the accompaniment of appropriate musical instruments.

Chryses: Trojan priest of Apollo.

Cimon (c. 512–450 BCE): leading conservative politician in Athens in the 470s and 460s before the ascendancy of Pericles.

Circe: powerful sorceress or witch; daughter of the Sun (Helios). She turns Odysseus' men into pigs, Odysseus rescues them, and she sends them to the Underworld to consult the seer Tiresias.

Clytemnestra (Greek, Klytaimestra): wife of Agamemnon, whom she murdered on his return from Troy; sister of Helen, Castor, and Pollux (Polydeuces), mother of Orestes, Electra, and Iphigenia. She was murdered by her son Orestes in revenge for his father's death.

Creusa: mother of Ion by the god Apollo.

Croesus (Greek, Kroisos): king of Lydia in the sixth century BCE.

Delos: an island in the Aegean that was sacred to Apollo; it was said to be the birthplace of Apollo and Artemis.

Delphi: location of the sanctuary of Apollo, seat of an influential oracle, and site of the Pythian games.

deme: a local territorial district in Attica.

Dionysia: a festival in honor of Dionysus. In Athens, there was the Lesser, or Rural, Dionysia, and the Greater or City Dionysia at which the major tragic and comic competitions were held.

Diagoras: a lyric poet who was active in Athens in the late fifth century BCE. Because of his atheism, he was forced to flee.

Diomedes: a Greek warrior fighting at Troy.

Diopeithes: Athenian who sponsored an impeachment procedure against impiety in the 430s BCE.

divination: (*mantike*): attempting to discern the will of the gods by the observation and interpretation of signs believed to have been sent by them. Divination was practiced by seers (*manteis*) who interpreted signs from thunder, lightning, the flight of birds, oracles, and the entrails of sacrificial animals, especially the liver. Divination was also practiced by means of lots, small pebbles or bits of wood that were shaken and drawn from a bowl.

drachma: a unit of money within the following system: 6 obols = 1 drachma; 2 drachmas = 1 stater; 100 drachmas = 1 mna; 6000 drachmas or 60 mnas = 1 talent. In the mid-fourth century BCE, the daily wage for a skilled laborer was between one and a half to two drachmas.

Dracon: magistrate, c. 621 BCE, who is said to have given the Athenians their first law code.

Eileithyia: goddess of childbirth.

Electra: a daughter of Agamemnon and Clytemnestra who, with her brother Orestes, devised revenge for her father's murder.

Eleusis: a sanctuary some twenty-two kilometers from Athens, where mysteries of Demeter were celebrated and initiations took place.

Epidaurus: location of a sanctuary of Asclepius, the god of healing, on a peninsula of the Saronic Gulf.

epiphany: the appearance or visitation of a god to a human.

ephebe: a young man between the onset of puberty and the age of twenty; also a group of Athenian young men between the ages of eighteen and twenty who were undergoing military training.

Erinyes: the Furies who avenge the shedding of blood by a blood relative, e.g., the Furies of Clytemnestra pursue Orestes after he has committed matricide.

expiation: an action aimed at making amends or atonement for an offense against the gods in order to win back their favor.

genos (pl. *gene*): clan or a small grouping of families within a phratry.

guest-friendship: see *xenia.*

hecatomb: literally a sacrifice of hundred oxen, but generally used of a large number of sacrificial victims.

Hector: son of King Priam of Troy, and Hecuba; hero of the Trojan War, who killed Achilles' companion Patroclus (Greek Patroklos) and was then killed by Achilles.

Hecuba (Greek, Hekabe): wife of King Priam of Troy, and mother of Hector and Paris (Alexandros).

Helen: sister of Clytemnestra and wife of Menelaus, king of Sparta who was the brother of Agamemnon; she was abducted by Paris (Alexandros) of Troy, thus causing the Trojan War.

Heracles: son of Zeus and Alcmene (the wife of Amphitryon), who performed twelve labors and was worshiped as a hero and a god after his death.

herm: sacred pillar, with head of Hermes on the top and an erect phallus in the middle, located outside a house.

hero-cult: the worship of heroes or heroines, beings intermediate between gods and humans. These are real or imaginary persons said to have accomplished superhuman deeds.

hierophant: the chief priest who revealed the sacred Mysteries.

Hippolytus: son of Theseus and an Amazon. He was destroyed by Aphrodite because he refused to worship her.

hybris: outrageous or excessive behavior that goes beyond the human norm, excessive pride that offends the gods.

ichor: the liquid that flowed in the veins of the immortals, corresponding to human blood.

incubation: a ritual whereby an individual who was sick would go to a sanctuary that was a place of healing and sleep overnight in the hope of being cured by the god.

initiation: a ritual whereby an individual underwent a purification, followed by revelation of "things that must not be spoken of." Thus he entered into a mystical communion with the divine that was thought to set him apart from non-initiates, conferring a state of blessedness both in this life and after death.

initiand: a candidate for initiation into the mysteries of a particular deity.

Ion: son of Apollo and a mortal, Creusa.

Ionia: the area along the central coastline of Asia Minor inhabited by Greeks.

Iphigenia: a daughter of Agamemnon and Clytemnestra, who, according to some sources, was sacrificed by her father at Aulis in order to obtain favorable winds to sail to Troy. Other sources say that she was rescued and taken to the land of the Taurians, where she was later discovered by her brother Orestes.

iunx or *iynx*: a magic disc or wheel, pierced by two holes in the center through which a looped thread was passed. When spun, it emitted a whirring sound that was spellbinding.

Jason: leader of the Argonauts in the quest for the golden fleece. He was helped by the Colchian princess Medea who possessed magical powers. She fled with him to Greece. But when Jason wished to marry a Greek princess, Medea took revenge on him by killing their children.

Jocasta: widow of Laius, mother and wife of Oedipus.

Laius: king of Thebes, husband of Jocasta, and father of Oedipus. The oracle of Apollo foretold that Laius would be killed by his son, who would then marry his mother.

Lacedaemonians: another name for the Spartans.

Lenaea: an Athenian festival in honor of Dionysus at which dramas were performed.

Leto: the mother of Apollo and Artemis by Zeus.

libation: pouring of liquid on an altar or the ground in honor of god(s), often wine, but could be milk or honey, or lustral water. The pouring of the libation would be accompanied by a prayer. The remaining liquid would often be consumed by the participants in the ritual. Pouring a libation could be a separate ritual or part of an animal sacrifice.

Loxias: Delphic Apollo.

lustral water: water reserved for purification before entering a sanctuary or making a sacrifice.

maenads: women inspired to ritual frenzy by Dionysus.

mantis: a seer, prophet, or soothsayer.

Marathon: a deme in Attica where, in 490 BCE, the Athenians defeated an enormous force of invading Persians.

Medea: the daughter of the king of Colchis; Aphrodite caused her to fall in love with Jason. Possessing magical powers, she helped him obtain the golden fleece by charming the dragon that guarded it. She fled with him to Greece. Later, when repudiated by Jason who wished to marry a Greek princess, she took revenge by killing the bride, the bride's father, and the children she had borne to Jason.

Menelaus: king of Sparta and brother of Agamemnon. His wife Helen was abducted by Paris.

metic: a resident alien (i.e., a non-Athenian citizen who was a permanent resident of Athens). Liable to military services and special taxes, but not allowed to own landed property in Attica. Resident aliens generally handled trade and commerce.

mna: a unit of money; see drachma.

Musaeus: a legendary singer, whose name means "he of the Muses", and who is said to have given oracles and cures for diseases.

Nicias: Athenian politician and general (470-413 BCE); commander in Sicily where he was defeated and died. He was extremely pious but also superstitious.

nomos: custom or law.

obol: see drachma.

Odysseus: Greek warrior who fought at Troy; the *Odyssey* is the story of his journey home.

Oedipus: (Greek, Oidipous): king of Thebes, who killed his father (Laius) and married his mother (Jocasta); father of Polynices, Eteocles, Antigone, and Ismene.

oikos: household or family, including property and slaves.

Olympia: a location in the western Peloponnese and site of the Olympic games.

Olympus: a mountain in northern Greece and home of the twelve Olympian gods.

omphalos: the navel stone at Delphi.

oracle: an utterance, regarded as sent by a god, usually delivered by a priest or priestess. The word also can apply to the priest or priestess, as well as to the place.

orchestra: circular space in the Greek theater, where the chorus performed the choral odes as they danced and sang to the accompaniment of music.

Orestes: son of Agamemnon and Clytemnestra who avenged his father's murder by his mother, thus incurring the crime of matricide. He was absolved by Apollo and finally by Athena. His bones were said to have been retrieved from Tegea and reburied in Sparta.

Orpheus: a legendary singer and poet, to whom are attributed a set of beliefs and religious practices.

paean: a song or hymn performed to honor a god in festal, political, military and personal situations.

Pallas: Pallas Athena.

Panathenaea: an Athenian festival held annually in honor of Athena, celebrated with greater magnificence every fourth year (the Great Panathenaea). There were processions, sacrifices, and contests that were open to all Greek-speaking males.

papyrus: writing material prepared from the papyrus rush.

Paris (also known as Alexandros or Alexander): prince of Troy, son of Priam and Hecuba. He abducted the wife of Menelaus, King of Sparta, thus causing the Trojan War.

Parthenon: the temple of Athena Parthenos (the Maid) on the Athenian acropolis, built 437–432 BCE.

Patroos: literally "of the father," used of gods in their role as protectors of the family and people.

Peloponnesian War: the war fought between Athens and Sparta from 431–404 BCE, in which Athens was defeated.

peplos: the sacred robe woven annually for the statue of Athena Polias and presented to her at the Panathenaea.

Pericles (c. 495–429 BCE): Athenian statesman and general who commissioned the building of the Parthenon; friend of many leading intellectuals of the day, e.g., Anaxagoras.

Phaedra (Greek, Phaidra): the wife of Theseus, whom Aphrodite caused to fall in love with her stepson Hippolytus.

Piraeus: the harbor of Athens.

Persian Wars: wars fought between Greeks and Persians between 490 and 480 BCE, particularly the battles of Marathon (490 BCE), Thermopylae (481 BCE), Salamis (480 BCE), and Plataea (479 BCE). All but Thermopylae were Greek victories.

phallus: representation of the male reproductive organ, often carried in processions, particularly those associated with Dionysus.

Philip II, reigned 359-336 BCE: king of Macedon, who unified Macedon and defeated the Greeks at the battle of Chaeronea in 338 BCE, thus ending Greek independence. He was the father of Alexander the Great.

Phoebus (Greek, Phoibos): a title of Apollo.

phratry: a subdivision of the tribe (*phyle*), a kin grouping or brotherhood, to which only Athenian citizens could belong. It had various religious functions, including the official acknowledgment of the newborn children of its members. It was often called upon to validate claims to legitimacy and thus rights of citizenship.

Pisistratus (Greek, Peisistratos): tyrant (sole ruler) of Athens in the mid-sixth century BCE. Under his rule Athens began to flourish as a cultural and commercial center.

Polias: title of Athena as guardian of the city.

polis: the *polis* or Greek city state developed in the eighth century BCE. The term designates a political community consisting of a principal city or town and its surrounding territory, which combined to form a self-governing entity.

Polynices (Greek, Polyneikes): one of the sons of Oedipus and Jocasta, who made war on his native Thebes in order to oust his brother Eteocles from the kingship. Both brothers were slain in the conflict and Creon, their uncle and the new king, forbade the burial of Polynices. Antigone, Polynices' sister, defied Creon and gave her brother token burial.

Priam: king of Troy and father of Hector and Paris (Alexandros).

Pythagoras: born in Samos in the mid-sixth century BCE, and migrated to Croton in southern Italy, where he founded a sect that bore his name.

Pythia: the priestess of Apollo at Delphi, through whom the god delivered his oracles.

Rhea: wife of Cronus.

sacred robe: see *peplos*.

seer or **soothsayer** (*mantis*): an interpreter of signs thought to be sent by the gods.

Socrates (470–399 BCE): the philosopher who turned Greek philosophical enquiry away from the nature of the physical world to questions concerning humans. He left no writings; for knowledge of his teachings, we are largely dependent on Aristophanes' comedy *Clouds*, and the dialogues of Plato and Xenophon. He was condemned to death on charges that were tantamount to impiety.

Solon: late seventh and early sixth century BCE poet, politician, and law-giver.

sophists: literally "wise men," the term was applied to traveling teachers who were prepared to impart knowledge for a fee. Some taught rhetoric, others engaged in discussions that challenged traditional views.

supplication: a ritual whereby an individual in need of help or protection would humble himself by sitting at a more powerful person's feet or at an altar and beg for assistance, while also invoking a god. The individual being supplicated (*supplicandus*) would thus be bound to grant the suppliant's prayer.

symposium: a drinking party celebrated by males of noble birth. Women, with the exception of female entertainers, were excluded

talent: see drachma.

Telemachus: the son of Odysseus and Penelope.

temenos: a sacred precinct of land consecrated to a god or hero, containing an altar and probably also a temple and other buildings essential for the administration of the cult.

Themis: daughter of Gaea and Ouranos (Earth and Sky); her name means Right or Established Custom. She becomes associated with the order or justice of Zeus.

Themistocles (c. 528–462 BCE): leading Athenian general in the late 480s. He advised the Athenians to build a navy and was instrumental in the strategy that resulted in the Greek victory over the Persians at Salamis.

Theseus: legendary king of Athens who performed various exploits including killing the Minotaur; father of Hippolytus and husband of Phaedra. Bones, said to be his, were brought from Scyros and interred in Athens by Cimon in 474 BCE, where he was worshiped as a hero.

Thesmophoria: a women's festival in honor of Demeter and her daughter Kore (Persephone).

Thetis: immortal sea nymph and mother of Achilles by the mortal Peleus.

Thirty Tyrants: thirty men appointed in 404 BCE by the Spartans to govern Athens and write a new constitution after Athens' defeat in the Peloponnesian War. They were overthrown in 403 BCE.

Tiresias: the blind prophet or seer in the story of Oedipus.

Titans: the generation of gods that preceded the Olympian gods and was overthrown by them.

The Twelve gods: Aphrodite, Apollo, Ares, Artemis, Athena, Demeter, Dionysus, Hephaestus, Hera, Hermes, Poseidon, Zeus. These are the twelve gods depicted on the Parthenon frieze, and altars were erected to this group in the agora in Athens and in other Greek cities.

votive offering: an offering made to a god either in fulfillment of a vow promising such a gift if the god granted a particular prayer, or in the hope of a prayer being granted.

xenia: guest-friendship, a form of ritual friendship, whereby a "stranger" (*xenos*) entered into a relationship of mutual friendship with an individual from another community or country, each becoming obliged to offer hospitality and aid when they visited the other's community. This bond endured from generation to generation within the two families.

Xerxes: king of Persia; leader of the invasion of Greece in 480s BCE. He defeated the Spartans at Thermopylae, but then lost the battles of Salamis and Plataea, after which the Persians withdrew from Greece.

CHRONOLOGY

All dates are BCE unless otherwise specified. Some of the earlier dates are traditional or approximate.

c. 1250–1225   Trojan War

c. 800   Greeks develop alphabet; earliest temples built

776   traditional date of the first Olympic games

c. 750   emergence of *polis*

overseas colonization of the West begins

c. 750–720   *Iliad* and Odyssey composed

c. 700   Hesiod, *Theogony* and *Works and Days*

650   colonization of Black Sea area begins

c. 621   law code of Dracon in Athens

600   beginning of science and philosophy (the presocratics)

594   Solon's political reforms in Athens

c. 585   Thales of Miletus active

582   Pythian games established at Delphi

581   Isthmian games established at Isthmia

572   Nemean games established at Nemea

c. 566   Pisistratus expands religious festivals at Athens

560–546   Croesus, king of Lydia

508   Cleisthenes' democratic reforms in Athens

490   Athenians defeat Persians at Marathon

480–479   battles of Thermopylae, Salamis, Plataea: Persians driven from Greece

474   Cimon brings bones of Theseus to Athens

470   birth of Socrates

early 450s   Anaxagoras takes up residence in Athens

458   Aeschylus' *Oresteia*

456   death of Aeschylus

447–432   construction of Parthenon in Athens

442/1   Sophocles' *Antigone*

440s–430s   height of Athens' "Golden Age"

mid–430s   Diopeithes' decree; departure of Anaxagoras from Athens

431–404   Peloponnesian War

430   outbreak of plague in Athens

429   death of Pericles

c. 429   birth of Plato

c. 428   Sophocles' *Oedipus the King*
         Euripides' *Hippolytus*

423   Aristophanes' *Clouds*

421   Peace of Nicias brings temporary end to Peloponnesian War
       Asclepius brought to Athens

415   Euripides' *Trojan Women*
       mutilation of the herms and profanation of the Eleusinian Mysteries
       Diagoras forced to flee from Athens

415–413   Athenian expedition to Sicily; Alcibiades defects to Sparta

407   return of Alcibiades to Athens; he provides escort for procession to Eleusis

406   deaths of Sophocles and Euripides

405   Euripides' *Bacchae*; Aristophanes' *Frogs*
       Sparta inflicts naval defeat on Athens

404–403   regime of Thirty Tyrants in Athens

401–399   Xenophon and the march of the Ten Thousand (*Anabasis*)

399   trial and death of Socrates

399-347   dialogues of Plato

359–336   Philip II rules Macedon

356   birth of Alexander the Great

338   battle of Chaeronea; end of Greek political freedom

336   death of Philip II of Macedon; accession of Alexander

331   Alexander founds Alexandria and visits oracle of Zeus Ammon

323   death of Alexander

322   deaths of Demosthenes and Aristotle

306   Demetrius the Besieger of Cities and his father Antigonus receive divine honors in Athens

292   cult of Asclepius imported to Rome

200   Roman invasion of Greece: Second Macedonian War

196   Flamininus proclaims the freedom of the Greeks at the Isthmian games

167   end of the Macedonian monarchy

146   sack of Corinth; Rome annexes Macedon and Greece

129   Asia Minor becomes a Roman province

44   assassination of Julius Caesar

31   battle of Actium

30   Rome annexes Egypt

27–14 CE   rule of Augustus

40s–50s CE   journeys of the apostle Paul

Maps

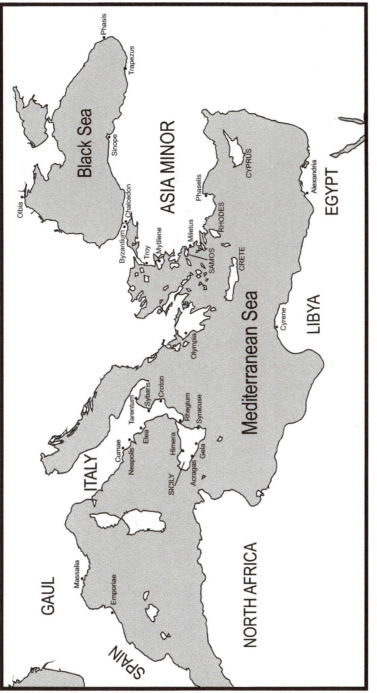

Map I. The Mediterranean World.

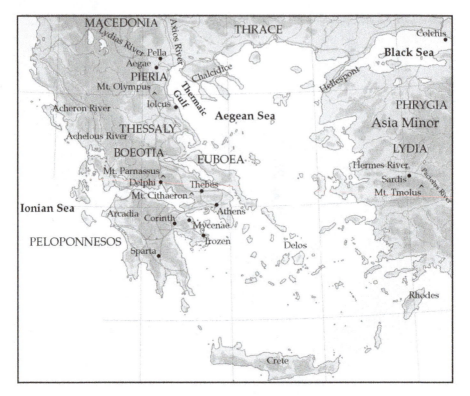

Map 2. Greece and Asia Minor.

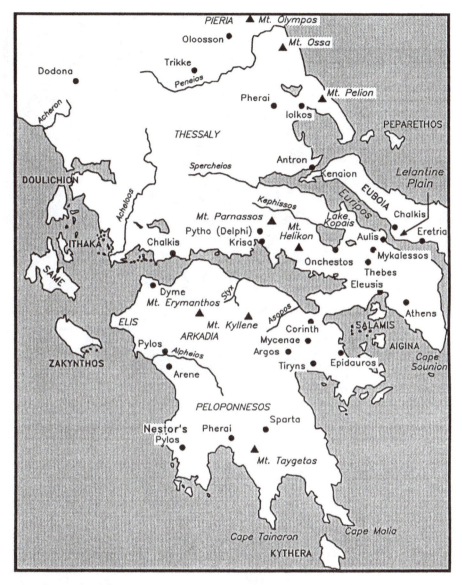

Map 3. Mainland Greece.

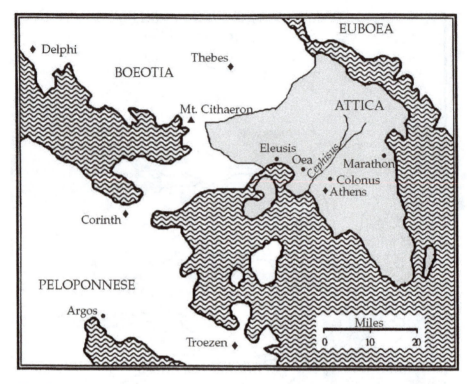

Map 4. Attica and the Environs.

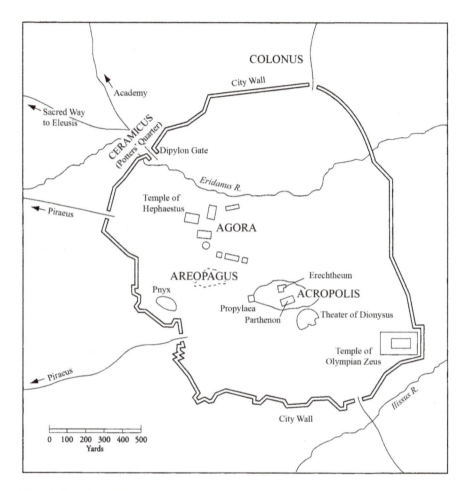

Map 5. The City of Athens.

Ancient Literary Sources

Most of the sources listed are available in the Loeb Classical Library.

Acts of the Apostles: the fifth book of the New Testament, a major source for the journeys of the apostle Paul in the 40s and 50s CE.

Aeschylus (c. 525–456 BCE): Athenian tragedian.

Anaxagoras (c. 500–428 BCE): Greek philosopher who came to Athens but was forced to leave because of his teachings to avoid the charge of impiety.

Anaximander: early sixth century BCE philosopher.

Antiphon (c. 489–411 BCE): Athenian orator.

Apollonius Rhodius: third century BCE poet who worked in Alexandria. His major work, the *Argonautica*, is an epic poem telling the story of the quest of Jason and the Argonauts for the golden fleece.

Aristophanes (c. 450–c. 385 BCE): greatest Athenian comic playwright; his plays reveal much about contemporary Athenian life and politics.

Aristotle (384–322 BCE): philosopher, joined Plato's Academy, and later founded his own school, the Lyceum.

Athenaeus c. 200 CE: author of the *Deipnosophists*, an account of a cultured conversation over dinner in fifteen books that is an invaluable source of quotations from authors whose works are now lost.

Callimachus *fl.* 280–240 BCE: Greek poet and critic, educated in Athens, but worked in the library of Alexandria that was established by Ptolemy II.

Cicero (106–43 BCE): Roman orator, politician, and writer of letters and philosophy that touch on religion and theology, notably *On divination* and *On the gods*.

Clement of Alexandria born c. 150 CE : Christian writer of *Exhortation to the Greeks*, a diatribe in which he makes various assertions about the Eleusinian Mysteries and the Thesmophoria.

Critias (460–403 BCE): friend of Alcibiades and associate of Socrates, generally included among the sophists. He was an oligarch, an extremist, and one of the Thirty Tyrants, probably the author of the lost tragedy *Sisyphus*.

Demosthenes (384–322 BCE): Athenian orator and politician.

Dio (c. 160–c. 235 CE): Cassius Dio, a Greek who wrote a history of Rome through to his own times.

Diodorus Siculus: a Sicilian who wrote a *World History* in the late first century BCE.

Diogenes Laertius (probably the third century CE): wrote a compendium on the lives and doctrines of ancient Greek philosophers.

Dionysius of Halicarnassus: a Greek resident in Rome 30–8 BCE, who wrote *Roman Antiquities*, a detailed account of Rome's early history and customs that emphasized the Greek origins of Rome.

Empedocles (c. 492–432 BCE): a philosopher from Sicily, who posited a theory of reincarnation.

Epictetus: a mid-first to second century CE Stoic philosopher.

Euripides (c. 485—406 BCE): Athenian tragic playwright.

Heraclitus: early Greek philosopher, active c. 500 BCE.

Herodotus (c. 480–420 BCE): historian who came from Halicarnassus, and lived for some time in Athens, wrote *Histories*, an account of how the Greeks and Persians came into conflict in the Persian Wars. He traveled widely in doing his research and is known as the "father of history."

Hesiod: late eighth to early seventh century BCE poet and farmer, who wrote in epic style *Works and Days* (a farmer's calendar and instruction manual) and *Theogony* (the birth of the gods).

Hippolytus (170–c. 236 CE): Christian apologist who, in *Refutation of all Heresies*, claims knowledge of the ultimate Eleusinian revelation.

Homer: late eighth century BCE poet, who imposed unity on the *Iliad* and *Odyssey*.

Homeric Hymns: a collection of thirty-four poems written in the same meter as the *Iliad* and *Odyssey*, but composed by different authors dating from the eighth century BCE to the Hellenistic period.

Isaeus: (c. 420–340s BCE): Athenian speech writer.

Isocrates (436–338 BCE): Athenian orator and advocate of panhellenism.

Julian "the apostate": Roman emperor from 361–363 CE who attempted to restore the old pagan cults in opposition to Christianity.

Livy (64 or 59 BCE–17 CE): Roman historian who wrote a history of Rome.

Lysias (459/8–c. 380 BCE): Athenian orator.

Menander (c. 342–292 BCE): writer of so-called New Comedy, set in contemporary Greece and dealing generally with domestic, i.e., non-political, situations.

Palatine Anthology: a selection of Greek poems by different authors, composed in the tenth century CE that drew on three older anthologies.

Pausanias: mid-second century CE Greek author of *Description of Greece*, a descriptive tour of the cities and sanctuaries of Greece.

Phanodemus: a fourth century BCE chronicler of early Athenian history, whose work only survives in fragments quoted by later authors.

Philochorus (340–260 BCE): a scholar-historian who was also a seer. His work only survives in fragments.

Philostratus: mid-third century CE author of *Pictures in a Gallery*, descriptions of paintings that elaborate the breadth of his knowledge.

Photius: a Byzantine lexicographer who wrote in the ninth century CE.

Pindar (518–c.446 BCE): lyric poet from Boeotia famous for the victory odes he composed for victors at the various games, e.g., Olympic games.

Plato (c. 429–347 BCE): influential Greek philosopher and pupil of Socrates, whom he made an interlocutor in many of his dialogues.

Pliny the Elder (23/4–79 CE): author of *Natural History*, an encyclopedic collection of contemporary knowledge; he died in the eruption of Vesuvius.

Plutarch (c. 50–120 CE): biographical historian, whose works include the *Parallel Lives of Greeks and Romans* and *Moralia*.

Porphyry (234–c. 305 CE): scholar, philosopher, and student of religion, whose works include *On Abstinence from Killing Animals*.

Prodicus: sophist and contemporary of Socrates.

Protagoras (490–420 BCE): most famous of the sophists; he made several visits to Athens.

Simonides: late sixth and early fifth century BCE poet.

Solon: late seventh and early sixth century BCE poet, politician, and law-giver; only fragments of his work survive.

Sophocles (c. 496–406 BCE): Athenian tragedian.

Strabo (c. 64 BCE–after 21 CE): author of *Geographia*, an important source for descriptions of Greek cities and sanctuaries.

Tertullian (c. 160–c. 230 CE): a convert to Christianity, who wrote many works about the history and character of the church.

Thales: early sixth century BCE Greek philosopher.

Theocritus: early third century BCE poet from Syracuse in Sicily who worked in Alexandria in the 270s.

Theognis: elegiac poet; a large body of verses attributed to him survives, of which many were probably by other elegiac poets. Scholars date the poems from the mid-sixth to the early fifth century BCE.

Theopompus: fourth century BCE historian; his work only survives in fragments quoted by later authors.

Thucydides (c. 460–400 BCE): Athenian who wrote the history of the Peloponnesian War as far as 411 BCE.

Timaeus (c. 350–260 BCE): important Greek historian who lived in Sicily; much of his work is lost, surviving only in fragments quoted by later authors.

Xenophanes (c. 570–c. 475 BCE): an early Greek philosopher who questioned several concepts of traditional Greek religion.

Xenophon (c. 430–c. 354 BCE): pupil of Socrates, Athenian soldier, and author of several works, including *Anabasis* (the expedition of a Greek mercenary force to Mesopotamia and their return journey, 401–399 BCE), *Memorabilia* (Memoirs of Socrates), and *Symposium*. His works reflect traditional piety.

Bibliography

Reference Works

Diehl = *Anthologia Lyrica Graeca,* ed. 1949 by E. Diehl, Leipzig.

DK = Die Fragmente der Vorsokratiker, 5th to 7th eds., 1951, by H. Diels, ed. with additions by W. Krantz.

DTAud = Audollent, A., 1904. Defixionum Tabellae quotquot innotuerunt. Paris.

FGrHist = Jacoby, F., 1923–1958. *Die fragmente der griechischen Historike*r. Berlin-Leiden.

GHI = Tod, M.N., 1946 reprinted 1985. *Greek Historical Inscriptions.* Chicago.

Graf and Johnston = Graf, F., Johnston, S., 2007. *Rituals of the Afterlife; Orpheus and the Bacchic Gold Tablets.* Routledge, London and New York.

IG = Inscriptiones Graecae. Berlin, 1893–.

KRS = Kirk, G. S., Raven, J., and Schofield, M. 1983. The *Presocratic Philosophers,* 2nd edition. Cambridge University Press.

LSCG Suppl. = F. Sokolowski, 1962. *Lois sacres des cites grecques. Supplement.* Paris.

ML = Meiggs, R. and D. Lewis, 1969, 2nd edn 1989. *A Selection of Greek Historical Inscriptions.* Clarendon Press, Oxford.

NGSL = Lupu, Eran, 2005. *Greek Sacred Law: A Collection of New Documents (NGSL).* Brill, Leiden and Boston.

OCD = Oxford Classical Dictionary, 3rd edition 1996, revised 2003, ed. Simon Hornblower and Antony Spawforth, Oxford University Press.

Parke 1967 = Parke, H. W., 1967.*The Oracles of Zeus: Dodona, Olympia, Athens.* Blackwell, Oxford.

PGM = Papyri Graecae Magicae, 1973, 2 vols, ed. K. Preisendanz et al. Stuttgart

RO = Rhodes, P. J., and Robin Osborne, ed., 2003. *Greek Historical Inscriptions: 404–323 BCE.* Oxford University Press.

SEG = Supplementum Epigraphicum Graecum, Amsterdam. 1923– .

SIG 3 = W. Dittenberger, (ed.) 3rd ed. 1915-1924, reprinted 1999. *Sylloge Inscriptionum Graecarum,* Leipzig.

Translations used in this volume

Aristophanes, *Clouds,* translated by Jeffrey Henderson, 1992. Focus Publishing, Newburyport, Massachusetts.

Euripides, *Trojan Women,* translated by Shirley A. Barlow, 1986. Aris and Philips, Oxford.

Euripides, *Medea, Hippolytus, Heracles, Bacchae,* ed. Stephen Esposito, 2002. Focus Publishing, Newburyport, Massachusetts.

Hesiod, *Theogony,* translated by Richard S. Caldwell, 1987. Focus Publishing, Newburyport, Massachusetts.

The Homeric Hymns, translated by Susan C. Shelmerdine, 1995. Focus Publishing, Newburyport, Massachusetts.

Sophocles, *The Theban Plays: Antigone, King Oidipous, Oidipous at Colonus*, translated by Ruby Blondell, 2002. Focus Publishing, Newburyport, Massachusetts.

Some Introductory Works on Greek Religion

Bremmer, Jan, 1994. *Greek Religion*, Oxford University Press.

Garland, R., 1994. *Religion and the Greeks*. Bristol Classical Press.

Mikalson, Jon D. 2005. *Ancient Greek Religion*. Blackwell, Oxford.

Price, Simon, 1999. *Religions of the Ancient Greeks*. Cambridge University Press.

Zaidman, Louise and Pauline Schmidt Pantel, 1992. *Religion in the Ancient Greek City*, translated by Paul Cartledge. Cambridge University Press.

Further Reading

Betegh, G,. 2004. *The Derveni Papyrus: Cosmology, Theology and Interpretation*. Cambridge University Press.

Betz, Hans Dieter, 1996, rev. 2nd ed. *The Greek Magical Papyri in Translation including the demotic spells*. University of Chicago Press.

Blundell, S., and Margaret Williamson, 1998: *The Sacred and the Feminine in Ancient Greece*. Routledge, London and New York.

Bremmer, Jan N., 2007. "Greek Nominative Animal Sacrifice" in Ogder, 2007: 132–144.

Broad, William J., 2006: *The lost secrets and hidden message of ancient Delphi*. Penguin Press, New York

Burkert, Walter, 1983. *Homo Necans*, translated by Peter Bing. University of California Press.

Burkert, Walter, 1985. *Greek Religion*, translated by John Raffan. Blackwell and Harvard University Press.

Burkert, Walter, 1987. *Ancient Mystery Cults*. Harvard University Press.

Burkert, Walter, 2001. *Savage Energies: Lessons of Myth and Ritual in Ancient Greece*. Trans. P. Bing. University of Chicago Press.

Buxton, Richard, ed., 2000. *Oxford Readings in Greek Religion*. Oxford University Press.

Camp, John M., 2001. *The Archaeology of Athens*. New Haven, Yale University Press.

Carpenter, Thomas H. and Christopher Faraone,1993. *Masks of Dionysus*. Ithaca, Cornell University Press.

Clinton, K., 1992. *Myth and Cult: The Iconography of the Eleusinian Mysteries*, Stockholm.

Cole, S. G., 1998. "Domesticating Artemis," in Blundell and Williamson 1998: 27–43.

Connelly, Joan Breton, 2007. *Portrait of a Priestess: women and ritual in ancient Greece*. Princeton University Press.

DeBoer, J.Z., J.R. Hale, and J. Chanton, 2001. "New Evidence for the Geological O of the Ancient Delphic Oracle (Greece)." *Geology* 29.8 (August): 707–710.

Detienne, M. and J-P. Vernant, 1989. *The Cuisine of Sacrifice among the Greeks*, translated by Paula Wissing. University of Chicago Press.

Dickie, M., 2001. *Magic and Magicians in the Greco-Roman World*, London and New York.

Dillon, Matthew, 1997. *Pilgrims and Pilgrimage in Ancient Greece*, Routledge, London and New York.

Dillon, Matthew, 2002. *Girls and Women in Classical Greek Religion*. Routledge, London and New York.

Dodd, David B. and Christopher Faraone 2003. *Initiation in Ancient Greek Rituals and Narratives: New critical perspectives*. Routledge, London and New York.

Dodds, E. R., 2004, first published 1951. *The Greeks and the Irrational*. University of California Press.

Donnici, L. R. 1995. *The Epidaurian Miracle Inscriptions: Text, Translation and Commentary*. Scholars Press, Atlanta, Georgia.

Dowden, K., 2006. *Zeus*. Routledge, London and New York.

Easterling and Muir, eds.,1985. *Greek Religion and Society*. Cambridge University Press.

Ekroth, G., 2007, "Heroes and Hero Cults," in Ogden 2007: 100–114.

Faraone, C. A., and D. Obbink, eds. 1991: *Magika Hiera: Ancient Greek Magic and Religion*, New York.

Faraone, C. A., 1999: *Ancient Greek Love Magic,* Harvard University Press.

Faraone, C. A., 2003. "Playing the bear and the fawn for Artemis: female initiation or substitute sacrifice?" in Dodd and Faraone 2003: 43–68.

Ferrari, G., 2003. "What kind of rite was the ancient Greek wedding?" in Dodd and Faraone 2003: 27–42.

Flower, M. A., 2008. *The Seer in Ancient Greece.* University of California Press.

Gager, J., 1992: *Curse tablets and binding spells from the ancient world.* Oxford.

Garland,R., 1985, 2nd edition, 2001. *The Greek Way of Death.* Bristol Classical Text.

Garland, R., 1990. *The Greek Way of Life: from conception to old age.* Cornell University Press, Ithaca, New York.

Garland, R., 1992. *Introducing New Gods: The Politics of Athenian Religion.* Cornell University Press, Ithaca, New York.

Goldhill, S.,1994. "Representing Democracy: Women at the Greater Dionysia," in *Ritual, Finance, Politics,* ed. R. Osborne and S. Hornblower. Oxford University Press.

Graf, F., 1997: *Magic in the Ancient World,* translated by Franklin Phillip. Harvard University Press.

Graf, F., and S.I. Johnston, 2007. *Rituals Texts for the Afterlife: Orpheus and the Bacchic Gold Tablets.* Routledge, London and New York.

Guthrie, W. K. C., 1969. *A History of Greek Philosophy,* vol. 3. Cambridge University Press.

Hamilton, Richard, 1992. Choes *and* anthesteria: *Athenian iconography and ritual.* University of Michigan Press.

Henderson, J., 1991. "Women and the Athenian Dramatic Festivals," *Transactions of the American Philogical Society* 121, pp.133–47.

Jameson, M. H., D. R. Jordan, and R. D. Kotansky, 1993: "A *lex sacra* from Selinus," in Greek, Roman, and Byzantine Monographs 11. Durham, N.C.

Johnston, Sarah Iles, 1995. "The Song of the *Iunx*: Magic and Rhetoric in *Pythian* 4," in *Transactions of the American Philological Society,* 125: 177–206.

Johnston, Sarah Iles and Struck, Peter T., 2005. Mantike: *studies in ancient divination.* Leiden, Boston, Brill.

Johnston, Sarah Iles, 2008. *Ancient Greek Divination.* Wiley-Blackwell pub., Oxford.

Jordan, D. R., 1999. "Three curse tablets," in Jordan D. R., H. Montgomery, and E. Thomassen, ed. in *The World of Ancient Magic.* Papers from the Norwegian Institute at Athens 4. Bergen.

Kearns, E., 1989. *The Heroes of Attica.* Bulletin of the Institute of Classical Studies, supplement 57, University of London.

Kearns, E., 1992. "Between Gods and Man: Status and Function of Heroes and their Sanctuaries," in A. Schachter and Bingen, J., eds., *Le sanctuaire grec.* Entretiens Hardt 37, Geneva.

Kearns, E., 1998: "The Nature of Heroines," in Blundell and Williamson 1998.

Lopez Jimeno, M. d. A., 1991. *Las tabellae defixionis de la Sicilia griega.* Amsterdam.

Larson, Jennifer, 2007. *Ancient Greek Cults: : a guide.* Routledge, New York and London.

Leduc, Claudine, 1992. "Marriage in Ancient Greece," 235–294 in Schmitt Pantel 1992.

Lefkowitz, M. and M. Fant. 3rd ed. 2005. *Women's Life in Greece and Rome: a sourcebook in translation.* Johns Hopkins University Press.

Lefkowitz, M. L., 2003: *Greek Gods, Human Lives.* Yale University Press.

Lloyd-Jones, H., 1979. Aeschylus, *Oresteia,* translation and commentary, 3 vols. Duckworth, London and Dallas.

Lloyd-Jones, H., 2nd edition 1983. *The Justice of Zeus.* Berkeley, University of California Press (first published 1971).

Lowe, N. J., 1998, "Thesmophoria and Haloa: Myth, Physics and mysteries," in Blundell and Williamson 1998: 149–173.

Meyer, Marvin W., 1999: *Ancient Mysteries a sourcebook: sacred texts of the mystery religions of the ancient world.* Philadelphia University Press.

Mikalson, Jon D., 1975. *The Sacred and Civil Calendar of the Athenian Year.* Princeton University Press.

Mikalson, J., 1991: *Honor Thy Gods,* University of North Carolina Press, Chapel Hill and London.

Miller, Stephen G., 2004a. *Ancient Greek Athletics.* Yale University Press, New Haven and London.

Miller, Stephen G., 2004b, 3rd ed., *Arete: Greek Sports from Ancient Sources.* University of California Press.

Mylonas, George, 1974, first published 1961. *Eleusis and the Eleusinian Mysteries*. Princeton University Press.

Naiden, F. S., 2006. *Ancient Supplication*. Oxford University Press.

Naiden, F. S., 2007. "The Fallacy of the Willing Victim," in *Journal of Hellenic Studies* 127.

Neils, J. 1992, *Goddess and Polis: the Panathenaic Festival in Ancient Athens*. Princeton University Press.

Oakley, John H. and Rebecca H. Sinos, 1993. *The Wedding in Ancient Athens*. University of Wisconsin Press.

Ogden, Daniel, 2002. *Magic, Witchcraft, and Ghosts in the Greek and Roman Worlds*, Oxford University Press

Ogden, Daniel ed., 2007. *A Companion to Greek Religion*. Blackwell, Oxford.

Parke, H. W., and D. E. W. Wormell, 1956. *The Delphic Oracle* (2 vols.) Oxford, Blackwell.

Parke, H. W., 1967. *The Oracles of Zeus: Dodona, Olympia, Athens*. Blackwell, Oxford.

Parke, H. W., 1977. *Festivals of the Athenians*. Ithaca, New York.

Parker, R., 1983. *Miasma: Pollution and Purification in Early Greek Religion*. (2nd edition 1996) Oxford.

Parker, R., 1985. "Greek States and Greek Oracles" pp. 298–326 in *Crux, Essays Presented to G. E. M. de Ste. Croix*, edd. P. Cartledge and F. D. Harvey, reprinted in Buxton 2000: 76–108.

Parker, R., 1996. *Athenian Religion: a history*. Oxford University Press.

Parker, R., 2005. *Polytheism and Society at Athens*. Oxford University Press.

Pedley, John G., 2005. *Sanctuaries and the sacred in the ancient Greek world*. Cambridge University Press.

Pedley, John G., 2007 3rd edition. *Greek Art and Archaeology*, Prentice Hall, Upper Saddle River, N. J.

Pickard-Cambridge, A 1988. *The Dramatic Festivals of Athens*, second edition, revised by John Gould and D. M. Lewis, Clarendon Press, Oxford.

Polinskaya, Irene, 2003. "Liminality as Metaphor: initiation and the frontiers of ancient Athens," in Dodd and Faraone 2003: 85–106.

Pulleyn, S. J., 1997. *Prayer in Greek Religion*. Oxford University Press.

Rice, David G. and John E. Stambaugh, 1979. *Sources for the Study of Greek Religion*. Scholars Press. Missoula, Mont.

Roller, L. 1999. *In Search of God the Mother: The Cult of Anatolian Cybele*. University of California Press.

Rosenzweig, Rachel, 2004. *Worshipping Aphrodite: art and cult in classical Athens*, University of Michigan

Schacter, A., and Bingen J., eds., 1992. *Le Sanctuaire grec*, Entretiens sur Antiquité Classique 37, Geneva.

Schmitt Pantel, Pauline, ed. 1992. *A History of Women in the West*, vol. 1. Harvard University Press.

Seaford, R. 2006. *Dionysus*. Routledge, London and New York.

Simon, Erika, 1983. *Festivals of Attica: An Archaeological Commentary*. University of Wisconsin Press.

Sourvinou-Inwood, C., 1991. '*Reading*' *Greek Culture: Texts and Images, Rituals and Myths*. Clarendon Press, Oxford.

Sourvinou-Inwood, C., 1995. '*Reading*' *Greek Death*, Oxford University Press.

Sourvinou-Inwood, C., 2000. "What is Polis Religion?" in Buxton 2000.

Sourvinou-Inwood, C., 2003. *Tragedy and Athenian Religion*, Lexington Books, Lanham, Boulder, New York, Oxford.

Swaddling, Judith, 2004. *The Ancient Olympic Games*. British Museum Press, London.

Van Straten, F. T., 1995. Hiera kala: *Images of Animal Sacrifice in Archaic and Classical Greece*. Brill, Leiden, New York, Köln.

CREDITS

Figure 1.1 the Gales Painter
Potter: Gales, *Oil flask (lekythos) with sacrificial procession.* Greek, Archaic Period, about 520–510 B.C. Place of Manufacture: Greece, Attica, Athens. Ceramic, Red Figure. Height: 31 cm (12 3/16 in.). Museum of Fine Arts, Boston
Francis Bartlett Donation of 1912. 13.195

Figure 1.2 *Mantiklos "Apollo"*
Greek, Late Geometric or Early Orientalizing Period, about 700–675 B.C. Place of Manufacture: Greece, Boiotia. Bronze. Height: 20.3 cm (8 in.). Museum of Fine Arts, Boston. Francis Bartlett Donation of 1900. 03.997

Figure 1.3 Family Tree, chart, from Bristol Classical Press, *Religion and the Greeks*, Garland. Used with permission.

Figure 1.4 Silver coin (tetradrachm). © istockphoto/Georgios Kolllidas

Figure 2.1 Genealogy of the Gods, chart, from *Hesiod's Theogony*, Focus Publishing. Used with permission.

Figure 2.2 Succession of Divine Rule, chart, from *Hesiod's Theogony*, Focus Publishing. Used with permission.

Figure 2.3 Wives of Zeus, chart, from *Hesiod's Theogony*, Focus Publishing. Used with permission.

Figure 3.1 *Loutrophoros depicting a bridal procession.* Greek, Classical Period, about 425 B.C. Place of Manufacture: Greece, Attica, Athens. Ceramic, Red Figure. Height: 75.3 cm (29 5/8 in.); Diameter of lip: 25.3 cm (9 15/16 in.); Diameter of body: 18 cm (7 1/16 in.). Museum of Fine Arts, Boston. Francis Bartlett Donation of 1900. 03.802

Figure 3.2 *Grave marker in the form of an oil flask (lekythos).* Greek, Classical Period, Late 5th century B.C. Place of Manufacture: Greece, Attica, Athens. Marble, from Mount Pentelikon near Athens. Overall: 76cm (29 15/16in.). Diameter and weight: 215.9 mm, 6 x 31.1 cm (8 1/2 x 2 3/8 x 12 1/4 in.). Weight: 129.3 kg (285 lb.). Mount (3/4" diameter brass rod / 7/8" brass nut): 1.9 x 35.6 cm (3/4 x 14 in.). Museum of Fine Arts, Boston. Anna Mitchell Richards Fund and 1931 Purchase Fund, 38.1615

Figure 4.1 The Kleophon Painter or his circle, *Mixing bowl (bell krater) depicting a sacrifice.* Greek, Classical Period, about 425 B.C. Place of Manufacture: Greece, Attica, Athens. Ceramic, Red Figure. Height: 42.3 cm (16 5/8 in.); diameter: 47 cm. Museum of Fine Arts, Boston. Catharine Page Perkins Fund, 95.25

Figure 5.1 View of Delphi. © istockphoto/ Benjamin Lazare

Figure 5.2 Kodros Painter (5th BCE), attributed to: Aegeus receiving the oracle of Delphi from the the priestess Themis who is sitting on the tripod. Kylix (drinking cup), from Vulci, c. 440 BCE. Diam. 32 cm. Inv. F 2538. Photo: Johannes Laurentius. Location: Antikensammlung, Staatliche Museen zu Berlin, Berlin, Germany. Photo Credit: Bildarchiv Preussischer Kulturbesitz / Art Resource, NY

Figure 5.3 Scene of divination. Black figure amphora, c. 520 BCE. Location: Chateau-Musee, Boulogne-sur-Mer, France. Photo Credit : Erich Lessing / Art Resource, NY

Figure 6.1 Close to: the Judgement Painter, *Mixing bowl (bell-krater) depicting Orestes at the Delphic Omphalos*. Greek, South Italian, Late Classical Period, Middle Apulian, about 370–360 B.C. Place of Manufacture: Italy, Apulia. Ceramic, Red Figure. Height: 36 cm (14 3/16 in.); diameter: 39.3 cm (15 1/2 in.). Museum of Fine Arts, Boston. Frederick Brown Fund, 1976.144

Figure 6.2 Delphi, Athenian Treasury. © istockphoto/Javier Garcia

Figure 6.3 Votive relief from a healing sanctuary. Greek, 100–200 CE. From the island of Melos, Aegean Sea. Marble, 12 x 8 in. Inv. GR 1867, 0508.117. Location: British Museum, London, Great Britain. Photo Credit: © British Museum / Art Resource, NY

Figure 7.1 The Villa Giulia Painter, *Stamnos depicting women congregated about an idol of Dionysos*. Greek, Early Classical Period, about 450 B.C. Place of Manufacture: Greece, Attica, Athens. Ceramic, Red Figure. Height: 47.4 cm (18 11/16 in.); diameter 33.4 cm (13 1/8 in.). Museum of Fine Arts, Boston. Gift of Edward Perry Warren, 90.155a–b

Figure 7.2 Central scene of the east frieze of the Parthenon, the Acropolis, Athens. 438–432 BCE. Inv. GR, East frieze V, 28–30. Location: British Museum, London, Great Britain. Photo Credit: Erich Lessing / Art Resource, NY

Figure 7.3 the Euphiletos Painter, *Panathenaic prize vase (amphora)*. Greek, Archaic Period, 530–520 B.C. Findspot: Italy, Etruria, Vulci. Place of Manufacture: Greece, Attica, Athens. Ceramic, Black Figure. Height: 60.7 cm (23 7/8 in.); diameter: 40.4 cm (15 7/8 in.). Museum of Fine Arts, Boston. Henry Lillie Pierce Fund, 99.520

Figure 7.4 The Parthenon. © istockphoto/ Stefan Matei

Figure 7.5 Athens, view from the Acropolis. © istockphoto/Styve Reineck

Figure 8.1 Theater of Dionysus. Focus Publishing. Used with permission.

Figure 10.1 Checker, *Skyphos (cup)*. Greek, Sicilian, Early Sicilian Period, about 400 B.C. Place of Manufacture: Italy, Sicily. Ceramic, Red Figure. 21.2 cm (8 3/8 in.). Museum of Fine Arts, Boston. Francis Bartlett Donation of 1900. 03.824

Figure 13.1 Execration figure stuck with needles. (Figure for ritual cursing). Terra cotta. Egyptian, Roman period. Photo: Herve Lewandowski. Location :Louvre, Paris, France. Photo Credit : Réunion des Musées Nationaux / Art Resource, NY

INDEX OF TEXTS CITED

Bolded numbers, e.g., **1.2**, indicates the chapter followed by the number of the excerpt in this text.

1. Literary Texts

GENERAL INDEX